Merry Xmas, Bill
Richard + Annie
1987

D1566806

TWILIGHT OF PROGRESSIVISM

THE JOHNS HOPKINS UNIVERSITY STUDIES
IN HISTORICAL AND POLITICAL SCIENCE

Ninety-ninth Series (1981)

1. Twilight of Progressivism:
The Western Republican Senators and the New Deal

By Ronald L. Feinman

TWILIGHT OF PROGRESSIVISM
The Western Republican Senators
and the New Deal

RONALD L. FEINMAN

THE JOHNS HOPKINS UNIVERSITY PRESS
Baltimore and London

The Johns Hopkins University Press, Baltimore, Maryland 21218
The Johns Hopkins Press Ltd., London

Library of Congress Cataloging in Publication Data
Feinman, Ronald L.
Twilight of progressivism.

(The Johns Hopkins studies
in historical and political science; 99th ser., # 1)
Bibliography: pp. 239-46.
Includes index.
1. United States—Politics and government—1933-1945.
2. Progressivism (United States politics)
3. Depressions—1929—United States.
I. Title. II. Series: Johns Hopkins University.
Studies in historical and political science; 99 ser., #1.
E806.F34   973.917   80-20124
ISBN 0-8018-2373-0

For Adria and David

Contents

Preface

The advent of the Great Depression in the fall of 1929 marked a turning point in American political history. The federal government was confronted with an economic and spiritual crisis of staggering proportions. President Herbert Hoover, the apostle of government-business cooperation and political conservatism, viewed the depression as a short-lived phenomenon that would correct itself through natural economic forces. An opponent of intervention by the national government in the economy, Hoover refused to consider large-scale government assistance to those in need, attacking the concept of a "dole" as the undermining of America's "rugged individualism." As Hoover proclaimed that prosperity was around the corner, members of his own party were calling for a change in priorities on the national level.

The most prominent and outspoken opponents of Hoover were the bloc of western Republican senators who proudly called themselves progressives and were labeled "Sons of the Wild Jackass" by conservatives. In alliance with a smaller number of progressive Democrats, these independent-minded, individualistic reformers demanded recognition of the need for federal action to combat the depression. The members of the progressive Republican Senate bloc, while not always in agreement as to the type and extent of reform legislation required, had not come to a sudden realization of the urgency of change. They had been the leading opponents of Republican administration policies during the 1920s and had kept reform sentiment alive in its period of declining fortunes.

As the 1930s began, the progressive Republican Senate bloc members were regarded as being among the leading reformers in American politics. Journalists, intellectuals, and fellow politicians were in basic agreement on this point. The proposals that the progressives set forth during the Hoover administration to combat the depresssion were later, in many particulars, adopted by the Democratic party under Franklin D. Roosevelt's New Deal. In this respect, the advent of the New Deal was a triumph for the progressive Republicans, who saw their long struggle for economic and social reforms come to fruition.

The New Deal was also a challenge to these Republicans, who witnessed many of their ideas and proposals being usurped by Roosevelt and the Democrats to their political advantage. Moreover, the New Deal came to represent a threat to the cherished ideals of many bloc members, as it advanced in several respects beyond the philosophy of western Republican progressivism. Then too, the growing menace of fascism in Europe and Asia confronted the progressive Republicans with a different type of challenge, and their response led to a rapid decline in public esteem. Between 1930 and 1945, the progressive Republican Senate bloc plummeted from a position as the forerunner of the New Deal to one of repudiated reactionaries in the public mind.

The purpose of this work is to examine how and why this decline occurred. The following chapters will trace how the progressives reacted to the domestic and foreign policies of the New Deal and will explore their relationship with Franklin D. Roosevelt. The president's role in attracting the progressives to his leadership, then ultimately alienating them, will be delineated. The weaknesses of the progressives as a group and as individuals will also be examined in detail. The aim of this work is to place the progressives in the correct historical perspective and clarify their significance as individuals and as a bloc in the history of the 1930s. As the following chapters will demonstrate, personality, as well as politics and principle, had a key role in their reactions to the New Deal.

The term "progressive" should be clarified. There has never been agreement among scholars as to the precise meaning of the term. The general ideas that progressives believed in and promoted are discussed in the first chapter. The author decided that, in doing research for this work, he would consider specific senators members of the progressive bloc if they were so labeled by journalists or historians, or if these senators proclaimed themselves to be progressives. Some scholars may disagree with the author's selections, but each of the twelve senators covered in this work has met at least one, if not more, of these three criteria for being considered "progressive."

Acknowledgments

This book could not have been written without the cooperation and assistance of the staffs of the various manuscript repositories that I either visited or had correspondence with over a period of years. I wish to express my gratitude to the following institutions for the cordial handling of my requests for manscript material: the Manuscript Division of the Library of Congress, Washington, D.C.; the Franklin D. Roosevelt Presidential Library, Hyde Park, New York; the State Historical Society of Wisconsin, Madison; the Bancroft Library, University of California, Berkeley; the Kansas State Historical Society, Topeka; the Minnesota Historical Society, St. Paul; the Manuscript Division of the New York Public Library, New York City; and the Oral History Collections, Columbia University Library, New York City.

I also extend my thanks to the following institutions for sending me useful information: the Herbert Hoover Presidential Library, West Branch, Iowa; the I. D. Weeks Library, University of South Dakota, Vermillion; the Michigan Historical Collections, Bentley Historical Library, the University of Michigan, Ann Arbor; the Western Historical Manuscripts and State Historical Society of Missouri Manuscripts, University of Missouri, Columbia; and the Western Historical Collections, University of Colorado, Boulder. I also wish to thank the many other repository staff members who sent me material that, unfortunately, I did not find useful, and those who informed me that their manuscript collections lacked material on the twelve senators discussed here.

Material from the Hiram Johnson Papers is quoted by permission of the director of the Bancroft Library, University of California, Berkeley. Permission to cite material from the Louis Taber Memoirs in the Oral History Collections, Columbia University (copyright 1972), has been granted by the trustees of Columbia University in the City of New York. Finally, permission to use material in the Frank P. Walsh Papers has been granted by the Manuscripts and Archives Division of the New York Public Library, and by the Astor, Lenox, and Tilden Foundations.

I was very appreciative of the warm reception and cooperation given me by those distinguished public figures who acceded to interviews on their recollections of the New Deal years and the role of the progressive Republican senators in the history of that era: the late Gerald P. Nye, Burton K.

Wheeler, Raymond Moley, James Farley, and Morris Rubin; and also Isen La Follette and Benjamin Cohen.

I am deeply indebted to my adviser during the dissertation stage of this manuscript, Prof. Arthur M. Schlesinger, Jr., for his advice on relevant materials and writing style. I have no doubt that this work has been vastly improved by his suggestions and through his guidance, and I feel honored to have had the opportunity to work with him. I also wish to extend my thanks to Prof. Michael Wreszin and Prof. Bernard Bellush, for their valuable comments and criticisms of my original manuscript. I also express gratitude to Prof. Frank Warren and Prof. Stanley Hirshson for their willingness to give me their assessments of the manuscript and how it might be readied for publication.

I wish to thank the editors of the journal *Mid-America* for permission to use material published in a 1977 article, cited in the bibliography. I know that I could not have produced as good a manuscript as this might be without the cooperation and assistance of Henry Y. K. Tom, the social sciences editor at The Johns Hopkins University Press, and his excellent staff.

Finally, I owe a debt to my family that cannot be adequately repaid. My father-in-law, Philip Osroff, carefully read the original manuscript and gave me feedback from the viewpoint of an amateur historian. My mother, Lillian Feinman, became involved with the project during the years that I was in the process of researching and writing my dissertation. Through my discussions with her, I believe she has become something of an expert on the progressive Republican Senators! I also wish to thank the rest of my family—Harry Feinman, Morton Feinman, and Hannah Osroff—for their constant moral support. Finally, my wife, Adria Osroff Feinman, encouraged me in the final stages of the dissertation and in the revisions undertaken for book publication. She boosted my spirits when necessary, prodded me to greater efforts, and lent her assistance in the proofreading of the manuscript, both in its original version and now in its revised form. She also presented me with my son, David Eric, who has made all of my labors worthwhile.

TWILIGHT OF PROGRESSIVISM

[1]

The Progressive Republican
Senate Bloc in 1930

On November 7, 1929, Sen. George H. Moses of New Hampshire, a conservative Republican, spoke to an audience of New England manufacturers. His topic was a group of independent senators from both major parties, whom he mockingly called "Sons of the Wild Jackass." He bitterly criticized these mavericks, mostly Republican, who refused to adhere to party loyalty. The term he coined drew public attention to these colorful, controversial men, who had been fighting various battles in the political, economic, and social spheres since the time of Theodore Roosevelt.[1]

Who were these senators who drew the ire of Senator Moses? They were individuals who had acquired a reputation as "progressive" in their political and economic outlook. They represented states in the Midwest and Far West that were primarily devoted to agriculture and small businesses, areas of predominantly small towns and cities, primarily Protestant and of old European stock. Large-scale urbanization and the "new" immigration had not affected these states to any great extent. As the 1930s began, the "Sons of the Wild Jackass" were in danger of becoming outdated and inconsequential by the turn of events. Could they adapt to the rapidly changing America of the 1930s? Only time would tell.

The general views of the progressive senators were well known through long years of struggle and oratory. Harsh opponents of special privilege, they denounced the encroachments of big business, banks, and utilities upon the public interest. To curb the power of these vested interests, the progressives actively promoted the passage and enforcement of antitrust legislation and public power projects, such as Muscle Shoals in Alabama. Representing the great agricultural heartland of America, they advanced the interests of farmers. Believers in political democracy and opponents of the power of political machines, they denounced the Teapot Dome scandals of the Harding Administration and the corruption inherent in the two major parties. Convinced that America should avoid involvement in other nations' power struggles,

1

they reminded the nation of the disastrous effects of the First World War, using that war as a justification for an isolationist foreign policy.

These beliefs and principles were to be sorely tested by the events of the 1930s, including the Great Depression, the coming of the New Deal under Democrat Franklin D. Roosevelt, and the threat to world peace of international fascism. The older generation of progressives, of whom only three were still in the Senate in 1930, had faced a somewhat parallel situation during the administration of Woodrow Wilson (1913-1921). Then, as in the 1930s, most of the progressives were Republicans, confronted by a Democratic President who called himself progressive. Would those Republicans join with Wilson to promote an advanced progressive program based on common principles, or would their well-known individualism and partisan political feelings prevent them from cooperating with Wilson? Would Wilson make a concerted effort to bring them within the Democratic fold? As James Holt's study shows, the progressive Republicans of that era failed to seize the opportunity to work with the Democratic administration on a close basis, and Wilson also did not make a strong effort to attract their support, because of large Democratic majorities in both houses of Congress. When foreign policy became the dominant issue after 1915, any semblance of cooperation between the two camps disappeared.[2]

During the 1920s, an era of conservative Republican dominance, the progressive Republicans renewed the struggle to promote their ideals; most of the members of the 1930s bloc entered the Senate during this decade. Being individualists and mavericks, most did not support the third-party candidacy of Sen. Robert M. La Follette, Sr., in 1924, and the Progressive party of that year was the last gasp of the group's acknowledged leader. With his death, in 1925, progressive Republicanism floundered, only to be revived by the Great Depression.

Twelve Republicans in the United States Senate in 1930 were regarded as progressives and lived to serve through at least part of the New Deal years of Franklin D. Roosevelt. Their dates of birth ranged from 1861 to 1895 and their first years in the Senate from 1907 to 1927. Some were more outspoken and attracted more public attention than others, but all were considered by their public statements and voting records to be members of the progressive Republican bloc. A brief examination of the background, beliefs, and mentality of each of these twelve men would be instructive. It would clarify the reactions of these senators to the events, both domestic and foreign, of the 1930s.

Probably one of the most prominent men in the Senate's history was William Edgar Borah of Idaho, who served from 1907 to 1940 and was dean of that body at his death.[3] Born on June 29, 1865, in Fairfield, Illinois, of an old American family of mixed German and Irish ancestry, Borah was the third son in a family of ten children.

Before entering the University of Kansas in 1885, young Borah joined a traveling Shakespearean troupe and assumed the role of Mark Antony, demonstrating his natural aptitude for oratory. He was later acknowledged as one of the great orators of Senate history.

Borah never finished college. Instead, he decided to become an attorney through the reading of law in a relative's office, and he met the Kansas bar requirements in 1887. In a time of agricultural depression in Kansas, he made plans to move west in 1890. Due to a shortage of funds, he settled in Boise, Idaho, rather than Seattle, Washington, his original goal. During the 1890s, he established a successful criminal law practice and became involved in politics. In 1892, he became chairman of the Republican State Central Committee. By 1895, he was secretary to the governor of Idaho and had married the governor's daughter.

In 1896, Borah bolted the Republican party for the first and only time in his career. A strong supporter of silver and a harsh critic of business trusts, he endorsed William Jennings Bryan for president. He was the leader of a Silver Republican convention in Idaho and ran for Congress on its ticket, losing to a candidate with Democratic and Populist support, although coming out ahead of the regular Republican candidate. By 1902, Borah was an acknowledged leader of the progressive faction of the Idaho Republican party and was considered for a United States Senate seat, but he was defeated in the Republican caucus in the Idaho legislature.

In 1906, Borah ran for the Senate as a supporter of Theodore Roosevelt and the direct primary. This time he was chosen by the legislature with a handsome margin. He proceeded to ignore the adage that freshman senators are seen but not heard. He sponsored a bill to create the U.S. Department of Labor, fought for the amendments promoting the direct election of senators and the income tax, and was an uncompromising opponent of the trusts. However, he supported William Howard Taft at a time when most progressives were bitterly critical of Taft's policies and moving toward a revolt against his leadership. Borah refused to bolt the Republican party in 1912 to support Theodore Roosevelt's Bull Moose Progressives, despite his liking for the former president. Soon it was recognized that he was a party maverick only between elections, always coming home in election years. For this, many progressives harshly condemned him.

During the Wilson administration, Borah opposed most of the reform legislation that became law. Attacking Wilson for his abandonment of America's neutral rights during World War I, he made the war a major issue in campaign speeches during the presidential campaign of 1916. In April 1917, he voted for American entrance into the war against Germany, based on the concept of national interest. He opposed involvement in the political affairs of Europe and was one of the leading members of the bloc of "bitter-end irreconcilables" opposed to Wilson's League of Nations and the Treaty of Versailles after the war ended.

During the 1920s, Borah became chairman of the Senate Foreign Relations Committee and the most powerful and influential spokesman in Congress on foreign policy. He believed in noninvolvement in international organizations, noninterference in other nations' controversies, and world disarmament and peace through the rule of law. He had an important role in bringing about the Washington Conference of 1921 and the Kellogg-Briand Pact of 1928. He also promoted United States recognition of the Soviet Union, which came finally in 1933. In domestic affairs, he was a vigorous critic of Presidents Harding and Coolidge but never bolted the party. In 1928, he was a strong supporter of Herbert Hoover. As a mark of his prominence, he was considered a number of times for the presidential or vice-presidential nomination of his party.

Borah was a Jeffersonian in his philosophy of government. He disliked the growth of bureaucracy and centralization of power in the federal government and desired a return to the egalitarian and competitive economy of the nineteenth century. He was thus opposed to federal regulation of the trusts, believing rather in a strict enforcement of the Sherman Anti-Trust Act. He was a firm believer in states rights and therefore opposed to woman suffrage by amendment and federal bills to end the lynching of blacks. But, ironically, he was a strong supporter of the Prohibition Amendment and its enforcement by the national government. Borah was truly an enigma, not always trusted by his progressive colleagues but not a favorite of conservatives either. Borah was the true lone wolf, the supreme moralist in domestic and foreign affairs, who claimed that his only guide was the United States Constitution.

Despite his great prestige, Borah was an ineffective leader. He tended to be rich in rhetoric but poor in action, often abandoning causes in midstream. No important piece of legislation could be called his own. His main contributions were in blocking legislation or programs that he considered undesirable or a threat to the Constitution. A master of oratory, a pleasant, honest, and sincere man, a person of imposing presence—yet he had a basically negativist role in American politics.

George William Norris of Nebraska,[4] the acknowledged leader of the progressive bloc after the death of Robert La Follette, Sr., in 1925, was born in Sandusky County, Ohio, on July 11, 1861. Experiencing poverty in his youth due to the untimely death of his father and the killing of his only brother during the Civil War, he had to help support his widowed mother and sisters. He attended Baldwin University in Berea, Ohio, and Indiana's Valparaiso University, and studied law, being admitted to the bar in 1883. After teaching for two years, he moved to Beaver City, Nebraska, where he practiced law and entered politics, winning local elections for prosecuting attorney and district judge. Settling in the town of McCook in 1900, Norris proceeded to win a seat in the U.S. House of Representatives in 1902 and was reelected four times.

As a member of the House, Norris tended to be a regular Republican until a battle developed over the powers of Speaker Joseph Cannon of Illinois in 1909. Under the prevailing House rules, the Speaker had the power to select the members of the Rules Committee, which determined the calendar on legislation; this gave him tremendous authority over House activities. Norris led the attack on the Speaker and succeeded in restricting his power; he thus gained a reputation as an insurgent and entered the progressive camp.

In 1912, Norris was elected to the Senate as a progressive Republican and was to serve in that body until 1942. During the Wilson administration, he became prominent as one of six members of the Senate who opposed the armed ship bill and American entrance into the world war. He also opposed the Versailles Treaty and the League of Nations and acquired a reputation as an isolationist.

During the 1920s, Norris became the symbol of the progressive movement on the national level. He fought for farm relief legislation in the form of the McNary-Haugen plan, vetoed by President Coolidge. He began his long struggle for conservation and the development of hydroelectric power sites and public control of utilities with his promotion of the Muscle Shoals project, temporarily stymied by the vetoes of Presidents Coolidge and Hoover. He championed the rights of labor unions and the average working man and became interested in the cause of good and efficient government in both the nation and his home state of Nebraska. He was the author of the Lame Duck (Twentieth) Amendment to the Constitution and of the unicameral legislature in Nebraska.

Norris became more liberal and independent as the years went by. In 1928, he supported Democrat Al Smith over Herbert Hoover and made no apologies for it, calling himself a better Republican than the party's presidential nominee. His career was a contradiction of the usual belief that one becomes more conservative with age. He was youthful in spirit and ideas, a man of complete sincerity, integrity, and unpretentiousness. Although his critics labeled him a radical, a fanatic or, an anarchist, he was simply a vigorous fighter for human rights and governmental reform. His philosophy included portions of the Jeffersonian and Jacksonian heritage of agrarianism and the common man, the moralistic conceptions of the social gospel and Christian socialism, and the propositions of the Populist movement, which, ironically, Norris had opposed in the 1890s. Norris was a rare progressive, looking to the future of the nation as well as the past. He had begun to accept the growing power of labor and the urban areas before the New Deal came along and spoke for these elements of American society. Earnest, pragmatic, and hard working, he drew attention because of his deeds, rather than through aggressive leadership of the progressive bloc or the force of personality or oratory. Norris was a visionary of the finest kind in the American tradition.

Hiram Warren Johnson of California, who came to the Senate in 1917, was born in Sacramento on September 2, 1866, the son of a corporation lawyer who served briefly as a congressman.[5] He studied law in his father's office and attended the University of California at Berkeley for a few years. Admitted to the California bar in 1888, he began the practice of law with his father and brother. By the turn of the century, he had acquired a reputation as an outstanding trial lawyer and became involved in a political reform movement in Sacramento. In 1902, he moved to San Francisco and became engrossed in a long struggle against the corrupt city government and the public utility corporations and railroad interests that controlled California's political machine.

In 1910, Johnson campaigned for governor of California, touring the state in a little red automobile. He ran on a platform of clean, reform government and a pledge to drive the Southern Pacific Railroad, for which his own father was an attorney, out of politics. Elected governor easily, he appointed a group of reformers as his advisers and proceeded to give California a reform administration for six years. Under his direction, the state adopted such proposals as a direct primary, referendum, recall, a shorter ballot, woman suffrage, prison reform, a workman's compensation law, shorter work hours for women, and regulation of railroads and public utilities.

In 1912, Johnson became a figure of national importance as the vice-presidential nominee on Theodore Roosevelt's Bull Moose party ticket. In 1916, he was elected to the Senate and served in that body until his death in 1945. There Johnson acquired a reputation as an obstructionist. Like Borah, he had few positive accomplishments, a rare one being his successful sponsorship of the federal Boulder Dam in 1928. Both conservatives and progressives regarded him as unreliable. While proclaiming his progressivism, he seemed to many to become more reactionary as the years went by. But all agreed that he would throw himself into any cause he believed in and against anything he hated. Certainly Johnson could not be safely ignored, as he was considered a potential presidential candidate many times during his career.

Johnson's greatest influence was in the field of foreign affairs. A stubborn isolationist and leading figure on the Senate Foreign Relations Committee, he fought against Wilson's League of Nations, the World Court, and any international involvements. Like Borah, he had supported American entrance into the First World War only on the grounds of national interest. He was a lifelong believer in a strong navy to protect America from foreign aggression.

Often depicted in photographs as in a fighting mood, with a clenched fist held in front of him, he was an extremely emotional speaker in Senate debate and on the stump, effective at dramatizing issues and attracting audiences.

Colleagues found him to be sensitive and thin-skinned, a man who could bear a grudge for a lifetime. He was also extremely moralistic, inflexible once he made up his mind, self-centered, egotistical, and cynical. He had few close friends in the Senate, preferring to be a bloc of one. Sarcastic in his private correspondence toward his fellow progressives, he was also envious of Borah, because the latter received more newspaper and periodical coverage. The California senator was indeed a man incapable of compromise.

Charles Linza McNary of Oregon was appointed to fill a Senate vacancy in May 1917.[6] Born on June 12, 1874, on a farm near Salem, Oregon, he was the ninth of ten children. His parents died while he was still very young, and his eldest sister reared the family. After finishing his secondary education, he entered Leland Stanford University in 1896, leaving after two years. In 1898, he was admitted to the practice of law in Oregon and worked in his brother's firm until 1913. During these years, he held various local public offices, and from 1908 to 1913 was also dean of the law school at Willamette University in Salem. Serving as a justice of the Oregon Supreme Court for two years and as chairman of the Republican State Central Committee, he was first appointed to, and then proceeded to win, a Senate seat, serving from 1917 until his death in 1944.

During his years in the Senate, McNary won respect from his colleagues. A moderate progressive in his political views, he acted as a bridge between the progressives and the conservatives in his party. He was regarded as a skillful parliamentarian, an able party strategist, and a realistic conciliator, always mild and pleasant in his manner. He tended to avoid oratory on the Senate floor, preferring to use his influence in the cloakrooms and in behind-the-scenes negotiations.

His main interests were agriculture and public power. The sponsor of the McNary-Haugen plan to aid agriculture, he also actively promoted major legislation to protect and preserve American forests and federal aid to build roads and bridges, improve harbors and waterways, and construct hydroelectric projects. In 1922, he joined George Norris in favoring public development of Muscle Shoals, and he also endorsed development of the Tennessee, Colorado, and Columbia Rivers.

McNary came into the 1930s with a reputation as a cautious reformer, not willing to go along with the programs of the progressive Republican bloc in all its particulars, but also unwilling to allow the conservatives to have total control over public policy. The failure of the McNary-Haugen plan due to presidential vetoes did not lessen his determination to aid American farmers in any possible way, since he regarded them as the chief victims of the conservative, probusiness philosophy of the Republican administrations of the 1920s. It was not part of his nature, however, to consider bolting his party's caucus in the Senate or to issue public denunciations of the party leadership.

Arthur Capper of Kansas was elected to the Senate in 1918 and served his state for thirty years.[7] Born in Garnett, Kansas, on July 14, 1865, of Quaker parents, he learned the printing trade while working on the local newspaper. After graduation from high school in 1884, he worked for the *Topeka Daily Capital* as a typesetter, reporter, and city editor. Also employed for a short time by the *New York Tribune*, he soon invested in the newspaper business, becoming the owner of a vast publishing empire, Capper Publications, including such journals as the *Topeka Daily Capital, Capper's Farmer*, and *Capper's Weekly*, all of which emphasized agricultural news. As the biggest publisher of farm journals in the nation and the owner of two radio stations, Capper gained significant political outlets for his views. Having acquired tremendous influence in the farm belt, he entered public life in 1910.

Capper was appointed president of the Board of Regents of Kansas State Agricultural College and held that position until 1913. During these years, with other Republican progressives such as William Allen White, Sen. Joseph Bristow, and Rep. Victor Murdock, he fought against boss rule and railroad control in Kansas. The Republican nominee for governor in 1912, he lost the election by only twenty-nine votes, but won two terms as chief executive of the state in 1914 and 1916. His administrations were regarded as reformist in nature and led to his elevation to the Senate in 1918.

Like McNary, Capper was regarded as a moderate progressive. He would not bolt his party in election years, would not abandon the party caucus, but would fight from within, in a mild, unassuming manner, for the cause of the American farmer and small businessman. William Allen White wrote of him: "His record is progressive but he has friends in both factions, dear friends whom he consults often and who respect him for his honesty and courage no matter whether he follows their advice or not." He was a conscientious, kind, gentle, modest person. Not a major Senate orator, he was content to speak out with brief comments, centered around his two major fields of interest, agriculture and foreign affairs.

Agriculture was his chief concern. In 1922, he wrote a book, *The Agricultural Bloc*, which set forth the aims of the bipartisan farm bloc, of which he was a founding member. During the 1920s, he sponsored a mass of farm legislation designed to aid the farmers immersed in the economic depression of the time. As a member of the Senate Foreign Relations Committee, Capper also became engrossed in foreign affairs. Basically fearful of international commitments, he fought against American entry into the League of Nations. In the late 1920s, he proposed a resolution to implement the Kellogg-Briand Pact by an economic embargo on nations that violated world peace.

Not a profound thinker, Capper was not considered a Senate leader. His personality and demeanor prevented him from becoming as controversial as other members of the progressive bloc. Although not always joining the progressives on key votes, he still shared many of their views and concerns on domestic and international issues. But he had a strong belief in party loyalty and party organization. Not a committed progressive as others were, Capper still contributed much to the progressive mentality of the 1930s.

Peter Norbeck of South Dakota was elected to the Senate in 1920.[8] Born on August 27, 1870, on a farm in the Dakota Territory, he was the oldest of seven children born to his Swedish father and Norwegian mother. His father was a Lutheran minister who held public office twice, one year in the territorial legislature and two years in the state body. Young Norbeck attended the University of South Dakota for a couple of terms but never received a degree. He became engaged in agricultural work and started a successful business as a contractor and driller of artesian wells for water, oil, and gas. By 1908, when he entered public life, he was an extremely prosperous businessman.

Norbeck identified himself with the progressive faction that was developing in the Midwest. He was elected to the state senate three times and as lieutenant governor of South Dakota in 1914. With the backing of the Non-Partisan League, a radical farmers' group, he was elected governor in 1916. As chief executive of the state, he was noted for promoting aid to the farmers and his two terms were regarded as an outstanding example of reform government.

Norbeck won election to the Senate as a "TR Republican." A strong supporter of the former president in the 1912 Bull Moose campaign against Taft, he permitted this as the only description of him in the Congressional Directory. He tended to ally himself with the progressive Republican bloc, although occasionally he exasperated the more advanced members of that group by his seeming regularity. His main concern was the welfare of the farmer and the promotion of conservation. A person who avoided flamboyance or personal publicity, he nevertheless was regarded as a good debater and the most important Republican in his home state. A major critic of Wall Street and of his party's neglect of the farm problem of the 1920s, he insisted that the party must become more liberal. A person of distinguished appearance but very limited interests, Norbeck should be classified as a moderate progressive. His service in the Senate lasted until his death in 1936.

James Couzens of Michigan entered the Senate through appointment in November 1922.[9] Born on August 26, 1872, in Chatham, Ontario, he was the eldest of five children of English immigrants and lived a modest existence, his father struggling to make a living. Despite his humble background, young Couzens showed marked self-assurance from an early age. After attending a business college for two years, he moved to Detroit, working for a fuel company as bookkeeper and office worker. He invested in the Ford Motor

Company and soon became its business manager. From 1909 to 1915, the company was practically a partnership of Ford and Couzens, with Couzens dominating the business affairs section. He suggested the five-dollar-a-day wage plan adopted by Ford in 1914. However, in 1915 Couzens resigned as business manager due to tensions between him and Ford. Selling his stock in 1919, he received nearly $30 million in return for an original investment of $2,500.

Interested in public service, Couzens served Detroit as chairman of the street railway commission from 1913 to 1915, as police commissioner from 1916 to 1918, and as mayor from 1918 to 1922. An independent, reform-oriented mayor, he achieved an unprecedented program of public improvements, including municipal ownership of the transportation system. Appointed to the Senate to fill a vacancy, he served in that body until his death in 1936.

One of the wealthiest men in public life, Couzens was nevertheless a progressive who fought bitter struggles against the conservatives who dominated the party hierarchy. He opposed the tax program of Harding and Coolidge and emerged early as a leading advocate of "soak the rich" taxation of the wealthy and low taxes on people of average income, thus coming into constant conflict with Treasury Secretary Andrew Mellon. He supported George Norris's plan to develop Muscle Shoals through a government corporation and was a pioneer advocate of the Federal Communications Commission. Always known for his outspokenness, a typical example was his statement in 1927 that senators were overpaid and underworked!

Couzens was always noted for his independence, brusqueness, and unpredictability. He came across to his colleagues, even the progressive group, as a bluff, blunt, and forceful personality who would ride over any opposition. Being a hard person to deal with, he made many enemies and was unable to become a leader of the progressive bloc. Sometimes he even surprised the progressives with his voting record. He lacked tact and the ability to compromise, functioning best when he worked alone. But despite his "grizzly bear" nature, Couzens could be a very kind man. A major philanthropist, especially for the health and welfare of children, he seemed to have a passion for social justice and economic opportunity.

Lynn Joseph Frazier of North Dakota was elected to the Senate in 1922.[10] Born on December 21, 1874, in Minnesota, his family soon settled on a farm near Hoople, North Dakota, where he lived for most of his life. After graduating from the University of North Dakota in 1902, he became a farmer and school teacher and was associated with various business enterprises. Involving himself in local politics, he identified with the growing Non-Partisan League in 1915 and won election to the governorship in 1916. Serving almost three terms as governor, until his removal in a recall election arranged by enemies of the Non-Partisan League, he compiled a record as a progressive reformer.

Serving in the Senate from 1922 to 1940, when he was defeated for renomination, Frazier was known as a strong supporter of the farmer's cause. He left the Republican party in 1924 to support the candidacy of Progressive party nominee Robert La Follette, Sr. Rejoining the Republicans after the campaign, he continued to be a major critic of conservatives.

Except for his statements on agriculture and his strong support of isolationism in foreign affairs, Frazier rarely spoke in the Senate. He deferred to other members of the progressive bloc in debates on domestic and foreign issues. Not considered a brilliant senator, having no original ideas, he was yet a sincere, earnest "plodder in the ranks." Leaving the initiative and drive for progressive causes to others, he was nonetheless reliable in his vote for their traditional beliefs. Frazier could be summed up as an ordinary, humble man of the Great Plains, certainly no shining star of the progressive Republican bloc.

Henrik Shipstead of Minnesota was elected to the Senate as its only Farmer-Labor member in 1922.[11] Born on January 8, 1881, of Norwegian immigrant parents, he was one of a family of twelve children. An excellent student, ready to debate and state his opinions at a young age, he was also an avid reader. Studying dentistry at Northwestern University, he engaged in a dental practice in Glenwood, Minnesota, from 1904 to 1920, but also became involved in public affairs. Elected to various local offices and to the state house of representatives between 1911 and 1917, he was supported by Non-Partisan League forces for Congress in 1918 and for governor of Minnesota in 1920. He lost both elections and decided afterward to leave the Republican party for the more radical Farmer-Labor party.

In 1922, Shipstead gained a Senate seat on the Farmer-Labor ticket. He served in that body until 1946 but rejoined the Republican party in 1938, after charges of Communist influence within the Farmer-Labor ranks in the state. Although not a Republican during most of the 1930s, Shipstead tended to vote with the Republican caucus on organization of the Senate, and his support often was very significant during the 1920s, when there was sometimes a close division of Democrats and Republicans.

Shipstead came to the Senate branded as a "wild-eyed radical." As the only member of his party, he could obtain little patronage or exert little influence on legislative matters. But he was also not subject to party discipline. Thus he was the epitome of the completely independent senator. He gained the cooperation and friendship of progressive senators of both parties. Many of them supported him in his reelection campaigns despite party ties.

Shipstead was a major champion of agricultural interests and of the working man. He was deeply concerned by, and wanted to curb, the power of railroads, banks, and manufacturing interests. In foreign affairs, Shipstead was an adamant isolationist, opposed to the use of American armed forces abroad and to American involvement in international organizations, such as the League of Nations and World Court. Criticized by some political observers as too cautious, a publicity seeker, and unwilling to exert himself for most causes, at the same time he was regarded by others as one of the most astute, best-trained legislators and as a brilliant parliamentarian. An impressive looking figure on the Senate floor, Shipstead certainly did not prove to be as radical as some of his Farmer-Labor supporters had hoped.

Robert Marion La Follette, Jr., of Wisconsin,[12] son of "Fighting Bob," the leading progressive of the first quarter of the century, succeeded his father in 1925, at the minimum age allowed for a Senator—thirty. Born on February 6, 1895, in Madison, Wisconsin, young Bob absorbed the doctrines of the "Wisconsin Idea" from his father at a young age. The father's belief that "the will of the people shall be the law of the land" was instilled in Bob and his younger brother Philip by the Senator and his wife, Belle Case La Follette, an exceptional person in her own right. His youth was spent watching his father bring Wisconsin a model reform government and fight national political and social issues in Washington.

Despite his exposure to politics and public affairs, young Bob had a greater interest in journalism and banking. But his attendance at the University of Wisconsin was cut short by a bout with pneumonia in his second year of college. After many months of convalescence, young Bob went to Washington to work as his father's secretary, later as chief clerk of the Senate Committee on Manufactures, and then as manager and chief spokesman for his father's campaign for the presidency on the Progressive party ticket in 1924. In June 1925, his father died, leaving a vacancy that he would fill.

Although his younger brother Phil was more politically ambitious, he was two years short of the minimum age needed to sit in the Senate. So young Bob ran for and won the seat his father had held. La Follette served in the Senate until the end of 1946, giving up his seat to Joseph R. McCarthy, who defeated him in the Republican primary election. His brother was to serve three two-year terms as governor of Wisconsin during the 1930s, and both men played a significant role in politics throughout that decade.

When La Follette entered the Senate in September 1925, he was the youngest member of that body since Henry Clay. He informed conservative Republicans that he was determined to carry on the insurgent role of his father. He was therefore denied his choice of the better committee assignments. He spoke out early for the rights of labor and farmers and against the taxation policies of Treasury Secretary Andrew Mellon. Like his father, he came out for an isolationist foreign policy, opposing American membership in the World Court and intervention in other nations' disputes. By 1928, he had established himself as a national figure.

During 1928, La Follette devoted himself to two subjects: taxation and unemployment. He proposed a national taxation system based upon the principle of ability to pay, according to income. He also proposed a serious examination of the national unemployment problem even before the depression hit America in 1929. At the 1928 Republican convention, he presented a minority report that urged farm relief, public ownership of utilities, higher income taxes, aid to the St. Lawrence waterway project, prohibition of injunctions in labor disputes, and the curbing of stock market inflation. He later attacked the Republican platform, minus his proposals, as reactionary and ignored the presidential candidacy of Herbert Hoover.

By 1930, La Follette was regarded as the progressive leader of the future and one of the prime movers of the progressive Republican bloc, along with Borah, Norris, and Johnson. La Follette had not reached this stage of prominence because of great oratorical ability, which he did not possess. Rather, it was through hard work in committees and on the floor, his fairness in debate, and his mastery of the subjects under discussion. He was a leading member of the Foreign Relations, Education and Labor, Finance, and Manufactures Committees of the Senate.

In addition to his activities in the Senate and his participation in his brother's plans to extend progressivism in Wisconsin, La Follette was also the owner of a weekly journal of opinion, *The Progressive*. This was the successor to *La Follette's Magazine*, begun by his father in 1909 and retaining that name until 1929. In newspaper format, the journal contained information about the activities of the La Follette brothers and other progressive reformers throughout the state and nation. Each issue had a series of editorials, sometimes written by the senator or his brother, detailing their views on major public issues of state and national importance. It was a major source of information on progressivism's fight for change in America's domestic and foreign policies.

La Follette, unlike most members of the progressive Republican bloc, was concerned with the problems of an industrial society. He was willing, by the late 1920s, to reassess modern capitalism and to develop a more pragmatic, realistic analysis of needed reforms. He avoided being doctrinnaire or dogmatic, and he demonstrated a better understanding of economics than most of his colleagues. One of the most conscientious members of the Senate, he commanded universal respect, even from those who opposed his ideas with vehemence. He was considered the most constructive and cohesive force among the progressive bloc members, and his name was already being proposed as a future candidate for the White House. Shy and reserved, in comparison with his brother Phil's outgoing, volatile personality, he tended to be less dynamic and more judicious than his father, but possessed his father's quick, nervous stride and gestures. Overall, La Follette was a worthy successor and would prove to be one of the most significant political figures of the 1930s.

Gerald Prentice Nye of North Dakota came to the Senate by appointment in November 1925.[13] Born on December 19, 1892, in Hortonville, Wisconsin, he spent most of his youth in Wittenberg, Wisconsin. His father, the crusading editor of a number of country weeklies, was a strong supporter of Robert La Follette, Sr. Nye returned to Hortonville in 1911 to take charge of one of his father's papers. Following a career in country journalism for the next fourteen years, he moved to Iowa and North Dakota and became a strong proponent of the rising Non-Partisan League movement, which elected Lynn J. Frazier governor of the latter state in 1916. A supporter of America's war effort in World War I, he attacked Senator La Follette for his opposition to American involvement. However, his foreign policy attitudes would undergo great change during his years in public life. By 1924, Nye, editor of a Non-Partisan League newspaper, was campaigning for La Follette and the Progressive party ticket in North Dakota.

Nye came to Washington, D.C., in December 1925 with a reputation as a "village Greeley," a country editor with a populist orientation. Journalists depicted him as a naive country hick, who wore "bulbous yellow shoes and an Old Oaken Bucket haircut." He won election to his seat in 1926 and was to serve in the Senate until 1944. He immediately gained fame by becoming involved in the investigation of the Teapot Dome oil scandal, as chairman of the obscure Public Lands Committee. This experience convinced Nye of the danger represented by moneyed interests. He acquired a reputation as a stubborn fighter for farm relief legislation and as a champion of the small shopkeeper and consumer. He declared his opposition to American entrance into the World Court and to any involvement in foreign crises. He attacked Secretary Mellon's taxation policies, declaring that the Coolidge administration was dominated by bankers and industrialists who had no concern for the welfare of the farmer. He reluctantly supported Hoover in 1928, after opposing his nomination.

Although called a liberal, reformer, and idealist by most observers, Nye also had his critics, who regarded him as an opportunist and a publicity seeker. Earnest, direct, and intense in his manner, he was an aggressive, outspoken, and vigorous advocate of the causes he believed in. Possessing considerable talent as a public speaker, Nye would rise to the leadership of the progressive Republicans during the 1930s, especially in the area of foreign affairs. He was to stir many emotions among his listeners and become one of the most controversial political figures of that decade. One of the Senate's most active speechmakers, Nye based his whole career on two main threads—agrarianism and isolationism. Anyone studying the 1930s cannot safely ignore him.

Bronson Murray Cutting of New Mexico was the last of the progressive Republicans to enter the Senate.[14] Born on June 23, 1888, at Oakdale, Long

Island, New York, to what had originally been one of Boston's oldest and wealthiest families, he was the second son and third of four children. The Cutting fortune had expanded from Boston into the West, going into railroads, timber, and mines. Son of William Bayard Cutting, a New York City lawyer and reformer, he was a nephew of a former chairman of the New York Citizens Union, Robert Fulton Cutting, and a descendant of Robert Livingston, Robert Fulton, and a number of other prominent American public figures dating back to the American Revolution.

Like Franklin D. Roosevelt, but a few years later, Cutting graduated from the Groton School in Massachusetts and went to Harvard, where he was elected to the Phi Beta Kappa society. Stricken with tuberculosis shortly before graduation, he traveled to southern California and New Mexico in 1910 to recover his health and made Santa Fe his home base. Taking an interest in the various Indian tribes of the area, he associated himself with the political, cultural, and commercial interests of the state, becoming one of its leading residents within a short time. In 1912, the year New Mexico became a state, he purchased controlling interest in a newspaper company that published three daily and weekly newspapers, including one in Spanish for the state's many Spanish-speaking residents. The most significant of the three newspapers was the daily *Santa Fe New Mexican*, which became a promoter of Cutting's budding political career.

A founder of the state's Progressive Republican League and a supporter of the candidacy of Theodore Roosevelt and the Bull Moose Progressives in 1912, Cutting remained active as the leading progressive in his state. After active service in World War I as a colonel in the New Mexico National Guard and an infantry captain in the U.S. Army (with time spent in military intelligence), and after service in London as assistant military attaché at the American embassy, he returned to New Mexico as a spokesman for the World War I veterans. He also cultivated good relations with the large Spanish-speaking population of the state.

Many Old Guard Republican opponents accused Cutting of building a political machine that could rival the great political bosses of the cities. A shrewd politician, he used his newspapers and his war record to attract political support for progressive ideas. Despite his scholarly nature, Ivy League background, and eastern heritage, he became an influential political force in the state during the early 1920s. Finally, in 1927, he was appointed to fill a vacancy in the Senate. The following year, he was elected to the Senate by a plurality of more than 18,000 votes. He was to serve until his tragic death in an airplane crash in 1935.

Cutting immediately joined the progressive bloc in the Senate, and became known as a strong spokesman for the "forgotten man." However, he had a shy, reserved nature and was not regarded as a good speaker, being somewhat hampered by a lisp. His weathy eastern heritage set him apart from the rest of the progressive Republican Senate bloc, but, like them, he was devoted to good government and equality of economic opportunity for all. Along with La Follette, Cutting was regarded as the most promising younger member of the progressive bloc, possibly a candidate for the nation's highest office someday.

The members of the progressive Republican Senate bloc were quite varied in their background. The group included four journalists (Capper, La Follette, Nye, and Cutting), four lawyers (Borah, Norris, Johnson, and McNary), two businessmen (Norbeck and Couzens), a farmer (Frazier), and a dentist (Shipstead). Four had served as governors of their states (Johnson, Capper, Norbeck, and Frazier); two were mayors (Couzens and Shipstead), although only the former headed a large city; and one (Norris) served ten years in the House of Representatives. With the single exception of Nye, all had held an elected or appointed political office on the state level before coming to the Senate. Four (McNary, Couzens, Nye, and Cutting) came to that body by appointment to finish an unexpired term.

All of the progressive Republicans, with the exception of Couzens (Canadian) and Cutting (New York), came from middle-class American families with small-town, agrarian backgrounds in the West and Midwest. All twelve had a northern or western European ethnic background and a Protestant religious heritage. Nine had at least some college education, while Capper, Couzens, and Nye finished high school. Only Couzens was ever exposed to urban problems on a first-hand basis, as mayor of Detroit. He and Cutting were the only ones of the group who possessed great wealth, the former by investment in the Ford Motor Company and the latter by inheritance.

Political commentators in the late 1920s and early 1930s speculated about the future of the progressive Republican Senate bloc. The major problem was whether they could play an effective role in American politics as a bloc, or whether they would continue to go their independent ways and fail in the leadership expected of them by many reform-minded people. How could the progressives be effective in their own party and in Congress without organization and unity? How could they lead the struggle for progressive ideals and goals if they continued to be suspicious and jealous of one another?

Early in 1929, T.R.B., a columnist for *The New Republic*, criticized the progressives for their individualism and lack of leadership: "To those who recall the power of these Senate independents under the late La Follette, and fully grasp the potentialities of a well-led, balance-of-power group swinging between the two parties, their present supineness is not without a tragic flavor. Sometimes it almost makes you weep to see the opportunities lost." The major weakness of the progressives was "that there is not among them a genuinely strong man who combines stability of conviction with a reasonably clear head and first-class political brains." Borah, Norris, Johnson, and La Follette, the so-called "stars" of the bloc, were incapable of imposing strong leadership over the group, and each member seemed interested only in promoting his own career.[15]

At the same time that T.R.B. was delivering a scathing critique of the progressives, an anonymous article in the *American Mercury* was labeling the group as "a sorry bunch of weaklings and timeservers." The author continued: "The principle of attack, of aggressive leadership, of purposeful endeavor is completely lacking among them." The article proceeded to draw unflattering portraits of most of the bloc members.[16]

Within the next few years, these men came under greater journalistic scrutiny, as Ray Tucker and Frederick R. Barkley wrote separate chapters on most of them in their book, *Sons of the Wild Jackass*, and Drew Pearson and Robert S. Allen also wrote about them in their *Washington Merry-Go-Round*. Tucker and Barkley tended to praise the group, declaring: "It is no exaggeration to suggest that the Senate Progressives possess most of the brains and brilliance to be found in that body." But the authors were concerned about the ability of the bloc to achieve any constructive change in the midst of the depression, and wondered whether its members were destined to remain lone voices in the wilderness.

Pearson and Allen praised the progressives for their sincerity, intelligence, and forward-looking ideas, but lamented their lack of planning and purpose, which made them ineffective. It seemed unlikely to these two journalists that the progressives could organize an independent political platform that would essentially transform the nature of American politics. If fundamental change was to come about, the progressives had to be in its forefront or perish.[17]

As the 1930s dawned, the members of the progressive Republican Senate bloc faced new challenges and new opportunities. With the coming of the Great Depression in the fall of 1929, they had history on their side if only they could mount an effective campaign for fundamental political, social, and economic reform. Would they be able to meet the challenge and the expectations of millions of Americans, including many intellectuals? That is the subject of this work. The nature of the progressive response to the domestic and foreign problems of the new decade would have a great effect on American history.

[2]

The Great Depression:
A Call for Action

The inauguration of Herbert Hoover caused no rejoicing among progressive Republicans. Hiram Johnson, who had an intense dislike for Hoover and had refused to campaign for him, expressed the feelings of many progressives: "I do not need to tell you the thoughts that course through my mind," he wrote his son ironically, "when the greatest Californian, who has ever existed, is about to be initiated into the Presidency of the United States. . . . We need not worry, for after the fourth of March God will reign." He confided to his sons that he was not optimistic about the future, thinking Hoover a ruthless man with ambitions to become a dictator.[1]

Any honeymoon period that Hoover may have wished for ended with the stock market crash in October 1929. Johnson, in a sarcastic reference to the president, told his sons: "The only good reason for the great slump in the market that I have heard is that god was absent for a few days sailing o'er the Ohio River, and could not, therefore, give the personal attention that otherwise he might have given had he remained in Washington." He criticized Hoover's slow response to the economic crisis and his practice of consulting with wealthy businessmen: "The President is the prince of bunk artists, and what he is doing now is to take political advantage of the situation. He calls here those who have much and have lost little. They make speeches from the White House steps about business is sound, there is no cause for worry, and that prosperity is with us, and the newspapers in their filthy lying way, tell those who have lost their all, that it is quite for the best, and they will soon recover it, and that everything is fine."[2]

With the worsening of the economic situation in 1930, the progressive Republicans demonstrated their discontent, and rumors spread of an open split in the party. In November, members of the progressive bloc held a meeting to map out a legislative program. They demanded a special session of Congress during the spring and summer of 1931 to deal with the economic emergency. Their platform called for the passage of unemployment relief legislation, an anti-injunction bill to help labor, a federal commitment to public power development at Muscle Shoals, and higher taxation of the wealthy. La Follette's journal, *The Progressive*, outlined these as the main issues of the new session. There was also speculation that the progressives might form a third party or work against Hoover at the 1932 convention. *The Nation* commented that the progressive bloc had an extraordinary opportunity to lead the nation out of the economic emergency, if only they could unite. But leadership and organization were lacking, and the individualistic nature of the progressives militated against their unity on a common program.[3]

The progressives began an attack upon Hoover's seeming indifference to the unemployment problem, and his refusal to promote federal relief. Henrik Shipstead offered a resolution that urged presentation of the report of the President's Emergency Commission on Unemployment to the Senate. He declared: "I fear we are making a very grave mistake in underestimating the national emergency and the economic depression. The longer we wait the greater will be the emergency and the more we will have to pay." Calling for unemployment relief, public works, conservation and control of natural resources, a lower tariff, a better balanced distribution of national income, and steps to prevent inflation or deflation of credit, Shipstead grew impatient at the lack of action by the Hoover administration, later declaring: "Before the Roman revolution, when the people became discontented and hungry, they were given a loaf of bread and a circus. Now we only give them a circus."[4]

It fell to Robert M. La Follette, Jr., to articulate the progressive Republican response to Hoover. La Follette, disturbed that the progressive bloc lacked a comprehensive program supported by all its members, wrote his sister as follows: "I am going to try and get the progressive group together soon to see if we cannot outline our position and a legislative program." He asserted a leadership role, introducing a resolution calling for an investigation of the effects of the depression on the American people—this in response to Hoover's charge that sponsors of relief measures were "playing politics at the expense of human misery." He was critical of what he saw as the president's greater concern for wealthy taxpayers.[5]

When the La Follette resolution was debated in the Senate, its sponsor declared that the unemployment problem had been minimized by the administration. The senator placed telegrams from labor leaders and community relief organizations in the *Congressional Record* to demonstrate the reality of widespread unemployment. If the victims of an earthquake were immediately assisted by the federal government, why not the victims of an economic earthquake? La Follette pointed out that the president's assertion that unemployment relief would be a "dole" had not been his view during 1919 and 1920, when Hoover was the leader of American economic assistance to the victims of the world war. La Follette demanded that the federal government appropriate funds for the needy to supplement the efforts of state and local governments and charity organizations. Senator Borah backed La Follette's demand that the federal government become involved in the unemployment problem, declaring: "For God's sake, get something done to feed the people who are hungry!"[6]

La Follette endorsed Shipstead's resolution and emphasized the need for expanded public works. However, Congress, anxious to adjourn for the Christmas holidays, passed the administration's program of minimal relief measures. La Follette denounced this action as totally inadequate to deal with the nation's economic distress. He expressed hope that his fellow legislators would examine the unemployment problem in their states during the recess and return with the same generous spirit toward average citizens that they regularly displayed toward corporations and wealthy taxpayers. To increase information about the unemployment crisis, he announced that he was sending questionnaires to the mayors of all municipalities of more than five thousand population.[7]

After the recess, La Follette continued the struggle against the administration, armed with extensive statistics from the questionnaire returns and the research assistance of the American Federation of Labor. He contended that his information demonstrated further the need for extensive federal appropriations to aid the unemployed. Congress must assert its leadership, he said, if President Hoover continued to lack the will or courage to deal with the problem. The Congress must provide food and clothing to sufferers from drought in the rural areas, give direct relief to the unemployed and their dependents, expand public works, and call upon the industrial and financial leaders of the nation to solve the problem of distribution as well as productivity. La Follette warned his colleagues: "The Congress, like Nero, is fiddling while Rome burns." He took his campaign for federal relief for the unemployed to the public during January 1931. At Town Hall in New York, he declared that Hoover had minimized the situation from the beginning and still persisted in refusing to recognize the ultimate responsibility of the federal government in this area.[8]

Other progressive Republicans joined La Follette's campaign. George Norris declared: "If we have reached the time when the United States Senate, right or wrong, can not express itself in favor of the appropriation of public funds to relieve human suffering, then we ought to abandon our form of government. What are we here for?" William Borah, in an impassioned speech, denounced administration forces in the House of Representatives for opposing a $25 million drought relief appropriation already passed by the Senate. He declared himself willing to aid in forcing a special session of Congress, by holding up appropriations bills until the administration agreed to help the hungry and unemployed. He pounded on his desk for emphasis as he spoke. Attacking those who called the relief concept a "dole," he said that the Red Cross was unable to meet the problem alone, people were starving, and the health of children was being undermined. Borah's oratory made a great impression on the Senate. Democrats applauded him, while conservative Republicans sat in silence, offering no response to his denunciations of the administration.[9]

In early February, a compromise $20 million drought relief bill to aid farmers was reported favorably to the Senate. La Follette indicated he would vote against it, because it showed "callous indifference to the needs of the hungry" in the cities. The administration seemed, he said, unconcerned about the suffering of millions of Americans. The senator demanded that the problem of relief for farmers and urban dwellers alike be squarely faced by Congress before the session ended. La Follette soon broadened his attack to include the opposition Democrats, criticizing them for surrendering their principles to support the administration's weak response to the unemployment crisis. After the 1930 congressional elections, the Democrats had control of the House of Representatives, giving that party a mandate, La Follette asserted, to fight for the people's interests. However, the Democratic leadership already seemed to be abandoning its mandate.[10]

The Senate passed the compromise drought relief measure by 67 to 15, and Hoover immediately signed the bill. Before the vote, Borah delivered another impassioned speech, appealing for government assistance to those unable to obtain loans under the terms of the legislation. He pictured the suffering of the starving in eloquent terms. Hiram Johnson joined the debate, recalling that the federal government had come to the aid of the victims of the San Francisco earthquake of 1906. Why, he asked, should the American people be denied aid in the present economic disaster? James Couzens was also critical of the bill, declaring in a sarcastic tone that a farmer had to admit he was a pauper before he could obtain a government loan.[11]

Only Arthur Capper and Charles McNary, the two progressives with the closest ties to the regulars in the Republican party, supported the Hoover proposal. Hiram Johnson wrote his son after the vote: "I think Hoover has driven another nail into his coffin by his action, and that when the thing is discussed so that our people know what it is, as it probably will be in the ensuing campaign, he will be in a particularly defensive position."[12]

With the session drawing to a close, La Follette introduced a resolution for hearings by the Committee on Manufactures, of which he was chairman, on a proposed National Economic Council to deal with the depression. After changes in the language of the resolution, the Senate passed it. La Follette then stated that the need for relief would be greatly increased by the opening of the next session in December. He again attacked Hoover—and the Democrats for surrendering their powers to him. Borah suggested that the Senate should try to force through a resolution appropriating $10 million for unsecured loans to those in need. However, no action was taken on this proposal, and Congress adjourned on schedule on March 4, 1931.[13]

The progressive Republicans had been unsuccessful in their first legislative attempt to obtain adequate federal relief for victims of the depression. During the congressional session, they had also learned of the complicity of the Republican National Committee in an unsuccessful attempt to defeat Senator Norris for reelection in Nebraska. This was clear evidence of the administration's antagonism toward the progressive bloc; many intellectuals and liberal spokesmen wondered if the progressives had a future in the Republican party.

The leading organization of liberal intellectuals who thought the progressives should leave the Republican party was the League For Independent Political Action (LIPA), led by John Dewey, the philosopher. This group was founded in 1929 to promote a political realignment in America. Its activities included lobbying, publishing literature on important public issues, and sponsoring public addresses by leading liberal spokesmen. The LIPA was critical of the two major political parties on economic grounds and condemned the unequal distribution of income in the country. Its members believed that progressives who remained within the two major parties compromised their liberalism. LIPA goals were considered advanced, even radical, for that time.[14]

In December 1930, LIPA issued a public call to Norris and other progressive Republicans to aid in forming a new progressive party. Dewey, in a public letter to Norris, urged that he sever his relationship with the Republicans and take on the leadership of a new party that agreed with his philosophy of life and government. "You do not belong in the Republican party," Dewey wrote. "You are too socially minded for it. Come out of it and participate in the thrill and enthusiasm of a great movement which is our own and which will realize for common men their rightful heritage. They will rally to your support. Will you help lead the march?"[15]

The day after the letter hit the front pages of the nation's newspapers, Norris issued a public reply. While praising Dewey's sincerity and patriotism, he declined the chance to lead a third-party movement. The way to gain their common goals, he said, would be better served through action to abolish the electoral college and thereby encourage independent candidacies for the presidency. However, Norris declared that he personally would not seek the presidency in 1932.[16]

Borah discussed the Dewey-Norris exchange with newsmen, indicating that he agreed with Norris that a third party was impractical under present conditions. A new party could only succeed if it came from the grass roots, but there did not seem to be a demand for such a third party. Borah concluded that progressives had to work for change within the traditional two-party system.[17]

The Dewey-Norris correspondence provoked much comment. The *New York Times* criticized the progressives for following a double standard. They were willing to remain Republicans so they could retain their committee chairmanships and influential voice in Senate affairs, said the *Times*, but they felt free to attack the president in order to advance their own careers. *The New Republic*, disappointed by Norris's response, commented that the progressives in the Republican party might indeed be incapable of formulating a program and philosophy that true liberals could follow. New leadership was needed, and it was obvious that liberals and progressives would have to turn elsewhere for it. *The Nation* stated that the Republican party hierarchy would do a service for the country if it forced the progressives out of the party. The progressives would then face the necessity of formulating an adequate and coherent economic and political philosophy if they wished to remain influential. The motives of the progressives were honorable and worthy, but "in tying themselves to the old organization they cut themselves off from the new movement and indicate that they do not belong in it."[18]

While two leading figures of the progressive Republican bloc had stated their unwillingness to consider a third-party movement for 1932, they, along with other progressives, *were* interested in developing a legislative program for the new session of Congress in December 1931. In an attempt to formulate a coherent program, arrangements were made for a Progressive Conference in Washington in early March. Co-sponsored by Republican Senators Norris, La Follette, and Bronson Cutting and by Democratic Senators Burton K. Wheeler of Montana and Edward P. Costigan of Colorado, the program was to center around five key topics: unemployment and industrial stabilization, public utilities, agriculture, the tariff, and a return to representative government. The senators denied that the gathering was a stage in the formation of a new political party, and Norris said that the conference did not have the purpose of furthering the political ambitions of any participant.[19]

La Follette, in a radio address, reiterated that the sole purpose of the conference was the formulation of a constructive program for which progressives in Congress could do battle in the upcoming session. Again criticizing Hoover and the hierarchy of the two major political parties for their lack of "enlightened leadership," he declared: "It is the hope, therefore, of those who have called the progressive conference that it may contribute to the solution of our present problems and thus materially aid in the maintenance of our democratic institutions and the creation of that equality of opportunity and richness of life promised by the Declaration of Independence."[20]

Among those who attended the Progressive Conference were noted labor leaders, farm spokesmen, journalists, intellectuals, and political and social reformers outside of Congress. Seven of the twelve progressive Republican senators took part, but a number of well-known progressive figures were missing. They included Senators Johnson, Norbeck, and Couzens; Govs. Franklin D. Roosevelt, Gifford Pinchot, and Philip La Follette; Rep. Fiorello LaGuardia; and journalist William Allen White. Roosevelt, already considered a possible Democratic presidential candidate, sent a message of regret that he could not attend, due to the fact that the state legislature was in session. The absence of Johnson and Couzens again demonstrated the maverick nature of the progressive bloc members. Johnson explained his absence to Harold Ickes:

> I told Norris and Cutting that they had my sympathies and I gave them my blessings, but that I expected in the few years remaining to me to continue to be a block of one, and to walk alone in my own path. I have been happier doing this, and I am sure I will be happier in the future by continuing.

The California senator asserted: "I am going ahead in my own fashion and do exactly as I damn please, and I do not want to put myself in a position where I might, although not wholly with justice, feel bound to any particular course." Couzens thought the conference was a mistake and ill advised. Dewey, who had urged Norris to help in a third-party movement, was not invited, so as to avoid speculation about that issue. Dewey's reaction was to attack the progressives for their weaknesses and unwillingness to fight harder for their views.[21]

On the first day of the conference, Norris, acting as chairman, delivered a stirring introductory address. He centered his attention on the power trusts, which he accused of interfering in the legislative process to prevent adoption of legislation that would promote federal development of cheap power and conservation of natural resources at Muscle Shoals. He warned that the major power companies were planning to use their influence to control the national conventions of both political parties in 1932.[22]

Borah then spoke on the farm problem. He was critical of the Hoover administration for its failure to consider agriculture on a equal footing with industry, especially in regard to the protective tariff. Denouncing monopolies and trusts, he blamed them for the sad economic state of the nation. Finally, Senator Cutting accused Hoover of an attempt to take legislative power into his own hands by running the government through commissions and bureaus. He called for measures to strengthen the corrupt practices law dealing with the use of money in political campaigns, recalling the administration's attempt to defeat Senator Norris's reelection bid in 1930.[23]

On the second day of the conference, Norris called for another Roosevelt in the White House, a leader in the mold of Theodore Roosevelt. This declaration caused speculation that Norris was endorsing Governor Roosevelt of New York for the presidency, which was denied. In addition, La Follette criticized Hoover's refusal to involve the federal government in unemployment relief and public works projects. A series of resolutions were adopted, calling for a study of the business depression and the convening of a special session of Congress to deal with the crisis via unemployment relief and public works legislation. Finally, the conferees demanded legislative action to lower the

Smoot-Hawley Tariff of 1930; to adopt an anti-injunction law for the benefit of labor; to prohibit "excessive and corrupt use of money" in primary elections; to abolish the electoral college; to adopt Senator Norris's Lame Duck Amendment to the Constitution (changing the presidential inauguration day and the opening date of a newly elected Congress from March to January); and to revise the rules of the House of Representatives. No resolutions were adopted on the issues of agriculture and public utilities. Instead, committees were organized to investigate these areas further and to recommend legislation in the fall. The conference ended with no overt attempt to form a permanent organization.[24]

Editorial reaction to the Progressive Conference was mixed. The *New York Times* asserted that the progressives would not cooperate on so-called "progressive" legislation, since each had his own "pet plan." The meeting was simply an opportunity for politicians to make speeches they had not had a chance to deliver during the recent congressional session. It was a publicity stunt, which demonstrated the inability of the progressives to influence events in Washington. The *St. Louis Post-Dispatch* hailed the conference for its main objective: "the well-being of the people as a whole." The conference might be "the foreword of a new historical volume." The *New York World Telegram* endorsed the results and requested a fair chance for the progressives to solve the nation's economic problems, warning: "If democracy cannot provide jobs and a decent living for the masses as the Progressives demand, this country is headed for Fascism or Communism."[25]

The New Republic hailed the endorsement of federal relief for the unemployed, public works projects, and compulsory unemployment insurance; it saw the general sentiment for national economic planning as the major significance of the conference. *The Nation* declared that the Washington meeting indicated the progressives were the only major group in Congress actively concerned with the economic crisis and that now it was easier to have faith in progressive leadership and programs. The socialist-oriented *New Leader* was extremely critical of the conference. The progressives had again demonstrated their lack of a comprehensive philosophy. Their solutions would ultimately fail because they were tied to the preservation of the capitalist economic system.[26]

After the Progressive Conference, speculation arose over the possibility of an alliance between progressive Republicans and the Democratic party in 1932. Norris now declared that he would not support Hoover. While denying that he had decided to back Franklin D. Roosevelt for the presidency, his statement that the country needed another Roosevelt in the White House was interpreted by political commentators to be an indirect endorsement of the New York governor. Norris reiterated his belief that there would be no third party in 1932. If the Democrats nominated someone unacceptable to him, he would simply refuse to endorse anyone for the presidency. The possibility of a Democratic-Progressive alliance seemed better when Sen. Cordell Hull of Tennessee praised developments at the conference as being in harmony with the views of many rank-and-file Democrats. Senator Borah refused to comment on the possible political effects of the meeting but said that it had aroused agitation for the legislative proposals promoted by the progressives. It seemed unlikely that Borah would bolt the Republican party as Norris had, but it was believed that he would aid the progressives in creating sentiment for their program.[27]

Other members of the progressive Republican Senate bloc avoided public comment, but it became obvious that a split was developing within the group over whether to attempt a fusion with the Democrats for 1932 or to encourage an insurgent Republican to run against Hoover in the primaries. Many of the bloc members wanted proof that Franklin D. Roosevelt was a true progressive—Senator Nye was specifically cited as being in this category. The *New York Times* noted the developing split:

> These personal divisions and collisions among the Progressives show at once their weakness and their strength. As troublemakers in Congress they are potent. They are able to unite behind a disturbing program, but cannot produce among themselves, or find elsewhere, a leader whom they will obediently and harmoniously follow. This makes the chief scene of their labor and their influence Congressional, not political in the sense of wielding great power in a Presidential campaign.

The *Times* believed that the major beneficiary of the conference had been Governor Roosevelt, since a third party was improbable and President Hoover was unlikely to experience a strong challenge for renomination at the 1932 Republican National Convention.[28]

Hiram Johnson issued a statement warning the Republican party to pay attention to the political unrest evident at the meeting. Political observers reported that many progressives both in and out of Congress hoped that Johnson, along with other bloc members, would enter various Republican presidential primaries in 1932 as favorite sons, with the aim of rounding up enough anti-Hoover delegates to force the Republican party to consider their demands on the platform and possibly the vice-presidency. T.R.B. of *The New Republic* wrote shortly after the Progressive Conference that the bloc would have a major effect on the next presidential campaign. Meanwhile, the progressive senators hoped to pressure the administration to call for a special session of Congress to deal with the unemployment problem.[29]

A few days after Congress adjourned, Shipstead called upon the president to summon a special session to consider a program to aid the hungry and bankrupt. Some weeks later, Borah joined in this demand, pointing to the increased number of unemployed reported in January. La Follette, however, was again the major spokesman for the progressive Republican bloc. "I suppose people will think I have an obsession on Hoover," he wrote, "but it does seem as though someone should keep after him and no one else in Washington appears to feel as keenly as I do about the shameful manner in which he has neglected his responsibilities in this economic crisis." La Follette made a series of speeches in Boston, Brooklyn, and New York City during April. Asserting that laissez faire was dead as an economic policy, he proposed a seven-point legislative program: (1) federal aid to the unemployed; (2) a shorter work day and week; (3) maintenance of wage levels; (4) the stabilization of industry; (5) unemployment insurance; (6) the rehabilitation of agriculture; and (7) graduated income and inheritance taxes to meet the increasing burdens and responsibilities of government. Such a program, La Follette believed, would result in a large reduction in unemployment, maintain the purchasing power of the masses, and provide a constantly rising standard of living. If the government did not do something, then revolution was in the offing. In New York City, he indicated that he might support a progressive Democrat for president in 1932 and defended the decision of progressive bloc members to avoid formation of a third party. He felt that they could be more effective in promoting legislation by remaining members of the two major parties.[30]

During May, La Follette renewed the call for a special session of Congress, but Hoover refused. Denouncing the president, La Follette expressed pessimism about the economic situation: "I take a very dark view of the future. I see nothing that promises to bring the much promised recovery. It looks to me like a long, long, pull with lowered standards of living for the masses of the people. I shall be happy if we can weather thru with out some big failures and a panic such as we have never known before."[31]

In late May, Senators Borah and Couzens criticized the Hoover administration on the subject of tax revision. Borah attacked Treasury Secretary Andrew Mellon's suggestion that tax exemptions be lowered on income, as this was equivalent to a decrease in wages for lower-income Americans. Couzens suggested a gift tax, an increase in the estate tax, and higher taxes on incomes over $100,000 as the means to finance economic recovery. Senator Norris came to Couzens's side. In a letter to an Omaha newspaper, he emphasized the need for public works projects to relieve unemployment, with the bonds to be paid by heavier taxes on large incomes. The government must end the concentration of wealth in a few hands, he insisted.[32]

During June, Couzens announced he would introduce a public works bill at the next session of Congress. Also advocating a federal and state system of unemployment insurance and old-age assistance, he declared that private charity alone could not handle the economic problems of millions of Americans. In August he told newsmen: "We've played ostrich long enough. Families cannot be allowed to starve and Red Cross and community funds will be insufficient." Senator McNary then wrote Couzens, expressing the view that Hoover was unlikely to heed the plea for a special session. Couzens responded that he did not expect his comments to have any influence on the president, but that he had to make a statement "on the subject which is nearest my heart and head, and that is, the condition of the unemployed." At the end of August, Couzens pledged $1 million of his personal fortune to aid the city of Detroit, if the city leaders could raise $9 million from private sources. He told Mayor Frank Murphy that he wished to help the city in a time of trouble, since the administration in Washington refused to do anything about the economic situation. In response to a citizen's letter, he wrote that he did not consider this grant as permanent relief, but simply as a temporary expedient for the forthcoming winter.[33]

During September, Senators Shipstead and Borah continued to agitate for immediate action to aid the unemployed. Shipstead delivered a radio address, again demanding a special session before December, and Borah stated that the rich must feed the unemployed during the coming winter or face forced action by Congress and the people. Supporting an increase in taxes on large incomes, Borah indicated in his personal correspondence that unrest and discontent against Hoover were widespread in the West, and that Governor Roosevelt of New York was likely to be the beneficiary of those feelings.[34]

Senator La Follette continued his campaign for unemployment relief during the second half of 1931. In July he wrote an article on Hoover's record on the unemployment issue for *The Nation*. In August he announced that he would fight for a relief bill at the next session of Congress. In October he spoke on public works programs to cope with unemployment. Asserting that the depression was not a temporary phenomenon and there would be no spectacular recovery, he said that drastic increases in income and inheritance taxes on the wealthy were essential for an economic recovery.[35]

While antagonism toward the Hoover administration's handling of the depression was widespread among progressives, it was not unanimous. Arthur Capper, regarded as a moderate progressive, kept up a correspondence with Hoover, in which he clearly indicated sympathy with the President's plight. Immediately after the congressional elections of 1930, Capper wrote Hoover about the election results in Kansas. The senator had won an easy reelection victory while commending the administration's program in his campaign speeches. Capper told Hoover in a frank manner that "the future—politically—looks rather gloomy, I regret to say." In June 1931, Capper informed the president that the political situation in the West for 1932 was not promising for the Republicans: "Yet I know of nothing that you or anyone else can do to better the situation. As long as we have low prices for farm products the party in power and the man in The White House will be blamed. This ought not to be, but unfortunately a majority of the people are up against it and do not stop to reason." He assured the president of his "cordial support" and declared: "Personally, I shall do everything I can to further your renomination and re-election. I think you have made the country a great President under most trying conditions. No one could have done a better job. You are entitled to another term. I still have faith in the American voters. I believe when they stop to think it over, they will reach the conclusion that it would be a mistake to make a change."[36]

In September, Capper told William Allen White of his pessimism about the political future of Hoover and the Republican party. The two agreed that the president had lost whatever progressive and independent followers he had acquired in 1928, due to his reputation as a friend of Wall Street bankers and industrialists. Capper predicted "another year of hard times" and the possible loss of Republican control of the White House and both houses of Congress. As 1931 ended, Capper wished the president a better new year and added: "It is my sincere belief that you have fought a good fight; have served your country and your people with ability, distinction, and sincerity of purpose."[37]

With the new congressional session approaching T.R.B. of *The New Republic* wrote as follows on the significant role the progressive Republicans might have in the new Congress: "It becomes clearer that the only group in the coming Congress with any sort of coherent program will be the progressives. . . . Not since anyone can remember have the progressives had quite so fine an opportunity to commend themselves to the country as in the coming session." The bloc members had a chance to show they were statesmen as well as crusaders and critics. T.R.B. believed they would hold the balance of power in the new Congress. He saw the session as a duel between the progressive Republicans and the administration, with the former likely to win some battles. They would also have the opportunity to challenge Hoover's renomination.[38]

At the end of November, Norris called a conference of Senate progressives. He declared that the group planned to be an aggressive force in promoting legislative proposals, including unemployment insurance, public works, and an anti-injunction bill. When the session opened, La Follette again took the initiative for the bloc. He released the report of the Unemployment and Industrial Stabilization Committee of the Progressive Conference, which recommended planning by a national economic board appointed by the president and representing labor, finance, and industry. National planning of the economy would regulate growth and stabilize the purchasing power of the masses. The committee's report also recommended wage increases, redistribution of income, stabilization of price levels, and unemployment insurance legislation. It came out in flat opposition to sales tax increases as an added burden on Americans during the depression.[39]

La Follette now resubmitted his bill to establish a National Economic Council to the Manufactures Committee of the Senate. He also proposed a $5.5 billion emergency public works program, to be financed by issuing so-called "prosperity bonds." And he suggested an additional surtax of 2 percent

on all incomes over five thousand dollars, the proceeds going toward redemp-
tion of the bonds. Some $3.75 billion would go to the states, and the rest
would be handled by the federal government.[40]

In a radio address, La Follette said that 4.5 million people would be employed under his public works bill, and that such a program could expand
purchasing power and break the deflationary cycle. He added that Hoover's
new Reconstruction Finance Corporation would not help the average American—only banks, insurance companies, and railroads. As an alternative, La
Follette and progressive Democrat Edward P. Costigan of Colorado co-sponsored an unemployment relief bill, with a proposed appropriation of $375
million in direct federal aid, the funds to be allocated to the states on a population basis. However, La Follette privately doubted that this bill would command enough support in the Senate.[41]

The La Follette-Costigan bill was opposed by the Hoover administration
as a "dole." It came before the Senate in February 1932 for consideration.
La Follette began the debate with a three-hour speech urging adoption of
the measure. He reminded his colleagues that the nation was confronted with
the most serious economic crisis in its history. He cited statistics to show that
more than 300 cities needed direct federal aid to help them with relief programs. Otherwise, municipalities would go bankrupt in their attempts to help
the needy. Denouncing the charge that unemployment relief was a "dole,"
La Follette said the bill under consideration was an emergency measure,
and was not designed to be perpetual. He quoted from testimony submitted
to him the previous year by labor unions, business leaders, social workers,
and mayors to demonstrate the desperate need for unemployment relief
from the federal government. Privately, the senator still doubted that this bill
had a chance of passage, but he felt that his address had piled up enough evidence to prevent the bill from being sent back to committee without a recorded vote on its merits.[42]

Borah, Johnson, Lynn Frazier, and Couzens took part in the heated debate
over the La Follette-Costigan bill. Borah clashed with Simeon Fess of Ohio, a
conservative Republican, over the use of the word "dole." Contending that
new conditions forced the setting of precedents, Borah declared that the
relief bill could not justly be called a dole. He criticized the willingness of the
federal government to give aid to banks and corporations through the Reconstruction Finance Corporation, while regarding aid to the unemployed as
a dangerous move. The issue, he stated, was one of humanity on the part of
government toward its citizens. The Fess-Borah debate caused much excite-
ment on the floor and in the Senate galleries, as both men became very
emotional in defense of their viewpoints. Hiram Johnson followed with a
plea for consideration for the welfare of women and children, as well as
corporations. He quoted President Hoover as being in favor of relief for
Europe after World War I. Why not the same feelings for an economically de-

pressed United States in 1932? All legislation passed since the depression began, Johnson contended, had favored the wealthy over the masses. It was about time this situation changed.[43]

Frazier, a rare speaker on the Senate floor, declared that it was the responsibility of the federal government to provide assistance to the unemployed. If the government did nothing, then the people might find an appeal in radical ideologies. Couzens now surprised the progressive bloc by saying that the states should have the primary responsibility for relief, not the federal government. It is difficult to explain why Couzens abandoned the La Follette-Costigan bill, but it gave further evidence of the inherent instability and unreliability of the progressive bloc's members.[44]

On February 16, the bill was defeated by 48 to 35. Couzens and the two moderate progressives with closest ties to the Old Guard, Capper and McNary, had abandoned the progressive bloc on this vote, and the group had failed in its major effort of the session. Shortly before the vote, La Follette delivered one last diatribe against opponents of the legislation. Centering his attack on conservatives like Fess who had spoken against the bill, he asserted that these senators were as blind as the Bourbons of France before the French Revolution. Privately, the Wisconsin senator still hoped that a substitute relief bill of a more modest nature, sponsored by Democrat Robert F. Wagner of New York, might be passed. During the spring of 1932, La Follette continued to struggle for his other major goals, a public works bill and the establishment of a National Economic Council.[45]

In May, La Follette and Borah, along with Bronson Cutting, again raised the issue of unemployment relief. Borah repeated his demand that the federal government should grant direct relief through the states to the unemployed. Speaking before a conference of the National Association for the Advancement of Colored People, La Follette attacked Hoover's lack of action. Cutting, who had not spoken out earlier, offered a bill calling for a $5 billion bond issue, of which $3 billion would be expended by the federal government on highways and the rest on rivers and harbors, public buildings, reforestation, and other worthy public projects. Assailing Hoover's program as "a wavering policy which left the country facing the alternatives of starvation or revolt," the New Mexico senator argued that a public works program inaugurated by the federal government and pursued as if there were wartime conditions would stop the downward spiral of the depression and start the country on the road to recovery. In another speech on his bill, Cutting declared that more attention should be paid to the restoration of purchasing power than to balancing the budget.[46]

During June, a $300 million unemployment relief bill, written by Democratic senators but satisfactory to the administration, was passed by 72 to 8 in the Senate. Hiram Johnson hailed the vote as a triumph because it finally demonstrated recognition of the federal government's obligation to the unemployed. However, the bill was of a limited scale, and Senator Borah again stressed the need for a greater commitment. The individualism and physical and moral fiber of the American people would not be harmed, he said, as so many conservatives had charged. La Follette asserted that the measure was too limited and had taken too much effort to gain the acceptance of a grudging administration.[47]

Later in June, the Senate debated the Wagner relief bill, which authorized $500 million for public works, much less than the La Follette and Cutting proposals. Various amendments were offered by progressive Republicans, who contended that this amount was inadequate. Norris introduced a bill providing for $3 billion for public works supported by bond issues. La Follette offered an amendment to the Wagner bill, raising the allotment for public works up to $5.5 billion and declared in a floor speech that the present situation was graver than that of the world war. The conference report of both houses deleted La Follette's amendment, and the Senate proceeded to pass the Wagner bill by 43 to 31 on July 9. Capper, Couzens, La Follette, and Shipstead voted against the final bill, while Cutting did not vote. The progressive Republican bloc was thus divided 7 to 4 on this bill, which Hoover proceeded to veto as unwise and unnecessary. Johnson declared that the president had to take personal responsibility for preventing relief from going to those who desperately needed it. In a quote later adopted by Franklin D. Roosevelt, the California senator said the bill was designed to help the "forgotten man" in American society.[48]

The progressive Republicans had fought vigorously for an adequate program of unemployment relief and public works. While they had basically failed in their legislative goals, they had brought a key issue to the forefront of public debate: that the federal government must be ultimately responsible for the welfare of its citizens in a time of economic distress. The fact that the progressives had not united on the details of the problem was a warning sign of possible ineffectiveness unless they gave up some of their cherished independence.

But progressives had some things to be happy about in 1932. A limited relief bill had indeed passed in June. The Norris-LaGuardia Act, banning injunctions against labor unions on an indiscriminate basis, had passed the Senate by a vote of 75 to 5 on March 1 and was now the law of the land. Senators Capper, Norbeck, and McNary had also successfully promoted the distribution of government-owned wheat to the Red Cross and other relief organizations to aid the needy. The struggle to change national priorities had just begun, and the progressive Republican Senate bloc hoped to play a significant role in that transformation. The 1932 election provided a golden opportunity, if only the progressives could take advantage of it.[49]

[3]

Alternatives in the 1932 Presidential Campaign

As the presidential campaign of 1932 approached, the members of the progressive Republican Senate bloc faced a choice of strategy among a large number of options. They could change their mind about the formation of a third party; encourage one of their own in or outside of Congress to challenge Hoover's renomination in the primaries and at the convention; support the Democratic party's nominee if he were a progressive in his views on the major issues; remain uncommitted to any candidate; or endorse Hoover for reelection. Their individualistic nature would make it difficult for the progressives to join together on any one option, thereby weakening their effectiveness in the 1932 campaign.

The third-party idea had been rejected twice. Senators Norris and Borah had rebuffed the concept when John Dewey suggested it as a progressive alternative in December 1930. Along with others, they had again avoided the issue at the Progressive Conference in March 1931. Some of the progressives, as veterans of earlier third-party movements in 1912 and 1924, were simply unwilling to indulge in a similar strategy again, seeing no chance for success.

With the third-party concept discarded, the progressive senators began considering a challenge to Hoover's renomination, despite the odds against success. Even former President Theodore Roosevelt had been unable to wrest the party's nomination away from President Taft in 1912, despite his widespread popularity within Republican ranks. But as early as November 1930, rumors began to spread of possible challenges by Senators Borah and Norris and by Gov. Gifford Pinchot of Pennsylvania, a leading spokesman for conservation and a close friend and adviser of the late President Roosevelt. In March 1931, Hiram Johnson was added to the list of possible rivals, and in May La Follette's name was suggested, although later discounted because of his youth and lack of experience.[1]

The first planning for a primary challenge was by Governor Pinchot. At the end of May 1931, the *New York Times* reported that he had made plans to enter Republican presidential primaries if the depression continued to grow in severity. Pinchot was depicted as confident that the progressive Senate bloc would back him. In early June, the governor sent spokesmen to confer with several members of the bloc, seeking support for his candidacy, which would be based on two major issues—agricultural relief and regulation of public utilities. The unidentified senators refused to comment publicly on the possibility of a Pinchot candidacy, but the feeling seemed to be that it would be a futile gesture, although it would give progressives an opportunity to promote their ideas in the Republican platform. Meanwhile, at the annual Governors' Conference at French Lick, Indiana, Governor Pinchot delivered a stirring speech on the subject of public utilities, calling for federal regulation. Senator Norris hailed the speech and said he would support Pinchot for the Republican presidential nomination, should the governor seek it.[2]

The possibility of a Pinchot presidential candidacy was further explored in late October in a series of conferences between the Pennsylvania governor and a group of Senate progressives, including Borah, Couzens, Frazier, and Nye. They told Pinchot the western states were anxious for an alternative to Hoover. Believing that a fight against the administration was worthwhile, they encouraged Pinchot to run, but the governor held off a final decision, wanting a public endorsement from bloc members before he committed himself to campaign in twelve state primaries. The group agreed to meet again at the end of the year, but at that time no final public commitments were made.[3]

In March 1932, Pinchot, still unannounced, requested that Harold Ickes, a progressive reformer from Chicago active in reform activities for twenty years, send out letters promoting his candidacy to leading progressives around the country. A letter was drawn up, mailed to thousands of people, and published in the nation's newspapers. Although Ickes agreed to help Pinchot, privately he had little hope that the governor's candidacy had any promise. To the progressive journalist William Allen White, he wrote: "Just between you and me, I agree with you that Gifford has not got a chance and that no one could take the nomination away from Hoover." Ickes told Pinchot of his willingness to help but added that the governor should not have any illusions of success.[4]

The response to the possibility of a Pinchot candidacy was poor. Ickes wrote Pinchot after the first batch of responses: "These letters so far mean to me that the Republicans are going to take their licking lying down. They are afraid of the future, they have no hope in the present and they regret the past four years. But most of all they are afraid to make a move for fear they may interfere with that return of prosperity which is 'just around the corner.' " At the beginning of May, Pinchot announced he was abandoning his effort. Ickes agreed that Pinchot was doing the wise thing, since "the whole thing is tied up for Hoover."[5]

Rumors of Borah's possible candidacy were rampant throughout 1931. When he agreed to make a speaking tour of the farm states during the summer and proceeded to criticize Hoover's farm policies, the press speculated that he might enter primaries. In September he declared that he had no objection to the formation of a Borah-for-President club in the state of Virginia. Progressives were divided on his candidacy, however, some thinking it a wasted effort, others asserting that if he did not run in 1932, he would have no further opportunities for the presidency, due to his advanced age.[6]

In early October, Sen. Smith Brookhart of Iowa and Senator Frazier claimed that Borah had presidential aspirations and might enter the western state primaries. In November, the newspapers reported the offer of a group of Republican businessmen to finance a Borah primary campaign. Although impressed, Borah indicated he was unwilling to run because of the advantages held by an incumbent president. The support of western delegates at the Republican National Convention would not be enough to stop Hoover's renomination. During the next few months, Borah received many letters urging him to run, but at the end of February, he made a final decision against it. Informing Pinchot of his decision, he said that Hoover could not be defeated and the progressives would be unable to determine the platform.[7]

Norris, another possible challenger, indicated at the end of 1930 that he would not be a candidate. During 1931, he expressed his willingness to support Gifford Pinchot or Franklin Roosevelt—or politicians with similar views. In November, he said the western states favored the nomination and election of any progressive over Hoover, but he continued to cite his lack of interest in running. At the beginning of 1932, Norris was depressed about progressive chances to deny Hoover the Republican nomination. He was coming to the conclusion that the best hope for all progressives, both Republican and Democrat, was the nomination and election of Franklin D. Roosevelt. Whatever funds the progressives could garner should be saved, he believed, for the election campaign, rather than used in a wasteful struggle against Hoover. However, he continued to be willing to make a fight for any progressive who decided to challenge Hoover.[8]

The most serious possibility of a challenger to Hoover lay not in Pinchot, Borah, or Norris, but in Hiram Johnson, the veteran of the Bull Moose campaign of 1912. Many progressives thought he had the best chance of stopping Hoover, and Johnson considered a possible race for many months. The major promoter of Johnson's cause was Ickes, who knew him from Bull Moose days and had worked for his nomination in 1924. For eight months, Ickes played the role of a self-appointed campaign manager, working very hard trying to convince Johnson to run. In June 1931, he wrote the senator that a Hoover renomination would lead to disaster for the Republican party, yet no one seemed willing to fight him for the nomination.[9]

In the fall, Ickes informed Johnson that he planned to meet with other progressive senators to promote the Californian's candidacy, since the progressives could not find a stronger challenger to Hoover. Johnson did not discourage Ickes's activities, apparently anxious to see if there was solid support for his candidacy. During November, Ickes spoke with La Follette, who agreed that someone should challenge the president and was receptive to a Johnson campaign. Citing his respect for Johnson, La Follette thought a good campaign could be made on the economic issues facing the country. Johnson's own contacts with his progressive colleagues, however, convinced him that "their peculiar individualism renders any concert of action well-nigh impossible." The major weakness of the progressives was obvious to Johnson, himself a supreme individualist: "I am perfectly satisfied that if we undertook anything we could not count upon anything like united action from those who call themselves Progressives here. A few individually would be glad to aid, but those are few. The difficulty with the so-called Progressives is that they are so very good, no individual except themselves can measure up to their standards."[10]

Speculation that Johnson might seek the Republican nomination increased despite his private doubts, when he declared in late November that the President should eliminate himself as a candidate for a second term. Such an act would earn the gratitude of his party, Johnson asserted, as well as the people of the nation. When asked by a newsman if he was announcing his candidacy for the nomination, Johnson replied: "Quit kidding me about the Presidential nomination. When I'm a candidate you'll know about it."[11]

During the next few months, Ickes continued to pressure Johnson, telling him that he had spoken with Bronson Cutting, who agreed that a progressive should challenge Hoover. Cutting thought Johnson an acceptable candidate, one whom he could support even though they did not agree on every issue. Ickes now assured Johnson that his candidacy would attract great support throughout the country and that he would sweep the primary states. He warned Johnson: "Unless you get into the fight Hoover is going to get this nomination by default, the Republican party will get a terrific licking in November and the organization will remain in the hands of the reactionaries." Ickes bombarded Johnson with letters for the next few weeks, but the Californian told his sons at the end of December that he was not inclined toward running because of his age and lack of funds to operate a decent campaign. Hoover was likely to lose the election, Johnson asserted, but he had the power to renominate himself, and any challenger was doomed to defeat. He also told Ickes of his feelings.[12]

In January, Colonel McCormick, the owner of the *Chicago Tribune*, increased the pressure on Johnson by offering financial aid to the senator if he would run in the Illinois primary. Johnson now wrote his sons: "I have been importuned day and night to go into the presidential preference primaries." But he remained convinced that no progressive had a chance of getting the party's nomination, that even if Hoover was denied renomination, a person of similar beliefs would be selected. Bronson Cutting, still hoping Johnson would run, wrote Ickes of his willingness to commit himself if only the California senator could be convinced. Ickes decided to make one last effort to draw Johnson into the primaries.[13]

Ickes wrote Mrs. Johnson, whom her husband called "The Boss," imploring her to convince the senator to announce his candidacy. Ickes also wrote three letters to Johnson during the next two weeks. Johnson's decision would be significant for the future of the progressive movement in the Republican party and the nation, Ickes asserted, continuing: "It seems to me that it is the inescapable duty of any man who can take this nomination away from Hoover and who can establish as the head of the government a tolerant, wise, humane leadership at this hour of great crisis to say the word that will release the forces that will bring about his nomination and election." Johnson's name would go down in history as the man who came to the rescue of the nation, Ickes declared, in the midst of its greatest crisis in many years. Cutting also took it upon himself to speak with Johnson about the financing of his campaign, but he came away with the view that Johnson was determined not to run, and that some progressives, including Borah and La Follette, were rather lukewarm about supporting Johnson.[14]

Johnson remained convinced that he should not run for President. He did not rejoice at the thought of fighting a primary campaign in his home state against another native son. He indicated his thinking in a letter to the publisher of the *Sacramento Bee*, a friendly newspaper. In February, the senator announced he would not enter the North Dakota primary, although he had been publicly encouraged by the progressive senators Nye and Frazier. While not making a formal statement of noncandidacy elsewhere, Johnson had made his final decision, and so informed Ickes.[15]

By the end of February, the progressives believed the chances of denying Hoover renomination to be hopeless. The refusal of Borah, Norris, and Johnson to commit themselves to an expensive, grueling campaign was due to personal factors, but also to their belief that the progressives would not stick together and could not gain enough support to threaten Hoover. Why run a martyred race with no chance of success? At the same time, Gifford Pinchot's eagerness to run failed to draw progressive commitments. The individualism of the progressive Republicans had led to indecision and lack of action. Again they had demonstrated more bark than bite.[16]

With the progressive Republican Senate bloc having abandoned thoughts of challenging the president, its members now faced a decision on whether to abandon their party ties and support the Democratic nominee. This was not an easy decision, as it could cause a revolt against their leadership role in various Senate committees after the election. The possibility of a party bolt made the progressives subjects of much political speculation throughout 1932.

Senator Norris, rumored to be in favor of the election of Franklin D. Roosevelt since his speech at the 1931 Progressive Conference, formally announced his support of the New York governor in May 1932. If Roosevelt failed to gain the Democratic nomination, Norris would refuse to support anyone for president. No other member of the progressive group endorsed Roosevelt before the conventions took place, but the favorable attitude of a number of them was predicted by some political observers.[17]

As early as September 1931, political speculation was that Senator La Follette and his brother Philip, the governor of Wisconsin, would support Roosevelt, due to similar views on public ownership and regulation of utilities. Meanwhile, early in 1932, Hiram Johnson wrote that Roosevelt was the one political figure in the Democratic party who had a chance of defeating the president. While Roosevelt was not an ideal candidate, Johnson asserted, he seemed to have great popularity and could probably attract the mass support necessary to win the election. By April, Johnson was certain that Roosevelt would be the Democratic nominee, declaring that "the people who are abusing Roosevelt, and the reasons for which he is being abused, are beginning to make me feel very, very kindly towards him." He indicated that he could not support Hoover or a conservative Democrat for president.[18]

Although by the spring of 1932 they had abandoned their fight for the party's nomination, the progressives continued to speak out against the incumbent. In March, La Follette issued a harsh denunciation of the administration and reactionaries in both major political parties, and he began a campaign to elect the largest possible number of progressive delegates to the national convention. Aware that Hoover's renomination could not be prevented, the Wisconsin senator still wanted publicity for progressive ideas, which he hoped to present as a minority report to the Platform Committee of the convention. Meanwhile, at the end of March, Senator Nye threatened to bolt the Republican ticket. Facing a reelection campaign, the North Dakota senator proceeded to criticize Hoover's agricultural policies.[19]

Political observers were most interested to see what Borah would do. The Idaho senator had a reputation for being a maverick for three and a half years of every four, returning to the party fold by election time. In late May, Borah announced his dissatisfaction with the prohibition resubmission plank formulated for the convention, and indicated he did not know whether he would attend. Hoover invited Borah to a White House breakfast to discuss the plank, but no agreement was reached. Borah refused to attend the convention and criticized the platform clause that condemned party irregularity. In late June, he announced that he would not support Hoover for reelection on the basis of the platform adopted by the convention. At this time, Norris again affirmed his refusal to support Hoover, and Frazier indicated similar views.[20]

Roosevelt, aware of the possibility of garnering significant progressive Republican support for his candidacy, welcomed them into his ranks in his acceptance speech at the Democratic convention. The convention extended a formal invitation to those Republicans who agreed with Senator Norris on the need for Roosevelt in the White House.

Hiram Johnson expressed happiness at Roosevelt's nomination. He believed the Democrats had made the best possible choice, and that Roosevelt could win the election if he overcame forces favoring the status quo. He planned to remain silent regarding his role in the campaign until he returned to California and consulted with friends and political associates. Despite these plans, on July 4, he issued a statement very complimentary to the Democratic nominee, causing many observers to speculate that he would throw his support to Roosevelt in the near future. Johnson praised Roosevelt's decision to come to the Democratic convention to deliver his acceptance speech, a break with tradition. However, Johnson refused to go further in his public statements on the campaign for the time being, and Senators Nye, Frazier, and Borah also refused to comment on what they might do. La Follette was depicted as unlikely to campaign for Roosevelt even if he endorsed him.[21]

Other than Norris, it was evident that the progressive Republican senators were not anxious to bolt their party hastily. However, no one except Capper was willing to endorse Hoover at this point. The Kansas senator issued a statement in mid-June predicting the reelection of the president "if the country exercises its sober judgment." He asserted that "history is going to record that Herbert Hoover served his country well and faithfully and courageously and ably during these times." As the 1932 campaign began, therefore, only Norris and Capper had definitely committed themselves.[22]

Shortly after Roosevelt's nomination, La Follette's publication, *The Progressive*, printed an editorial advising watchful waiting on the part of progressives. Although pleased by Roosevelt's nomination, the journal declared that he had been weak and vacillating in his attitudes on various issues: "*The Progressive* believes that Progressives and liberals everywhere should await the future pronouncements of the Democratic nominee before enlisting under his banner in the coming campaign." However, the magazine admitted that Roosevelt was bitterly opposed by "the forces of organized greed," which made him an appealing candidate to progressives.[23]

As the presidential campaign went into full swing in September, Roosevelt undertook a series of actions designed to attract the support of progressive Republicans, including those senators believed to have a major influence on the voting patterns of western states. During a campaign tour of the West, he appealed to progressive elements to join his bandwagon. Among the states he visited were California, New Mexico, and Nebraska, the home states of Hiram Johnson, Bronson Cutting, and George Norris.

On September 22, Roosevelt spoke in Sacramento, inviting the Johnson followers into his camp. He praised the senator as a "warrior for progress,"

who had done much during his years in public office to further progressive
ideals and goals. The next day, Johnson issued a statement expressing ap-
preciation for Roosevelt's tribute. While not endorsing the Democratic
nominee, he declared that Roosevelt was a progressive. Johnson vowed that
he would continue to fight for progressive goals as long as he sat in the
Senate. His statement was considered helpful to the Roosevelt campaign, but
he was not expected formally to endorse and campaign for the Democratic
nominee.[24]

A few days later, Roosevelt was in Lamy, New Mexico. Cutting was there
to greet the presidential contender, who delivered a speech calling for support
of all liberals. Roosevelt invited the senator on the platform to make some
remarks; Cutting instead simply waved to the audience and sat down again.
Roosevelt then proceeded to tell the crowd that his family and Cutting's had
been friends for generations in New York. Cutting had resigned his position as
Republican national committeeman a few days earlier, indicating he would
refuse to support Hoover's reelection. But he held back from any immediate
endorsement of Roosevelt, although it was believed that he would eventually
support the New York governor.[25]

The next day, Roosevelt was in McCook, Nebraska, where he met with
Norris. The two men exchanged compliments about each other before a
crowd, expressing their approval of common goals and beliefs. They also
spoke of the need for voters to ignore party lines in the forthcoming presidential election. Norris declared that the nation needed Roosevelt in the
White House, while the candidate eulogized the Nebraska senator as "the very
perfect gentle knight" of American progressivism and as a better Republican
than President Hoover. Norris made a special point of praising Roosevelt's
views on the issue of public utilities. The meeting ended with Roosevelt's
personal appeal to western progressives to support his candidacy.[26]

Roosevelt also worked at gaining the support of progressive Republicans
via establishment of the National Progressive League for the Election of
Roosevelt and Garner. Formed on September 25, 1932, with Senator Norris
as its chairman, the organization was designed to attract independent support
to Roosevelt's candidacy. The possibility of such an organization was thought
of by Harold Ickes as early as April, when he saw that Roosevelt was the only
hope for progressives in the 1932 election.[27]

The formal move to establish it, however, was on the part of Frank P.
Walsh, head of the New York State Power Commission under Governor
Roosevelt and a close friend of many progressives across the country. Walsh
had arranged for a letter to be mailed to a select list of people in late August,
to get their views on the formation of a group independent of the Democratic
party organization to support Roosevelt's presidential candidacy. The letter
produced responses from many progressive spokesmen, including Ickes and
Norris. Norris indicated his belief that "there ought to be some kind of a

movement, nation-wide in its scope, to bring the Progressive vote of the country to Roosevelt where it naturally and logically belongs. This organization ought to be controlled and handled preferably by Republicans of the Progressive wing." Upon receipt of Norris's letter, Walsh called a series of conferences with various public figures between September 7 and 13. A plan of organization was drawn up, and Walsh visited Roosevelt in Albany to discuss his activities. Roosevelt was shown Norris's letter, and the candidate agreed on the plans for such an organization.[28]

Walsh decided that the National Progressive League should have offices in Washington for publicity; in New York for the speakers' bureau, radio operations, and finance; and in Chicago for membership and field work. A national committee of progressive Republicans and progressive Democrats, representing at least three-fourths of the states, was to be arranged. Progressive spokesmen would make public appearances at political gatherings in the Midwest and West, under the auspices of the league. Norris, as chairman of the organization, agreed to make a speaking tour of the nation on behalf of Roosevelt during October. Progressive Democrat Edward P. Costigan was selected as vice-chairman, to take the organizational burden away from Norris. Donald Richberg and Frederic C. Howe were named chairman of the Executive Committee and secretary, respectively; Ickes agreed to take charge of the western headquarters.[29]

The formation of the National Progressive League was announced on September 25. Among the members of the organization were such public figures as Henry Wallace, Frank Murphy, Bainbridge Colby, Felix Frankfurter, Ray Stannard Baker, and Amos Pinchot. Others who later joined the group included progressive Democrats Burton K. Wheeler of Montana, Clarence C. Dill of Washington, and Tom Connally of Texas.[30]

The *New York Times* commented that the National Progressive League seemed especially designed to appeal to progressive Republicans. Norris seemed ideally fitted to attract western Republican votes to Roosevelt. *The Progressive* saw the new league as an obvious attempt to garner progressive support around the Democratic nominee. T.R.B. of *The New Republic* felt that Roosevelt was certain to gain the outright support of many progressive Republicans, as a result of his western trip and the formation of the league. The result of these endeavors was endorsement of Roosevelt by six of the twelve members of the progressive Republican Senate bloc—Norris, Johnson, Cutting, La Follette, Frazier, and Shipstead.[31]

Before the formal announcement of the founding of the National Progressive League, Walsh had sent a representative, Robert G. Sucher, to speak to various progressive Republican senators. On September 16, Sucher met with the La Follette brothers in Milwaukee, informing them of Norris's plans to head the new organization. On September 22, Sucher met with Hiram Johnson in his San Francisco office. The conference lasted several hours, with Johnson making it clear that he was awaiting an appropriate opportunity to lend at least indirect aid to Roosevelt's candidacy. Roosevelt's references to him the next day in Sacramento led him to praise the Democratic nominee publicly, but he still held back from commitment to a formal endorsement and campaign speeches in Roosevelt's behalf.[32]

Meanwhile, Sucher had journeyed to New Mexico, where he spoke with Bronson Cutting in Santa Fe. This meeting occurred shortly after Cutting's public appearance with Roosevelt at Lamy. Told of Norris's plans for the campaign, Cutting said he wished to confer with Senator La Follette before making a public statement of support. He indicated that he had no objections to the use of his name by the National Progressive League.[33]

Returning eastward at the end of September, Sucher met again with the La Follette brothers in Madison. Both were interested in the views of Johnson and Cutting. Neither was yet willing to commit himself to Roosevelt or the league. Although still hesitating at the end of September, it seemed likely that these progressive Republicans would eventually endorse Roosevelt and possibly speak for him at public meetings.[34]

On October 12, Johnson received a telegram from seventy Southern California newspaper publishers, calling upon him to declare his support for the national and state Republican tickets. Johnson responded that he would not and could not endorse Hoover. He would not mar his progressive record by working for a president who was in alliance with the wealthy and powerful interests of the country. Progressives, he said, were concerned with the human needs of the majority of the nation's population, rather than the welfare of the privileged. While there was no comment from the Roosevelt camp, conjecture increased that the California senator had been provoked enough to come out with a strong endorsement of the Democratic nominee. Ickes went to California, at the request of Frank Walsh, to confer with Johnson about the possibility of campaigning for Roosevelt. Johnson finally agreed to speak publicly—twice in California and once in Chicago.[35]

In his first speech in San Francisco, Johnson bitterly attacked the Hoover administration and called on all progressive Republicans to support Roosevelt. Hoover was incapable of understanding the economic problems faced by the nation, he charged, and Republicans should not feel bound to party loyalty under the present circumstances. Loyalty to America must come before loyalty to bankers and the power trust. In a Los Angeles speech a few days later, Johnson said California progressives should give Roosevelt the same support they had given him when he ran for governor back in 1910. Attacking Wall Street, big business, party regularity, and the leadership of the national Republican party, he spoke of Roosevelt's philosophy, which "speaks the hopes and aspirations of this common humanity, demanding for all alike, rich and poor, high and low, big and little, the same rights in government, and insisting that the blessings of government shall not be showered upon a selected class." In his last campaign speech, in Chicago, Johnson reviewed President Hoover's career and philosophy and said that the president had been wrong many times and broken many promises to the American people. He declared that the economic crisis demanded a change in the White House.[36]

In letters to progressive colleagues Peter Norbeck, Charles McNary, and Bronson Cutting during October, Johnson said he expected Roosevelt to carry the country on Election Day, unless big business and the power trusts were somehow able to turn the tide with their funds. He told Cutting of his lack of concern over threats of various supporters of Hoover that they would work against his reelection to the Senate in 1934: "I infinitely prefer to take the present abuse and suffer the consummation of the threats of what will happen in the future than always or at any time to be in the attitude of running with the hare and hunting with the hounds."[37]

Cutting spent a few weeks after his meeting with Roosevelt before he decided to endorse him formally. In early October, he wrote his mother about his indecision over the campaign. He would definitely repudiate the Hoover administration, but he actually believed that Norman Thomas, the Socialist party presidential nominee, would make the best chief executive. However, he agreed that the best practicable alternative to Hoover was Roosevelt. Cutting expressed doubts, nevertheless, about the extent of the Democratic nominee's progressivism: "The . . . immediate question to decide is, whether Roosevelt or Hoover is the lesser of two evils, and whether, if I believe the former, I am not under some moral obligation to say so." The New Mexico senator finally decided to endorse Roosevelt, convinced that he would carry the state in November. Cutting authorized the National Progressive League to release a statement of support on October 21. Asserting that Roosevelt was for the average American, that his career had been devoted to improving the living conditions of the masses, and that he was "an idealist who has sought to put his ideals into practice," Cutting urged a vote for the Democratic national ticket.[38]

On October 26, Cutting spoke in Denver under the auspices of the National Progressive League. He criticized Hoover's record and depicted Roosevelt as an independent Democrat who would not be accountable to political bosses, but only to the American people. On November 6, Cutting renewed his appeal for those who supported his ideals to back Roosevelt. In a speech at Albuquerque, he said the major issue of the campaign was that one candidate thought it too expensive to put the unemployed to work, while the other made it the main item of his platform. The masses should ignore Hoover's appeal to their fears and pay attention to Roosevelt's appeal to their hopes.[39]

After Sucher's meetings with the La Follette brothers during September, the senator wrote Cutting, indicating that he was undecided as to his activities during the campaign. While certain that he would issue a statement giving his reasons for rejecting Hoover's candidacy (similar to his declaration in the 1928 campaign), he was doubtful about supporting Roosevelt wholeheartedly. La Follette wrote: "I sense in his speeches confirmation of my estimate of the lack in depth and breadth of his fundamental progressivism." He was concerned that support of Roosevelt would be interpreted as backing for Democrats in Wisconsin, who were regarded as reactionary by progressives in the state. The latter had lost their hold on the Republican organization to the conservatives in the 1932 state primaries, with the surprising upset of Governor Philip La Follette's bid for a second two-year term. The senator wanted to remain out of the state election but knew this would be difficult if he endorsed Roosevelt.[40]

Despite his doubts, La Follette issued an endorsement of Roosevelt, as well as the Democratic candidates for governor and senator in Wisconsin, on October 19. A few days later, his brother similarly endorsed the Democratic candidate when he addressed a Springfield, Illinois, rally as a replacement for Senator Norris, who had taken ill in his tour across the country for Roosevelt. The La Follette paper, *The Progressive*, published an editorial of support in its October 22 issue. While supporting the Democratic nominees for governor and senator, the La Follette brothers backed progressive candidates for Congress and the state legislature, wherever they had a chance of victory. The senator said he was supporting Roosevelt as the only immediate hope for the relief of 10 million unemployed people. He would, however, feel free to oppose any Roosevelt policies that he felt were harmful to the nation's interest, and he continued to harbor no illusions about the reactionary nature of the two major party organizations.[41]

La Follette expected a new party alignment in the near future because of the depression. He was the only one of the four progressives most actively courted by Roosevelt who refused to speak in his behalf on the campaign trail. Norris, who had set up a grueling schedule of eleven major speeches from October 17 to November 7, in cities ranging from Philadelphia to Long Beach, California, had to ask both Philip La Follette and Bronson Cutting to replace him because the traveling wore down his health.[42]

The other two progressive senators who endorsed Roosevelt did so without public notice. Lynn Frazier said in a September interview that he would not support Hoover, reaffirming his earlier statements, but he refused to commit himself publicly to Roosevelt. Henrik Shipstead predicted shortly before the election that Roosevelt would carry Minnesota and win election to the White House by the most decisive majority in many years. He agreed to preside at a political rally addressed by Norris, but he refused to clarify his attitude toward the campaign in any explicit manner. Since both senators were listed as members of the National Progressive League, despite their unwillingness to make a clear public endorsement or speak for Roosevelt, they were regarded as supporters of the Democratic nominee in 1932.[43]

Four progressive Republican senators—Borah, Nye, Couzens, and Norbeck—chose to remain neutral in the 1932 campaign. Borah naturally attracted the most journalistic scrutiny. At the beginning of August, the Idaho senator said he would not support either ticket but would back the Republican state organization. He continued to be critical of the Republican platform, especially its prohibition and economic planks.[44]

Sen. Arthur Vandenberg of Michigan, a moderate with close ties to both progressive and conservative leaders of his party, attempted to gain Borah's endorsement for the president. He wrote Borah in late August: "I am impatiently waiting for your Republican commitment in the present campaign. Some how or other I have a feeling that it is on the way. I can think of nothing more important at the moment, not only to the Party, but particularly to the country."[45]

After Borah replied that he could not endorse Hoover, Vandenberg again wrote him, indicating that he could certainly state his disagreements with the president but declare that he preferred him over Roosevelt. Vandenberg believed that Borah's support could swing many undecided voters to Hoover. He suggested that Borah deliver a brief radio speech during the last week of the campaign or send a letter of endorsement to the Republican National Committee for release shortly before the election. However, Borah was unrelenting in his determination to avoid endorsement of the president. He wrote an Idaho editor who urged him to come out for Hoover: "I am perfectly aware I am being criticized because of my silence. . . . whatever the result may be to me politically, I will not advocate a program in which I do not believe nor prostitute my intellect in defense of policies which I believe unwise, if not unpatriotic." He said he believed the Republican party was wandering away from its long-held principles.[46]

At the end of October, the Associated Press quoted Borah as saying he would vote for Hoover but not campaign for him. The Idaho senator issued a statement, claiming that he had made no such comments to anyone. As the issues developed in the remaining days of the campaign, he would make a determination on how to vote, said Borah. Casting an absentee ballot a few days before the election, he refused to indicate how he had voted, maintaining his noncommittal attitude toward the presidential campaign to the very end. After the election, he wrote columnist Walter Lippmann: "I found myself out of harmony with both the candidates in this campaign, particularly upon economic and monetary questions. It did not seem to me there was any program whatever before the people purporting toward relief,—and this vote was a protest vote. However, I sincerely hope that the new President will be equal to the task."[47]

Gerald Nye had indicated in the spring of 1932 that he would concentrate on his own reelection campaign in North Dakota and ignore the presidential race. His attitude had not changed by the fall. He indicated his views in a letter to Senator Norris: "I could not and would not support Hoover so long as his administration withheld from agriculture as much in the way of relief as was being granted to the big and selfish interests." Nye avoided mention of Hoover or Roosevelt in his campaign speeches. His attitude toward the Democratic nominee was summed up in a comment to Norris: "As for Roosevelt I do not and could not enthuse over him as you do." In late October at a campaign rally in Bismarck, Nye condemned the political leadership of the nation for its ineffectiveness in the economic crisis. He confronted criticisms of his neutral stand on the presidency a week later in Minot, saying that any Republican in the state who endorsed Roosevelt was foolish, because it would only serve to put more voters into the Democratic column in the statewide races. On the other hand, he could not support Hoover and speak for the farmers of his state. Nye remained neutral to the very end of the campaign and won reelection handily.[48]

James Couzens also refused entreaties that he endorse Hoover. Vandenberg urged him, as he had with Borah, to issue a simple statement of support. Donald Richberg of the National Progressive League attempted to enlist Couzens in a Roosevelt campaign rally in Michigan, at which Senator Norris was to speak. His Senate secretary, John Carson, tried to convince him that he should go to the Norris gathering. But Couzens refused to commit himself to either candidate in any way. He wrote Vandenberg: "I can get up no enthusiasm for either candidate. I have received some letters from out in the State asking me to make some speeches but I have declined and intend to remain out of the campaign." He told his secretary that he did not see how anyone could expect him to endorse Hoover after he had been so critical of his record in the White House. He expressed the belief that he was a senator for all the people of Michigan, not just the Republicans of that state. Therefore, he refused to engage in a campaign for others seeking high office. He wrote Richberg that he would take no role in the campaign and was completely unenthusiastic about it.[49]

Despite all this, the *New York Times* reported that Couzens was seen on the platform when President Hoover delivered a campaign speech in Detroit. Couzens said nothing publicly and seemed anxious to leave the meeting as soon as possible. Apparently, he had believed it only proper to pay his respects to the president while he was in Michigan; this incident did not change his public position of neutrality.[50]

Besides Nye, Peter Norbeck was the only other progressive Republican senator to face a reelection contest in 1932, and he had a similar dilemma. Should he endorse an unpopular President, of whom he had been critical? Norbeck decided that his conscience would not allow it. On the other hand, his opinion of Roosevelt was definitely unfavorable. He wrote a friend after Roosevelt's nomination: "I have absolutely no confidence in him or his party, and I know the party and its leaders thoroughly." In his campaign speeches, he blamed the Democrats during the Wilson administration for the farm depression of the 1920s and implied that Hoover was not solely responsible for the harsh economic conditions facing the nation. At Sioux Falls, he declared that, as a Republican, he hoped for the success of the entire ticket. But he avoided a flat endorsement of the president, admitting only that he would feel less comfortable with the Democrats in power. Norbeck was attempting to run an independent campaign so that he could survive the expected Democratic landslide. His tactics proved correct, as he won reelection while the Democrats swept the state, including most local offices.[51]

Charles McNary and Arthur Capper were the only two members of the progressive bloc to endorse and make campaign speeches for Hoover. Both moderate in their progressive views, they had the closest ties to the regulars in the Republican party. McNary delivered two radio speeches in Chicago, as well as an address at Madison Square Garden in New York City, during the last week of the campaign. Praising Hoover's programs for the farmer, he called Roosevelt "ambiguous or evasive on controversial issues" and said the people were still unaware of his stand on many major questions. Predicting Hoover's reelection by a substantial majority, he warned the people that a new president with plans for radical policy changes would only further depress industry and thus retard economic recovery.[52]

Capper, one of the most active campaigners for Hoover's reelection, said in his speeches that the president had "courage and backbone" and that the American people should not abandon him. The reins of government should not be placed in the hands of a far less qualified and experienced man, vowed Capper. In radio speeches over his own Topeka station, in addresses in Ohio and Iowa, and in his editorials in *Capper's Weekly* and other of his farm publications, Capper emphasized that Hoover was from the West, while Roosevelt was an easterner. Despite his valiant efforts, Capper privately was pessimistic over Hoover's chances. He wrote Borah that it would be difficult for the President to carry Kansas.[53]

On Election Day, Roosevelt swept the nation, winning forty-two of the forty-eight states. Now the members of the progressive Republican Senate bloc, having split over their stand on the election, faced a new challenge. How much influence could they, liberal members of the minority party in Congress, exert over a president who claimed that he agreed with many of their ideals and principles? Would they lose their identity and merge with the Democratic party? Would they revolt against him on party grounds? Would the progressive Republicans play an important role in the advancement of the New Deal, or in its demise? The progressives looked to the advent of a new administration with feelings of both optimism and concern.

[4]

The Cabinet Overtures
and the Hundred Days

Franklin D. Roosevelt's accession to the presidency promised a bright future for progressive goals. Hiram Johnson thought the election results were evidence of a political revolution of the common people, determined that the federal government should pay attention to their needs rather than the demands of the wealthy. Challenging the leadership of his party to recognize the aspirations of the average American by adopting progressive programs, Johnson dismissed criticism by conservative Republicans of Senators Norris, La Follette, Cutting, and himself for having supported Roosevelt. He also scotched rumors that he would accept a committee chairmanship as his reward for endorsing the president-elect. The progressive Republicans, he said, had two major goals for the future. They wished to aid Roosevelt in the formulation and implementation of his programs, but at the same time, they wanted to liberalize their own party to make it competitive with the Democrats in future elections. The key issue of the moment was the unemployment problem, Johnson declared, rather than prohibition, which had received too much emphasis during the campaign. He reaffirmed that he had no interest in patronage, that he had supported Roosevelt on principle, rather than for the hope of political gain. He believed Roosevelt was faced by a crisis never equaled in American history.[1]

George Norris agreed that the progressives had supported Roosevelt "with a zeal and unselfishness which I think is remarkable. Not one of them, so far as I know, was guided in the slightest degree, by any thought of personal gain or advancement." The La Follette brothers sent telegrams of congratulations, to which Roosevelt responded that he would like their support and counsel in the days ahead. A *Progressive* editorial declared that "Progressives in Wisconsin and throughout the nation generally will rejoice in the election of Franklin D. Roosevelt and the smashing repudiation of Hooverism." The Republican party was warned to turn toward liberalism or face the drift of all progressives either to the Democratic party or a third-party organization.[2]

Of those progressives who had endorsed Roosevelt, the least optimistic was Bronson Cutting. He told Philip La Follette of his doubt that the Democratic party would promote liberal programs. To his mother he wrote: "I wish I felt a little more real confidence as to what the new administration will do." He considered Roosevelt's landslide victory undesirable and noted that he had "no confidence in the Democratic party as a whole. Perhaps they will give us a pleasant surprise but I confess that I rather doubt it."[3]

Other progressive Republicans now pledged support to the new president. Arthur Capper offered Roosevelt "my whole-hearted support in the mighty task you must undertake." The president-elect thanked Capper and expressed a desire for cooperation. Charles McNary was invited to visit Roosevelt to discuss politics and agriculture. The Oregon senator wrote his brother afterward: "He is very affable and I think him much on the square and I am sure it will be a pleasure to work with him." James Couzens wrote: "I will be in a friendly atmosphere if a majority of the Democrats go along with legislation to better provide for our countrymen than has been done heretofore." But he doubted the Democrats would stay united long enough to accomplish the passage of much reform legislation. Peter Norbeck, relieved that he had survived the Democratic landslide in South Dakota, expressed the view that Roosevelt had failed to be frank with the voters, but that no one should consider the election results a fluke.[4]

The president-elect, wanting to retain the bridge built to the progressive Republican camp during the campaign, decided within a few weeks of his election to offer cabinet posts to some of them. While reporting rumors of such offers, the *New York Times* indicated that those who had endorsed Roosevelt were on record as unwilling to leave the Senate and join Roosevelt's administration. They wished to preserve their identity and independence and be free to criticize any policies with which they disagreed. Norris spoke for the group when he said he would not consider a cabinet appointment and advised his colleagues to do likewise, so as not to cast doubts on their motives during the campaign. The progressive bloc was too small to permit any to leave without harming the liberal-conservative balance in the Senate, Norris asserted. He believed the progressives could best help the new president by fighting for good programs and insisting on good personnel in high government positions. They must ensure that Roosevelt stayed on a progressive path, avoiding the advice of reactionary Democrats who now wished to advise him.[5]

Despite the publicized sentiments of these Republicans, Roosevelt was determined to invite them into his cabinet. He spoke first with Bronson Cutting in early December. The New Mexico senator was queried about his availability for secretary of interior, although not formally offered the post until late January. Cutting did not commit himself and told newsmen that the progressive Republicans should prepare their own legislative program, which would be submitted to the president for his consideration. Indicating he was prepared to support Roosevelt on progressive legislation, he stated that the progressive Republican bloc in the Senate did not expect patronage and would not consider leaving the party to become Democrats. On January 19, Roosevelt formally offered the Interior Department post to Cutting, indicating that he did not want a final answer until Cutting had some time to consider it carefully.[6]

A few days later, Cutting and Senator La Follette conferred with Roosevelt on unemployment relief and the cabinet. Rumors that Cutting would be the next interior secretary were widespread, but he remained undecided. Despite a front-page story in the *New York Times* predicting that Cutting was certain to be in the cabinet, he ultimately decided to turn down the offer. Cutting's privately expressed doubts about Roosevelt persisted in his mind. He later told a staff assistant that he had rejected the president-elect's offer because he wanted to remain a "free agent" and that he "could not, somehow, trust Franklin." The New Mexico senator's suspicions and distrust of Roosevelt were to be reciprocated by the president and cause troubled relations between the two men.[7]

In mid-January, Hiram Johnson was also offered the post of secretary of the interior. As early as December, various unnamed individuals had asked him if he was interested in an administration appointment. No definite offer was tendered, however, and Johnson responded that he would not consider such a proposition until it was a reality. However, he confided to his sons that he had given much thought to the question of working for Roosevelt. He declared: "I have lived so long in absolute independence that it is a very difficult thing for me to see myself a member of any group where I would discipline myself to the views of any one, or any few men. . . . I have never been able to take my politics or my governmental policies from others. And this is why, perhaps I have been in rebellion and opposition so much. . . . I know myself well enough to know that I could not change, . . . I do not think therefore that there would be any real charm for me in any Cabinet position, nor do I believe that such small ability as I may have, could be best thus employed."[8]

At a conference with Roosevelt, the president-elect greeted Johnson warmly, with flattering personal comments and praise for the strong support California had given him in the election. Telling him they had similar views on most issues, Roosevelt asked Johnson to become his interior secretary. Roosevelt was well aware of Cutting's reluctance to consider the post and therefore felt free to offer the job to another progressive at the same time. His motives are not clear in this matter. Was he interested more in gaining political points with progressive Republicans than in having them in important positions in his administration? This seems quite plausible, since, according to Roosevelt adviser Raymond Moley, the president-elect had considered naming a progressive Republican to the more significant post of attorney general but never offered any of them that position.[9]

Roosevelt told Johnson he was perfectly equipped to handle the Interior post. Thanking him for his kind words, Johnson declared that he did not want and would not accept any cabinet offer. He spoke of his desire to maintain his individualism, but Roosevelt told him that he hoped to increase the responsibilities of the job and wanted Johnson to avoid a final decision until he had some time to think it over. Johnson left the conference with a very favorable impression of the president-elect. "He is genial, kindly, and sympathetic. I think I may sum up the impression that he made upon me by saying he is just a human being, and because he is just this, he is vastly different from the man who now occupies the White House. . . . He presents . . . as fair a hope for us as during my political career has been presented by any man." He was pleased by Roosevelt's expressed desire to maintain cordial relations with the progressive bloc in the Senate.[10]

With Cutting and Johnson refusing the Interior post, Roosevelt now determined upon Harold Ickes as his progressive liaison with the Republican senators who had endorsed him for president. Ickes had been involved in the National Progressive League and wanted the Interior position, so indicating his interest in letters and phone calls to Senators Johnson, La Follette, Cutting, and Nye. While all expressed their support, they contended that it was not proper for them to suggest his name to Roosevelt. However, when Raymond Moley asked the progressives to suggest someone to represent their interests at a policy meeting on the London Economic Conference, they recommended Ickes and this convinced Roosevelt that Ickes should be offered the job.[11]

Before Ickes met with Roosevelt, the four senators who had backed the president-elect in 1932 were asked their opinion of his qualifications to be interior secretary. With their endorsement, he was offered the position in late February and gladly accepted. Hiram Johnson was especially happy at the turn of events: "I think his selection is probably the best he could have made. There is no question of Ickes' ability and integrity. He regards the place as a great opportunity, and he has had sufficient experience to know how to conduct himself under the circumstances. I really look to see him make as good a secretary of the Interior as we have ever had." T.R.B. of *The New Republic* called Ickes's selection "the real surprise" of the cabinet and declared: "Quite clearly the Ickes appointment is due to the influence of Senator Hiram Johnson of California, and is competely progressive."[12]

Roosevelt also considered Philip La Follette for a number of government positions. Aware of rumors that he was being considered for a position in the new administration, Philip wrote his brother in early December that he would give serious thought to any offer but would make no final decision without consulting with him, Cutting, and Norris. In mid-December, a spokesman for the president-elect wrote Senator La Follette, informing him that his brother was being considered for attorney general and that Roosevelt wished to know the reaction of the Senate progressives to this possibility. The senator spoke to Roosevelt's representative over the phone, informing him that such an offer would require a great amount of analysis.[13]

While in the process of preparing for a European tour from January to March, Philip La Follette met with Col. Edward House, a former adviser to Woodrow Wilson who was working for Roosevelt during the transition period before inauguration. House gave him information and letters to assist his travel through Europe and also spoke of Roosevelt's need for the support of the western progressives. La Follette replied that the progressives would act as a guard against extreme reactions to the left or right. They should not join Roosevelt's administration, however, unless "he was willing to apply courageously and intelligently the remedies that would at least try to get to the guts of the depression." The La Follette brothers had spoken earlier with Cutting about the cabinet speculation, and the former governor now sailed to Europe with a clear indication that if the proper situation developed, he would be willing to consider working for Roosevelt. After he left, his brother received a telegram from Roosevelt adviser Henry Morgenthau, indicating the president-elect wished to speak with Philip. The senator wired back that since his brother was in Europe, he would speak for him in his absence.[14]

Informed that Roosevelt wanted to see him, La Follette responded that he was not seeking an interview but was ready to consult with the president-elect on any matter of public affairs. Roosevelt spokesman John F. Sinclair sent on this letter to the president-elect, observing: "It seems to be the attitude of the Progressives that they will cooperate in every way, but they do not want to be making suggestions to you with reference to public policy unless you ask definitely for their cooperation."[15]

At the conference, La Follette was ushered into a room where Roosevelt and Sen. Burton K. Wheeler of Montana were talking. Roosevelt told La Follette in front of Wheeler that he wanted the Wisconsin senator's brother in his administration. La Follette told the president-elect he wished to discuss the matter further in private; Roosevelt then invited La Follette to join Cutting in a visit to Warm Springs. It was not long before news leaked out that Philip La Follette was being seriously considered for an administration post. Moreover, *The Progressive* noted that the position of attorney general would be a major goal for the progressives, as this office opened up the possibility of antitrust enforcement.[16]

At the Warm Springs meeting, La Follette came to the conclusion that Roosevelt's attitudes on public power, farm relief, unemployment relief, and public works were similar to the progressive positions. Roosevelt informed him that he planned to offer the attorney general post to La Follette's brother if Sen. Thomas Walsh of Montana, a progressive Democrat, turned down the job. In any case, he wanted to know what positions were acceptable to Philip La Follette, since he wanted him as a part of his official family. The senator declared that he doubted his brother would be willing to leave Wisconsin unless the opportunity offered him for public service was outstanding.[17]

Meanwhile, Senator Cutting hinged his decision on entering the cabinet on whether former Governor La Follette also joined the administration. But regardless of whether his brother joined Roosevelt, Robert La Follette made it clear that he would support the new administration as long as it pursued progressive goals. He expressed no expectation of being consulted on policy, however. He also warned the president-elect that pursuing progressive programs would divide the Democratic party down the middle, but he saw this as an opportunity for Roosevelt to make his party a progressive one. Roosevelt, indicating that he was aware of this possibility, said this was the reason he wanted the support of the La Follettes and Cutting.[18]

Writing his brother in Europe, La Follette indicated that he expected Senator Walsh to accept the offer to become attorney general, and that Roosevelt was offering Philip the position purely as a means of gaining the support of the La Follettes for his administration. In a letter to his sister, the Wisconsin senator wrote: "The chances of Phil's being offered a place in the cabinet are now very remote. Everything I hear indicates Walsh will accept and that eliminates Phil as I see it. If it works out this way Cutting will decline and that's that."[19]

At the beginning of February, Philip La Follette wrote from Berlin. Indicating his approval of the course followed by his brother in conferring with Roosevelt, he noted that Cutting was correct in refusing to join the cabinet unless another progressive Republican was also selected. Philip La Follette believed that

> the big central question is *we must not* be maneuvered into a situation which will divide our forces.—Hence I think it will be for the best if it works out that none of us are in his cabinet, and are left free to use this year to organize ourselves into a closer and more definitely organized group.—There is real danger that by going into his cabinet we would become prisoners to his future—that danger is *greatly* augmented if one of us goes alone.

Senator La Follette responded a few days later, agreeing with his brother's views and speculating that Philip might be offered the Interior post if Cutting declined it.[20]

Once Cutting had turned down Roosevelt's offer to be secretary of interior and Walsh had accepted the post of attorney general, Roosevelt asked Senator La Follette whether his brother would consider accepting the chairmanship of the Federal Power Commission or membership on the Federal Trade Commission. A final answer was delayed until Philip returned from his European trip. Finally, in mid-March, after Roosevelt's inauguration, the two La Follettes went to the White House at the new President's invitation for a one-hour conference.[21]

The senator's brother prepared a nine-page memorandum summarizing the subjects discussed at the meeting. The foreign situation, including the rise of Hitler in Germany, was discussed, as well as the relief program plans of the new administration. The main topic of the hour, however, was the president's wish to have the former Wisconsin governor in his administration. Philip replied that he was not interested in leaving Wisconsin at that time, but that he would make himself available later if there were an urgent need for his services. He believed that other people were better suited to handle a position on the Federal Power Commission or Federal Trade Commission, or in the public works and relief program. Roosevelt requested that the brothers keep in touch with the White House and visit him often. The La Follettes considered the overall atmosphere of the meeting very pleasant.[22]

So, after courting the progressive Republicans for four months after the election, Roosevelt succeeded only in getting Harold Ickes, a close friend of the senators, to accept a cabinet post. Henry Wallace's appointment as secretary of agriculture, while generally applauded by progressives, was not intimately connected with their influence or special desires. Roosevelt's attempt to fortify the bridge built between him and the progressives during the campaign had only partially succeeded.

The President was aware of the nature of the progressive personality. Shortly before the election of 1932, he had spoken at length about the progressives with one of his advisers, Rexford Guy Tugwell, a close friend and associate of many of them. He had declared at that time that the progressives "were wonderful people, but they did have the general characteristic of complete unreliability." As supreme individualists, they were unwilling to accept the leadership of others or to work effectively as a group. Political leaders must make deals to gain their ends, Roosevelt told Tugwell, but the progressives were reluctant to condone this. As Tugwell later expressed Roosevelt's thoughts: "They insisted on dictating means as well as defining ends; they'd sacrifice the cause if the strategy happened not to please them, and they would be noisy and accusatory." Roosevelt believed that he would be unable to retain the support of the progressive Republicans through two terms in office. While expressing admiration for individual progressives, he also distrusted them. He hoped, however, that Tugwell would be able to firm up their support for the administration for as long a period as possible.[23]

Roosevelt made one other attempt to gain progressive support for his administration before he was inaugurated on March 4. The progressives, led by Norris, had long been promoting government ownership and operation of the power and nitrate plants at Muscle Shoals, Alabama, designed to bring electricity and improved economic conditions to the Tennessee valley. Norris was with the president-elect in Montgomery, Alabama, in late January when Roosevelt announced that he would support formation of a Tennessee Valley Authority (TVA) to operate the facilities at Muscle Shoals. The TVA would provide economic stimulation and capital improvement, boost the region's economy, save soil from erosion, prevent floods, and increase enormously the electrical energy supply of the nation. Norris's eyes were welling with tears as he told reporters that his dream was finally coming true. Hiram Johnson cheerfully declared: "Roosevelt has taken such a remarkable position concerning Muscle Shoals that we can forgive him many other things."[24]

A few weeks before the inauguration, T.R.B. of *The New Republic* declared that the progressives expected to be able to work in a harmonious manner with the new president. This would be a unique experience for the group, which had always worked in opposition to every president since Taft. Another promising sign for the future was the bloc's reaction to the Roosevelt cabinet. Although only Ickes was a close friend of the progressive Republicans, the cabinet also included Henry Wallace, Frances Perkins, Cordell Hull, and Thomas J. Walsh (until his tragic death two days before the inauguration)—all regarded as liberals. Borah, outgoing chairman of the Senate Foreign Relations Committee, had special words of praise for the new secretary of state, calling Hull "an able, cultured gentleman, a deep student of international affairs and a man of fine courage."[25]

Although the progressive Republicans were happy at the inauguration of a progressive-minded chief executive, they did not wish to lose their identity as a separate force in the Senate and in national politics. This explains the refusal of those senators who had supported Roosevelt to accept patronage, the retention of their committee chairmanships under the Democratic Congress, or a position with the administration. The progressives, in their pursuit of independence, attempted in the early months of 1933 to form a permanent organization to serve as a vehicle for their political activities—what they hoped would be an extension of the National Progressive League of 1932.

The progressives had never succeeded in forming a permanent organization that lasted beyond a presidential campaign. But Governor Pinchot of Pennsylvania decided to try again. In December 1932, he asked a friend, Rep. Philip D. Swing of California, to consult with Johnson and La Follette about calling a conference of progressive office holders to discuss future approaches toward the new administration. Johnson expressed interest, but La Follette seemed doubtful, thinking it better to await events after the inauguration before deciding on future strategy. Swing wrote that La Follette believed "that if Roosevelt was fortunate in having the Country return to some degree of prosperity, the probability was that the progressive rank and file would stay merged in the Democratic party, at least for another election. If Roosevelt's program failed to produce results, then the situation would be different." La Follette did believe, however, that the progressives should announce their own legislative proposals before Roosevelt usurped their goals. This would demonstrate that the progressives were not just effective as critics, as in past administrations, but were out to lead Roosevelt along the right path. Roosevelt could thus be judged by his adherence to progressive ideals. Pinchot was disappointed by La Follette's expressed reluctance to form a permanent organization, but he still wanted to hold a conference on the matter.[26]

Before his appointment as interior secretary, Harold Ickes was also a major promoter of a progressive conference to unite the group behind a common program and goals. In mid-January, he wrote Johnson, urging him to join in a conference of progressive senators, for which plans were being formulated by Senators Norris, Cutting, and La Follette, as well as Democrats Wheeler and Costigan. Despite Ickes's statement, Norris seemed strangely reluctant, as head of the progressive bloc in a nominal sense, to call such a conference. Ickes now prodded La Follette to chair such a meeting if Norris continued to be reluctant, and he suggested Cutting as a good choice for the leadership of any permanent organizational structure. The final result of Ickes's efforts was that Norris agreed to call an informal meeting for January 28, but Johnson now refused to attend! Ickes wrote Johnson of his disappointment: "I do think it of tremendous importance for the Progressives to make common cause and undertake to work together where and when they can."[27]

Norris, La Follette, Cutting, Wheeler, and Costigan attended the meeting along with only four other senators—Nye, Frazier, Shipstead, and John J. Blaine of Wisconsin (a lame duck). Norris expressed the desire to continue the National Progressive League as a vehicle to promote liberal reform. But no definite actions were taken, except that a subcommittee consisting of La Follette, Cutting, and Wheeler was formed to examine the prospects and practical concerns in forming a permanent organization—concerns such as funding and literature needs and the formation of a nationwide committee with representatives in every state. Ickes felt the main goal of a new organization should be to "at least create a skeleton organization so that two years from now or four years from now we won't have to start from scratch or act as individuals without a common understanding or a common objective."[28]

In early February, the subcommittee met and agreed on the concept of a progressive organization but expressed doubts about the ability to raise enough money to finance it. Norris announced at the end of the month that the progressives would encourage the administration toward progressive goals through the establishment of a national committee. Columnist Robert S. Allen wrote in *Common Sense* magazine at this point: "The Progressives . . . still hold to their belief that Roosevelt will display a militant liberal leadership. But they frankly are taking no chances. If he lives up to their expectations, well and good. If not they propose being ready to abandon ship and set out on their own again." However, Norris's announcement was premature, since a number of progressives refused to join any movement for a permanent organization. Among these were Borah, Johnson, Couzens, Norbeck, Capper, and McNary.[29]

Even those senators who had agreed to support a new organization could not be counted on to give up their highly cherished individualism. La Follette, for example, believed that Norris was too intent on cooperation with the Roosevelt administration and "reactionary Democrats." "I shall not be able to follow Norris's leadership," he told his brother, "if he persists in his adherence to the policy of silent cooperation which he has outlined." Hoping Roosevelt would succeed, La Follette yet was unwilling to tie the future of progressivism to his star. "I dread any open break with Norris and I know it will weaken the movement at least temporarily; but I would rather go on alone, if need be, than to have the movement destroyed." Once again, as many times in the past generation, the progressive Republican Senate bloc lacked unity. Would this group of twelve mavericks be able to exert any leverage on Roosevelt and the New Deal? This was a question not only asked by political observers but by the progressives themselves as the New Deal administration began in March 1933.[30]

A few weeks before the inauguration, Hiram Johnson predicted to his sons that "you'll see some of the most bizarre and fantastic legislation that ever was enacted." The California senator was impressed with the serenity and confidence of Roosevelt in the face of the nation's most significant crisis since the Civil War. It was because of prevailing conditions that Senator Borah publicly expressed concern that the Congress might confer dictatorial powers upon the new President, which he feared would upset the constitutional balance of power. The president could deal with the economic crisis by using the constitutional powers already granted the executive branch but unused by Hoover, Borah asserted, and Congress should not give up any of its cherished rights to the president—even for an emergency period. Thus there was evidence that progressives were both expectant and concerned about what the New Deal would mean to American traditions.[31]

Roosevelt's inaugural address attracted widespread interest among progressives. *The Progressive* praised it for its optimistic note and its call for action. This was not the time to be partisan, the journal declared, but rather to unite behind the president in the special session called to deal with the urgent economic problems of the nation. The general feeling among progressives was that Roosevelt had made a good beginning. Hiram Johnson, who attended the first presidential inauguration in his career and then went to the White House for tea, praised the section of the address where Roosevelt attacked the "moneychangers" who had led the nation into economic ruin. Certain that no Republican president would have dared to utter such a statement, Johnson told his sons: "The Lord only knows what is going to be done, but that he is going to endeavor to do something quickly is certain."[32]

On his first night in office, Roosevelt directed the secretary of the treasury to draft an emergency banking bill in time for the opening of the special session on March 9. Proclaiming a national bank holiday on March 5 to end the run on banking deposits, he also halted all transactions in gold. This was the beginning of the First Hundred Days of the New Deal, a period when Congress and the president together worked to accomplish more significant and numerous pieces of legislation than had ever been achieved in American history.

Immediately after the special session opened on March 9, the banking bill was passed by a unanimous voice vote in the House of Representatives and by 73 to 7 in the Senate, with practically no time for discussion and debate. The Emergency Banking Act granted the President authority for the banking orders he had already issued, established a means to help banks in trouble, and provided a method for reopening the closed banks. Many progressives favored the nationalization of the banking structure of the nation, but this was not part of the bill.

The progressive Republicans were far from united, with four (Couzens, Johnson, McNary, Norris) voting with the majority, four voting against (Borah, La Follette, Nye, and Shipstead) out of the total of seven nays cast in the Senate, and four not voting (although Norbeck and Frazier were listed as against and Capper for the bill). Norbeck expressed great concern over the passage of a bill without adequate time for debate: "When we undertake to frame important banking legislation in an hour we are liable to get ourselves in trouble." La Follette said he believed that no more important vote had been cast since the declaration of war in 1917. He was unhappy that, under the terms of the bill, the large New York banks would exercise practically dictatorial controls over the nation's banking system. The president, he said, should have greater control over banking than he had under the terms of the bill. Borah voted against the bill for similar reasons. In a letter to a constituent, he wrote that the bank bill was "laying the foundation for the creation of a financial dictatorship with headquarters in New York."[33]

Johnson, who had been invited to consult with Roosevelt the night before the opening of the special session, admitted that no one knew much about the banking bill, but he was impressed by Roosevelt's commitment to action and had determined that he would support the president's judgment on the matter. Capper, although announced as in favor of the legislation, served a warning on the administration later in the session that the president should not try to force a general banking reform bill through Congress as he had done with the emergency banking measure.[34]

On March 10, Roosevelt sent his second message to Congress, requesting power to cut $400 million from the payments to veterans and $100 million from the pay of federal employees. This economy bill passed Congress after only two days of debate, with only three progressive Republicans (Capper, Johnson, and McNary) voting with the majority, four voting against (Borah, Couzens, Frazier, Nye), and the remaining five not voting, although at least two (Cutting and La Follette) were known to oppose the legislation. Capper said he was supporting the grant of emergency powers to Roosevelt because there was no time for petty politics during a period of economic hardship. He hoped that Roosevelt would be fair in applying the law, which was essential to avoid bankruptcy. Couzens, on the other hand, considered the bill "iniquitous" and one that would be enforced by government bureaucrats, who lacked concern about the effect of pension cuts on veterans, rather than by the president or his lieutenants, who would be too involved in other matters. Borah asserted that an across-the-board percentage reduction for all government workers was unjust to those at the bottom of the scale. After its passage, he denounced the bill as "clearly in violation of the Constitution" because of its grant of new powers to the President.[35]

La Follette introduced two amendments to the bill, both of which were defeated. One would have limited the veterans' pay cut to 15 percent, while the other would have prevented a flat cut in the salary of government employees. La Follette regarded both the banking and economy bills as deflationary. While he wanted to support the president, he would not do so if he felt Roosevelt was steering in the wrong direction. Cutting, who had been absent for the vote, later declared that the bill was "the most indefensible piece of legislation ever passed by Congress." He did not intend to sit back and allow the bill to stand as it was.[36]

A number of progressives fought for reinstatement of veterans' pensions to the old standard rate later in the special session. Hiram Johnson pointed out that the early days of the special session had been ones of "hysteria," in which bills had been thrown at Congress in a bewildering fashion and pressure had been applied to pass them without any substantial debate. He had not known, Johnson said, that the Economy Act would have such a drastic effect on veterans, and he appealed for action to restore the cuts. Borah stated that a great injustice had been done: "The supreme question here is whether we are willing to retrace our steps, assume the power given to us by the people and retrieve the authority we have delegated to the President." La Follette also called for modification of the Economy Act to avoid putting tremendous hardship on veterans.[37]

But it was Cutting who led the progressive fight to alter the Economy Act. While offering an amendment to limit the pension cuts to 25 percent, he indicated that he felt the cut should be a maximum of 15 percent or be abolished altogether. Calling the legislation "the most infamous act ever passed," he told his colleagues that his bitter criticism was not personal, as he had known the president for many years and had "the highest affection and admiration" for him. Cutting asserted that the way to balance the national budget was not through cutting the income of the poorest members of the community, but through building up their purchasing power and that of all citizens.[38]

Despite Cutting's determined effort and a further plea from Johnson, the Cutting amendment, co-sponsored by Frederic Steiwer, Republican of Oregon, was ignored by the Senate. The progressives had lost a hard-fought struggle. The effects of this battle were to strain relations between Roosevelt and Cutting for the future. Privately, Cutting declared: "The veterans' fight has been extremely wearying, but I felt that it was up to me to make it, especially in view of the fact that I was not here to make a fight on the economy bill in March. We got nothing substantial in the way of legislation, but I do think the Administration will henceforth be rather leery about perpetuating the same kind of outrages which have been the rule in the last two months."[39]

The first actions of the new administration had been heavily oriented toward deflation, which led to expressions of displeasure by the progressives. Cutting was angered that Roosevelt was using a "steamroller" approach, insisting on action without careful thought and discussion on the part of Congress. The administration, he believed, was wasting its energies on harmful measures and losing the great opportunity afforded by the election mandate to introduce constructive programs. He was relieved that he had rejected a cabinet post, telling his mother: "How glad I am not to be a part of it!"[40]

The reaction of Hiram Johnson to the early trend of the New Deal was more favorable, and yet cautious, concern about the trend of events. While expressing admiration over Roosevelt's manner of taking hold of the presidency and pleasure that a "regular human being" had replaced "a direct descendent of God" in the White House, he admitted that most members of Congress did not fully understand the measures presented to them for action. The administration's proposals had not been "thoroughly digested," and Johnson was sure that the president's program would be "scrutinized now with much more care, and they will not be passed with the same celerity which characterized those of the financial crisis."[41]

The president's next move was to introduce a farm bill, destined to be known as the Agricultural Adjustment Act (AAA), which provided for reduction of farm mortgages, restriction of acreage, the levying of a tax on the processors of agricultural commodities, and the payment of fees to farmers who agreed to limit production. The AAA was the culmination of farm measures and proposals going back to the Populists. Its purpose was to create a balance between the production and consumption of farm products so that farm income would have the same relative purchasing power or parity that existed from 1909 to 1914. While the progressives were pleased that attention was being given to the plight of a large majority of their constituents, there were many misgivings about the effectiveness of the legislation.

Norris doubted that the bill would restore prosperity, but he admitted that no one else had suggested a better alternative. He regarded the AAA as an important first step in curing the evils the farmer had to contend with. He was not disturbed by the tremendous power given the president and the secretary of agriculture under the legislation, because he believed that Roosevelt and Wallace were "moved by the very highest of motives." Borah thought that the only acceptable portion of the AAA was its farm refinancing section. The legislation would not succeed, he claimed, in restoring the price of farm goods over the long term, and a sound method of ensuring higher farm prices was essential. Frazier declared that, in order to increase the purchasing power of farmers, the bill needed a provision for a reasonable profit as well as an average cost of production.[42]

Capper thought the AAA a step in the right direction but not a solution. It was an experiment in national planning that granted unusual powers to the executive branch of government. He also saw Wallace as well fitted to carry out the intent of the legislation. Norbeck viewed the bill as necessary, but he had misgivings about the effectiveness of the farm mortgage provision. Finally, Nye called the AAA a "glorious experiment" that at least promised an improvement in commodity prices. But he was dissatisfied with the overall nature of the bill and, along with Borah and Frazier, voted against the final draft of the legislation, while the other nine progressive Republicans in the Senate supported it.[43]

Two other key bills of the First Hundred Days were the Tennessee Valley Authority legislation and Sen. Hugo Black's bill for a thirty-hour work week, which was sponsored by the American Federation of Labor and designed to spread available jobs by banning interstate shipment of goods produced by labor working more than thirty hours a week. All the progressives rallied around the TVA, long the major effort of most progressives who believed in the concept of public power. But the Black bill was opposed by two progressives, Borah and McNary. The former explained his vote to an Idaho union leader by claiming that the proposal was unconstitutional. The bill failed of passage because the president also considered it unconstitutional and instead moved for the enactment of a general recovery bill, one that would regulate both industry and labor. The main emphasis for the rest of the session was on passage of the National Recovery Act and unemployment relief legislation.[44]

Unemployment relief came first, with the president proposing a Civilian Conservation Corps (CCC), an extremely popular proposal that took 250,000 young men from relief families and put them to work under the direction of the War Department at soil conservation and reforestation projects. However,

Roosevelt expressed reluctance to promote an extensive program of public works and federal grants to the states for relief. But he came around to support of these concepts under pressure from progressives in both parties. Senators La Follette and Costigan renewed their demand for an adequate relief bill, which passed on March 30 with the support of all progressive Republicans except McNary. While rejoicing over this hard-won accomplishment, which had been stalled in the interim between election day and the inauguration, the progressives had to lobby actively for the public works bill. La Follette wrote his sister at the beginning of April that the Roosevelt cabinet was bitterly divided on the issue of public works programs, with many advocating a balancing of the budget and the restoration of business confidence, in the spirit of the Hoover administration. La Follette felt that Roosevelt must swing away from a deflationary policy and use public works to stimulate the purchasing power of the masses. Otherwise, a sharp recession leading to a new bottoming of the economy was likely within a few months.[45]

La Follette was giving up hope that Roosevelt would support "an *adequate* program to restore purchasing power." However, along with Senators Wagner, Costigan, and Cutting, he went to the White House on April 14 to discuss a program to create jobs for the millions of unemployed. Roosevelt gave the senators the impression that he had committed himself to a large public works program and that he wanted them to formulate the details. But after the conference, the president told newsmen that little could be accomplished by such a program, a statement that upset La Follette. He wrote a friend that he was disappointed over Roosevelt's lack of planning and organization: "It . . . seems to me clear that in a crisis of this gravity, with mighty economic forces at play, the policy of leaping and looking afterwards may very easily prove disastrous." Philip La Follette offered to help his brother present his plans for public works in greater detail at another meeting with Roosevelt. The former governor told his brother: "If R. *sees* it, and *wants* it, we are rapidly approaching the time where our crowd can not only be of help to him, but can help push some of the reactionaries out, and at the same time pick up enough substantial, open-minded conservatives to put a real program over."[46]

On May 8, Costigan, Cutting, and La Follette introduced a public works bill calling for a $6 billion outlay, with all power over programs granted to the president. Meanwhile, the administration had formulated a more modest program as part of its recovery bill, calling for an investment of $3.3 billion. La Follette thought this inadequate, but Roosevelt's proposal which became the Public Works Administration (PWA) was accepted as part of the National Recovery Act (NRA) by Congress. Although the progressives had failed to see their money level accepted, they had certainly played a key role in impressing upon the president the necessity for a major commitment to public works projects. *The Progressive* proudly pointed out that Roosevelt's plan was modeled on that of Governor Philip La Follette's administration in Wisconsin during 1931 and 1932. The unemployment relief legislation was also copied from the La Follette experience in Wisconsin.[47]

The National Recovery Act, an experiment in business-government planning, was the most significant piece of legislation of the First Hundred Days. The final bill had something from each of several schools of economic thought. For business, there was a section providing for codes of fair competition and exemptions from the antitrust laws. For the national planners, there was government licensing of business through government approval of the codes written by industry. Labor got minimum wages, maximum hours, and section 7-A, which promised collective bargaining. Finally, title 2 established the Public Works Administration.

The NRA was a carry-over of the New Nationalism philosophy of Theodore Roosevelt and Herbert Croly. The progressive Republicans, however, for the most part were suspicious of any cooperation between the federal government and the "trusts and monopolies" of the country, and they insisted upon enforcement, rather than suspension, of the antitrust laws.

La Follette, concerned over the implications of the NRA, convinced the senators drawing up the bill to include a business licensing provision, which could be used as a weapon by the administration to protect the public interest. But despite the Wisconsin senator's misgivings, it was Borah who was the leading progressive critic of the bill, especially its provision for suspending the antitrust legislation, including the Sherman and Clayton Acts. He alleged that the bill was a serious step toward further concentration of wealth and that it weakened the terms of the Sherman Act. Quoting from the writings of Louis Brandeis on the dangers of monopolies, he said that the Democratic party had promised to strengthen and enforce the antitrust laws during Roosevelt's campaign for the presidency. Borah was also suspicious of the amount of power that would be given to the administrator of the NRA, Hugh Johnson. The Idaho senator proposed an amendment to the bill, stating that the industrial codes were not to be construed as allowing the establishment of combinations in restraint of trade, price fixing, or other monopolistic practices.[48]

All of the progressive Republicans present, with the exception of Borah, voted in favor of the NRA when it came up for passage on June 9. Although the Borah amendment was made part of the Senate bill, the Idaho senator so loathed the bill that he cast his vote against it. When the conference report on the bill came up for a Senate vote on June 13, however, seven progressives switched sides, joining Borah in opposition and leaving only Capper and McNary still in favor of the NRA. The progressive Republicans had changed their minds because the Borah amendment was deleted in the Senate-House conference committee for all practical purposes, as language referring to combinations in restraint of trade and price fixing was dropped.[49]

Borah, declaring that consumers and small businessmen would have no chance to compete with big business under the NRA, denounced the congressional action as an emasculation of the Sherman Act. Later, he wrote: "The masses will pay for it in the end. There may be a temporary revival, but in the end, the price fastened upon the great body of the people will amount to nothing less than a crime." Another reason for the progressives' abandonment of the administration on the NRA was the failure of La Follette's amendment, requiring public disclosure of the income tax returns of businesses under NRA supervision, to be accepted by the conference committee. The Senate had agreed to the amendment by a vote of 56 to 27. The final NRA vote was much closer, 46 to 39, as the progressive Republicans, nurtured on the antitrust laws and suspicion of Wall Street, expressed their displeasure over the possibility that the federal government was going to ignore the abuses of big business. They were ready to criticize the NRA as soon as its weaknesses became apparent.[50]

While Congress was in session, President Roosevelt, faced with the necessity of selecting a delegation to attend the London Economic Conference dealing with the world depression, decided to ask a progressive Republican to serve as one of its members. Roosevelt first asked Ickes to persuade his good friend Hiram Johnson to accept the position. At a White House meeting of the three men on May 21, however, Johnson spoke of his independent role and asserted he could not yield his individualism to serve the president in London. Roosevelt then asked Johnson to think about a European vacation after the conference, but Johnson refused to reconsider. The senator wrote his sons that his decision had been a difficult one, as the president had been very gracious and Johnson wanted to travel throughout Europe. But he felt that his independence would have been compromised had he gone to London, and that he could not permit.[51]

With Johnson out of consideration, Roosevelt turned to La Follette, who also refused to serve, despite a telegram from his brother urging him to accept. The Wisconsin senator contended that it was essential for him to remain in Washington and concentrate on the legislation being considered during the special session, especially that relating to industrial recovery and public works. Roosevelt finally succeeded in urging Senator Couzens to go as the progressive Republican representative at the conference. Again, the president had experienced difficulty in gaining the cooperation of progressives for a role in his administration.[52]

As the First Hundred Days came to an end, reaction among progressive Republicans to administration policies was mixed. As a group, the progressives had not been very effective, often dividing their bloc's votes on the major legislation. They had again demonstrated that they were supreme individualists, incapable of using their potential power and influence toward the fomulation of national policy based on their ideals. However, it must be said that even had they been truly united, they were faced with the realization that the Democratic party held an overwhelming number of seats in both houses of Congress, a factor that made any attempt at political leadership unlikely to succeed.

Most of the progressives disapproved of the Banking and Economy Acts, as well as the NRA, as these laws were perceived as deflationary and as aids to big business. The bloc was more pleased with the unemployment relief legislation, Black's thirty-hour bill, Roosevelt's promotion of TVA, section 7-A of the NRA (as well as its public works provisions), and the AAA. Although these laws were not seen as the solution to the nation's problems, at least these issues long promoted by the progressives had finally found a sympathetic friend in the White House, after years of conservative government. In the minds of the progressives, however, the extent of the administration's commitment to public works, workers, and farmers was yet untested. There was a long road to go before social justice was achieved. The progressives, therefore, had ambiguous feelings about the First Hundred Days of the New Deal.

Hiram Johnson was highly optimistic about the future and very positive toward Roosevelt. Detecting a definite change in the atmosphere of government in Washington and considering the progressive philosophy of government closer to fulfillment than at any point in his lifetime, he indicated that he was willing to go along with the president in almost anything he desired to do for the country. He praised the president's capacity for hard work, his energy and his willingness to experiment with new ideas. He told his fellow Senators:

> I am glad to pay my small tribute to the fine and gallant gentleman who sits in the White House . . . He has the adventure of youth and he has the wisdom of age. . . . we can thank God that there was a man in the White House who had the guts to do and go forward and to strive and to try and to take the responsibility of striving and trying.

In private, however, Johnson expressed concern to his sons that too many things were being attempted without real understanding of their implications by the Congress. He admitted: "We are shooting in the dark." But these concerns were mitigated by his genuine admiration for Roosevelt.[53]

La Follette's reaction to the First Hundred Days was one of pleasure, laced with dissatisfaction over some trends and a belief that the New Deal must go much further along the road to social justice before it could be labeled a success. *The Progressive* declared that the New Deal was succeeding in changing the face of government in Washington, but it warned that the "big interests" still had a major role in government through the NRA. In an editorial, the senator asserted that the battle against the depression had just begun:

> With the general purpose of some of these measures I was in hearty sympathy. To the extent to which they attempted to promote a more orderly economic system, to bring about inflation in its proper sense, to restore purchasing power and to raise the standard of living of the great mass of families who depend for their livelihood upon the effective functioning of industry and agriculture, they had my support.

However, La Follette strongly attacked the banking and economy measures and said the only good aspect of the NRA was its labor provisions.[54]

Arthur Capper felt that the New Deal must be given every chance to succeed. In an interview, he predicted increasingly better times and said he expected commodity prices would continue to rise, which would lead to a rise in employment and wages. Praising the president's leadership and expressing his confidence in Secretary of Agriculture Wallace, he asserted that America was obliged to experiment and that he was willing to support any program that promised improvement in the economy. As one of only two progressive Republican supporters of the conference report on the NRA, the Kansas senator admitted it was an experiment that might indeed fail, but, as he wrote in a *Capper's Weekly* editorial: "It will require the co-operation of industry, of labor, of a majority of people in the country, to give it a chance to work successfully. In my judgment it is necessary to try the experiment." He also called upon his constituents to give the AAA a chance before criticizing it: "Whether we approve entirely of the plans worked out by Secretary Wallace and his assistants or not, it is up to us to give those plans every chance to succeed. The measure was written in our interest. . . . Our co-operation is essential to its success."[55]

Other progressive Republicans generally optimistic about the thrust of the New Deal were McNary and Norbeck. McNary wrote of the feeling of optimism again evident in the nation's capital: "I think out of this legislation Congress has passed at the suggestion of the new President, that benefits nation wide will ensue." Norbeck believed Roosevelt had done a better job than he had expected and admitted to a friend: "I occasionally find myself singing faint praises. Yes, I know he is making a mess of a lot of things, but, My God, he is trying. What is more . . . they are introducing a little humanity into government . . . where it has been outlawed for some time."[56]

Other progressives expressed concern about various aspects of the First Hundred Days. Couzens, although agreeing to attend the London Economic Conference by appointment of the president, worried about the rapid pace of legislative action: "The legislation being proposed, the demands for more legislation, and further demands for government aid are almost bewildering." Borah was unhappy about the powers given up by the legislative branch of government to the chief executive and his appointees. He hoped that Congress would begin to demonstrate its independent judgment on New Deal programs. While he felt uneasy criticizing an administration that had such great popularity and support, and a president who seemed to possess genuine sincerity, he remained suspicious of the new powers granted to the executive branch.[57]

Finally, Nye was, like Borah, very unhappy about the passage of the NRA. He said that Congress had passed the law with feelings of fear and trepidation. It was up to the Roosevelt administration to demonstrate that the NRA was not an unwise action, that it would protect small businessmen and consumers from the tentacles of big business. Nye remained pessimistic about the NRA, warning that already there were indications that big business was going to dominate the codes mentioned in the law. He called for the federal government to take over control of the nation's banks.[58]

With the Hundred Days completed, optimism reigned in Washington and throughout the country that the nation was on the road to economic recovery. But passage of legislation did not guarantee that it would work. The progressive Republicans were hopeful but cautious about the future. Even if a comparatively good start had been made, there was much left undone and there were outright doubts as to the value and intent of some of the legislation. The New Deal was indeed on trial. Only the passage of time and new developments would indicate the ultimate response of the progressive Republicans to Roosevelt and the New Deal.

[5]

Growing Discontent and Disillusionment, 1933-1935

During the second half of 1933 and 1934, progressives drew attention to the faults they saw as inherent in the legislation of the First Hundred Days. While anxious to cooperate with the president, they expressed concern about various aspects of the administration's recovery program, specifically the NRA, AAA, Economy Act, and the extent of federal public works projects. They expected to move Roosevelt further to the left, away from cooperation with big business. They also assumed the president would endorse the reelection in 1934 of those members of the bloc who were facing the voters. In both areas the progressives were to be disappointed, and the result was growing discontent and disillusionment toward Roosevelt and the New Deal by early 1935.

Within a few months, after the NRA was passed, code agreements with major national industries were negotiated, Gen. Hugh Johnson was appointed NRA administrator by President Roosevelt, and the Blue Eagle was adopted as the official symbol to promote industrial recovery. By the fall of 1933, the NRA was provoking hostile commentary from many politicians, including progressives who had been critical of the law when it was first proposed.

The Progressive declared that the NRA was on trial. The way it was administered, especially in regard to its treatment of organized labor under section 7-A, would be a good indication of the extent of the president's progressive instincts. The journal was concerned over reports that the NRA was likely to be dominated by "millionaire manufacturers" and contended that the small businessman should be given a "square deal." Indications that big business was gaining control of the NRA machinery disturbed Senator La Follette.[1]

Senator Couzens, although agreeing to a radio address in support of the NRA, indicated that he had grave reservations about its efficacy, as it was attempting to encompass every aspect of business enterprise and centralized too much power in Washington. The NRA administration needed to be simplified, he said, and Roosevelt must avoid making this an issue of political loyalty. Couzens declared: "The cause is too big to argue about who should get credit for it—the people will decide that when we find the results."[2]

Senators Capper and McNary also spoke out on the NRA. Capper, in a radio address, said the NRA deserved the support of the American people because it was an expression of hope in the future. Roosevelt had stopped the drifting of the American economy, and he deserved the undivided support of all Republicans and Democrats as he worked to revive the nation's business, industry, and agriculture. In a newspaper interview, McNary said he heartily approved of the NRA, but believed more emphasis should be placed on the public works program.[3]

As the months went by, the NRA was attacked on its purposes, policies, and tendencies, with Senators Borah and Nye becoming its leading critics. In November, Borah called for revival of the antitrust laws, claiming that NRA codes were promoting monopoly and failing to aid recovery. He also said farmers were being victimized by the higher prices they had to pay for consumer goods. Nye wrote to Hugh Johnson at the end of November, charging that the NRA was "failing to accomplish through its codes that which the Congress intended should be accomplished" because it was failing to protect small independent businessmen against monopolistic practices.[4]

La Follette was also having doubts about the NRA. He wrote his wife: "People are losing faith in the N.R.A. and unless Roosevelt cuts loose on this recovery program and pumps out purchasing power and relief in other agencies, my judgment is that his administration is going to fail tragicly [sic]." Despite his private doubts, he declared in a speech that the NRA was a "great step in the right direction" and that the American people were behind it.[5]

At the end of December, NRA administrator Johnson invited Borah and Nye to become members of a board designed to guard the interests of small businessmen under the NRA codes. Both progressives had suggested such an idea, but they rejected membership on the board because it would compromise their independence.[6]

As the new session of Congress convened, *The Nation* speculated on the role of the progressives in 1934. The journal quoted Hiram Johnson as saying he would continue to support Roosevelt as the only alternative to "economic hell," but "a number of the other independent spirits in Congress have, however, remained ominously silent, while a few have broadly intimated that they will seek to modify the Roosevelt recovery program and restrain the President. Senators Borah and Nye, for example, have been agitating for a restoration of the antitrust laws to their former standing, and they apparently mean to carry their agitation to the floor of the Senate."[7]

In a Senate speech, Nye accused the NRA of being a huge government machine with greater power over the economy than in any other country, with the exception of the Soviet Union. He felt the legislation should be amended so that the NRA would serve the people, rather than monopolists. He supplied facts and figures to prove the NRA was harming small businessmen and increasing the cost of living. Borah also contributed to the attack, calling again for reinstatement of the antitrust laws and pointing out that prices had risen from 67 to 120 percent in various industries since the codes were enacted.[8]

When Hugh Johnson defended the NRA operations, Nye increased his attack, demanding that the New Deal divorce itself from the "industrial pirates." General Johnson now asked Senator Norris to set up a meeting so that he and Nye could discuss changes in the NRA machinery. After the conference, Nye expressed satisfaction that Johnson was trying to deal with the criticism of opponents, but he insisted that the machinery of the New Deal was being captured by "Old Dealers." Columnist T.R.B. of *The New Republic* noted that many progressive Republicans, besides Nye and Borah, were restive over the "lack of clear purpose" of the New Deal, especially as it related to the NRA.[9]

Progressives continued to attack the NRA. Borah submitted a resolution calling on the Federal Trade Commission to investigate the steel code for fixing and raising of prices. He also wanted an investigation of the petroleum code, as it related to the increased price of gasoline to consumers. The Senate proceeded to adopt the Borah resolution. Capper also joined the attack for the first time, accusing the New Deal of seemingly forgetting smaller businessmen and industries in its pursuit of prosperity. However, he pledged continued support of the administration so long as it promoted the public interest. Friendly criticism of the NRA codes would bring about necessary reforms, Capper believed, as he was certain that Roosevelt and his associates had the welfare of the masses in mind.[10]

Nye introduced a resolution requesting a list of all persons employed in responsible positions under the NRA. He wanted their present and past business connections, along with the codes they had helped to prepare. Any officials who had left the government since the NRA codes were finalized should be investigated as to whether they were now employed by code authorities who administered the agreements between business and the government. Finally, a complete roster of all code authorities and their members was requested, so that the extent of big business control over the NRA could be determined. Shipstead, in support of the Nye resolution, said the NRA was not restoring purchasing power and providing new jobs; rather, it was proving to be a "price-gouging program, permitting monopolistic practices and going back to the practices that brought on the depression."[11]

The Senate initially rejected the Nye resolution, sending it back to the Finance Committee by a vote of 41 to 33, with all the progressive Republicans (ten out of twelve, with Norbeck and Shipstead not present) in the minority. However, the next day, after the proposal was modified, the Senate adopted it. The wording of the resolution left it up to the NRA director, Hugh Johnson, as to whether the data requested would be supplied. Nye insisted that the Roosevelt administration should make Johnson comply with the resolution. As the NRA debate grew in ferocity in the Senate, T.R.B. of *The New Republic* commented that the progressives were never going to be satisfied so long as General Johnson continued in supreme command of the NRA.[12]

After months of attacks, the Roosevelt administration finally created a National Recovery Review Board to study monopolistic tendencies in the codes. Clarence Darrow, the noted attorney, was appointed head of the investigating committee. Progressive critics were pleased by the development, but they still persisted in their own investigation of the NRA. Borah publicized the findings of the Federal Trade Commission on the steel code. The report, he asserted, demonstrated the need to restore the antitrust laws. Borah pleaded for the Senate to reconsider his antimonopoly proposal.[13]

Nye predicted a vast shakeup of the NRA by Roosevelt and continued to voice criticism of General Johnson's handling of the recovery machinery. Capper attacked the NRA again for favoring the concentration of wealth. No longer able to support this aspect of the New Deal, he still indicated his willingness to endorse other legislation that would benefit farmers, small businessmen, and consumers. Nye now wrote the president, indicating the need for strong action to restore the nation's faith in the NRA. Roosevelt indicated willingness to consider changes, and the imminent issuance of the Darrow Report certainly demonstrated the need for action.[14]

The Darrow Report concluded that giant corporations were indeed dominating the code authorities and squeezing labor, small businessmen, and consumers, just as the progressives had been contending for many months. Hugh Johnson now became politically expendable. Declaring the Blue Eagle a "bird of prey" on the masses, Nye accused Johnson of dismissing underlings who tried to administer codes fairly, and he suggested the NRA administrator might like to abolish Congress and send the president to exile in Hawaii while he took control of the government and proceeded to destroy all small businesses. Nye believed the NRA's labor provisions were worth saving, but there must be a complete overhaul of personnel in the agency. Borah again tried to force action on his antitrust bill, but the Congress adjourned without taking action. As the session ended, Senator Cutting indicated he had always doubted the value of the NRA once he saw that prices were rising faster than wages, the purchasing power of the masses was not increasing appreciably, and labor was not getting the same rights and protection as employers under section 7-A.[15]

In a series of speeches during the summer of 1934, Borah spoke of the dangers of monopoly and the absolute need for restoration of the antitrust laws. He assailed the Democratic party for agreeing to a suspension of those laws. Demanding that small businessmen be released from a maze of laws, regulations, and restrictions, he called upon his own party leadership to end its silence on the NRA. Monopolies were "economic Hitlers" that retarded economic progress. Borah said he was not attacking the New Deal, as he believed its real aims were opposed to those of big business. Borah, as well as Nye, was hopeful that Roosevelt would bring about necessary changes in the NRA that would make it acceptable to them. Both senators were certainly pleased when General Johnson resigned as NRA head in September 1934.[16]

The two men were disappointed, however, that no fundamental action to change the NRA was taken after Johnson's resignation. When the new 74th Congress convened in January 1935, they again publicized the monopoly issue. Borah proposed a bill requiring all but a few corporations engaged in interstate commerce to prove, as a condition of continued operation, that they were innocent of monopolistic practices or trade restraints. Corporations would be required to obtain licenses from the Federal Trade Commission. Borah also pushed his proposal that the antitrust laws be restored under the NRA machinery. At the same time, Nye co-sponsored a resolution with Democrat Patrick McCarran of Nevada, calling for an investigation of the administration of the NRA codes. After a legislative struggle as to which committee should handle the resolution, it was finally adopted unanimously by the Senate.[17]

Borah, placed on the investigating committee, advocated that Congress abandon the codes entirely, with the labor provisions to be replaced by new statutes dealing with wages, hours, and child labor. He expressed the belief that Roosevelt agreed with him that the antitrust laws must now be enforced. But Borah's attempt to add an antitrust amendment to a relief resolution was defeated by a vote of 43 to 33. By this time, Senator Norris had joined the attack. He wrote a Nebraska constituent that "the N.R.A. has not in my judgment been a success. The tendency has been to give the big fellow an advantage over the little fellow, and I think mistakes have been made in trying to enforce rules which have been adopted." Norris still expressed confidence that the Roosevelt administration would correct the NRA errors and indicated he remained unwilling to criticize the codes publicly.[18]

With the NRA due to expire in June 1935, the administration was in the process of considering a renewal bill. Borah now called on the Supreme Court to decide the constitutionality of the legislation. Roosevelt held a White House conference with a large group of senators in an attempt to produce a renewal bill that would satisfy all factions. Among those present were progressive Republicans Borah, Couzens, La Follette, Nye, and McNary. No compromise was reached, and Borah indicated that the struggle against the NRA would continue until price fixing was eliminated. With the logjam on extension legislation, business and industrial representatives organized a march on Washington, which Borah and Nye criticized. Nye even introduced a resolution calling upon the NRA to supply to the Senate within three days any information indicating whether the individuals promoting the march were employed by that agency.[19]

The controversy over the NRA ended on May 27, 1935, when the Supreme Court declared the legislation unconstitutional in a unanimous 9 to 0 decision in the case of *Schechter Poultry Company* v. *United States*. The Court ruled that the Congress had given over too much legislative power to the executive branch, and that the federal government had no authority to regulate intrastate commerce. The Court was interpreting the commerce clause of the Constitution in a narrow sense. Hiram Johnson wrote his son that the NRA decision "was an absolute knock-out to the administration. Apparently, those in command had given little or no thought to the possibility of a decision, which would upset the entire industrial recovery organization."[20] Roosevelt held a press conference in which he denounced the Supreme Court decision. This marked the beginning of the administration's attacks on the Court, which were to result in a major confrontation between president and Congress in 1937. Certainly, the destruction of the NRA must be laid at the hands of its congressional critics, such as Borah and Nye, as well as the Supreme Court. Many progressives, always suspicious of any cooperation between government and big business, had resolved that the main underpinning of the president's recovery program must go if they were to push him toward necessary economic and social reforms.

Although the NRA was the major focus of progressive criticism during 1934 and early 1935, some of the bloc's members also had complaints about the Agricultural Adjustment Act. In the summer of 1933, Senator Capper urged the readers of *Capper's Farmer* to avoid partisanship and to give total support to the administration's farm program: "We know this legislation is an experiment. . . . This farm bill is only a part of the big experiment in government toward which we are heading." But the administration's decision to plow up the cotton crop and slaughter pigs to create a shortage that would raise prices caused a tremendous controversy. In the fall of 1933, *The Progressive* said it was ironic that farmers were being told to curb production at a time when many Americans lacked essential food and clothing. Former Gov. Philip La Follette criticized the crop reduction program as "cock-eyed." Destroying wealth, he maintained, was not a way out of the depression.[21]

Borah was the major critic of the AAA. The view that overproduction was one of the contributing causes of the depression was false, said Borah, and the policy of destruction, of restraint upon initiative and production, would only delay recovery. The real problem lay in underconsumption and distribution. The purchasing power of the masses must be restored, and the disparity of wealth and inequality of distribution must be overcome. Borah believed the restoration of the antitrust laws would lead to a successful solution of the farm problem. He wrote: "We ought not to seek to produce less, but more. The farmer ought to be encouraged to extend his production rather than to reduce it. Limitation of production is death to any industry."[22]

Norris, reluctant to criticize the administration, did agree that a policy of crop destruction, when many Americans were lacking the necessities for life, was a mistake. He concurred with Borah that permanent recovery would come only when steps were taken to ensure an equitable distribution of wealth and property. He believed, however, that Roosevelt and Wallace and their subordinates were honest, sincere men with good intentions. Most progressives agreed with Norris during 1934 that the AAA was not the perfect answer, but should not be abandoned until a better solution to the farm problem had been found.[23]

The progressive senators also worked during 1934 to ameliorate the effect of the Economy Act on veterans pensions. Frazier endorsed the Steiwer-McCarran proposal for increased pensions, saying it was a disgrace for veterans to have to depend upon charity. Norris said that although he supported the administration in most of its programs, he could not accept the Economy Act's devastating effect on veterans. Recalling that financiers had lived in luxury during the world war while American servicemen had risked their lives, many of them coming home with permanent disabilities, he vowed he did not care if the pensions increased the budget. Capper claimed he had been fooled into voting for the bill, and that the broad powers given to the president and his assistants in the Economy Act had been abused.[24]

When the Steiwer-McCarran proposal passed both houses, Roosevelt vetoed it, but Congress proceeded to override the veto by margins of 310 to 72 in the House and 63 to 27 in the Senate, with all twelve progressive Republican senators voting against the president. Cutting was the most vocal critic of Roosevelt's action. He told his colleagues that the president's veto message was similar in nature to Hoover's rejection of relief programs for the needy. He had no apologies to make for having supported Roosevelt in 1932 and wished to maintain his friendship, but he could not overlook the shabby treatment being accorded to veterans.[25]

Cutting, along with La Follette, led the progressive Republicans in urging a greater investment in public works programs than the administration seemed willing to promote. La Follette felt that the $3 billion provided for public works in the NRA legislation should be doubled. In July 1933, he appealed to Roosevelt to "prime the pump." At the end of that year, he expressed disappointment at the president's decision to set aside only $2 billion for all emergency expenditures in the second half of 1934. The following February, La Follette and Cutting introduced amendments to increase appropriations for public works, at a time when the administration was thinking about slashing funds. Cutting and La Follette were very critical of this plan. The purchasing power of the masses must be increased, and concentration of wealth in the hands of a few must come to an end; a public works program that provided work for everyone who wanted to work was their goal. In April 1934, La Follette urged that $10 billion be spent on public works projects during the next two years. Advanced progressives like La Follette and Cutting were never satisfied with the extent of the New Deal's commitment to public works as a way to bring the country out of the depression.[26]

The progressive Republicans advocated higher taxation of large incomes as the best way to finance the large public works program they desired. During 1934 Norris called for publicity of income tax returns and for a levy on the profits of holding companies. La Follette made a concerted effort to have the Congress adopt his amendments for a graduated increase in income taxes and higher estate taxes, as well as to make tax returns part of the public record. Although all progressives except McNary, the Republican minority leader, supported the La Follette proposals, they failed of passage during 1934.[27]

During 1934, the progressive Republicans, with the exception of McNary, supported the administration's Gold Reserve Act, which set the price of gold at thirty-five dollars an ounce and reduced the dollar's value in gold. They were unanimous in backing the Securities Exchange Act, which created the Securities and Exchange Commission to administer the stock market. As longtime opponents of Wall Street, they were pleased by this legislation, which placed trading practices under federal regulation. However, there was great controversy and opposition to the Reciprocal Trade Agreements Act among the progressives. This legislation empowered the executive branch to negotiate agreements with other countries to change by as much as one-half the existing American duties on imports, in exchange for reciprocal concessions by the other nations on their duties on American products. Such agreements did not need Senate ratification.

The trade bill easily passed the Senate 57 to 33, but the progressives split down the middle on it. Borah, Cutting, Frazier, Johnson, McNary, and Nye voted against, while Capper, Couzens, La Follette, Norbeck, Norris, and Shipstead supported the bill. After the legislation was introduced, Johnson wrote a journalist friend of his fear that Roosevelt was obsessed with a love of power. Convinced that Roosevelt had been swayed by Wallace and Hull, the two internationalists in his cabinet, to ask for this extraordinary and dangerous control over tariff rates, Johnson stood ready to oppose such a grant of power and was a major Senate critic during the next few months until passage of the bill.[28]

Borah and McNary used different arguments in voicing their opposition to the reciprocal trade law. Borah saw further proof that Congress was surrendering its constitutional power to the executive branch. Declaring that he was not opposed to a reduction in the tariff rates, he said only Congress could make the reduction, since it held the treaty-making, taxing, and legislative powers under the Constitution. The integrity of constitutional government was at stake, Borah asserted, and no emergency situation should be allowed to modify the basic traditions of American government. McNary wished to exempt agricultural products from the law, so that farmers would not be harmed by imports. He wanted reciprocal trade agreements only for those items that America did not produce, rather than those for which this country was competing with foreign nations. He feared that the president, unable to devote enough time to the details of reciprocal agreements, would delegate authority over rates to administrators who would have little concern for the American farmer.[29]

As the final vote on the bill neared, Hiram Johnson repeated the Borah argument that the legislation was unwise because it would alter the balance between the legislative and executive branches. Bronson Cutting called the bill dangerous to American interests. Until domestic purchasing power was provided for all of the people, the nation should not be selling its products abroad. Borah, summing up the debate for the progressive opponents of the legislation, declared he believed the president's motives were the highest and that he had the interests of the American people at heart. He was voting against the bill not because of lack of respect or confidence in Roosevelt, but simply because he refused to endorse the surrender of congressional power to the executive branch.[30]

Arthur Capper spoke up for the progressive Republican supporters of the legislation, indicating his belief that Congress could not, from a practical standpoint, negotiate tariff agreements with foreign nations. Willing to grant limited powers to the president to arrange these treaties, he would, however, hold Roosevelt responsible for protecting the interests of the agricultural states. The peak of the progressive bloc's disagreement on a bill during the second year of the New Deal was evident on this issue.[31]

As one would expect from a group of mavericks, the personal attitudes of the progressive Republicans toward Roosevelt and the New Deal varied during the early stages of the administration. Charles McNary, who served as the link between progressives and conservatives in his party in his role as Senate minority leader, found himself in an awkward situation, "criticized by some for being too close to the President, by others for being too friendly toward the Conservatives and by some for being too friendly toward the Progressives." By the end of 1934, he had criticized the AAA, reciprocal trade agreements, and tendencies toward excessive government regulation and regimentation. Yet he called upon the Republican party to liberalize itself to meet the problems of the depression. The eastern Republicans, he asserted, must make concessions to the West and Midwest to ensure party unity in 1936. Meanwhile, he urged Roosevelt to cut down on government bureaucracy and to reassure businessmen of his future plans so that confidence could be restored in the value of new business investment.[32]

Arthur Capper declared in July 1933 that he would not play politics, that he intended to support the New Deal, which was "simply the good old 'square deal' of another and former Roosevelt, under a new label." Early in the following year, he told a radio audience of his admiration for Roosevelt: "You know, that man fascinates me. He covers so much territory. He has so many ideas." Due to such comments, Capper was passed over by the chairman of the Republican Senatorial Campaign Committee as a member of a special executive committee to take active leadership in the 1934 congressional campaign. Capper seemed too "Democratic" in his utterances to suit many Republicans' tastes. On the first anniversary of the president's inauguration, Capper nevertheless reaffirmed his nonpartisan support of the Roosevelt program, reserving the right, however, to issue constructive criticism. He saw promise of better times for agriculture, his major concern. In May 1934, Capper declared that the business situation was greatly improved.[33]

Beginning in June 1934, however, Capper expressed concern that Roosevelt's program was becoming "bewildering" to himself, as well as to businessmen. The NRA was very unpopular in the Midwest, and the farm problem remained to be solved. Capper told William Allen White, the progressive journalist: "We should be prepared to make a fight for the Republican ticket all down the line this fall and need not hesitate about fair criticism of Roosevelt's program." He grew to be deeply concerned about three aspects of the New Deal: the great increase in the national debt, the growth of government bureaucracy, and the large-scale patronage program that Postmaster General James Farley was instituting at all levels of government. Regarding the latter, Capper told a radio audience: "Nearly 100,000 non-civil service appointments practically all Democrats have been made since President Roosevelt took office. New bureaus and commissions are being created outside the civil service. . . . The Democrats now have the greatest army of political workers ever possessed by any party in this country. That has been one of the abuses of the near-dictatorial powers given this Administration."[34]

Capper was not the only member of the progressive bloc unhappy about political appointees. Norris, one of Roosevelt's most ardent supporters, wrote Farley and the president as early as September 1933, criticizing the administration for discharging Republican postmasters. The Post Office was becoming a large political machine, but should be operated on a nonpartisan basis, Norris asserted, and if Farley was unwilling to arrange this, he should resign. Although his suggestions were ignored, Norris still believed President Roosevelt came closer to conducting the national government on an efficiency basis than any previous chief executive in the twentieth century.[35]

In a long letter in June 1934, Norris outlined his views on Roosevelt and the New Deal. Indicating his pleasure at the administration's record, he noted that the honesty, sincerity, and good intentions of the president were well known and documented. His major fault was a tendency to appoint some people solely on a partisan basis, but the senator believed that Roosevelt was really nonpartisan in his heart. Norris refused to ask the president for patronage despite his vocal support of the Democrats in 1932. He evinced willingness to ignore the administration's mistakes because of his belief in Roosevelt's good motives. His confidence in the President was demonstrated when he voted to give the executive branch the power to negotiate trade agreements, a grant of authority that he would have opposed for any other president.[36]

James Couzens expressed his feelings about Roosevelt in a letter to a constituent in February 1934: "Our President is displaying fine leadership and I am glad to support him whenever possible." That summer, he wrote McNary that there was much one could criticize about the New Deal, "but I am reluctant to do it because we seemed so impotent before the President took office." In a newspaper interview, the Michigan senator declared the president should inform the people more clearly of his plans and policies. However, at the same time, he rebuked administration critics who criticized and condemned the president without offering substitutes for his programs. Adjustments and compromises in the present system were necessary, he affirmed, but the days of laissez faire and "rugged individualism" were over forever. While he refused to endorse the entire New Deal program, Couzens felt that Roosevelt should be given credit for doing everything he could to find work for the jobless. During the fall of 1934, Couzens made numerous speeches in which he praised the president and the New Deal. He wrote Senator McNary: "I have simply said that I have served in Washington under four Presidents and that Roosevelt is the only one who has indicated a keen interest in the common people whom Lincoln pleaded for."[37]

William Borah feared the New Deal was departing from the principles of the Constitution. He wrote a constituent in the fall of 1934: "I feel very strongly that the situation in this country is critical in more ways than one. It is critical economically and governmentally. . . . If I am not mistaken, the trend in some respects is absolutely at war with the fundamental principle of American institutions, and will ultimately undermine many of the rights of the citizen." Borah remained the outstanding progressive critic of New Deal tendencies.[38]

Five progressive Republican senators faced reelection contests during 1934, and all had supported Roosevelt's election. Lynn Frazier and Henrik Shipstead had not actively campaigned but had been listed as members of the National Progressive League. Hiram Johnson, Robert La Follette, Jr., and Bronson Cutting had announced their distinct preference for Roosevelt, abandoning their party ties. During 1934, the Roosevelt administration faced the question of whether to endorse the progressive Republicans over Democratic party opponents or to turn against them.

At the beginning of 1934, T.R.B. of *The New Republic* asserted that although the progressive Republicans might be few in number, "it is quite clear that their support is indispensable to the Roosevelt program. They are, for one thing, easily the most forceful and articulate group in the Senate, and their effectiveness has been demonstrated a good many times in the past." Both *The Nation* and *The New Republic* agreed the progressives were still in a dilemma. Should they accept support from the Democrats and leave the Republican party, or should they run independent campaigns? The *New York Times* reported in January that the Roosevelt Administration was ready to take the progressive Republicans facing reelection under the wing of the Democratic party. But some of them were reportedly unwilling to leave the Republican party and to accept direct support from the administration. If these progressives ran as Democrats, the Republican party would be completely taken over by conservative elements.[39]

Ultimately, the Roosevelt administration took no role in Lynn Frazier's reelection battle in North Dakota. Frazier went on to win without assistance from the president. In Minnesota, Roosevelt straddled the fence, refusing to commit himself behind Senator Shipstead or his Democratic opponent. In a June press conference, the president did say that Shipstead was a good friend but indicated he was in a quandary about this particular race, as the Democratic nominee (Hoidale) was also a good man. Shipstead proceeded to win a new term without any further commitment from the New Deal.[40]

There was no question, on the other hand, of the administration endorsing Hiram Johnson for reelection. Relations between Roosevelt and the California senator were extremely warm during the first two years of the New Deal. Johnson evinced willingness to support the president's programs most of the time because he felt Roosevelt's motivations were good. He had high praise for the president's performance in office, and Roosevelt cultivated his friendship. Interior Secretary Ickes, whom Johnson had recommended to Roosevelt, wrote the senator after the end of the special session in July 1933 that Roosevelt had "referred to you in affectionate terms. There isn't the slightest doubt of his very real feeling for you." *The New Republic* reported a rumor during the same month that Johnson might be considered for a future vacancy on the Supreme Court. During August, Johnson wrote the president, praising the actions he had taken during the First Hundred Days: "It is the glory of this Administration, of which all of us are so proud, that it has dared to do and has gallantly embarked upon an economic adventure the most astounding the world has ever seen; . . . How heartily I congratulate you upon the work you are doing I cannot adequately express! May your heart continue strong in your good deeds and your high achievement."[41]

Roosevelt invited Johnson to visit him in December so that the two men could spend a few evenings discussing "the big things we are both working for." Johnson was very pleased that Roosevelt had written him in the midst of many problems and burdens, and he expressed a willingness to fight with the president against those who opposed what the administration was trying to accomplish. In a warm letter to the president, Johnson said:

> I hope to be in Washington just after your return there. Of course, I've followed your gallant fight, and nothing like it in courage and high endeavor has this country witnessed during my time. I'm eager to do my small part; and I return to Washington with my faith in my President strengthened, my pride in his achievements increased, and with whole hearted devotion to his great purposes.

Ickes wrote Johnson at the end of November 1933 that the president had been pleased with the senator's letter, and that he respected Johnson's ability and willingness to fight for a cause. During December, Johnson lunched with the president at the White House, which the senator later declared to be "a delightful and an unforgettable hour."[42]

In January 1934, the *New York Times* reported that the administration had decided to exert its influence among Democrats in California to bring about an uncontested reelection of Johnson to his Senate seat. Farley had already indicated that most Democrats desired Johnson's return to the Senate. Johnson, naturally, was gratified at the development. He proceeded to win reelection by a landslide, with the support of the Republican, Democratic, and Progressive parties of California. The senator continued his close relationship with Roosevelt throughout 1934, visiting with him a number of times and issuing statements of support for the New Deal. On the first anniversary of Roosevelt's inauguration, he criticized a Republican National Committee statement attacking the New Deal as overly partisan. Praising the president's audacity and the results he had achieved, Johnson declared: "We are better, and our country is better, and our people are better, and our times are better for what the President has done during the past year."[43]

In a Labor Day address in San Francisco, Johnson ridiculed cries of unconstitutionality raised against the New Deal. Some of Roosevelt's policies were frankly experimental and might not be desirable as to their end or objective, he said, but at least the administration had made an effort. Johnson criticized conservatives who made themselves guardians of the Constitution while refusing to take any action to solve the depression. The relief programs of the New Deal were not desirable as a general policy over an extended period of time, but they were indispensable now to aid the jobless and hungry. Overall, the senator considered that the accomplishments of the New Deal far outweighed the faults, such as the reciprocal trade legislation.[44]

Robert La Follette, Jr., and his brother Philip made a decision early in 1934 to leave the Republican establishment and form the Progressive party of Wisconsin as a vehicle for their political ambitions. While the two brothers remained hopeful that the New Deal would do what they considered necessary to take the country out of the depression, they were clearly suspicious of the reform commitment of Roosevelt and the Democratic party. They made plans for a meeting of progressives in Chicago in December 1933, to discuss future strategy. The senator suggested the meeting to his brother in October, indicating it would serve as a means of restating and reaffirming progressive goals. It would also serve as a way to "place the burden of proof on Roosevelt." The senator was pleased by Fiorello LaGuardia's election as New York City mayor in November, because "It confirms my judgment held right along that if there is a reaction against Roosevelt it will not be back to reactionarism but to more fundamental progressivism than he is providing."[45]

During November, Philip La Follette invited progressives in the fields of government, journalism, and education to the Chicago conference. Six of his brother's Senate colleagues were invited, including Cutting, Frazier, Johnson, Norris, Nye, and Shipstead. The conference was held in private, with twenty-five to thirty progressive leaders attending and discussing the virtues (or lack of them) of the New Deal. *The New Republic* reported that many doubts had been expressed about Roosevelt's commitment to reform:

> They do not believe the President's measures will be sufficiently drastic to get the country out of this depression, and keep it out of the next one. They are, of course, in sympathy with many ideas of the liberal wing of the administration; their pessimism is based on the fact that they do not feel that the President will adopt these ideas soon enough or completely enough to attain the all-important objective of greatly increased purchasing power among the masses of the American people.

There was talk of nationalization of the banks and public utilities by many of those present at the meeting, but it was considered unlikely that these ideas would gain a sympathetic hearing from the New Dealers.[46]

After the Chicago conference, the La Follette brothers debated whether they should leave the Republican party. In February 1934, Philip wrote his brother of his conviction that a new political party must eventually be established, and that the present situation was propitious for such an undertaking. But he did not wish to harm his brother's chances for reelection. The senator was uncertain about the virtues of a new party, but he agreed to sign a letter calling for a state conference of progressive leaders during March to consider formation of a Progressive party. Philip suggested that an endorsement from President Roosevelt would be valuable if the senator ran for reelection on an independent ticket. He urged his brother to request an appointment with the president to discuss political matters. If the president seemed hesitant to commit himself, however, the senator should not press for an endorsement.[47]

Senator La Follette met with Roosevelt at the White House on February 26. The president indicated that he wanted to support him for reelection but was experiencing opposition on that point from the Democratic party in Wisconsin. La Follette said he was unwilling to support the Democratic state ticket in exchange for an endorsement of his candidacy. La Follette had the distinct impression that Roosevelt would not alienate his own party members to endorse him for the Senate, were he to remain a Republican. It would be easier for the president to back him if he ran as an independent. In early March, the senator went back home to discuss the political alternatives with friends and supporters.[48]

The state progressive convention had five to six hundred people attending, and the sentiment was strong for a third party. Philip La Follette was now convinced that he should proceed with the necessary steps to form the Progressive party. Senator La Follette, still not convinced of the virtues of a new party, indicated that he would not interfere with his brother's plans. He told the delegates that they should not consider his Senate race as a deciding factor in the best strategy for Wisconsin progressivism's future. The convention proceeded to adopt a resolution authorizing a committee to go to the state supreme court for a decision on whether a new party could be legally established. On April 30, the court ruled that a third party could indeed be formed under state law. A statewide progressive conference consisting of four hundred delegates was now arranged for May 19 at Fond du Lac to inaugurate the new party formally.[49]

Senator La Follette announced his candidacy for reelection as a Progressive, rather than as a Republican or Democrat. At the Fond du Lac convention, the delegates voted to break away from the Republicans and form the Progressive party. A platform was adopted and the state Democratic party was attacked as reactionary. Senator La Follette claimed that the principal achievements of the New Deal had been originally promoted by progressives in both major parties before 1932. Senate progressives, led by Borah, Nye, and Norris, announced their support and intentions to campaign for the senator on the new party line. The *Madison Capital Times* declared in an editorial that the new party might be the forerunner of a national realignment: "If President Roosevelt continues his battle for progressive and liberal principles, the movement nationally may be held in abeyance. If on the other hand, President Roosevelt begins to yield to reactionaries in his own party and follows a middle of the road policy in which he attempts to hold reactionaries and liberals together in his own party, the movement started here in Wisconsin will assume national proportions."[50]

In early June, Roosevelt told Senator Norris he was interested in La Follette's reelection campaign and indicated his intention of endorsing the Wisconsin senator in the near future. On June 27, while holding a press conference, Roosevelt said that personally he would like to see the senator reelected, but he could not prevent the Democrats in Wisconsin from challenging him. Meanwhile, the Progressive party had adopted a fourteen-point declaration of principles that promoted public ownership of utilities and the banking system, the right of tenure for land owners through moratorium legislation, employment for everyone capable of working, unemployment insurance, sickness and accident insurance, old-age pensions, legislation guaranteeing the right for workers to organize, opposition to the sales tax, and support of a levy on corporate dividends and inheritances to bring about redistribution of wealth and increased purchasing power.[51]

In mid-July, Agriculture Secretary Henry Wallace praised the La Follette brothers and the Wisconsin progressive movement in a Madison speech. Wallace's statement gave additional strength to reports that Roosevelt would endorse Senator La Follette over his Democratic opponent. The president came to Wisconsin in the middle of August; at Green Bay, he praised La Follette and his Democratic colleague in the Senate, F. Ryan Duffy, for their cooperation and termed both of them "old friends of mine." He proceeded to endorse La Follette's candidacy and to recommend the political background of Wisconsin progressivism as a model for the national government. A few days later, the senator opened his campaign with a declaration of support for Roosevelt and the New Deal, "as long as he is right." He congratulated the president for having successfully taken power away from the reactionary Democrats, but he warned that they remained in the wings, waiting for the opportunity to assume anew their control of the Democratic party machine.[52]

Meanwhile, Philip La Follette had announced his candidacy for governor, the office he had held as a Republican in 1931 and 1932. The La Follette brothers ran their campaign on the concept of a general political realignment as essential to protect American democracy. Philip La Follette wrote an article for *Common Sense*, in which he emphasized the necessity of an equitable distribution of wealth and purchasing power if the nation was to escape from the throes of the depression. During October, many progressives from both major parties came to Wisconsin to speak for the La Follette brothers, and others sent letters of endorsement. Among the progressive figures aiding the La Follettes and their new state party were Frazier, Johnson, Norris, Nye, Shipstead and Democrats Wheeler, Costigan, Bone, and Wagner.[53]

The president sent two notes expressing his interest in how the senator's campaign was progressing but did not endorse Philip's candidacy for governor. He did, however, invite Senator La Follette to visit him after the election contest. These presidential letters were published in Wisconsin newspapers as further evidence of the White House's desire to see the senator reelected. In November, the La Follettes swept to victory, and the Progressive party was an established political force to be reckoned with. After visiting with the president, Senator La Follette declared that the state party was a permanent fixture and the beginning of a political realignment. This was a warning to the president to steer to the left if he wished to retain progressive support. Otherwise, the brothers from Wisconsin were waiting in the wings to take over the leadership of American progressivism.[54]

The manner in which the Roosevelt administration handled the reelection campaign of Bronson Cutting caused a major controversy, leading to bitterness and suspicion on the part of progressive senators toward the White House. Cutting and Roosevelt, although from similar wealthy New York backgrounds, had temperaments and personalities that clashed. Cutting was reserved and introverted, the opposite of the outgoing, exuberant president. Cutting was always somewhat suspicious of Roosevelt's motives and had been reluctant to endorse him in 1932, finally deciding to do so more as an anti-Hoover gesture than a pro-Roosevelt one. Roosevelt's offer to make Cutting secretary of the interior had been rejected by the New Mexico senator, who did not wish to tie his future to Roosevelt's fortunes. At that time Cutting had told his staff assistant, Clifford McCarthy, that he "could not, somehow, trust Franklin."[55]

Cutting had been absent from Washington during the early days of the New Deal, when he was on vacation recovering from poor health. However, he returned to Washington in time to denounce the effect of the Economy Act on the veterans' bonus and to speak out for greater government spending on relief and public works than the administration had called for. Otherwise, Cutting supported the basic New Deal structure in 1933 and 1934, although he aroused the president's ire when he denounced Roosevelt's veto of restoration of the veterans' bonus in 1934, later overriden by Congress. Rumors spread early in 1934 that the administration and the Democratic National Committee planned to finance and endorse a Democratic opponent for Cutting's Senate seat.

Privately, Cutting expressed reservations about the New Deal that he avoided saying publicly. He told Philip La Follette in November 1933: "Franklin's program is not working, . . . it cannot work without a fundamental revision of the aims as well as methods, and . . . such a revision is getting harder every day." He told his mother that he had been asked to give some speeches on behalf of the NRA and had been "sorely tempted to tell them just what I think of the President's program." He reiterated his firm conviction that he would accept no favors or positions from Roosevelt. At the end of January 1934, Cutting delivered a strong public criticism of the tendencies of the New Deal. "I am for the new deal," he declared. "I believe, and I think an overwhelming majority of this country believe, in the sincerity and good faith of the President, . . . But I think there are too many people in the ranks of the administration who are at heart not 'new dealers' at all, but old dealers in some other form." He praised the president's willingness to experiment, but he warned Roosevelt that "the time is coming when the people of this country are going to demand results. We have as yet few results to show them. We have got to get results, and we cannot afford to postpone them until it shall be 'too late.' "[56]

In the same month as Cutting's public criticism of the New Deal, Senator Norris heard rumors that Roosevelt had plans to oppose Cutting's re-election. He wrote the president, questioning why all federal appointments in New Mexico seemed to be offered to political enemies of Cutting. Roosevelt's response was to express his fondness for Cutting but to add that "a lot of Bronson's retainers in New Mexico are not considered especially fine citizens." He also hinted that he would refuse to endorse Cutting. In March, the New Mexico senator was told that Roosevelt would only support him if he became a Democrat, something Cutting would not do because of his long-standing criticisms of the state party. He wrote his mother: "On any other ticket I shall be anathema. This certainly is a fine type of non-partisan states-manship, and makes me feel like swallowing the Old Guard at their worst."[57]

Cutting's criticism of the president's veto of veterans pensions during March 1934, hastened the administration's plan to deny him his Senate seat in the fall elections. Congressman Dennis Chavez was now boomed for the Senate and was to receive extensive financial support from the Democratic National Committee. Cutting became more bitter toward Roosevelt at this time, writing a friend: "I have not yet met anyone who could explain what is going on in his mind, and I doubt if he can, . . . I doubt if either Benny or handsome Adolf have as much actual power. It is a pity he doesn't think up something sensible to do with it."[58]

In July, James Farley made a political visit to Albuquerque. Praising Senator Cutting's record and thanking him for his role in the 1932 election, he yet pointed out that the administration believed in a "home rule" policy and therefore would not interfere with the state Democratic party's right to select a candidate to oppose Cutting. No more overtures to Cutting to become a Democrat were made. Cutting was angry over the visit and wrote a friend that Farley had "consorted entirely with my enemies. I think there is no chance to do anything with the Democrats, even if I felt disposed to." Meanwhile, the state Progressive party had reunited with the Republicans after a series of meetings on July 20 and 21. But a number of influential Old Guard Republicans immediately announced they would support the Democratic candidate, Chavez, against Cutting in the fall election. Cutting now believed a successful reelection campaign was doubtful, but he pledged he would make a good fight.[59]

In September, Cutting and Chavez were duly nominated by party conventions to run against each other. In his acceptance speech, Cutting declared that he was for the New Deal so long as it dealt with the problem of relief for human misery, promoted employment for all, and increased the purchasing power of the masses. He had gone down the line with the administration, he asserted, except when it had pursued policies contrary to these goals, such as the Economy Act. He attacked the state Democratic party's claim that New Mexico's share of relief funds depended on the election of a Democratic senator.[60]

At the beginning of October, Albert G. Simms, the Republican national committeeman for New Mexico, announced he would support Chavez for the Senate. This symbolized the desertion of many conservative Republicans from Cutting's campaign because of his refusal to support his party in 1932. Cutting's reelection chances seemed poor; however, he gained vocal support from progressives in and out of Congress. Letters of support came from Borah, Capper, Frazier, Johnson, the La Follette brothers, McNary, Norbeck, Norris, Bone, Costigan, Wheeler, and Gov. Gifford Pinchot of Pennsylvania. Hiram Johnson even sent a wire to Farley about the Cutting-Chavez contest late in October, protesting the administration's handling of the situation. Johnson believed Cutting was being persecuted by both party organizations because of his progressive stands and his fierce independence. Cutting was a valuable senator, Johnson told Farley, a legislator with such courage that he had put himself in jeopardy to render important service to Roosevelt in 1932. This was certainly no way to repay such loyalty.[61]

Johnson also wrote Norris of his concern over Cutting's struggle and expressed hope that the Nebraska senator would display his displeasure over the administration's handling of the New Mexico election. Johnson later spoke with Farley over the telephone, again protesting the administration's intervention in the campaign. He also gave a radio address from San Francisco supporting Cutting's candidacy. Norris sent a telegram that was publicized before the election, appealing to the voters of New Mexico to return Cutting to the Senate. The liberal journals, such as *The Nation* and *The New Republic*, endorsed him for reelection and criticized Roosevelt's campaign against Cutting.[62]

In one of the closest races in the history of the United States Senate, Cutting defeated Chavez by a little more than 1,200 votes. It took a week after the election until all precincts reported the results, this due to the paper ballot system prevalent in the state. Chavez then claimed that the election results were not genuine, that he had been robbed of victory, and that he would challenge the results in a petition to the state courts and to the Senate, if necessary. He claimed to have evidence of irregularities and buying of votes by Cutting supporters. Cutting responded with a demand that Chavez produce proof to back up his allegations of fraud and bribery. Chavez went to Washington to confer with Democratic leaders, and Borah now wrote to Cutting that Chavez had indicated he was prepared to file charges that the New Mexico senator had bought the election. Johnson gave encouragement to Cutting at this time, telling him he should not "permit a lot of rogues to take your hard won laurels." When the complete official returns were issued on November 21, Cutting was ahead of Chavez by 1,291 votes.[63]

Norris, angry over the impending challenge to Cutting's reelection, publicly criticized Roosevelt for his intervention in the contest. He contended that Farley could not have pursued his strategy in New Mexico without the knowledge and approval of the President. Norris believed Roosevelt had made a serious mistake that might affect his legislative program. He again called for Farley to resign from one of his two posts, either the postmaster generalship or as head of the Democratic National Committee. The Nebraska senator also expressed concern that Chavez might successfully unseat Cutting through false charges. In late November, Sen. J. Hamilton Lewis of Illinois confirmed that Roosevelt had opposed the reelection of Bronson Cutting because of his attack on the president's handling of the veterans' pensions issue. Cutting had accused the president, Lewis declared, of "a want of humanity."[64]

The New Mexico election controversy was now assigned to the Senate Committee on Privileges and Elections. Borah said he expected the committee to delve into all aspects of the campaign, including the relief expenditures and contributions made by the Democratic National Committee in its attempt to defeat Cutting. Norris expressed hope that the progressive protest over the handling of the Cutting situation would lead the administration to abandon the fight to deny Cutting his seat in the Senate. T.R.B. of *The New Republic* wrote that a continued fight by the administration against Cutting would lead to damage in the relationship of progressive Republicans with the New Deal.[65]

During December, Chavez proceeded in his challenge to the election results. He brought a writ of mandamus before the state supreme court, calling for returns to be thrown out in some counties because of alleged stuffing of ballot boxes and illegal or unregistered voters. The state's highest court dismissed the suit on December 31, and Senator Cutting received a certificate of election from the state canvassing board. However, Chavez refused to give up the fight, bringing the case formally before the full Senate. Progressives were furious with Roosevelt for remaining silent. The *New York Herald Tribune* declared in an editorial: "Senator Norris and his friends cannot understand why the President long ago did not stop the Farley opposition to Senator Cutting. They look upon it as base ingratitude to a faithful friend. If the matter goes much farther it may be too late to make amends." The *New York*

Times asserted: "The subject should and presumably will be dropped. If it isn't, the Progressives will again turn fiercely on their Democratic allies."[66]

Hiram Johnson personally spoke with the president about the Cutting matter when he dined at the White House in mid-December. Johnson saw that Roosevelt exhibited hostility and resentment toward Cutting, that he had forgotten Cutting's courageous decision to abandon his party in 1932 to support him. All the president seemed able to recall was Cutting's denunciation of the administration's handling of the veterans. Johnson came away convinced that Roosevelt had personally endorsed the Chavez contest against Cutting. He considered the president's actions "small, and ungrateful, and cruel, and what little I can do to prevent an injustice being done Cutting . . . will be done." Johnson told two members of Cutting's staff that he saw no way to derail the Chavez challenge. When one of them asked if it was Farley's fault, the California senator leaped to his feet and shouted that such disgraceful activities could not be pursued without endorsement from Roosevelt.[67]

Interior Secretary Harold Ickes had informed the President of his view that opposition to Cutting's reelection was unwise, as it would create an unfriendly feeling among the progressives, whose support Roosevelt needed for his legislative program. After the election, Ickes and Henry Wallace, the two cabinet members with progressive Republican backgrounds, had a conference with the president about the Cutting controversy. What transpired at that meeting was never revealed, but the administration never discouraged Chavez in his challenge.[68]

Cutting was seated at the opening of the new Congress in January 1935, but Chavez filed a formal petition the following month, alleging fraud in Cutting's vote total. He claimed that children, the deceased, repeat voters, and noncitizens of the state were included in the victory margin of Cutting. He also accused Cutting of giving money to voters to gain their support. The senator now demanded that a total recount of the entire election be held, not just those counties that his opponent wished to investigate. The Privileges and Elections Committee held brief hearings, immediately dismissing accusations of unlawful expenditures but calling for Cutting to present evidence in his defense from New Mexico records. Therefore, the senator began traveling back and forth to New Mexico to gather material to show the validity of the election results.[69]

Hiram Johnson worked for Cutting's interests as a minority member of the Privileges and Elections Committee. He denounced the challenge as "a contest of bad faith and harassment. . . . I'm getting bitterer and bitterer because of the iniquity and the fraud, and the malice of the contest." He wrote his son: "I can assure you that they will not break this young man unjustly without this country knowing of it."[70]

Cutting continued his Senate activities as his hold on the seat was being challenged. He had two contacts with the administration that was trying to oust him from office. Rexford Tugwell, a key Roosevelt adviser, met with him to ask if he would introduce a banking bill for the administration. Tugwell hinted that if Cutting agreed to do this, something might be done about Chavez's challenge. The senator was displeased by the tone of this incident but was even more disturbed by a brief confrontation he had with the president himself shortly before the Senate took a vote on the World Court issue in January 1935. As Cutting entered the White House, Roosevelt greeted him warmly, said he was always glad to see him, and hoped that the senator would "drop around occasionally." He told Cutting that he hoped he did not believe the rumors going around that the White House was involved in Chavez's challenge of his reelection. Roosevelt said he was certain that the situation would be resolved in some way that would satisfy Cutting.[71]

Angry over what he regarded as presidential deceit, Cutting excused himself from the conference, but as he left, Roosevelt indicated he would be much obliged for any aid the senator could give him on the World Court vote. Cutting favored American membership in that world organization but was sorely tempted to change his vote. Deciding to follow his convictions rather than his emotions, he supported Roosevelt when the Senate voted on the issue. Cutting informed Norris of his meeting with the president, and Norris again expressed anger and bitterness over what the White House was doing to the New Mexico senator.[72]

While enroute to Washington from New Mexico, Senator Cutting was tragically killed in a plane accident over Missouri on May 6, 1935. At the announcement of his death by his New Mexico Senate colleague Carl Hatch, the Senate adjourned as a mark of respect to his memory. The scene in the Senate was one of extreme sorrow and shock. The progressive bloc was especially affected. Borah, Norris, and Johnson were visibly emotional, with tears welling up in their eyes. La Follette was so overcome that he left the Senate chamber during the brief session. The progressives renewed their harsh criticism of Roosevelt for having supported Chavez in the election challenge. Had this not happened, it would have been unnecessary for Cutting to travel back and forth from his home state to gather evidence for his defense. Five progressive Republicans—Borah, Johnson, La Follette, Norris, and Nye—were among those named to represent the Senate at Cutting's funeral services, acting as honorary pallbearers.[73]

Roosevelt spoke with regret of the tragedy, telling Ickes that he had opposed Cutting for reelection because of his dislike of the type of people Cutting was allied with in New Mexico. The president was concerned his good friend, Senator Norris, would feel bitterness toward him over Cutting's death. Ickes replied that he thought the progressives would be estranged temporarily from Roosevelt but would continue to support New Deal programs they considered worthwhile. The interior secretary was convinced that Roosevelt was conscience stricken over the tragedy. Roosevelt told him that he had been willing to give Chavez another position and to call off the challenge, but Cutting had refused to concede anything, insisting on retaining his independence. The president proceeded to send condolences to Cutting's mother.[74]

Bronson Cutting's death was mourned by many people of liberal persuasion, and he was eulogized in numerous editorials and articles as a major loss to the progressive movement. When Dennis Chavez was sworn in as Cutting's successor, five progressives walked out of the Senate chamber in silent protest—Johnson, La Follette, Norris, Nye, and Shipstead. Borah, given the credit for organizing the demonstration, was in the Supreme Court chamber when Chavez was called to be sworn in, but he later declared he had been with the others in spirit. The progressives made it clear that they felt bitter over the administration's handling of the whole affair. Norris commented: "I left the chamber because it was the only way, in my helplessness, that I could show my condemnation of the disgraceful and unwarranted fight made to drive Senator Cutting out of public office. The determined oppositon of the Democratic National Committee and its chairman to bring about the defeat of Senator Cutting is the greatest case of ingratitude in history. It is a blot upon the record of the administration."[75]

So ended an unfortunate incident that put Roosevelt in a bad light. It is difficult to measure the precise effect the Cutting tragedy had upon relations between the progressives and the president. The liberal flowering of the New Deal immediately followed the death of Cutting, and the progressive Republicans were to have an important role in pushing Roosevelt toward this Second New Deal. Thus, in terms of short-range cooperation and promotion of significant reform legislation, the Cutting death did not seem to impede progressives' principles and goals.

The long-term effect is harder to gauge. Certainly, Roosevelt's poor handling of Bronson Cutting must have increased distrust and suspicion of the progressives toward the president. He did not appear to be a man of honor, one who believed in reciprocal loyalty to people who had sacrificed for him politically. He seemed willing to allow partisanship and pettiness to affect his relationship with others. He appeared reluctant to accept constructive criticism from his friends and apparently had a tendency to hold grudges. Finally, he had given evidence that he would strike back with his executive power if he could not get people to do things his way, and yet would attempt to deceive his intended victim by claiming innocence of any "purge" attempt. Roosevelt's handling of the Cutting affair seemed a warning sign to some of his lust for power. The future reaction of the progressives to the New Deal was certainly, at least unconsciously, affected by the Cutting tragedy.

[6]

The Triumph of Progressivism, 1935-1936

The early months of the first session of the 74th Congress gave evidence of two trends: the growing sense of disillusionment toward Roosevelt and the New Deal on the part of the progressive Republicans, only heightened by the controversy over Bronson Cutting's Senate seat; and the floundering of the president, uncertain of the direction in which the New Deal should go. Despite these trends, the year 1935 was to witness the full flowering of the progressive movement, the accomplishment of the long-held dreams of the progressive Republican Senate bloc for social justice legislation. Despite their discontent with Roosevelt's handling of the Cutting affair, the progressives were to push Roosevelt toward his strong promotion of the legislation that has come down in history with the label of the "Second New Deal." At the same time, attempts were being made to reform the Republican party to make it an alternate vehicle to the New Deal. The failure of this effort led most of the progressive Republicans either to remain neutral or to support the reelection of Roosevelt in 1936.

During the first few months of 1935, the only major piece of legislation passed into law was the work-relief bill that created the Work Projects Administration (WPA). The WPA was the biggest, most ambitious, and generally most successful relief program the federal government had ever undertaken. More than eight million people worked for the WPA by 1941 on various construction, conservation, and public service projects. Roosevelt called upon Congress to permit the federal government to spend about $5 billion on emergency public employment, enough to give work to 3.5 million people. The executive branch was to have control of the funds and to determine how they should be spent, a significant shift of power from the Congress to the White House.

Senator La Follette was dissatisfied with this proposal and introduced an amendment to the bill calling for an appropriation of more than $9 billion,

91

nearly double what the president requested. His proposal was defeated by an overwhelming vote of 77 to 8, with only three progressive Republicans (Cutting, Frazier, Nye) joining in support of the Wisconsin senator. However, all members of the bloc voted in favor of the administration bill and the conference report. But Hiram Johnson expressed discontent with the president's control over the relief funds, telling his son: "I may accept this because I don't know what to do myself in curing our country's ills, and inasmuch as I am unable to present a plan, I may be justified in giving to him the purse strings of the nation for the consummation of any plan which he may devise. I do, however, hesitate in a matter of such transcendent importance." Johnson wanted the appropriation cut in half and confined to one year's duration, but the Congress went along with Roosevelt's plan. After the bill became law, Johnson wrote his son: "I did not feel with the views I have about relieving distress, feeding the hungry, etc., that I could vote against relief, and so finally I voted for the bill, but with many misgivings. We are in the Hands of the Lord . . . and I am perfectly certain that He, alone, and no earthly personage, has any knowledge of what will be done or what may ultimately occur."[1]

Roosevelt's lack of direction in early 1935, along with his attempt to hold on to conservative and business support, alarmed many of the progressives. Hiram Johnson believed Roosevelt was "not quite sure of himself and . . . his plans for the future are wholly nebulous and inchoate." The government was at a standstill, he said, while Roosevelt was deciding how to handle the extremist challenge of Sen. Huey Long of Louisiana and Rev. Charles Coughlin, the "Radio Priest" Charles McNary wrote his brother: "The President has lost considerable of his influence with his Party and has developed recently a rather childish peevishness." In March, T.R.B. of *The New Republic* declared: "To some extent, at least, he has lost the confidence of the progressive group in the Senate. It is, in my judgment, a much more serious loss than is generally appreciated because the progressives were his only convinced supporters."[2]

During May, Roosevelt finally lost support of the business community, as the U.S. Chamber of Commerce, the major spokesman for American business, denounced the New Deal. The progressives now saw their chance to direct the president's thinking. Within days after Bronson Cutting's death, despite their bitterness over Roosevelt's handling of the affair, a group of progressives led by La Follette went to the White House for a conference. The legislators urged the president to assume the leadership of a new reform program and to end the First New Deal program of cooperation with big business, as personified by the NRA. Norris spoke of the need to put the Post Office Department under the merit system. The progressives were confident that Roosevelt had been convinced of the need to assert a strong progressive leadership in the coming months. La Follette believed it to be "the best, the frankest, the most encouraging talk we have ever had with the President. . . . The President was fair, and frank, and I felt greatly encouraged that he is going to go into the stride of his old aggressive leadership."[3]

With Congress planning to adjourn after an unproductive session, Roosevelt now went into action. In June he announced a new program, which he insisted Congress should act upon before adjournment. Five major pieces of legislation were proposed: social security, a labor relations bill, a wealth tax, a public utility holding company measure, and a banking bill. Roosevelt also asked for action on a number of minor measures, including the Guffey-Snyder coal bill. These proposals were the basis of the Second New Deal.

The progressive Republicans were unanimous in their support of the social security legislation, having long advocated old-age pensions and unemployment insurance, as well as national aid for care of the needy. The Social Security Act provided funds to be granted to the states on a matching basis for the blind, for occupational training of those otherwise physically handicapped, and for indigent dependent children. The final Senate vote of 77 to 6 indicated that a turning point in American history had been reached, that it was now generally accepted that the national government had ultimate responsibility for the welfare of the people. President Roosevelt had, meanwhile, changed his attitude toward labor legislation, which had been promoted since 1934 by Democratic Sen. Robert Wagner and his progressive colleagues. The Senate passed the Wagner Labor Relations bill by a vote of 63 to 12 on May 16, with all the progressive Republicans supporting it. Roosevelt now indicated that he favored the bill, which gave labor the right of collective bargaining, compelled employers to agree to union organization of their plants, and set up a National Labor Relations Board to investigate and settle disputes between labor and management. Spurred on by the progressives in Congress, Roosevelt said he regarded House passage as essential. The bill won final approval of Congress on June 27 and was another great victory for social justice. Indeed, the Wagner Act did more for trade unionism than any other federal law at any time.[4]

On June 19, Roosevelt sent a tax message to Congress, calling for the beginning of redistribution of the nation's wealth. He recommended increased taxes on inheritances, a gift tax, graduated taxes on large incomes, and a corporation tax. This proposal led to large-scale denunciations by business interests, and rejoicing among the progressive Republicans. La Follette, who had long been in favor of heavier taxation of the wealthy, was especially pleased. Earlier in the session, he had called for fullest publicity of income tax returns, a proposal that had failed passage by 51 to 25, although all of the progressive Republicans present had supported the concept. At the end of April, the Wisconsin senator declared that the progressives in the Senate intended to make a major effort for passage of drastic increases in the taxes on wealth, regardless of the administration's actions. Continuation of the public works program depended upon such legislation.[5]

Immediately after the president's tax message, the progressive Republicans joined with other liberal senators in issuing a statement, which affirmed: "We believe that the tax program presented by the President to the Congress should be disposed of before this session adjourns. We are willing to stay in session until action is taken upon this vitally important question." The statement was released to the press with the signatures of twenty-two senators, including Borah, Capper, Frazier, La Follette, Norbeck, Norris, Nye, and Shipstead from the progressive Republican bloc. The idea of this public declaration was conceived at a luncheon attended by Norris, Johnson, Borah, and La Follette. The four legislators felt that the president had finally espoused their cardinal political philosophy and that they were ready to fight for the tax bill. Senator Nye saw the declaration as a means to test the sincerity of the president, indicating that some independent senators who had been supporting Roosevelt might turn away from him in 1936 unless he played a vigorous role in promoting the tax legislation. Nye thought the progressive Republicans who had supported the president in 1932 or had remained neutral would return to the Republican fold if that party nominated a progressive candidate.[6]

As the Democratic leaders of Congress seemed to waver on the tax bill, Borah publicly defended the Roosevelt tax program. He called the legislation a program to "share the burden of government"—one that was sound both economically and morally. *The Progressive* hailed the bill as pointing the way to "a genuine 'new deal' for America, based on sound economic policy and offering the most promise for permanent improvement." Capper delivered a radio address in support of the president's tax program. But despite the progressive support, Roosevelt seemed reluctant to commit himself to an all-out fight for the wealth tax proposal. When a drive to adjourn developed in the House of Representatives in mid-July, Senate leaders made a promise to the progressives, headed by La Follette, that they would not adjourn until the president called for it or the progressives gave up the struggle for the tax legislation. However, Norris and La Follette were determined to force tax action. The latter even proposed an amendment to the tax bill to increase the rates beyond the Roosevelt levels, so that an additional $500 million would be available for public works. His amendment was defeated, but the Senate passed the less extensive bill by a vote of 57 to 22 on August 15. Ten progressive Republicans were in the majority, with Couzens absent and only McNary voting against.[7]

After final passage by both houses, the Wealth Tax Act turned out to be less than the progressives had wanted. The president had made compromises and seemed to have lost enthusiasm for the fight. The inheritance tax had been eliminated, and the graduated corporation tax had been reduced to only a symbolic levy. However, estate, gift, and capital stock taxes had been increased, an excess profits tax had been levied, and the surtax had been raised to the highest rates in American history. Progressives who had wanted greater changes in taxation were disappointed, but the Wealth Tax Act was certainly an improvement on earlier tax legislation.[8]

The progressive Republicans, long enemies of the electric power monopolies that seemed to be beyond state regulation, unanimously backed the Public Utilities Holding Company bill, which included a "death sentence" provision empowering the Securities and Exchange Commission, after January 1, 1940, to dissolve any utility holding company that could not justify its existence. The Senate approved the "death sentence" by the bare majority of one vote, 45 to 44, in June, with ten progressive Republicans in the majority and only McNary voting against. Final passage of the bill in the Senate was by a 56 to 32 vote, with all of the progressive Republicans in the majority and the rest of the Republicans in opposition. Before the final vote, Norris and Borah issued attacks upon the public utilities. The former labeled the holding companies as robbers, thieves, and swindlers in the course of a five-hour speech, and the latter demanded that holding companies beyond the second stage should be eliminated entirely. The House, however, refused to pass the "death sentence" provision, and Roosevelt now compromised, angering some of the progressives. Norris reluctantly accepted the loss of the "death sentence," declaring that a good beginning had been made toward an ultimate goal. The legislation did eliminate all companies more than twice removed from the operating ones, and it represented a major attack on big business and monopoly, something the progressive Republicans had attacked over the years.[9]

The Banking Act of 1935 enlarged government control over currency and credit. It was a reform measure designed to centralize control of national banking in Washington. The Federal Reserve Board had increased authority, including the ability to set reserve requirements for member banks and control of open market operations. Senators Cutting and Nye had published articles on the dangers of private banking in *Liberty Magazine* and *Common Sense*, respectively and progressives had long spoken of the need to control banking practices. Cutting had even introduced legislation to change the American banking system twice in the last year of his life. The banking bill that the Roosevelt administration proposed passed without a recorded vote. However, a La Follette amendment to strengthen the bill by banning a director of one bank from sitting on the board of directors of another was defeated by a vote of 39 to 22, with all progressive Republicans present except McNary backing the Wisconsin senator's proposal. The conference report on the banking bill was agreed to without a recorded vote.[10]

Finally, the Guffey-Snyder Coal Act finished the legislative agenda for 1935. The legislation, reenacting the old bituminous coal code under the

NRA, guaranteed collective bargaining, uniform wages and hours, and set up a national commission to fix prices and allocate production. The Senate vote of 45 to 37 for the bill showed progressive Republican division on the greatest level for any of the session's legislation, with six supporting (Capper, Frazier, Johnson, La Follette, Norris, Nye), three opposing (Borah, Norbeck, Shipstead), and two not voting (Couzens, McNary).[11]

The first session of the 74th Congress had indeed been historic. Although the progressive Republicans alone were not able to push through reform legislation without the support of many Democrats, they had prodded the president toward the promotion of these basic changes. They had played an especially significant role in the passage of the wealth tax legislation and the public utility holding company measure. The Second New Deal undoubtedly had been much more to their liking than the First New Deal. The most outstanding advances of any congressional session in American history up to that time had been due partially to the progressive Republicans, who had pushed a wavering Roosevelt to the left.

During 1936, Roosevelt did not encourage further reform legislation, as it was a presidential election year, a time to avoid alienating moderates by an appearance of radicalism. However, in January, the Supreme Court declared in *U.S.* v. *Butler* that the Agricultural Adjustment Act was unconstitutional, because of its processing tax. By a vote of 6 to 3, the nation's highest court voided a mainstay of the First New Deal, a law that had been reenacted in 1935 by a Senate vote of 64 to 15 and strong support in the House. All of the progressive Republicans present and voting had supported renewal of the legislation. Peter Norbeck felt the AAA had improved conditions for the farmer, and Arthur Capper termed the Democratic agricultural program a "godsend." Capper added that the Republican party could not win the farm vote in 1936 if it condemned the AAA, which had given farmers a measure of justice they were unwilling to give up.[12]

A new farm bill had to be formulated to replace the repudiated AAA. The administration came up with the Soil Conservation and Domestic Allotment Act, which offered farmers bounties for deciding not to plant soil-depleting commercial crops and instead agreeing to grow soil-enriching grasses, clover, and soybeans. The bill passed the Senate by a 56 to 20 vote, with six progressive Republicans (Capper, Frazier, Johnson, La Follette, Norbeck, Norris) voting in support, and the other two progressives present (Couzens, McNary) voting against. Nye, Shipstead, and Borah were not present for the roll call, but the former two indicated they would have supported the bill, while the latter said he would have joined the opposition. Norris, Capper, Frazier, Norbeck, and La Follette all spoke of the necessity to pass some farm measure to replace the AAA. Although none considered the legislation the final answer, they saw it as an acceptable temporary measure until more permanent legislation could be enacted. At the same time, Borah considered the bill unconstitutional because it continued to allow federal control over farm production, and McNary regarded the proposal as simply the AAA in a different form, an attempt to ignore the Supreme Court decision.[13]

The other major legislation of the 1936 session was the passage of a modest tax on undistributed profits, a bill that only four progressive Republicans supported on original passage (Frazier, La Follette, Norbeck, Norris). However, Borah, Nye, and Shipstead supported the bill when the vote on the conference report came up. The other four progressives (Capper, Couzens, McNary, and Johnson) voted against the bill, with Johnson not present to vote on final passage of the conference report.[14]

The 1936 presidential campaign was on the minds of the members of the progressive Republican Senate bloc throughout 1935 and 1936, with their major goal being to liberalize the Republican party so it could act as an alternative to the New Deal. Failing this, the result would be a decision either to endorse Roosevelt for reelection or remain neutral during the campaign—a decision that would, in effect, benefit Roosevelt.

Immediately after the 1934 congressional elections, which saw a surprising and unprecedented gain for the party in power in both houses, Senator Borah vowed that the Republican party must be rehabilitated for 1936 if it hoped to have a chance to win the White House and control of Congress. Fresh leadership and new issues were essential, he said, for the party's survival as a viable force at the state and congressional levels. Borah called for the end of reactionary and big business control of the party apparatus and for reorganization along liberal lines. His fight for the restoration of the antitrust laws was intimately connected, he declared, with his struggle to take away the power that big corporations and monopolies had over the political and economic structure of the nation. In December, renewing his demand that the Republican party be liberalized, Borah suggested that if the Republican National Committee refused to reorganize the party apparatus, then the Young Republican clubs throughout the nation must assert their leadership and force changes in the party organization.[15]

Minority leader Charles McNary endorsed Borah's statements. Republicans must steer away from rhetoric about the Constitution, the Founding Fathers, and government bureaucracy and devote attention to everyday human problems, McNary asserted, and the only way to bring about a change in the priorities was through new leadership, planning, and ideals. The response of Republican National Chairman Henry P. Fletcher to the Borah and McNary statements was to declare that he had no intention of allowing the independents to take over the party apparatus. Borah countered that the fight for the soul of the Republican party had just begun. Senators Couzens, Cutting, Norbeck, Frazier, and Nye, as well as Gov. Gifford Pinchot and Sen.

Arthur Vandenberg, said they were with Borah and McNary on the issue of party reorganization. However, Couzens suggested that Borah write a platform for a liberal Republican party, posing practicable alternatives to the New Deal, rather than simply acting as a leading critic of the administration, as Borah had done in the 1934 congressional campaign. Couzens, never one to control his tongue, was calling on Borah to talk less and produce more in the way of action.[16]

On December 13, 1934, Borah and Gerald Nye carried their struggle for liberalization of the Republican party to a New York City platform. Speaking before the New York County Republican Committee, they demanded that younger, more liberal elements take over control of the party apparatus. Their speeches were broadcast nationally over the radio. Borah said that the party must move to the left if it was to meet the nation's economic crisis effectively. The party could only survive as a viable alternative to the Democrats if it stood for economic and social justice and a more equitable distribution of wealth. The supreme issue for a new party platform was, he declared, "protection of the rights, liberties and economic privileges of the average man and woman" against monopoly and privilege. Nye emphasized that western progressive Republicans might bolt to a new progressive party if their interests were not represented in the leadership of the Republican party, and if its policies and platform continued to be oriented toward big business rather than farmers, workers, and consumers. Both senators paid tribute to Roosevelt's leadership but found fault with the mainstays of the First New Deal, the NRA and the AAA. Nye declared the president could not bring about a permanent liberalization of the Democratic party, that reactionary views would return to control the party apparatus after he left office. Therefore, there was an urgent need for liberalizing the Republican party to bring about continued progressive policies after the New Deal ended. Senator Capper agreed with the Borah and Nye addresses: "If the last two elections mean anything, they mean, I think, that our program has got to change if we are to again become the dominant political party in this country."[17]

During 1935, Republican spokesmen who were concerned about Roosevelt's criticisms of the Supreme Court for declaring the NRA unconstitutional, fearful of too much centralization of power in the hands of the chief executive, and yet desirous of liberal reform on the national level, began to examine Senator Borah as a possible presidential candidate, one who could run on a platform of preserving the Constitution and liberalizing the Republican party. Progressive editor William Allen White wrote Borah in July: "Of course you can be President if you want to. You are the only Republican who could at this minute beat Roosevelt. And I am becoming more and more persuaded that he must be beaten and that only a big man can do the job." Two months later, White told Borah he believed the senator could win the party's presidential nomination if he was willing to seek the office. Borah replied he had no plans to run for president and would not even consider it so long as reactionaries retained the power to control the party apparatus and write the platform.[18]

Despite these claims, discussions of Borah's possible candidacy spread. *The Nation* considered the Idaho senator's lone-wolf nature, his age (seventy), his unwillingness in the past to carry through various progressive causes, and his lack of administrative and executive experience as points against him, but the journal still regarded him as a significant potential threat to Roosevelt's reelection. Although *The Nation* no longer considered Borah a progressive, it admitted that he had great prestige among the mass of the American people. *The Progressive* stated that Borah would probably gain the support of many progressive Republicans, although it was expected that La Follette and Norris, at least, would support Roosevelt's reelection.[19]

During October, in an interview with the *Washington Post*, Borah indicated a change of heart in his intention to rally public sentiment against eastern domination of the 1936 campaign. He was vague as to whether his fight against conservatism would include a challenge in the presidential primary states. In November, he further criticized Old Guard Republicans and former President Hoover specifically for following policies that led the country into the depression. He was willing to have his name entered into any primary state that wished to place him on the ballot but had no plans to seek the nomination actively. Borah warned that western Republicans would back Roosevelt if the Old Guard tried to control the party convention. He also expressed concern that if Roosevelt was reelected, he would take the mandate as an endorsement to change the American form of government to a "federal dictatorship" with all powers centered in the executive branch.[20]

Borah now called reporters into his Capitol Hill office and subtly hinted that he was indeed planning to seek the Republican presidential nomination, with the dangers of monopoly as the key issue in the primaries. In December, he addressed the nation over the radio, offering an alternative to the basic philosophy of the New Deal and that of Hoover Republicanism. He announced later that he wanted the support of all liberal delegates, and a campaign board to direct his presidential drive was now organized. Borah contended he was primarily interested in holding the balance of power at the Republican convention and thus ensuring a liberal platform and candidate, whether or not he was the nominee. A number of progressive Republicans, including Pinchot, Frazier, Nye, Norbeck, and Shipstead announced their endorsement of the Idaho senator for President. Finally, on February 4, 1936, Borah formally declared he was a presidential candidate and made plans to enter various western state primaries.[21]

Borah campaigned throughout the Midwest during the spring of 1936. On March 19, in a speech at Youngstown, Ohio, he defined his platform.

He was critical of the New Deal farm policy, of monopoly in all forms, of the growing bureaucracy in the federal government, and of the politics involved in the administration of New Deal relief programs. He called for adherence to the precepts of the Constitution, the complete independence of the federal judiciary, and a policy of complete neutrality by the United States in all European and Asian quarrels. In Chicago, Borah warned the Old Guard that he would walk out of the party if the corporate interests dictated the party platform and nominee. While reasserting his criticism of the New Deal, he defended the support he had given to many of the president's programs.[22]

Borah's candidacy caused much controversy among progressive and liberal spokesmen. Many leading progressives, including Norris, La Follette, and Johnson, remained silent while Borah made his effort for the Presidency. Liberal journals such as *The New Republic, The Nation*, and *Common Sense* indicated they did not regard Borah as a true, committed progressive. Hiram Johnson expressed the widespread cynicism that existed about the Idaho senator's campaign. Always jealous of the greater press attention devoted to Borah, he expressed doubt that Borah would reamin an active candidate until the convention in June. Borah was primarily interested in publicity, Johnson believed, and he was certain that his "vacillations, and apparent streak of laziness" would prevent him from gaining the nomination. During April, Johnson wrote as follows: "Borah as a candidate has been a dud. I think he is a complete 'flop', so far as the convention is concerned, . . . He labored under the delusion that there would be a popular uprising, which would overwhelm the electorate and carry him upon a tumultuous popular wave to success. He has not amounted to a last year's bird's nest, and his utterances have been really pitiful."[23]

Borah's quest for the presidency was indeed a failure by the end of April. With Gov. Alf M. Landon of Kansas moving toward the Republican nomination, Borah's friend William Allen White urged the Idaho senator to join the platform committee, so as to aid in the formation of an acceptable progressive platform. Borah rejected the idea, and with his fortunes sagging even further during May, he also declined to become a delegate to the convention. He threatened to withhold support from the Republican ticket if corporate interests shaped the platform. He did not like the fact that various oil interests were backing Landon. Arthur Krock of the *New York Times* called Borah "the Republican mystery man" who would play an important role at the convention despite the fact that he was not a delegate.[24]

Borah's planks on monopoly and foreign affairs were adopted in their basic form by the Republican convention, marking the high point of his influence at any convention during his career, but Borah remained unwilling to endorse Landon for president, stating that he wished to observe the candidate's campaign activities before making a statement. It was obvious that

Borah was bitter about losing this, his last opportunity for the presidency, an office he had been mentioned for many times during his career. Thus ended a hopeless campaign for reform in the Republican party. Although Landon had been a Bull Moose Progressive in 1912, he would be unable to attract the support of any progressive senator, with the exception of those two with the closest ties to the party machinery, Arthur Capper and Charles McNary. They were the only members of the bloc to support Hoover in 1932.[25]

Capper had been a strong supporter of much of the New Deal. During 1935, he had praised Roosevelt for a willingness to experiment and had specifically thrown his support to the president's proposal for a wealth tax. However, he expressed misgivings about the "spending spree" in which the New Deal was engaged and said the taxpayers' money was being spent in a reckless and extravagant manner on relief. Capper wrote Amos Pinchot in July: "Roosevelt is losing ground. He has gone too far in usurping power that was never intended the President should have." He believed the American people were losing faith in the New Deal. He thought certain programs, such as the AAA, still had their value as emergency measures, but the increasing centralization of power around the president, the growing public debt, and the burgeoning bureaucracy concerned Capper. In September the Kansas senator wrote Victor Murdock, a former progressive congressman from Kansas: "I think Roosevelt is slipping. If the Republicans put up a good man next year there is a fair chance that we can beat Roosevelt." Since Capper faced a re-election campaign in 1936, he defended his support of various New Deal programs while at the same time promoting fellow Kansan Alf Landon for the Republican nomination for the presidency. He predicted a close race between the two major parties in the Midwest heartland of the nation and thought the nomination of Landon would benefit himself and the Republican party.[26]

Capper attempted to act as an intermediary between Landon and Borah during the months before the convention, hoping to avert the possibility of the Idaho senator refusing Landon his endorsement during the campaign. Capper was very happy at Landon's victory and expressed the determination to do whatever he could to promote his presidential bandwagon. Capper gave a series of speeches for Landon, his main points being that the Republican candidate would loosen the concentration of power in Washington; cut down on extravagant federal spending; curb the federal government bureaucracy; and operate a more efficient administration based upon common sense, integrity, and liberalism. Landon would keep the good things the New Deal had brought, and for which Capper made no apology for supporting, and at the same time rid the federal government of the bad tendencies that had developed under Roosevelt's regime. The Kansas senator, easily reelected to another six-year term, was sorely disappointed over Landon's failure to carry Kansas and his disastrous national showing, winning only Maine and Vermont. He wrote William Allen White after the election results were in, claiming the administration's control of relief funds had been a major factor in the result. He was critical of the Republican party establishment, declaring that Roosevelt had "captured the imagination of the common, everyday folks because he convinced them that he was thinking of them and doing his best to see that they got an even break, while the Republicans were accepting immense sums from the Duponts and other Wall Streeters who would use the party in the future."[27]

After the 1935 congressional session, Charles McNary said that an improvement in the economy had taken place under the New Deal, but he was unhappy about Roosevelt's desire for more power over government affairs and thought the president's attempt to deal with so many issues at once was causing a loss of confidence that anything lasting was being accomplished. He believed the 1936 election would be decided in the Midwest and the West. The Oregon senator remained strangely silent as Landon won the Republican nomination to oppose Roosevelt. The *New York Times* pointed out in mid-October that he had not yet issued a definitive statement regarding the presidential campaign. Finally, in late October, in the midst of his own re-election campaign for another six years in the Senate, McNary's campaign manager announced that the senator was supporting Landon. The recent death of the senator's brother apparently prevented any further commitment to Landon other than this lukewarm endorsement, which stated that Landon would improve upon Roosevelt's farm program and would conserve the gains made under the New Deal. On Election Day, McNary swept to victory for another six-year Senate term without any major challenge.[28]

Lynn Frazier of North Dakota was the only progressive Republican senator to endorse the third-party candidacy of his state colleague, Rep. William Lemke, on the Union Party ticket. This party was promoted by such critics of the New Deal as Gerald L. K. Smith and Father Charles Coughlin. Frazier had, of course, worked with Lemke in the promotion of farm moratorium legislation to halt the foreclosure of mortgaged property during the height of the depression. The Supreme Court had invalidated the Frazier-Lemke Act by the time of the 1936 election, and Frazier felt that neither major political party was truly representing the interests of the common people, including the farmers. When he announced his endorsement of Lemke, he criticized the two major party platforms and denounced corporate contributions to both campaigns.[29]

Three progressives—Borah, Nye, and Johnson—remained publicly neutral during the presidential campaign. Borah returned to Idaho to campaign for reelection to the Senate and remained silent on the part he would take in the presidential campaign, although indicating he had no intention of bolting the Republican party. In late July, he praised the tone of Landon's acceptance speech but went no further toward a commitment to back him in the fall campaign. By early September, with no further statement by Borah forthcoming, doubts began to be expressed in news articles that the Idaho senator would actively support the Republican nominee. He had, for example, refused to meet with the Republican national chairman while the latter was visiting Idaho during August.[30]

The mystery over Borah's intentions seemed to be solved in early October when a Philadelphia newspaper reported that the senator had told one of its correspondents that he would not support Landon. Should the Republican leadership attempt to force an endorsement, Borah was supposed to have said, then he would issue a statement they would regret. His plans were to confine his campaigning to his own reelection contest. If the party leaders denounced him as a secret supporter of Roosevelt, then he just might announce an endorsement of the president. The reactionary forces backing Landon had better leave him alone if they wished to avoid a controversy. Borah repudiated this published article the next day, claiming he had never made such a statement nor had he authorized such a declaration to be made in his name.[31]

A few days later, while visiting Spokane, Washington, Borah finally confirmed that he would make no campaign speeches for any presidential candidate, confining himself to a discussion of issues of national importance. His campaign was based on a strong defense of those votes he cast for New Deal measures during the previous four years. Many of the motives and objectives of Roosevelt's program were worthy of support, Borah contended, while at the same time he had acted as one of the leading critics of those New Deal concepts that disturbed him. Above all, he had retained his fierce independence and would continue to fight for necessary reforms. Borah's neutrality did not hurt him at all, as he won reelection over Gov. Ben Ross without any major difficulty.[32]

Gerald Nye, who had supported Borah in his unsuccessful quest for the Republican presidential nomination, was not surprised by the Idaho senator's failure to win. He stated during 1935 that the Republican platform was more likely to be controlled by eastern reactionaries than by western progressives. Nye was critical of the Republican convention for ignoring the problems of farmers and workers and catering to the power trusts and other corporate interests. Roosevelt and Ickes, aware of Nye's discontent, now attempted to encourage him to endorse the president. In early August, Ickes asked Nye if he would be willing to take over the leadership of a progressive league that would be formed to promote the president's reelection. Nye replied in the negative, indicating he planned to remain neutral but would avoid speaking out against Roosevelt during the campaign.[33]

Roosevelt now decided to try the personal touch, inviting the senator to his estate at Hyde Park later in August. The president did not personally press the senator for his endorsement, but Nye certainly was aware of what was on his mind. The senator chose to regard it as a pleasant social visit that required no commitment for the fall campaign. Ickes still persisted, trying to convince Nye to attend a progressive conference organized by Senators Norris and La Follette to establish a campaign committee in support of Roosevelt. Nye refused, and in early October he declared publicly that he intended to follow a "hands off" policy with regard to the presidential race, confining his campaigning to the gubernatorial contest in his home state and to Senator Norris's independent race for reelection in Nebraska. Despite further efforts by Ickes to draw an endorsement from Nye, the senator continued his neutrality up to Election Day. Roosevelt's landslide victory was no surprise to him, Nye said, but it placed a tremendous responsibility on the president to prove that the welfare of America in both domestic and foreign affairs was safe in his hands. Nye wondered whether the president would now move to the left or right politically. The senator believed that if his own party did not rapidly reorganize along liberal lines, then a new progressive party seemed inevitable.[34]

Hiram Johnson had begun to undergo a change of attitude toward Roosevelt and the New Deal beginning in 1935. Unhappy over the president's sponsorship of American entrance into the World Court during 1935, as well as his handling of Bronson Cutting's reelection contest, the California senator began to suspect the president's motives. In addition, Johnson suffered from poor health during 1936, apparently incapacitated by a stroke, and this did not improve his state of mind, instead accentuating his crotchety, bad-tempered, sarcastic personality.

During 1935, Johnson became deeply disturbed by the increasing level of government spending, saying that "it leaves me jittery, . . . it is not difficult for our legislators to embrace any new, dazzling expedient of tremendous and unheard of cost." He told his son, regarding Roosevelt: "He has increased in the minds of many people, like myself, friendly to him, the feeling of uncertainty concerning him, and some think that his love of the dramatic has overcome his sense of proportion and his ideas of policies." He also concluded that the president would easily win reelection because the Republicans would not offer a viable alternative.[35]

Despite his growing suspicions of Roosevelt's motives, Johnson met a number of times with the president, including once with Mrs. Johnson on a cruise on the presidential boat. The senator's impression of the president at this time was that he had "something of a will power about him that very few human beings possess. . . . his mind is very active. . . . Now and then, he goes off on a tangent on a more or less startling proposition, with which one cannot agree, but when he observes the disagreement, immediately he shifts to another topic." When the 1935 congressional session ended, Johnson visited the White House before returning to California, and in November the president asked Johnson to visit him when he returned to Washington. Roosevelt was obviously attempting to maintain a close relationship with the California senator.[36]

Returning to the nation's capital at the end of December, Johnson asserted that business conditions were the best they had been since 1929, obvious words of approval for the basic thrust of the New Deal. He wrote his son that the upcoming campaign for the presidency "will be the bitterest we have ever encountered. It will develop, before its conclusion into a class war." Admitting that at times he was disturbed by the president's attitudes and approaches to such issues as neutrality, he declared: " . . . however, I compare him to those who are his opponents, either as candidates or advocates, and I must say that, generally speaking, he is so infinitely better than those who are yapping at him, or those who are seeking the nomination, that I feel there is little or no comparison." It was Roosevelt's fortune, Johnson asserted, that no strong Republican candidate was appearing to challenge him:

> What a child of destiny Roosevelt is! He blunders along here with half-baked and oftentimes half-finished policies, and I give him due credit for his adventurous spirit, and desire to accomplish things, . . . I do think if there were a Republican party and a real Republican candidate there might be a fight this year that would gladden the disinterested onlooker.

The senator was greatly concerned over what would happen after Roosevelt won reelection, as "he is so vain now of his powers."[37]

After Johnson suffered what were termed brain spasms, he became more isolated from political events. "The events of the days seem far removed," he wrote his son in August, "and the election something of which I am no part. . . . A strange feeling comes over one in contemplating himself, a forgotten man, unable to do the things that he was accustomed to do and most desirous of doing. The doctor has said I must not indulge in the campaign at all." Johnson did not attend the progressive conference set up by La Follette and Norris, giving as his reasons his poor health and his desire to remain a "lone wolf." He wrote his son: "I will soon be put on the spot in the presidential contest, which I have delayed as long as I could. Various individuals have been ringing me up, men in authority and I have been stalling."[38]

The president personally telephoned Johnson, but the house servant indicated he was asleep and could not be disturbed. Johnson's silence led to speculation that he might eventually endorse Landon before Election Day. The *New York Herald Tribune* reported that Johnson had not seen visitors or personally answered the telephone for many weeks, but that close friends were convinced he had turned against the president and the New Deal and would speak up for Landon. However, the *New York Times* noted in late October, the senator had not yet issued a statement on the presidential campaign.[39]

The president and Harold Ickes knew that Johnson had avoided a commitment to the Roosevelt campaign. While Ickes was aware of Johnson's illness, he could not understand why the senator had not issued a simple endorsement. The president decided to make one last attempt for the Californian's support, sending a letter inquiring about Johnson's health and inviting the senator and his wife to dinner at the White House after the election campaign was over. Regarding the election, Roosevelt wrote: "Apparently California remains safe but, of course, any statement by you, Hiram, would put the finishing touches to the picture, not only in California but in Oregon and Washington." Mrs. Johnson called Roosevelt's secretary to inform the president that her husband was in a very nervous state and had been ordered by his doctor not to read his mail. It seemed obvious that Johnson had decided to avoid an endorsement of either Landon or Roosevelt. However, the senator did send for an absentee ballot and told his son that he had voted for the president, "although with many misgivings."[40]

Johnson's decision to avoid an endorsement of the president surprised many people. The senator's California colleague, William Gibbs McAdoo, for example, wrote James Farley after the election of his astonishment "that my distinguished colleague never said a word for Roosevelt. I thought, at least, he would make a public statement in his behalf." Johnson himself was astonished at the magnitude of the president's victory and expressed concern over what the landslide might do to Roosevelt's plans for the future. While he did not look forward to the future with great hope, the Californian wished to resume an active political role after recuperating from his stroke.[41]

Roosevelt gained the support of the other five members of the progressive Republican Senate bloc for his reelection. Peter Norbeck supported Borah for the Republican nomination but admitted he was quite pleased with Roosevelt's record. In July 1935, he wrote a friend that "In spite of a deep conviction that a lot of unnecessary blunders are being made, I find myself today more disposed to support Roosevelt than I have had any time during the whole administration." In August, he warned the Republicans that "The New Deal is full of mistakes, but the Old Deal is no substitute. . . . The Republican party must offer something more than criticism of Roosevelt and the scare about losing the Constitution. Above all, they cannot win without inviting the progressives into the party and giving them a voice in party affairs." Norbeck remained silent after the party conventions until about three weeks before the election. Then he announced he was supporting Roosevelt, crediting the president with a substantial business recovery and an improved agricultural situation. Two months later, Norbeck died.[42]

James Couzens urged after the 1934 congressional elections that partisanship be abandoned and that the president be given the necessary support to guarantee success for his New Deal programs. During the following year, the Michigan senator was seriously ill, spending an extended period of time at the Mayo Clinic. Roosevelt sent a number of telegrams asking about his condition. Substantially recovered by the beginning of 1936, the senator now faced a tough reelection contest, which included a serious challenge for the Republican nomination from conservatives who felt he was too attached to the New Deal. In February, he declared: "While I have never stated that I am in favor of all of 'The New Deal' I was, and still am in favor of *a* new deal, because of the great distress that many millions of my countrymen have had to go through and to a large degree due to the conduct of and control of the management of the Republican party."[43]

Because of his own reelection campaign in Michigan, Couzens refused to involve himself in the presidential contest. If the voters of his state decided to abandon him in the Republican primary because of his independence, that would be all right with him, because "My country and the welfare of my countrymen is much more important to me than any party or any political honors that I may secure." He would remain a Republican but would feel free to endorse much of the New Deal and also to criticize it where he felt it was going wrong, as with the handling of relief funds. Couzens added: "I will not pussyfoot, I will say frankly as I hope I always have, what I believe about party policies. . . . I hope that I will be able to remain a liberal Republican and I hope I will be able to 'use my party as a "reform channel" ' through which to bring to the people more social justice." He had no intention of "criticizing a man who has tried to relieve the distress to a much greater extent than any President we ever had."[44]

In May, the *New York Times* reported that Couzens might be offered the chance of running for the Senate on the Democratic ticket. The Old Guard and industrial spokesmen in Michigan were united in their opposition to his selection by the Republican party and were planning to give strong financial backing to former Gov. Wilbur M. Brucker in his challenge to Couzens. Couzens held, however, to his original determination to seek reelection only on the Republican line, and so stated when he officially announced his candidacy for another six-year term on June 15. In the course of the primary campaign, Couzens told a Detroit audience he did not believe the Republican contention that President Roosevelt was leading the nation down the road to bankruptcy. He also ridiculed the notion that many Republicans held, that the federal budget could have remained balanced despite the depression's effect on the country. The primary contest became more and more one of bitter attack against Couzens's record by his primary opponent. In the midst of this tough struggle, Couzens demonstrated courage when he changed his mind about being noncommittal on the presidential race and instead declared on August 22 that he would support Roosevelt for reelection. His own campaign was not as important as the victory of the president, Couzens declared, and certainly this endorsement killed the senator's chances for renomination.[45]

Shortly before the Michigan primary, Roosevelt wrote a letter of thanks to the senator. Praising Couzens for his courage and fierce independence, he declared:

> It is one of the fine things about public life that every once in a while the usual rules of the political game are not followed! Your announcement is not only fine in itself but it is especially so because it came without solicitation or suggestion on my part or on that of any member of the Democratic organization. Frankly, I was just as much taken by surprise as, I imagine, Brother Landon was. I want you to know that I appreciate not alone what you have said and done but also your manner of doing it—for you have shown a very deep courage based on conviction and may lose your Primary as a result.

Couzens did indeed lose the Republican nomination by more than 120,000 votes, a result attributed largely to the senator's decision to declare for Roosevelt. The president now offered Couzens the chairmanship of the U.S. Maritime Commission, but the senator declined the position. Taken ill again, he entered the hospital for treatment. When Roosevelt was campaigning in Detroit in mid-October, Couzens left his hospital bed to meet with him at a dinner party and a public rally. The crowd cheered him when he was introduced. The president had offered to visit him at the hospital, but Couzens had rejected the idea. After Couzens returned there, Roosevelt sent a telegram wishing him a speedy recovery. However, the senator's condition turned for the worse and he died on October 22 from uremic poisoning, following an emergency operation for a kidney ailment.[46]

Henrik Shipstead continued to have good relations with President Roosevelt during 1935 and 1936, despite the administration's decision to remain neutral during the Minnesota senator's 1934 reelection campaign. Before returning to his home state after the 1935 congressional session, Shipstead wrote a note of thanks to Roosevelt "for the many courtesies that I have been shown by you during the past session of Congress. . . . I hope that you will have a good rest, which you so richly deserve." Shipstead did not attend the progressive conference organized by Senators La Follette and Norris in September 1936 but told La Follette that "Roosevelt is safe anyway." He had a conference with Roosevelt in the middle of September. After the meeting, he predicted to newsmen that the president would win the Midwest by the same margin as in 1932. When Roosevelt visited Minneapolis during October, Shipstead introduced him at a public rally and was given a seat in the presidential automobile. On October 20, he gave a formal endorsement of the New Deal in a broadcast speech to eight midwestern states. This was the first time since 1924 that he had publicly declared for a presidential candidate.[47]

Shipstead said Roosevelt had made mistakes and that all programs of the New Deal were not equal in their value, "but I am going to vote for Roosevelt because I believe he has been more often right than wrong, and he has looked upon the problems of the Mississippi Valley and the Northwest with greater sympathy and understanding than any other President in my time." The Minnesota senator specifically praised the administration's farm legislation, the holding company law, and its rural electrification policy as constructive measures. The establishment of conservation laws and the passage of the Wagner Labor Relations Act were also mentioned as outstanding achievements. Roosevelt sent a note of thanks to Shipstead for his "eloquent defense of the Administration."[48]

Robert and Philip La Follette remained strong supporters of the New Deal during 1935 and 1936. They consulted frequently with the president, prodding him toward the left and emphasizing the necessity of ever higher levels of government spending on public works, these to be financed via higher taxes on the wealthy. After the brothers won election as progressives in Wisconsin in 1934, Roosevelt invited them to the White House. The subject of the 1936 campaign came up during their conference. Governor La Follette informed Roosevelt that if he was willing to promote a true progressive program, then progressives would rally around him. But the brothers felt an obligation to work for a new national Progressive party for the long term. Roosevelt indicated he desired the brothers' support for 1936 and intended to cooperate with them on the formation of an advanced progressive program. He said independent progressive support was essential for the success of the New Deal.[49]

The friendship between the La Follette brothers and the president became so close that, in the spring of 1935, rumors began to spread that the senator was being considered as a possible vice-presidential nominee for the Democratic ticket in 1936, with the aim of holding on to the western progressive vote. La Follette responded to these rumors with the comment that he preferred to remain in the Senate. At this time, a journalist wrote about the relationship of Senator La Follette and the President: "Today La Follette has the ear of the President. Not that he is a New Dealer, for there has been much under the Roosevelt administration which he could not approve, but that with the spirit of the man in the White House and with his general purpose the Senator finds himself in sympathy. Furthermore, some of the most important New Deal legislation closely resembles proposals which La Follette was making in the days of Herbert Hoover." The senator, who had been one of the leading progressives to prod Roosevelt toward the necessity of a Second New Deal, was extremely pleased by the results of the 1935 session of Congress. Further evidence of the president's high regard for La

Follette was Felix Frankfurter's comment to the senator in the spring of 1936: "I verily believe there are not half a dozen men who leave the same impact on him that you do, and fundamentally because he knows that your downrightness and simple honesty are used for wholly disinterested ends." The La Follette brothers were ready by the beginning of 1936 to promote the president's reelection, and they would play a significant role in the gathering of progressive support via the formation of the Progressive National Committee.[50]

George Norris continued as a confirmed supporter of Roosevelt during 1935 and 1936. He told an interviewer in July 1935 that he had no regrets over having supported the Democratic candidate in 1932. More social legislation for the benefit of the common man had been passed in the previous two and a half years than in any previous period since he came to Washington in 1903. The president had met the problem of the depression, Norris said, with determination, courage, and a willingness to employ new methods. "In my judgment, he is absolutely sincere. He means to do the right and to help the underdog. His sympathies are with the common man. That's what I like about him. With all his mistakes, I believe that he has made life a little easier, a little more comfortable, for the common man." Norris was especially pleased with the labor, social security, banking, and public power legislation of the New Deal. His main criticism continued to be the power that James Farley held over patronage as postmaster general and Democratic national chairman.[51]

In October 1935, Norris formally announced he would support the president for reelection. Certain that Senator Borah would not be the Republican nominee, he indicated that he would be unable to endorse any other Republican for the presidency. The next month, Norris shocked many political figures with his decision to retire at the end of his Senate term in 1936. President Roosevelt immediately urged Norris to change his mind. At a press conference, he asserted: "If I were a citizen of the State of Nebraska, regardless of what party I belonged to, I would not allow George Norris to retire from the United States Senate, whether he wanted to or not, for the very good reason that I feel he is necessary not only to Nebraska but to the United States as long as he lives." The president also wrote Norris, imploring him to change his plans;

> You do not have to be as physically active as in bygone days, nor do you have to engage in nearly as much detail work or connect your activities with every legislative subject which comes up. The point is just one thing—your own broad, basic principles and point of view. The country needs your principles to be set before the nation from time to time—an occasional statement or speech to clarify our thoughts, to keep our perspective, and to encourage us. The fact that so many young men in public life rely on your leadership and help is the final argument from which you cannot escape!

Norris reiterated his intention to retire in a public statement in December, however.[52]

Norris presented various suggestions for inclusion in the Democratic party platform in a letter to Sen. Robert Wagner in June 1936. He thought emphasis should be placed on the Tennessee Valley Authority (TVA), Rural Electrification Administration (REA), and the merit system in all branches of government. He had been primarily responsible for the first two developments and had long promoted the third. The fact that a non-Democrat was giving advice on what should be emphasized by Roosevelt in the party platform demonstrated the great respect and prestige that Norris enjoyed under this Democratic administration. After Landon's nomination that same month, the Nebraska senator criticized the Republican nominee as an unknown quantity who was controlled by the special interests.[53]

During the following month, Norris reached the age of seventy-five. A drive was now begun by Nebraska volunteers to draft him for the Senate race by the circulation of petitions. In late August, Norris finally consented to the entrance of his name as an independent candidate for reelection. Forty thousand citizens of his home state had signed the petitions urging his candidacy. It seemed like a tough reelection battle, with Norris facing competition from Democrat Terry Carpenter and Republican Robert Simmons. Henry Wallace campaigned for Norris in early October and was followed by President Roosevelt himself, who deserted the Democratic candidate as he had done in the cases of Hiram Johnson and Robert La Follette, Jr., in their reelection campaigns in 1934. In Omaha, he called the Nebraska senator a major American prophet whose candidacy transcended party lines. In November, Norris was reelected to his fifth term in the Senate as its only Independent member.[54]

Senators Norris and La Follette decided that a progressive league similar to the one organized in 1932 was an appropriate means to draw the support of independents to Roosevelt in 1936. The president recalled the effectiveness of the National Progressive League, and in January 1936, his leading progressive spokesman, Harold Ickes, publicly urged progressive Republicans to support Roosevelt's campaign for a second term in the White House. Donald Richberg, one of the leaders of the 1932 organization, contacted Norris about reviving the idea for the upcoming campaign. During May, a group of progressive senators of both parties, including Norris, La Follette, and Shipstead, had a three-hour conference at the White House, the president obviously attempting to solidify his standing among this group. That same month, Roosevelt arranged for Farley to speak to Frank P. Walsh, another organizer of the 1932 league, about convincing La Follette and Norris to lead a new league. Walsh found both men willing to do their part in supporting Roosevelt, as long as it was on an independent basis, rather than through the Democratic party organization. Walsh then met with David K. Niles, who had been the director of the earlier league, to make further plans. La Follette, meanwhile, spent much of the summer contacting progressives in all areas of public life who might be willing to work with an independent committee for Roosevelt's reelection. He spoke with Roosevelt about plans for a general conference during September, and Richberg sent La Follette the draft of a proposed progressive statement to be issued at the meeting.[55]

LaFollette and Norris were to be the national chairman and honorary chairman of the group, which would be called the Progressive National Committee. Norris was unable to attend the national conference that set up the organization on September 11 in Chicago, but he sent a message stating he would do everything possible, considering his advanced age and own reelection contest in Nebraska, to promote the reelection of the president. It would be a "national calamity" were the Republicans to win control of the national government, said Norris, and therefore independents must unite behind the president's candidacy for another term.[56]

The "nonpartisan conference of progressive minded citizens to consider joint action in this vitally important national campaign" attracted more than one hundred progressive figures, including Mayor LaGuardia of New York City; Sens. Lewis Schwellenbach and Homer Bone of Washington, and Hugo Black of Alabama; Governor La Follette of Wisconsin; many of the Wisconsin progressives in the House of Representatives; Congressman Maury Maverick of Texas; and labor leaders John L. Lewis and Sidney Hillman. However, no other members of the progressive Republican Senate bloc joined La Follette at the meeting. The conferees issued a ringing endorsement of the president, discussed the possibility of an eventual political realignment along liberal and conservative lines, and concluded by sending a telegram to the White House, informing the president of their support and intention to campaign for him among independent voters. La Follette, Bone, LaGuardia, and Lewis then broadcast short radio speeches explaining the purposes of the organization to the American people.[57]

Norris and La Follette took an active role in the campaign under the auspices of the Progressive National Committee. The former, involved in his own reelection race, delivered a few major speeches, but La Follette carried the bulk of the effort to gain independent support for Roosevelt. He arranged a series of daily addresses by progressive leaders over the radio, so as to attract maximum exposure to the message of the Progressive National Committee: that Roosevelt had saved the country from the depths of the depression, that he had a genuine interest in the common man, and that the Republican opposition represented the forces of reaction.[58]

Norris and La Follette continued their speechmaking right up to Election Eve. La Follette made a final appeal for support on November 2, at the same time accusing Roosevelt's enemies of distorting the issues and concentrating on personalities: "Never in my experiences has there been such wanton distortion of truth, such reckless attempts to light the fires of blind prejudice and such vile attacks upon the character of a man who has spent a lifetime in public service." He urged support for Roosevelt "because I believe that if reelected he will carry on for four years using his great abilities and the power of the high office of the Presidency to the end that the people may share more equitably from year to year in the national income which they produce." The senator and his brother sent a telegram to the president that evening which read: "Every progressive in America is proud of you and will be at the polls tomorrow with his coat off to give the reactionaries the licking they so richly deserve for their rotten campaign."[59]

The election results seemed to ensure four more years of New Deal reform, if only Roosevelt knew how to manage his mandate. The landslide victory certainly gave the president the belief that bold action could be taken. Whether the progressive Republicans were prepared to support the new initiatives was another question that was yet to be answered.

Sen. William Borah, Idaho

Served 1907 to 1940. Former chairman of the Senate Foreign Relations Committee. Acknowledged orator and leading "lone wolf" of the Senate. Courtesy of the Library of Congress.

Sen. George Norris, Nebraska

Served 1913 to 1943. Regarded as the dean of Senate progressives. Foremost independent member of Congress, and sponsor of many major reforms. Courtesy of the Library of Congress.

Sen. Hiram Johnson, California

Served 1917 to 1945. Former reform governor of his state. A leading maverick who played a key role in many significant Senate debates. Major spokesman for isolationist foreign policy. Courtesy of the Bancroft Library, University of California, Berkeley.

Sen. Charles McNary, Oregon

Served 1917 to 1944. Republican minority leader in the Senate during the New Deal. Vice-presidential nominee in 1940 election. Courtesy of the Library of Congress.

Sen. Arthur Capper, Kansas

Served 1919 to 1949. Former governor and major spokesman for the Senate farm bloc. Leading farm journalist and promoter of isolationism. Courtesy of the Kansas State Historical Society.

Sen. Peter Norbeck, South Dakota

Served 1921 to 1936. Former governor and major farm spokesman who was proud to call himself a Theodore Roosevelt Republican. Courtesy of the South Dakota State Historical Society.

Sen. James Couzens, Michigan

Served 1922 to 1936. Former partner in the Ford Motor Company and mayor of Detroit. An absolute independent in the Senate. Courtesy of the Library of Congress.

Sen. Lynn Frazier, North Dakota

Served 1923 to 1941. Former governor and Non-Partisan League leader. Spokesman for farmers and isolationist foreign policy. Courtesy of the Library of Congress.

Sen. Henrik Shipstead, Minnesota

Served 1923 to 1947. Leading figure in his state's Farmer-Labor party. Supreme independent and die-hard isolationist who became a Republican in 1938. Courtesy of the Minnesota Historical Society.

Sen. Robert La Follette, Jr., Wisconsin

Served 1925 to 1947. Son of famous "Fighting Bob" and founder, with his brother, of the Progressive party in Wisconsin. Leader of Senate progressives and major isolationist spokesman. Courtesy of the Library of Congress.

Sen. Gerald Nye, North Dakota

Served 1925 to 1945. Head of munitions committee that recommended neutrality legislation in the 1930s. A leader of the America First Committee and probably the Senate's most controversial and outspoken advocate of isolationism. Courtesy of the Herbert Hoover Presidential Library.

Sen. Bronson Cutting, New Mexico

Served 1927 to 1935. Considered a progressive with a bright future at the time of his tragic death in a plane crash. Courtesy of the Library of Congress.

[7]

The Progressives' Revolt:
The Supreme Court Controversy of 1937

Franklin D. Roosevelt began his second term as president in 1937 with the bloc of progressive Republicans in the Senate diminished from twelve to nine by the death of Bronson Cutting in 1935 and of James Couzens and Peter Norbeck in 1936. Of the nine remaining, the three who had supported Roosevelt's cause in 1936 were not regarded as loyalist Republicans, as they called themselves Progressive (La Follette), Independent (Norris), and Farmer-Laborite (Shipstead). However, they did ally themselves with the Republican minority for the purposes of Senate organization. Still, the reality was that the Republican party had only twenty-one members in the Senate, including the nine progressives. With an all-time record majority of seventy-five members, the Democratic party was dominant in the upper house, and it was equally so in the House of Representatives. Obviously, if the president handled his mandate properly, he did not need any minority party support to push his programs through Congress. He no longer needed to consult with progressive Republicans so long as he controlled his own party.

Roosevelt had become cocky by this time of his ability to achieve whatever he set as his goals for the nation. He would discover during the course of the next two years that he had ruined his mandate, lost control of his own party majority, and provoked a progressive Republican revolt against the extension of the New Deal. The issue that would bring about these trends in American politics was Roosevelt's decision to propose a reorganization of the Supreme Court, which would be called by his opponents "the court packing plan."

The Supreme Court in 1937 had three distinct blocs: four rock-ribbed conservatives (James McReynolds, George Sutherland, Willis Van Devanter, and Pierce Butler) who saw the New Deal as a challenge to the virtues of nineteenth-century, laissez-faire capitalism; three advanced liberals (Louis Brandeis, Benjamin Cardozo, and Harlan Fiske Stone) who endorsed much of the New Deal legislation as a desirable intervention into the operations of the American economy and society; and two moderates (Chief Justice Charles Evans Hughes and Owen Roberts) who cast the swing votes and were therefore least predictable as to their stand on New Deal legislation.

During the second half of Roosevelt's first term, the "Four Horsemen" (as the conservatives were known) often gained the support of the moderates in voiding New Deal laws as an unconstitutional extension of federal power. The best-known and most significant cases were those that struck down the NRA (*Schechter* v. *United States*) in 1935 and the AAA (*Butler* v. *United States*) in 1936. Decisions outlawing such state legislation as the New York minimum wage laws (*Morehead* v. *New York*) in 1936 gave indications that the Supreme Court would eventually get around to a declaration that the Wagner Labor Relations Act and the Social Security Act were unconstitutional, and that the federal government could not regulate the wages and hours of workers.

Roosevelt had pondered the problem of the Supreme Court's hostility to the New Deal ever since the first hints of difficulties arose in 1935. A constitutional amendment did not appeal to him because of the complexities of ratification and his feeling of the need for an immediate, rather than long-range, solution of the issue. Rumors that the president was thinking of enlarging the membership of the Supreme Court were repudiated by Roosevelt at a press conference. Other than denunciation of the Court for its backward views on the question of the government's role in the economy, no action was promoted by the administration until the president won a landslide reelection victory in 1936. In his second inaugural address on January 20, 1937, Roosevelt spoke of a third of the people as "ill-housed, ill-clad, ill-nourished." He hinted that he was planning a radical move to improve the economic and social conditions of the nation. Two weeks later, on February 5, he shocked the Congress and the country with his proposal to reorganize the Supreme Court.[1]

The progressive Republicans had often been critical of the Supreme Court's role in American government. George Norris, William Borah, Hiram Johnson, and Robert La Follette, Sr., had led the progressive attack on the judicial branch as an undemocratic means of thwarting the will of the people. Many suggestions had been made to alter the nature of the nation's highest court. It had been difficult, however, to gain the cooperation of the progressives behind any one program, and of course it had been impossible to attract support from conservatives who saw the Court as the bulwark of the Constitution.

The Supreme Court's NRA decision in May 1935, led to division in progressive Republican ranks, with Borah and Norris heading the two factions. Roosevelt's statement at a press conference that the Court was relegating the nation "to the horse-and-buggy definition of interstate commerce" increased the controversy over the judiciary. Borah applauded the decision and indicated the Congress could remedy any problems that the invalidation of the NRA created in government's relationship with industry. Declaring that criticism of the NRA decision was unjustified, he praised the judicial branch for "jealously guarding" the Constitution and the rights of the states from encroachment by the executive or legislative branches of government. Voicing his opposition to a constitutional amendment that would give the federal government increased control over interstate and intrastate commerce, Borah said that emergency conditions did not justify hasty change of the underlying principles of the Constitution, which were indispensable to the republican form of government.[2]

Norris was critical of the Court's decision. The American government, he said, had become a government based upon injunctions, as the federal courts had blocked the execution of laws passed by Congress to benefit the mass of Americans. He called for an amendment to the Constitution that would take away from the courts all power to hold any federal law unconstitutional. Other suggested amendments by Norris would require a four-fifths majority of the Court to declare a law unconstitutional, and would speed decisions by giving the Supreme Court greater original jurisdiction over federal legislation, abolishing its passage for review through lower courts. In June 1935, he offered a further modified amendment, which would require a two-thirds vote of the Supreme Court to declare an act of Congress unconstitutional, with action against the legislation being initiated within six months after the law had taken effect. The Court would also have exclusive jurisdiction in cases involving constitutional questions.[3]

Other progressives expressed their views of the NRA decision, seeming to side with either Borah or Norris but avoiding definite stands on the Court— with the exception of La Follette, who positively agreed with Norris. Hiram Johnson said the decision against the NRA was a "body blow," but he felt that it would do no permanent damage to the New Deal program. Charles McNary asserted that Congress could easily pass legislation that would bring the NRA within the limits of the Constitution, so long as the antitrust laws were restored. An amendment might be acceptable in the long run, he added, but action should be taken without delay to reestablish the NRA through voluntary agreements by business. Arthur Capper expressed little fear that the NRA decision was a sign that the AAA might also be declared unconstitutional. The NRA had attempted to cover too much ground, he said, and had ignored the needs of small businessmen, farmers, workers, and the small cities and towns. That was why the Court had turned against it. Legislation to meet Supreme Court standards was preferable, Capper believed, over a constitutional amendment, which would take years to ratify. Gerald Nye doubted that an amendment calling for centralized power over interstate and intrastate commerce could be ratified. Robert La Follette, Jr., condemned the NRA decision in an editorial in *The Progressive*, declaring that the "nine old men" were acting as the nation's rulers, and that the Supreme Court was "one of the most formidable barriers to progress along social, economic, and political lines."[4]

Controversy over the Court increased in 1936 when the AAA was declared unconstitutional because of its processing tax on middlemen. The AAA had not had the unqualified endorsement of the progressives, but certainly it had improved the economic conditions of the American farmer, although favoring the large ones over tenant farmers and sharecroppers. While all the progressives were disappointed at the decision, a number of them were more angry than the rest. Peter Norbeck, for example, introduced a bill providing that no act of Congress could be held unconstitutional unless seven or more of the Supreme Court justices agreed. (The Butler decision on the AAA had been based on the concurrence of only six of the nine justices.) Lynn Frazier said he would support any bill that curbed the power of the Court, which he felt had never had the right to declare laws unconstitutional, if one carefully examined the words of the Constitution. Hiram Johnson saw the decision as one based on politics rather than the Constitution:

> To a body whose members are responsive to no one, who . . . are subject only to their own self-restraint, comes that which the other two branches of government have decided must be done, perhaps for the preservation of the Republic, and one man, if the decision be five to four, may exercise a super-veto power. . . . it is the system that ought, in some fashion, to be altered.

La Follette assailed the Court decision as "a serious blow to agricultural recovery" and demanded that the Constitution be interpreted in light of modern conditions, so that the economic and social conditions of the depression era could be dealt with. If the Supreme Court resisted change, then constitutional changes would be necessary. An editorial in *The Progressive* read: "It is evident that eventually the American people will demand a showdown on the usurpation of legislative authority by the courts."[5]

Capper and McNary were less upset by the Court decision. Capper said that the AAA need not be put out of business entirely, that state organizations could be set up to continue the program, and that Agriculture Secretary Wallace might be able to develop a new program that would be acceptable to the Supreme Court. He did not believe that a constitutional amendment was necessary. McNary concentrated on the need for a new farm program, rather than denouncing the Court for the Butler decision.[6]

Shortly before the Butler case was decided, Borah wrote an article on the judiciary for *Redbook* magazine, in which he again criticized demands for restrictions on the power of the Supreme Court. Any amendment that further increased federal power to control national economic conditions was undesirable in his view, as he wished to preserve the rights and powers of the states, rather than further restrict them. Borah wrote: "The Supreme Court is not a divine institution, and its members are not always wholly exempt from influence of politics. But, in my opinion, it is the most nearly perfect human institution yet devised by the wit of man for dispensation of justice, and for preservation of liberty as defined by the people themselves in the charter under which they have declared their desire to live." He saw the Court as an anti-Fascist bulwark that prevented the possibility of dictatorial leadership by the executive branch of government, as in Italy and Germany. Borah admitted, after the AAA decision had been released, that narrow decisions of 5 to 4 and 6 to 3 were great evils needing correction, but he could not think of a solution. He rejected the kinds of proposals introduced by fellow progressives Norris and Norbeck. Ironically, the *New York Times* now recalled, Borah had proposed back in 1923 that a minimum of 7 to 2 decisions be required before a law could be declared unconstitutional. Borah had lost a great deal of his anti-Court feeling in the ensuing thirteen years.[7]

Norris continued his attack on the Supreme Court. He warned that the Butler decision gave indications that most New Deal laws would be declared unconstitutional. He was especially concerned about the Tennessee Valley Authority, the Social Security Act, and the Wagner Labor Relations Act. The Court could not be allowed to make decisions based on an inflexible view of what the Founding Fathers of one hundred forty years earlier would have thought. The Constitution had to be adapted to modern conditions. The Court, he alleged, was acting as a legislature superior to Congress. Norris now advocated that a unanimous vote be required to declare a law of Congress unconstitutional, just as a unanimous vote of a jury was required in a criminal trial. Norris pointed out that Presidents Jefferson, Lincoln, and Theodore Roosevelt had been major critics in the past of the power of the judiciary. He urged that the problem be made a major issue in the presidential campaign and said that work should begin to formulate an amendment that could pass Congress, rather than wasting time on legislation that could only be a temporary solution. He saw the Court as "an impediment, not an aid, to human freedom and liberty, and an instrument of oppression."[8]

Thus, the progressive Republicans were divided over the issue of the Supreme Court's proper role in American government. Some, led by Norris and seconded by La Follette, believed action had to be taken to curb its power. Others, led by Borah, were unwilling to attack the highest judicial body, because of their belief that it was the bulwark of the Constitution and prevented executive dominance of the federal government. As on so many other issues, the progressives were unable to achieve a consensus. The question that would arise in 1937 was how the progressives would react to Roosevelt's "court-packing" proposal.

After Roosevelt's landslide victory, Hiram Johnson expressed fear that the president "will really feel that he has been given a mandate by the people to do as he pleases, and there will be enough people in Congress anxious to truckle to him, that will enable him to do just as he desires." Norris, on the other hand, looked forward to action against the judiciary as a result of the presidential mandate. He was ready to fight for an amendment to the Constitution that would allow federal legislation to deal with industrial and agricultural problems, and he emphasized that there was definite need for a curb over the power of injunction lodged in federal courts, which was hindering the operation of many federal agencies and laws—one example being the TVA. Norris demanded the formation of a special court, in which would be vested sole jurisdiction over suits involving the constitutionality of federal laws. Appeals would be taken from that special court to the Supreme Court, rather than through the maze of federal courts, which slowed up action for months and even years. The time between the granting of an injunction and the disposition of the case would be drastically shortened.[9]

Roosevelt's Second inaugural address gave hints that he planned major changes. Borah sensed the president was planning a bill to curb the court system, and he therefore confronted the issue squarely in a radio address. He demanded that the administration make a direct appeal to the American people for the strong central powers it claimed were necessary to carry out its program, rather than tampering with the courts in an unconstitutional manner. Constitutional amendment, not congressional legislation or executive action, was the only acceptable means of reforming the Supreme Court, in Borah's view. Insisting that the Court had been correct in its interpretation of the Constitution when it voided New Deal laws, he pointed out that the NRA decision, which had been roundly condemned by the president, had been a unanimous verdict. Borah used historical examples to demonstrate his contention that the Court was the bulwark of American democracy. He concluded with a reference to the sad fate of democracy in Europe and Asia, given the growing ascendancy of Germany, Italy, and Japan, and he warned against the establishment of a similar situation in the United States.[10]

Four days after Borah's radio address, the president asked Congress to approve reorganization of the judicial branch of the federal government. He discussed the problem of aging justices on the various federal courts, including the Supreme Court, which had six of its nine members over the age of seventy. He recommended that when a federal judge who had served at least ten years waited more than six months after his seventieth birthday to retire or resign, then the president should be permitted to name another person to that court. This proposal, if approved by Congress, would give Roosevelt the immediate opportunity to select six more justices for membership on the Supreme Court, as well as forty-four judges on the lower federal courts. This would, Roosevelt declared, increase efficiency of the court system. He left unsaid the fact that he would be able to mold the federal courts in his own liberal image by the power to appoint so many judges in such a short period of time. His opponents would see the Roosevelt court plan as an attempted "packing" and a danger to the constitutional separation of powers.[11]

Roosevelt's proposal came as a major surprise and shock to many, including the members of the progressive Republican Senate bloc. The first reaction of those progressives who were questioned by newsmen was to avoid public comment. Borah, McNary, Johnson, Capper, and Nye had nothing substantive to say. Johnson wrote his son, however, that it seemed the president was attempting to make the Supreme Court subservient to the executive branch. He indicated plans to fight Roosevelt all the way on his proposal, vowing: "I will try to prevent the President's sinister grasp of power. . . . I fear that the next few years, . . . we'll be very close to a Dictatorship. The Congress, of course, is worse than subservient, and no one man can prevent what is happening, but at least, an official as old as I am, with little in the future for him, can stand on his feet and make clear the situation." Capper arranged for the reprinting in the *Congressional Record* of a critical editorial by William Allen White taken from the *Emporia Gazette*.[12]

Only Senator Norris had anything significant to say immediately. Expressing surprise at Roosevelt's action, he indicated that he did not approve of the president's plan. Someday a majority of a larger Supreme Court might also "see through glasses fitted to meet needs of another generation, just as is true today with only nine members." Age was not the key factor, Norris declared, but rather a forward-looking progressive attitude toward the role of government in modern American society. It would have been far simpler, he claimed, to have suggested that action be taken to require at least a two-thirds majority of the Court in cases regarding the constitutionality of federal laws. Norris's expressed reservations about Roosevelt's plan were a warning sign of trouble ahead. If such a strong Roosevelt loyalist as Norris was unhappy, it meant that strong opposition was in the making, not only from progressives in the Republican party but also from conservatives in both major parties.[13]

Shortly after the president's Court message, McNary, Borah, and Arthur Vandenberg of Michigan met informally and agreed that the Republicans would avoid a heavy attack on the proposal for the time being, instead allowing Democratic opposition to have a chance to develop. This would prevent the issue from becoming partisan in nature. As adverse reaction rolled in from Democrats, it became obvious that the progressive Republicans' attitudes toward the president's plan might play a crucial role in its fortune in the Senate, despite their small number. Democratic congressional leaders failed to share Roosevelt's assumption that he could count on the progressives for support. When bloc members failed to comment immediately on the virtues of the proposal, some political observers began to recall the many examples of rebellion by the bloc in previous administrations. The president had made a major error in his decision to avoid consultation with the progressives in advance.[14]

Three days after the president dropped his bombshell, Hiram Johnson publicly announced his opposition and hinted that Roosevelt could not expect support from most of the progressives. The issue, he said, was whether or not the Congress was going to permit the Supreme Court to become subservient to the wishes of the president. He considered such a development ominous for the future of American democracy. Johnson consulted with Borah before he issued his statement, reviving memories of the many times that the two old warhorses had joined together against various causes over the years. A number of unnamed progressives were reported to be against the increase in presidential authority that Roosevelt's plan would bring about, preferring a constitutional amendment which curbed the Court and increased the power of Congress rather than that of the chief executive. The reported dissatisfaction of many progressives with the president's proposal indicated that Roosevelt had provoked the most memorable political controversy since the Versailles Treaty debate of 1919-1920.[15]

The next day, McNary indicated he was opposed to the Court plan, when asked for his views by the *New York Times*. At the same time, Capper asserted that an increase in the number of justices on the Supreme Court would not resolve the problem of interpreting the Constitution according to modern needs over the long term. Although personally disappointed by some of the Court's recent decisions, he contended that the answer was not to give the president the power to coerce the judiciary, but to submit a constitutional amendment to the people. Indicating that he had already received many letters and telegrams from farmers, businessmen, and ordinary citizens protesting the Court proposal, the next day he began a campaign in his farm publications, including *Capper's Weekly* and *Capper's Farmer*, urging that the public express its views on this crucial question.[16]

Meanwhile, Norris proposed another constitutional amendment, this one calling for limiting the terms of all federal judges to nine years, so that a constant turnover would be possible. On February 11, he met with the president to discuss the Court plan, and the White House inner circle was reportedly disturbed by Norris's misgivings. After the conference, the senator reaffirmed his opposition to the Roosevelt program because it did not go to the heart of the issue and was only a temporary solution. He suggested instead three additional constitutional amendments. One would allow a Court judgment to be overturned by a two-thirds decision of both houses of Congress. A second would require a 7 to 2 vote to void a congressional law. The third would provide for general election of justices, rather than their appointment. These amendments, along with the earlier suggestion of a nine-year term, would bring about a taming of the Supreme Court's tendencies toward aggrandizement of power. Norris refused to clarify whether or not he would support the Roosevelt plan if it reached the floor of the Senate. It certainly was constitutional in his opinion, but he pointed out: "Another Congress might come along and increase the court again, until it's as big as the House of Representatives. Then, we'd have to build another marble palace."[17]

On February 12, Lynn Frazier added his voice to the progressive opposition to the Court bill. "Packing" the Court might solve the immediate problem, he acknowledged, but a long-term solution that limited and defined the power of the judiciary had yet to be suggested by the administration. With the leading progressive Democrat, Burton K. Wheeler of Montana, also announcing his bitter opposition to the Roosevelt plan by this time, Charles McNary predicted that the proposal would never be reported for a vote by the Senate Judiciary Committee. Wheeler, a close associate of many of the progressive Republicans and a leading supporter of the president before the election of 1932 and during his first term, indicated his intention to lead the legislative struggle against Roosevelt. If Wheeler could gather the backing of most progressive Republicans and add a large number of conservative votes on the issue of too great a concentration of presidential power, then the proposal would certainly be defeated.[18]

Robert La Follette, Jr., became the first and only progressive Republican to back the Roosevelt plan. He did so with a whole-hearted commitment. In a radio address on February 13, he insisted that this was "a government of law, not of men" and that Congress must not permit "forces of reaction" to prevent progress toward victory over the depression. Accusing the Supreme Court of "judicial usurpation," he challenged those Republican senators opposed to the plan to lead the fight against it, rather than remaining on the sidelines and allowing the Democrats to divide over it. La Follette contended that the president's proposal was "nothing more or less than a call to Congress to exercise its power under the Constitution to prevent a majority of the Court from thwarting the popular will." The issue was not whether the Court was to be "packed," he declared, as the economic royalists and the Liberty Leaguers had had a Supreme Court "packed" in their interests for many years. Reaction and laissez-faire beliefs had been repudiated in the 1936 election, and it was now time, vowed La Follette, for the Court to be responsive to the needs of the American people. The amendment procedure was not the answer to the problem for the short term, as one-fourth of the states with a small percentage of the total population could successfully block any reform that pased through Congress. He concluded with an appeal to liberals and progressives to unite behind Roosevelt:

Liberals—be realists—don't let a lot of professional legalists—paid to do the job—blind you to the woods while they are showing you the trees. Progressives who hesitate or divide upon this issue must assume full responsibility if the mandate registered by the overwhelming majority of the voters at the last election is thwarted.

This statement was a reaction to the defection of most of the progressives from the Roosevelt camp during the previous week. It would not sway any attitudes or votes, to La Follette's chagrin.[19]

On February 15, the *New York Times* published a poll of senators' views of Roosevelt's Court bill. Borah, Capper, Frazier, Johnson, and McNary were listed as definitely in opposition, while La Follette and Norris were put in the president's column, although it was quite obvious that Norris was unenthusiastic about the White House program and would only support it reluctantly if no better action were taken by Congress. Only Gerald Nye and Henrik Shipstead remained to be heard from.[20]

In an attempt to recruit support behind his plan, Roosevelt held a conference with a group of senators on February 20, including progressive Republicans La Follette, Frazier, and Nye. Afterwards, Frazier declared that his inclination to vote against the proposal had not been changed by the meeting. Nye gave the president a respectful hearing but went ahead with plans to deliver a radio address attacking the Court proposal on the night of February 21. Many years later, Nye indicated that Roosevelt had expressed the view that a speech on the Court issue might create political problems for the North Dakotan. He urged Nye to "sprain his ankle," to plead inability to give his speech, and to enter the United States Naval Hospital for the weekend! Nye brushed off the president's suggestion. The next morning, Bill Thatcher, a leader of the Farmers' Union, visited Nye at his home. He told the North Dakota senator that he was not qualified to speak out on questions of law, as he had no legal training. The president had obviously sent Thatcher in a last attempt to prevent Nye from speaking out against the Court bill.[21]

In his nationwide radio speech, Nye asserted that the president had not been given a mandate to transform the basic nature of the court system. Roosevelt had avoided suggesting such a radical proposal during his 1936 reelection campaign, and he had given no hint of such plans in his meetings with congressional leaders. Nye did not regard the Court as sacred or beyond criticism, but he strongly believed that only via the amending process should the judiciary be reformed. He did not approve of lengthy court delays, such as the use of injunctions, which prevented operation of federal laws and agencies, but the Supreme Court remained as the only redress for the American people against the excesses of the legislative or executive branches. Packing the Court in a liberal direction now meant that the precedent would be set for a future conservative president to turn the judiciary in the opposite direction. An ambitious, power-hungry chief executive would have the means to sacrifice the constitutional rights of American citizens. Nye spoke of the administration's pressure on legislators to support the president's proposal, and said the plan would not change the powers of the Supreme Court, only its personnel. Instead, Nye supported the efforts of Democratic senators

Wheeler and Homer Bone for a constitutional amendment, which would permit Congress to override a Supreme Court veto by a two-thirds vote of both
houses.[22]

Shipstead was unaccounted for on Roosevelt's Court bill before early
May, as he was ill at home in Minnesota until then. Arriving in Washington,
he announced that he was joining the opposition to the proposal, because
the powers of the judiciary should be the question at issue, not the specific
membership of the Supreme Court. Shipstead warned: "What you can do today for a good purpose, some one else can do for a bad purpose tomorrow."
A few days later, he wrote to Norris saying he was disturbed that the controversy over the president's proposal was obscuring the urgent need for
fundamental reform of the judicial system. Judges had too often been appointed on the basis of political influence and economic interests, and the
federal courts had introduced great confusion by their contradictory decisions over a period of years as to the powers of the federal government. "I
shall be very much disappointed," Shipstead declared, "if this opportunity
to rejuvenate and clean up the judiciary from top to bottom shall be permitted to be defeated over a bitter personal and political controversy over
the appointment of six new judges." He urged Norris to attempt to bring
together the opposing sides on the Court issue on the need to reform the
method of judicial selection.[23]

With seven of the progressive Republicans having come out against the
president, one extremely unhappy with the nature of the administration
bill but considering support if no better alternative were formulated, and
only La Follette enthusiastically backing it, it was obvious that Roosevelt
had made a major tactical error in springing the Court bill on the country
without prior consultation with those whom he regarded as his natural
allies. He had taken the support of the progressive Republicans for granted.
This controversy was, in retrospect, the crucial turning point in the relationship between the progressive Republicans and the New Deal. Although
limited by their own meager numbers and the overwhelming Democratic
party majority in the Senate from taking an active role in the Court fight,
at least in its early stages, the progressive Republican opponents of Roosevelt's plan did not remain silent. Evidence of their thoughts on the controversy is available in their private letters and in occasional public statements
and actions.

Nine days after Roosevelt announced his proposal to a startled nation,
Hiram Johnson wrote his son that he feared the establishment of a dictatorship if Roosevelt won his cause. He expressed doubt that the opposition
would win the struggle. Arthur Capper wrote Amos Pinchot in mid-February,
informing him that the Court proposal "has stirred up more opposition in

Washington than I have ever seen at any time during the Roosevelt administration." Borah, a member of the Senate Judiciary Committee, announced
at this time his opposition to the Sumners-McCarran bill being considered by
a subcommittee. This proposal called for encouraging the voluntary retirement of justices at seventy years of age on full pay. Borah, himself over
seventy, maintained that the retirement age should be seventy-five, and that
a retired justice should not be permitted to try cases in lower courts. He indicated that when the bill covering the Roosevelt program came before the
Judiciary Committee, he would vote to split it into two sections, one dealing
with proposals to change court procedures, which he favored, and the other
dealing with the increase in Supreme Court justices, which he hoped to defeat
in committee. A few days later, Borah endorsed a proposal made by Sen.
Edward Burke of Nebraska that Congress specify that any constitutional
amendment dealing with the Court issue be ratified by state conventions
instead of state legislatures. This method had been used to ratify the Twenty-
First Amendment repealing prohibition and had taken only eighteen months.
The administration's argument that an amendment was only a long-range
solution to the judicial problem would thus be overcome.[24]

Borah was convinced that Republicans must remain out of the public
spotlight as long as possible, so that Roosevelt could not make the Court
issue a partisan question. He wrote a friend: "The *NOW* business must be
modified to some extent by reason of the situation here. If you were on
the ground and wanting to secure votes for the proposition, I think you
would do what I am doing. As you must fully realize, the party situation can
not be ignored. If this is beaten, it must be beaten by Democratic votes."
Borah telephoned former President Hoover three times to implore him to
avoid a partisan attack on the Court bill. The Idaho senator, meanwhile,
was planning much of the antiadministration strategy in the offices of Democratic opponents, in order to avoid press speculation and publicity as to his
role in the struggle. Borah made plans to filibuster the Court bill to death
if enough Democrats did not defect from Roosevelt. He would talk about
constitutional law and history for a month if necessary. One of his associates
declared many years later that Borah had planned to fight the Court bill
with his voice until he fainted from exhaustion! Borah pictured the death
of liberty and the establishment of dictatorship in America if Roosevelt had
his way.[25]

Norris wrote a constituent in mid-February that he forecast an extended
debate on the president's Court proposal. Personally confident of the chief
executive's sincerity, the senator admitted that many people who were
criticizing Roosevelt for only offering temporary relief for the problem were
correct. "If the power for which he has asked," Norris asserted, "were to be
placed in the hands of one whom I did not absolutely trust, I would not
consider it for a moment. The great danger, it seems to me, comes from the

precedent it establishes." In late February, Capper issued the first of a series of editorials in *Capper's Weekly* that were highly critical of Roosevelt's plan. He also delivered a radio address in which he spoke in favor of an amendment to resolve the problems created by recent Court decisions and urged that the crisis be settled rapidly. The American people did not like the idea of 5 to 4 decisions upsetting legislation that may have had great support in Congress, claimed Capper, but they also did not want one man in the White House to gain the power to dictate the decisions of the nation's courts.[26]

On February 22, the Senate Judiciary Committee approved the Sumners-McCarran bill for voluntary retirement of justices by a 9 to 5 vote, with Borah in the minority and Norris, the only other progressive Republican on the committee, joining the majority. The Senate proceeded to pass the bill by a 76 to 4 vote, with Johnson the only progressive Republican in opposition. It is not clear why neither Borah nor any other progressive joined Johnson. The California senator declared that the bill was "bait" held out to the present Court justices so that they would retire. He would retain no respect for any of them who left the bench because of the financial attractions. The legislation was designed, Johnson told his son, "in the hope it would save timid, shrinking souls, from having to take a stand, . . ." While inclined to back some of the constitutional amendments that Norris, Wheeler, and others had proposed, he still believed Roosevelt would succeed in his demand for six new justices, a "shot-gun" means of solving the Court problem.[27]

Fresh from his unsuccessful actions to block the Sumners-McCarran bill, Borah proposed another constitutional amendment, this one to redefine the due-process clause of the Fourteenth Amendment so that the states would have undisputed power to act upon economic and social problems, rather than permitting the further centralization of power in Washington. Such an amendment would prevent federal courts from declaring null and void such state legislation as the New York minimum wage law. The procedure by which such legislation was enacted in the states would be subject to court review, but not the substance of the laws themselves. Although this proposal attracted some supporters, it did not seem a likely solution to the crisis in the minds of many political observers.[28]

During the last week of February, journalist William Allen White urged the progressives "to offer an alternative solution rather than to be put in a position of mere opposition. Our group has not been opposers ever. We have been constructive and we should be constructive now." White was incorrect in his sentiments. The progressives had always been better known for their opposition than for constructive achievements, with the exception of senators like La Follette and Norris. They were always better able to unite against a program than to agree on an alternative. White made the suggestion that an amendment with a clear definition of interstate commerce be formulated by the progressive bloc, with the intention of giving the national government the power to pass legislation for the social and economic welfare of the people without the danger of rejection by the Supreme Court.[29]

Ironically, White's proposal was precisely opposite the Borah suggestion, demonstrating once again how progressives could not agree amongst themselves as to the extent of federal intervention that should be allowed in social and economic affairs. Such an amendment could only gain the support of a few of the progressives like La Follette and Norris. It could not unite the progressives as an alternative to the Roosevelt plan. In defense of his proposal, which he hoped would be voted on directly by the people in the 1938 congressional elections, White contended that packing the Court would be unnecessary with the enactment of a liberal definition of interstate commerce. He commented: "I would like to see Roosevelt try to get around the wisdom, justice and essential democracy of a popular referendum on a constitutional amendment."[30]

Norris, one of the recipients of the White suggestion, spoke with the president about it but was noncommittal about his reaction. Although he personally expressed approval of the idea, Norris told White: "The remedy is not so easy to attain as your letter might indicate. Your suggestion is rather a simple one, and yet I doubt very much whether it could ever be put into law in the form of an amendment, and I have no doubt but that it would take quite a number of years, at best, to bring it about." Arthur Capper informed White that he had spoken with other progressives who were opposed to the president's proposal, but they had expressed an unwillingness to formulate a specific progressive strategy on the matter.[31]

Roosevelt received endorsement of his Court proposal from a progressive outside the Senate ranks on February 27. In a nationwide radio address, Gov. Philip La Follette of Wisconsin agreed with his brother that immediate action was necessary against the Supreme Court, which was amending the Constitution by judicial decree. Scoffing at the charges that the Roosevelt plan would give the executive branch dictatorial authority, he predicted that Congress would pass the measure, and he challenged Senator Borah and other critics of the measure to offer a constructive, plausible alternative.[32]

The fierce opposition of most of the progressive Republicans to Roosevelt's Court bill was of great concern to administration supporters as the issue began to divide the country. Sen. William Gibbs McAdoo found it difficult to understand Hiram Johnson's opposition, "in view of what I have always understood to have been his views about the courts of the country. I vaguely recall his campaigns in California and his statements about the judiciary." Harold Ickes was equally mystified at the senator's harsh attack on the president and his proposal. Ickes believed that Johnson was becoming more conservative as he aged, and that perhaps he saw an opportunity to finish his long career in a "blaze of glory." The interior secretary wrote William Allen White in late February of his concern that Johnson and other progressive Republicans were doing considerable damage to the president's cause: ". . . the sickening thing is that the so-called liberals are doing worse damage to the President's cause than even the reactionaries." Josephus Daniels, a leading member of the cabinet under Woodrow Wilson, wrote President Roosevelt of his distress at the opposition of men like Borah and Johnson, who had attacked the Supreme Court's power many times in the past. *The New Republic* warned the progressive opponents of Roosevelt's Court bill that they should separate their views from those of reactionary elements. The progressives had the responsibility to unite behind an alternative program or else support the president, rather than allow the reactionaries to block essential reform of the Court and the Constitution.[33]

On March 4, Borah began his thirty-first year in the Senate with an allegation that President Roosevelt was attempting to destroy the Constitution. He quoted James Madison on the Supreme Court as "an impenetrable bulwark against every assumption of power." Newsmen found the Idaho senator working at a desk stacked with books on law and history, from which he was gathering notes for possible future use in a filibuster, if that was necessary to stop passage of the Court bill. Also at this time, Capper called upon Roosevelt to give up his attempt to force through his undesirable Court bill which, he said, had caused such widespread opposition among the American people.[34]

But the president was not about to give up. In a speech at a dinner celebrating his reelection landslide, he gave a powerful address, which La Follette called "An inspiring, fighting speech!" Norris said it was the best speech the president had ever delivered, and McNary said it was obvious that there would be no compromise move to appease the critics, and "Therefore, the issue is drawn and his plan must be resisted with the same earnestness" that was evident in his address. Nye claimed that Roosevelt's words had not changed any votes, and Johnson concluded that the president was "drunk with power, I am sorry to say." Roosevelt was likely to triumph, but "it will be a Pyrrhic victory."[35]

In an address before a conference of Labor's Non-Partisan League on March 8, La Follette termed the forthcoming legislative struggle as one in which "the strength of popular democratic government in America will once more be pitted against the organized forces of reaction." The Supreme Court's outmoded philosophy threatened the security and well-being of all Americans. The Constitution was meant to be a flexible document, adaptable to the conditions of the twentieth century. The issue, La Follette declared, was "simply whether a handful of judges ought to be allowed to exceed their lawful authority by paying more attention to their own personal economic and social beliefs than to the Constitution." Regarding his fellow progressives who were opposing the administration proposal, he said they were "sincere but misguided liberals whose intentions are worthy." A few days later, La Follette took part in a meeting of administration supporters who agreed to reject any suggestion of compromise and to continue the struggle for the president's bill. Ironically, he was the only non-Democrat who attended the informal caucus. Continuing his campaign for the Roosevelt Court plan, he spoke in late March in New York at a rally of the American Labor Party. Discussing the sit-down strikes then taking place in American factories, he said this was the response of the working people of America to the "sit-down strike" of a majority of the Supreme Court against the New Deal's social and economic reforms.[36]

The president's determination to carry on the fight for his proposal despite widespread opposition did not change the attitudes of the rest of the progressive Republican Senate bloc. Norris, for instance, still regarded the administration bill as undesirable and continued during March to offer alternative legislative and constitutional remedies. He suggested that inferior courts should be denied the power to declare legislation unconstitutional, thus taking away the appellate jurisdiction of the Supreme Court. Again, he promoted his other ideas for constitutional amendments, which he had spoken about in February. Johnson, meanwhile, grew more bitter toward the president. He wrote Raymond Moley, the former New Deal adviser: "With my anger at the shuffling and the pretense is a very great sorrow that the President has proposed this. It has forced me into a position of opposition to him, which will widen as the days pass." Because of his fragile health, he turned down an opportunity to deliver a radio address on the subject of the Supreme Court. Leadership of the opposition would have to be in other hands. Johnson believed that the president's ability to use patronage would bring about an administration victory eventually, and he still held the belief that dictatorship was likely within a year after the adoption of the Court bill.[37]

Johnson proved wrong in his view that Roosevelt had the support needed for his Court proposal. Popular support ebbed away during March and April while the Senate Judiciary Committee conducted hearings on the controversial legislation. At one committee session, Senator Wheeler produced a letter from Chief Justice Hughes which declared that the Supreme Court was able to manage its workload without any major hardship and that, therefore, a larger Court was unnecessary and would only lower efficiency. This repudiation of the president's arguments was a tremendous psychological boost for the bill's opponents.[38] A second blow to the administration was the sign of a switch in the swing votes on the Court toward affirmation of the New Deal. Between the end of March and mid-April, the Court, with Justices Roberts and Hughes joining the three liberals, upheld a Washington minimum wage law (similar to the New York law that had been declared unconstitutional) and the Wagner Labor Relations Act. This could be regarded as the crucial turning point in the Supreme Court struggle. Roosevelt was now forced to the defensive by his congressional opponents.

McNary called upon the president to withdraw the Court bill, but Borah said he doubted that Roosevelt would abandon his cause. The Idaho senator served warning that he would oppose any compromise calling for a smaller number of justices to be added to the Court, instead of the six that Roosevelt had requested. The La Follette brothers were pleased by the decisions of the Court on the Washington minimum wage law and the Wagner Act, but they felt that the future of American democracy could not be left to chance, to be based on the whims of Justice Roberts or anyone else. Johnson told his son that he had little respect for Hughes and Roberts, because they had allowed themselves, in his view, to be pressured into supporting the Wagner Act's constitutionality. The members of the Court were not worth fighting for, but the principle of an independent judiciary and the need for a restrained presidency was essential. Roosevelt already had control of Congress, "and he whips it about as a schoolmaster would whip a recalcitrant boy. Give him now the judicial branch and all the power of government would be his. This way dictatorship."[39]

Johnson was critical of La Follette because he supported the president no matter what the issue. Johnson also thought that "a man could not die in any better cause" if he participated in a nationwide campaign against Roosevelt's Court bill, as he had personally done in the struggle against Woodrow Wilson's Versailles Treaty in 1919 and 1920. He told his son that he had received seventy-five thousand signatures on petitions opposing the president's scheme. Johnson's absolute refusal to accept any compromise was evident when he wrote: "The President is using all the reprisals that he can, but if he shall use them until Hell rolls over on me of course I would not change my views." Capper was pleased by the switch of the Court to the liberal side, but still believed in mid-April that Roosevelt's program would pass by at least a six-vote majority. But on May 1, reflecting the rapidly changing situation, he wrote Alf Landon that the president was losing ground. By mid-May, even Norris admitted that he did not know what the ultimate outcome of the Court fight would be.[40]

On May 18, Justice Van Devanter announced his retirement, giving Roosevelt the opportunity to make his first appointment to the Court. Borah and Wheeler had convinced Van Devanter that retirement at this time would be advantageous to the cause of the president's opponents. With the Court upholding the Social Security Act on May 24, there seemed to be no need to pack the Court. Upon Van Devanter's retirement, McNary again called upon Roosevelt to withdraw his proposal. Johnson, however, criticized this suggestion, vowing that the issue should be fought out on the floor of the Senate. Norris moved for a favorable report within the Judiciary Committee, but his motion was defeated by a vote of 10 to 8, with Borah in the majority. The committee issued a forty-six page adverse report and rejected Norris's proposal that an amendment requiring the concurrence of more than two-thirds of the Supreme Court to invalidate an act of Congress be considered by the entire Senate. Johnson remained concerned that a compromise plan to add the two new justices might succeed. He issued a statement criticizing this strategy, calling upon the opponents of Roosevelt's Court bill to remember the principles for which they were fighting. The president's plan to nominate Senate Majority Leader Joseph Robinson of Arkansas to the Court vacancy angered the California senator, as Robinson was already sixty-five years old, which certainly seemed to weaken Roosevelt's argument that younger men were needed on the bench.[41]

In early June, La Follette and Borah indicated their unwillingness to settle for a compromise of two additional justices, but they did so from different sides of the issue. Meanwhile, the White House's hopes of changing the minds of Senators Nye, Frazier, and Shipstead, all of whom had remained silent after their original statements against the president's plan, had dissolved after unsuccessful efforts by adviser Thomas Corcoran. The president was hoping to avert a total defeat; as Hiram Johnson put it: "He is engaged in saving his face now." Johnson, Capper, and Borah declared they would filibuster the bill to death if necessary. The Senate struggle over the Court bill came to a head in early July, when Wheeler and Borah formed a steering committee to plan the filibuster. On July 15, Shipstead broke the silence since his original statement to announce his opposition to the substitute bill calling for only two additional justices. Shortly before the Senate vote on the bill, Capper told the readers of *Capper's Weekly* that the Senate struggle was a "war to save the constitutional form of government for this United States." Borah wrote a constituent that the Court struggle was "a fight we can not afford to lose."[42]

The death knell of the Court plan came on July 14 with the sudden passing of Senator Robinson. The Arkansas legislator had worked very hard to gather support for the president, but with his death, which many claimed was caused by the extra pressures brought on by the Court fight, a number of senators began to abandon the administration. On July 22, the Senate voted 70 to 20 to recommit the Court proposal to the Judiciary Committee, which effectively shelved the bill. La Follette was the only progressive Republican to support the president. Norris was absent due to illness, and he did not leave word as to how he would have voted had he been present. During the final debate before the vote, the seven progressive Republicans opposed to the bill remained silent, a course they had successfully pursued in the Senate chamber since the beginning of the controversy. When the vote had been cast and announced, however, Johnson rose to his feet and exclaimed: "Glory be to God!" As he dropped into his seat, the people in the galleries burst into applause. Later, weeks after the end of the controversy, McNary paid tribute to those Democratic senators who had abandoned the White House on the issue, acknowledging that the Republicans, whether conservative or progressive, could not alone have prevented passage of the proposal.[43]

William Allen White wrote to Felix Frankfurter three months after the Court fight ended, expressing the disappointment and disillusionment with Roosevelt that many progressive Republicans, including Senator Norris, had volunteered to him during the months of the controversy. Regarding the president, White wrote: "To break their heart and drive them away from his leadership was a tragedy. They will come back, perhaps I should say, we will come back, but not with the same full faith in his judgment that we had before." Whether the progressive Republicans would indeed regain their confidence in Franklin Roosevelt's leadership or instead become part of the great conservative coalition that was forming in Congress against the New Deal remained to be seen. It would soon become obvious that the latter path would be the one for the progressive Republican Senate bloc, except for Norris and La Follette.[44]

[8]

The Progressives' Abandonment of the New Deal, 1937–1938

The controversy over the Supreme Court weakened the mandate Roosevelt had won in 1936 for increased social legislation and a more responsive government. Proposals to enact laws giving the federal government extended powers over labor and agriculture, as well as plans for executive control over reorganization of the federal government, were first stalled by the Court dispute and then bitterly attacked by opponents of the president, both old and new, as part of his plan for complete control over the federal government. Stunned by the opposition, Roosevelt would respond with a sudden retreat in the controversial area of government spending in mid-1937, provoking a new recession that would wipe out much of the economic gains since 1935 and lead to a revolt against his leadership by his most avid Court reform supporters in the progressive Republican camp, Robert and Philip La Follette. By the end of 1938, Roosevelt had lost the support of all members of the progressive Senate bloc except George Norris. The formerly close and cooperative relations between the members of the progressive Republican Senate bloc and the Roosevelt administration had been destroyed, and the field of foreign policy would only accentuate the conflict in goals and ideals that had developed between the progressives and the New Deal.

The field of labor relations, which had received a major boost from the federal government with the passage of the Wagner Act in 1935, had become a subject of great controversy by the fall of 1937. The campaign by the newly organized Congress of Industrial Organizations (CIO) and its president, John L. Lewis, to recruit members from the vast industrial working class in auto and steel factories provoked resistance from the major corporations and resulted in sit-down strikes that aroused great animosity in the nation against organized labor. One of the leading congressional critics of Lewis's sit-down tactics was the increasingly conservative Hiram Johnson. He saw the strikes as evidence that law and order was breaking down and was critical of President

Roosevelt for avoiding involvement in the crisis, ostensibly because of the generous financial support that Lewis and the CIO had given the Democrats during the 1936 campaign.[1]

Fellow progressive William Borah disagreed with his colleague about where the blame for the sit-down strikes lay, asserting that big business must share the responsibility. Although not considering the strikes to be legally justified, he said the nation could not expect labor to obey the law if monopolies were permitted to ignore it. But Johnson did not end his denunciation of labor. On the floor of the Senate, he declared: "I am opposed to the idea that any body of men can come into my house or to yours, can shut the door and lock it, and say that they will keep possession of our homes during the time while we are determining whether we will yield to some demands of theirs." The president had the authority to send militia to end the illegal strike, Johnson asserted, if only he wished to do so. Borah denied that Roosevelt had such power, indicating his belief that only state authorities could deal with the situation. Human rights were just as important, he said, as property rights. Senator Norris entered the debate at this point, admitting his bias toward labor in this struggle to improve its conditions against the organized antilabor campaign of the large corporations. La Follette commented that the sit-down action was the reply of labor to the reactionary Supreme Court.[2]

Sen. James F. Byrnes of South Carolina proposed an amendment to an impending bill that called for denunciation by the Senate of the sit-down strikes. On April 5, the Senate voted the Byrnes Amendment down by a vote of 48 to 36, with only McNary joining Johnson in support of the proposal, while four progressives (Borah, Frazier, Norris, Nye) voted against and the three other progressives (Capper, La Follette, Shipstead) were absent for the vote. Johnson was angry at the action of the Senate, calling his colleagues a group of "cowards." He told his son that he believed John L. Lewis was desirous of becoming the nation's dictator, and that Roosevelt seemed to be willing to go along with whatever the CIO wanted. The California senator, already distrustful of Roosevelt's motives because of the Court controversy, had obviously moved further to the right on the question of labor relations, contrasting sharply with his wholehearted support of the Wagner Act in 1935.[3]

While the sit-down strikes encountered the opposition of only Johnson and McNary, the Roosevelt administration's promotion of a minimum wage and maximum hours law encountered strong attacks from six of the nine progressive Republicans, all but Shipstead, La Follette, and Norris. Johnson saw no need for further labor legislation. He said the Fair Labor Standards bill was "attacking a subject . . . that is an extremely difficult one, and because of the difference in localities in this country and their varying interests, it is almost impossible to accomplish. It ought to require a year's study of perfectly disinterested economists, not a couple of weeks investigation by a blatherskite committee." Borah said he was for a fixed minimum wage, rather than for allowing a Fair Labor Standards Board to decide wages for different regions of the nation. He expressed reluctance to grant authority to any board or commission selected by the president and said he was opposed to arbitrary government control of the economic life of the American people.[4]

Two votes were taken on the bill on July 31, indicating that most progressive Republicans had become indistinguishable from conservatives in Congress. Six progressive Republicans supported a motion to recommit the legislation to the Education and Labor Committee, a move that would have temporarily shelved and possibly killed the bill permanently. Only La Follette and Shipstead voted against recommittal, which was defeated 48 to 36. Norris was not present for the vote but indicated he would have joined with his two colleagues in voting against recommittal. The Senate proceeded to approve the legislation 56 to 28, with the same 6 to 3 progressive split. Strong opposition in the House prevented passage of the Fair Labor Standards Act until 1938.[5]

The extent of progressive Republican alienation from the New Deal was now clear-cut. No longer could Roosevelt count on the bloc's support for liberal legislation. Arthur Capper indicated that he could not support hastily drawn and carelessly written legislation that gave discretionary power over industry to a government board. Fear of continued government centralization of power over the economy was also evident in Hiram Johnson's comment to his son: "I would be very glad to make a minimum wage, and prescribe hours, but to leave it to a board in Washington would be one more way of turning over the economic life of the country to the President for him to exercise at his own sweet will. I decline to do this." Gerald Nye also voiced his general disapproval of a new labor board. He felt that the National Labor Relations Board had already shown its bias on the side of labor regarding the question of the CIO sit-down strikes, and he issued a strong attack on that board during debate on the Fair Labor Standards bill. *The Progressive* criticized Nye for this denunciation and questioned whether he was still a progressive in his thoughts and actions. This was a question that could well have been asked of many progressive Republicans by the end of 1937.[6]

The administration's dissatisfaction with the congressional reception of its labor, farm, and government reorganization proposals convinced Roosevelt to call a special session in November and December 1937. The proposal for new farm legislation was a major subject of controversy during the session. The farm legislation of 1936 had not worked out as well as hoped for by its sponsors. Senator Borah remained critical of the tendency of the administration farm program to encourage reduction of crops. Capper said most of the farmers of his section were opposed to compulsory crop control and federal regimentation and would prefer a program that would be administered locally. He also believed that at least two-thirds of the farmers should be required to approve any measure before it was set up as a control over all farmers.[7]

The new farm bill was subjected to attacks by Borah, Shipstead, Johnson, Nye, and Frazier on various grounds. First, it placed the American farmer under the control of Washington bureaucrats. Secondly, it failed to accomplish the goal of raising the income of farmers to the level of the rest of the population. Thirdly, it contributed to scarcity of farm goods. Finally, there were doubts that the new bill would give any further benefits to the farmer beyond the existing legislation. When the final vote came, however, three progressive critics of the New Deal farm program—Capper, Nye, and Frazier—joined with La Follette and Norris in support of the legislation, while Borah, McNary, Johnson, and Shipstead joined the opposition. The Senate approved the measure on December 17, 1937 by a 59 to 29 vote.[8]

The House did not approve the farm bill until February 1938. In the Senate debate on the conference report, Norris defended the legislation. Some compulsion was necessary if the program was to succeed, he contended, and he firmly believed that the farmers would benefit from the law. Shipstead attacked the conference report, asserting that agriculture should not be regulated unless industrial production and prices were also controlled. McNary denounced the bill because it gave too much power to Secretary of Agriculture Wallace over farm prices and production levels. The American farmer, the Oregon senator asserted, was losing his freedom, individuality, and independence under the terms of the bill. The only part of the legislation that he could approve was the section on soil conservation. He would not support the legislation, however, so long as Henry Wallace was permitted to be "the autocrat of the breakfast table." Hiram Johnson said the farm bill would harm American democracy and transform the nation's economy in an undesirable way. He had supported every farm bill in the past, but he valued his independence too much to vote for this dangerous bill.[9]

The restriction on production contained in the final version of the bill apparently displeased two supporters of the Senate version, La Follette and Nye. They joined the original four progressive critics of the legislation in opposition to the conference report, leaving only Norris, Capper, and Frazier in support of the administration's program. The Senate accepted the conference report by a vote of 56 to 31. Again, two-thirds of the progressive Republican Senate bloc had deserted the administration on a significant piece of legislation. The trend was unmistakable.[10]

The controversy over the administration's government reorganization proposal came to be connected with the Court bill in the minds of Roosevelt's opponents. Both seemed to be examples of the president's thirst for power, of his attempt to destroy democratic institutions in America. Roosevelt called for expansion of the White House staff; the strengthening of management agencies, including the substitution of a personnel director for the Civil

Service Commission; the extension of the merit system; and the establishment of new cabinet departments, with independent agencies placed under various departments. Congress would be allowed to reject presidential reorganization proposals, but only if a two-thirds vote of both houses was achieved.

The president's proposal did not receive much attention in the Senate until early 1938, when it came up for discussion and debate. Capper indicated his opposition to presidential appointment of a personnel director to replace the Civil Service Commission. He also was critical of the idea of putting the comptroller general, the individual responsible for handling government funds, under executive control. And he wanted independent bodies like the Interstate Commerce Commission and the Federal Trade Commission, to retain their status, rather than come under the control of the executive branch of government. Capper wanted to ensure that Congress would not give up its power to control any plan of government reorganization.[11]

As controversy began to rage around the reorganization proposal, La Follette and Norris came to the defense of the president. Reorganization of government was "too unwieldy" a job for Congress to be able to handle, La Follette asserted, and it was preposterous to claim that Roosevelt would become a dictator if the bill passed. Hiram Johnson, however, considered the bill an "iniquitous measure" and a "companion bill to the Court Bill." It was further proof, he wrote, of the president's desire for dictatorial powers and his attempts to diminish the powers and prerogatives of Congress. McNary was concerned that Congress would lose any power temporarily conferred to the president, as had been happening since 1933. Congress must retain the final right to veto the president's plans, he concluded. Borah also warned of the danger of Congress voting away its powers to the executive branch. He believed the Congress was just as capable of making judgments on government reorganization as the president. Lynn Frazier agreed with his fellow progressives that any plan should require congressional assent. No chief executive, the North Dakotan declared, should have such control over government reorganization as Roosevelt was requesting.[12]

During March 1938, Borah joined with Burton K. Wheeler as the leader of the opposition to the bill. Both men alleged that the administration was applying pressure to win votes for the legislation. A Wheeler amendment, proposing that Congress must approve all presidential orders on reorganizing the government, was defeated in the Senate by a vote of 43 to 39 on March 18. All of the progressive Republicans, except for Norris and La Follette, supported the defeated amendment. Hiram Johnson wrote his son after the defeat of the proposal: "Undoubtedly, we would have won, if the vote could have been taken forty-eight hours earlier, but the pulling and hauling, the downright bribery by the Administration in arranging for projects, gifts, et cetera, to different States, did the job. We've by no means surrendered, but will continue fighting, but I have little hope."[13]

Capper continued to denounce the administration bill as unsound and re-pugnant to representative government. Borah wrote a constituent: "It seems almost impossible to stay the march of centralization and of arbitrary power. Unless the people are thoroughly aroused upon this matter, there is little hope of preserving the fundamental principles of our government." Johnson had the feeling that the reorganization bill was "the small crack in the dike that will let through the torrent." Although the bill had been amended, it still had the potential, he concluded, of making the executive a dictator. He thought the proposal would pass because those Democrats who had abandon-ed Roosevelt on the Court bill were now "trying to crawl back into good favor with the President on this Bill."[14]

When the bill came up for a final vote at the end of March, Shipstead spoke of the need for congressional approval of any executive reorganization pro-posals, and Johnson, Capper, and Borah added last-minute warnings about the dangers of such a proposal becoming law. La Follette responded to these progressive critics by saying that the bill under consideration was the most ef-ficient and satisfactory method available to reorganize government agencies. He remained satisfied that adequate safeguards existed to prevent the establish-ment of a totalitarian form of government in the United States.[15]

All the progressive Republicans except La Follette and Norris supported a motion to recommit the reorganization bill, but it failed by a vote of 48 to 43. The Senate proceeded to pass the bill by 49 to 42, with the progressives again dividing 7 to 2 against it. Johnson, bitter over the support given the administration by La Follette and Norris, wrote blistering attacks on them to his son. He alleged that La Follette was always willing to advance his family's fortunes at the expense of principle. He called Norris "a sad figure these days because of his insanity over the TVA." Norris had always been a senator "who wanted to go to the stake, and who took a real pleasure in being burned alive, but now in his old age, while senile, because of Roosevelt's gift to him of the TVA, . . . anything that Roosevelt does, or anything that he says, Norris will defend, although at variance with all his former life. He is truly a pathetic figure now."[16]

With the reorganization proposal facing stiff opposition in the House of Representatives, Roosevelt went on the defensive. He negotiated some con-cessions, including one that called for a majority vote, rather than two-thirds, as enough to defeat any presidential reorganization plans. He also issued a public statement denying that he wished to become a dictator, crit-icizing his opponents in both houses who had conjured up such "silly night-mares." Johnson denounced the president for his temperamental statement, and the senator wrote his son that he doubted the president's powerful ego could be controlled any longer: "He has reached the place where he thinks he is so damn smart that he can do anything and pass it off as cleverness, but I do not think that he could accomplish many more so-called cunning things without an explosion on behalf of our people."[17]

On April 8, the House returned the reorganization bill to committee by a vote of 204 to 196, effectively killing the bill for that session of Congress. Borah now urged that a new bill giving Congress a proper role in the reorganization of government be formulated as soon as possible. Johnson, joyous over the unexpected defeat of the legislation in the lower house, termed the result the prevention of one-man government. Norris, disappointed by the bill's defeat, blamed it on a large-scale propaganda campaign and its claim that the president would assume dictatorial powers once the bill had passed. This fear of increased executive power had indeed alienated all of the progressive Republicans in the Senate, save La Follette and Norris, by the beginning of 1938. Increased executive power, which many of them had wholeheartedly endorsed as necessary for the survival of the nation in the early days of the Great Depression, had become anathema within a few short years. Their faith in the president's good motives, once so definite, had been permanently lost. Roosevelt's blunders were now a serious threat to the continuation of the reform spirit of the early years of the New Deal.[18]

Another development that estranged relations between the progressive Republican Senate bloc and Roosevelt was the economic recession that hit the nation in August 1937. Although the depression had not ended by 1937, economic statistics showed that by January of that year, the country had reached 1929 levels of economic performance and was continuing to make progress. Mass unemployment still existed, however. The question of what economic policy to follow became one that divided the Congress as well as the country. Concern over the large national debt built up by the government's policy of deficit spending through such organizations as the PWA and WPA led many conservatives, as well as many of the progressive Republicans, to urge an end to this policy. Capper, for instance, told a Kansas radio audience that the federal government must end its policy of "extravagant expenditures in public funds." Johnson wrote his son: "No government can withstand forever paying two dollars out and taking one dollar in. Even the President is beginning to see this and to worry about it."[19]

Roosevelt, himself concerned about the danger of inflation, made a decision in the middle of 1937 to cut government spending by slashing the WPA rolls and turning off the pump-priming of the PWA. This decision, so fervently advanced by many as necessary, resulted in the nation entering a new recession within a few months. By early 1938, all gains made since 1935 in the various economic indicators had been wiped out. A struggle developed within the administration over what to do about the new recession. One group, led by Treasury Secretary Henry Morgenthau, Jr., urged that business leadership be allowed to take the nation out of the recession, while others, led by Interior Secretary Harold Ickes and WPA head Harry Hopkins, wanted to increase government spending again, as well as begin a trust-busting program. As the debate went on, Charles McNary criticized the administration for creating an unfavorable business climate.[20]

In April 1938, Roosevelt finally decided to resume a large lend-spend program, and he requested that Congress pass legislation providing for appropriations of $5 billion for public works and other federal relief projects. Progressive Republicans who had been critical of the large-scale government spending program wondered whether a return to the same policy was justifiable. Nye, Borah, and McNary all said they would support a "reasonable" amount of new public spending but did not see that five years of such programs had done anything to solve the depression. Johnson saw the new spending program as a diversionary tactic to take away attention from the defeat of the president's reorganization bill. Capper said that only private enterprise could take the country out of the economic doldrums. He called for government cooperation with business, the elimination of government competition with private enterprise, a revision of the tax system to encourage business growth, and amendment of the National Labor Relations Act of 1935, which the Kansas senator believed had proved to be heavily in favor of labor unions and detrimental to business interests. The views of these progressive Republicans were indistinguishable from those of conservatives of both parties in Congress. It was obvious that most of the members of the progressive bloc had joined a conservative coalition against the purposes and policies of the New Deal.[21]

When the vote on the spending bill came on June 3, 1938, only Hiram Johnson and Charles McNary voted against it, with Capper, Norris, and La Follette voting with the majority in the 60 to 10 vote. Four other progressive Republicans (Borah, Frazier, Nye, Shipstead) were absent, with the latter three indicating they would have supported passage had they been present. The bill's humanitarian image had made it difficult for many of the progressives to vote against it. But their antagonism to the operation of the federal relief programs had been obvious when all of them had supported an amendment, introduced by Democrat Carl Hatch of New Mexico, which prohibited political activity by persons who worked for the various federal relief agencies. Even La Follette and Norris, who had long been critical of this aspect of the operation of the PWA, WPA, and other agencies engaged in providing work for the unemployed, supported this proposal. The amendment failed to pass the Senate by a 40 to 37 vote, but the unanimity of progressive Republicans behind the Hatch proposal demonstrated their determination to prevent the Democratic administration from gaining political points by dispensing relief funds and public works projects on the eve of the congressional elections of 1938.[22]

During the fall campaign, only Gerald Nye faced reelection, but other progressive Republicans spoke out against the New Deal. Nye ran his campaign with a more conservative orientation, attacking large-scale government spending and increased presidential power. His reelection victory set the stage for his leading role in the struggle against American involvement in World War II. Capper, meanwhile, continued to criticize the centralization of power in

Washington and what he saw as the heavy tax burden being imposed on the American people. He found fault with the economic situation, specifically with the high unemployment rate five and a half years after the New Deal came to Washington, and the administration's policies toward business and agriculture. McNary called upon the voters to elect a Congress that would stand as guardian of the Constitution. He also expressed concern about the threat to civil liberties of a strong central government. Johnson denounced Roosevelt's attempted purge of conservative Democrats during the 1938 congressional primaries, which turned out to be an unmitigated disaster. Johnson wrote Sen. Harry Byrd of Virginia that the president's "ruthless-ness . . . seems to me compelling proof that he has reached such a despotic and unreasonable state of mind that he will tolerate no man who disagrees with him at all." He was determined to help restore the old balance between Congress and the executive branch.[23]

The election results of 1938 showed that a new conservative coalition had formed in Congress. Made up of greatly increased Republican representation and southern Democrats, it would be able to thwart any further major domestic initiatives of the Roosevelt administration. A very disturbing aspect of this new political development was that seven of the nine members of the progressive Republican Senate bloc were regarded as recruits in this new conservative coalition. Their alienation from New Deal liberalism seemed complete and irreversible.

George Norris and Robert La Follette, Jr., were the only progressive Republicans who supported the controversial Supreme Court and government reorganization proposals of the president. Not officially Republicans anymore, they certainly showed they were not in tune with the views of the other members of the progressive Republican Senate bloc during 1937 and 1938.

Norris remained among the most loyal of the president's supporters in Congress. His strong doubts about the Roosevelt approach to Supreme Court reform were tempered by his close association with the chief executive. Because of illness, he had been able to avoid casting his vote on the Court bill, but no one doubted that he would have backed the White House had he been in Washington. While Hiram Johnson, William Borah, and other progressives were denouncing Roosevelt during 1937 and 1938, Norris always rushed to his defense, considering him the savior of liberal thought and action. Norris's loyalty provoked criticism from progressive colleagues, but he clearly saw no viable alternative to Roosevelt's leadership. During 1938, he attacked reactionaries in both major political parties for blocking liberal reforms, and he was obviously disturbed by progressive Republican abandonment of the New Deal. Norris warned that Roosevelt might be compelled to seek a third term as president if the stalemate over liberal reform ideas continued. He believed that no man could compete with Roosevelt for popularity among the

American people, and he continued to defend the president against charges of dictatorship.[24]

When the president cut funds for the WPA and PWA and other relief programs in mid-1937, La Follette began to have doubts about Roosevelt's commitment to economic recovery through government spending for public works and relief. His brother Philip, reelected governor of Wisconsin in 1936 on the Progressive party ticket, had even stronger doubts and great ambitions to run for president in 1940. As the recession of 1937-1938 hit the country, the Wisconsin governor, with the grudging assent of his brother, made preparations for the founding of a new national party, the National Progressives of America, which he hoped would drain away liberal and progressive support from the New Deal and focus it on the La Follette brothers, just as earlier in the century their father had made attempts to unite progressives around his own candidacy for president. It would be a hard, disillusioning struggle that would result in utter failure. But it would signify that another part of the progressive Republican coalition had abandoned the New Deal and Franklin D. Roosevelt.

Speculation about a new national party patterned after the successful Wisconsin progressive organization began immediately after the La Follette brothers won the Senate and governor's races on the third-party ticket in 1934. Both brothers were regarded as prime presidential prospects, although Philip was obviously more ambitious and aggressive. Senator La Follette predicted an eventual realignment of political parties in the near future, and the national press began to devote more attention to the Progressive party phenomenon. Governor La Follette told an interviewer from *The Nation* that his immediate ambition was to make Wisconsin an example of what progressive leadership could do to better economic and social conditions. He did not wish to discuss the future presidential elections, as they were too remote from his present-day challenges. The governor came across as a radical who believed that the government should own the utility companies; that farmers and workers (rather than corporations and banks) should own their own homes, land, and factories; and that the government should control distribution of the national income. He denied, however, that he was a Socialist.[25]

In July 1935, Governor La Follette predicted that a new left-wing party would form in America by 1940. A third national party would take time to form, due to the vast differences in state laws, but he believed that such progressive groups as the Wisconsin Progressives and the Minnesota Farmer-Laborites would achieve the goal of a new party by that date. A modification of the economic system, moving away from the private profit motive, was necessary, he asserted, but must come about through democratic means. Later he indicated that he expected to support Roosevelt for reelection in 1936 unless the Republicans nominated a liberal. But he was critical of restrictions on agricultural production and what he called unproductive spending by the national government.[26]

During 1936, the La Follette brothers endorsed and actively campaigned for Roosevelt. But speculation about a new national party continued, with Governor La Follette's bid for reelection regarded as significant for future third-party politics. To many people, the Wisconsin Progressives seemed to be the leading progressive beacon for the future, with no one in the Democratic party apparently able to fill the president's shoes, with the Republican party apparently remaining in reactionary hands, and with the widespread assumption that Roosevelt would adhere to the two-term tradition of the presidency. After his reelection victory, the Wisconsin governor spoke again of the coming realignment in American politics, and Senator La Follette warned of the danger of a new economic downturn if Roosevelt cut government spending. Sensing such a policy change, the senator delivered a warning to the administration in March 1937. Increased federal taxation and public works were integral parts of any lasting recovery program, he said, and talk about cutting the costs of government were therefore unwise.[27]

On the third anniversary of the founding of the Wisconsin Progressives in May 1937, Governor La Follette declared: "The Progressive party looks forward to a national existence and to a national political realignment." He predicted a national progressive party would sweep to victory over the "reactionary forces of America." In early June, the governor sent a letter to President Roosevelt, asking the federal government to cooperate with state and local governments on an expanded program of public works and relief for the needy and unemployed. When the administration ordered a cutback in government spending the same month, Senator La Follette accused the federal government of backing down on its promise to restore prosperity and employment. Dissatisfied with the administration's request for relief expenditures, he wrote: "Roosevelt is certainly driving the wedge deep into his own party. If he keeps on he may bring about the party realignment so essential if democracy is to work in the future." Governor La Follette, disgusted at not receiving a reply from Roosevelt on his proposal for federal-state cooperation on relief, wrote his brother: "Criticism against him grows—about labor difficulties, WPA retrenchment & lack of program. It looks from here like a retreat on the Court issue. A great mistake." Phil La Follette later wrote in his memoirs that Roosevelt's retrenchment of the WPA was "crass and cruel." His conclusion was that "Roosevelt had no more real interest in the common man than a Wall Street broker. . . . I would never again support him politically; he was just not aiming at the ends that Bob and I had been taught from childhood were the objectives of progressive government."[28]

Governor La Follette now began an active quest for expansion of the Wisconsin Progressives into a national movement. He requested proposals on the mechanics of organizing a national party, as well as planks for a platform, from a close associate. The advice given included the idea of a National Progressive Committee to act as a clearing house for progressive thought and action; the formation of a national party after the election of 1940 and before the congressional campaign of 1942; and a platform based upon the principles of aid to labor and farmers, large-scale public works, higher taxation of the wealthy, antimonopoly legislation, and avoidance of involvement in foreign controversies. La Follette received great encouragement to pursue the goal of forming a third national party and set about during the fall and winter of 1937 to gain supporters for such a venture. He held a series of meetings with progressive leaders and followers in his office in Madison. In addition, farm, labor, small business, and white collar groups met with him. The governor also worked to gain the backing of progressive groups in Iowa and California; however, he never consulted with major national progressive spokesmen, with the single exception of Mayor Fiorello LaGuardia of New York City. The advent of the recession in the fall of 1937 spurred the governor to greater efforts, and he urged his brother to increase his attacks on Roosevelt's economic policies. By early December, the governor had concluded that "FDR is drifting, and confused."[29]

Senator La Follette had prepared, with the assistance of progressive associate David K. Niles, a list of people who might be invited to a conference to discuss the future of the Wisconsin progressive movement. The list included the names of Senators Nye, Frazier, and Shipstead, as well as labor, intellectual, journalistic, and political leaders from around the country. The senator believed that careful planning for such a meeting was necessary if it was to be a success. The proposed conference was never held, however.[30]

As 1937 ended, the La Follette journal, *The Progressive*, issued a warning to President Roosevelt. If he did not change his policies on the economy, he would rapidly lose all the liberal support he had held for five years. The La Follettes hoped and expected that in such an eventuality, the liberals and progressives would come to them and back their movement.[31]

At the beginning of 1938, Senator La Follette gave a radio address in which he outlined the economic problem, which he regarded as the major question facing the nation. He was critical of the Roosevelt administration, accusing it of bringing on the new recession by reacting to opponents of large-scale government spending with attempts to balance the budget through cuts in relief and public works spending. Unemployment was still the major enemy, he asserted, and the only way to find work for the millions who needed it was by higher taxation of the well-to-do and a higher level of government spending than the administration had yet committed itself to follow. In a later radio address, the senator pointed out that the business community and conservatives had demanded a balanced budget and reduced expenditures between 1929 and 1932, which had led to disaster, putting the American economy at its low point as Franklin Roosevelt came into office.

La Follette continued to criticize the government's relief commitment, characterizing it as "an attempt to bail out this ocean with a tin dipper." He urged the establishment of a permanent public employment agency and also suggested a broad program of conservation and construction activities. Housing, education, health, and food distribution were other areas, added La Follette, in which people could be employed by the federal government.[32]

While the senator was speaking out on government spending and the recession, his brother continued to work toward his goal of a new third party. At the end of February, the Wisconsin governor announced in a radio address that a new political movement was under way with the purpose of preserving American democracy from foreign entanglements and assuring its viability at home. Unemployment must be ended, he declared, even if the American economic system had to be modified. He implied that neither major party had the ability to solve the nation's economic problems. The Democrats only thought of the present and not the future, and the Republicans looked only to the past, refusing to deal even with the present. Dictatorship, whether of a Communist or Fascist variety, was only attractive to discontented people. The federal government must avoid increasing the appeal of such movements at all costs, by dealing with the economic problems rather than avoiding them. The governor also held a meeting with the Wisconsin Progressive State Central Committee, requesting its assistance in making a decision on what the future of the state movement should be. But, in reality, he had already decided that he would take immediate action to form a new national party.[33]

The governor asked his brother during March to return to Madison to discussion the situation, but the senator pleaded a busy schedule. Therefore, the organizational work for the new party was done solely by Philip La Follette and his close associates. Apparently Senator La Follette was not keen about his brother's plans. Basically more shy and cautious than Philip, he had been less eager than his brother to organize the Wisconsin Progressives in 1934. While disillusioned with Roosevelt's economic policies, the senator did not believe a new party could succeed under the political circumstances in 1938. When the president announced in early April that he planned to resume large-scale government spending, the senator expressed his pleasure. Meanwhile, Phil La Follette had held more meetings with rank-and-file members of the state progressives, as well as farm and labor groups. He had also prepared rough drafts of four radio speeches, as well as an address announcing the formation of a national party. He passed these on to his brother for comment.[34]

The last ten days of April were hectic ones for the Wisconsin governor. He delivered his radio addresses on consecutive nights and announced that a meeting of progressives would be held in Madison on April 28, marking the inauguration of a new movement. In his radio speeches, he was critical of the Roosevelt administration for its economic policies, claiming the recession could have been avoided had the president prepared a constructive program

to solve the depression, rather than following a policy of "tinker and patch."
He said he and his brother had become alienated from the New Deal when
Roosevelt changed his economic policy in June 1937. Able-bodied men and
women, he asserted, must be put to work at productive enterprises to ensure
the return of prosperity. La Follette also indicated that four thousand people
had been invited to the Madison meeting and that he had consulted with
about 1,200 people in his office over recent months. But it was obvious by
his refusal to give names that no figures of national repute had spoken with
the governor about his plans.[35]

Senator La Follette indicated he stood behind his brother's plans and said
the formation of a new party was "inevitable." Columnist Arthur Krock expressed the view that the La Follette brothers were making a move to split
the Roosevelt coalition and to succeed him as the heads of liberal and radical
groups in America. Senator Norris urged those who sought to form a third
party to wait and see whether Roosevelt would seek a third term before going
ahead with their plans. The president indicated that he had no plans to send
any representatives to the Madison meeting, but it was known that Adolf
Berle, the assistant secretary of state and a close personal friend of the La
Follette brothers, planned to attend as Mayor LaGuardia's representative.
Roosevelt said he had no objection to a new liberal organization's formation, declaring that it was good for America.[36]

Madison's progressive newspaper, the *Capital Times*, edited by *The
Progressive*'s editor, William T. Evjue, was critical of Governor La Follette's
plans, calling them divisive. If the venture required a repudiation of the president, then the paper would not back the governor. His action would only aid
conservatism in the nation. The La Follettes should work with Roosevelt to
improve the New Deal, Evjue indicated, rather than abandon him in a time of
trouble. The strong opposition from *The Progressive*'s own editor certainly
was a sign that Philip La Follette had not done enough planning and consultation before going ahead with his bold venture for a new party. Other unidentified progressive leaders thought a new third party would have the
effect of pushing the president further to the left, therefore regaining for him
the support of many disillusioned progressives.[37]

On the evening of April 28, 1938, before an audience of approximately
7,500 people in Madison, Philip La Follette formally declared the establishment of the National Progressives of America. No nationally known progressive figures were present, however, including Senator La Follette, who remained in Washington to debate the naval appropriations bill submitted by
the Roosevelt administration. The senator sent a telegram that declared:
"Today it is an issue between progressives, who favor the widest possible
enjoyment of our abundant wealth, and reactionaries in both old parties,
who would go back to the discredited system of withholding the very neces-
saries of life by monopolistic control of production and distribution, in order

to maintain unlicensed profits. The outcome of this contest will determine whether the American people are to go forward with an ever higher standard of living and wider opportunity, or remain chained to a system that sacrifices human values to speculative gain."[38]

The governor, in his hour and a half speech, blamed both major parties for the continuing economic depression. Roosevelt had basically good intentions, said La Follette, but he was hamstrung by reactionaries within his own party. A new party was necessary to alter the American economic system. The policies of this new party were contradictory and vague, as the governor attacked socialism, said he was against "coddling" and "spoonfeeding" of farmers and workers, and contended he was against efforts to manage and control business and industry. Wealth must be produced through useful work, not by curbing production on the farm and in the factory, or by public and private borrowing of funds.[39]

Few progressives understood what Philip La Follette was advocating. His most clear-cut statement was the belief in a stronger executive branch. He also spoke of government ownership and control of money and credit and warned against any foreign power trespassing in the Western Hemisphere. He called his party the equivalent of a religious cause. The party emblem—a blue cross on a field of white and surrounded by a circle of red—and the dominant role of the governor in the ceremonies made many observers feel uneasy. Soon La Follette would be accused by critics of having formed a fascist-type party, its main goal being the acquisition of national power, not the promulgation of a legitimate program of ideas.[40]

Reaction to the new party was not long in coming. Charles McNary thought the party was a sign of the "retreat of the liberal forces from the Roosevelt banner." Norris was fearful that the new party would divide liberal and progressive forces and assist in the election of a reactionary president in 1940. He would only endorse the new party if it promised to extend the president's policies and consolidated with Roosevelt liberals. Wisconsin Progressive Congressman Thomas R. Amlie thought the new party would divide the progressive strength in Wisconsin, as the Socialists could not be expected to back a leader who had attacked their philosophy. Socialist party leader Norman Thomas criticized La Follette for his refusal to repudiate capitalism and his willingness to attack socialism. Senator Borah said his main interest still lay in the reorganization of the Republican party, not a new organization. Labor leader John L. Lewis refused to commit labor to support of the National Progressives, and Minnesota Farmer-Labor party leaders doubted a merger of their organization with the new party. Senator Shipstead saw the movement as weakening the liberal cause. Mayor LaGuardia indicated he was not ready to join the new party. The New York mayor still considered President Roosevelt the leader of the progressive forces of the nation, despite his close friendship with the La Follette brothers, which had caused him to send Adolf Berle as his personal representative to the Madison meeting. Senator Wheeler saw no chance of success for the new party unless both major parties nominated reactionaries in 1940. Meanwhile, he was remaining a Democrat. It was quite apparent that there was no rush to the bandwagon of Philip La Follette by liberals and progressives of national stature. In fact, not one major reform spokesman came out in support of the new party.[41]

The nation's leading newspapers and columnists devoted much attention to an analysis of the new party. The governor's statements seemed to have "a strangely conservative ring" to the *New York Times*, and they indicated a final break of the La Follette brothers with the New Deal. The *New York Herald Tribune*, a conservative Republican newspaper, strangely hailed the advent of the new party in an editorial entitled "Fresh Air From Madison." Walter Lippmann saw the new party as one different from traditional progressive thought, irreconcilable with the philosophy and practices of the New Deal, most farm and labor organizations, and liberal periodicals such as *The Nation* and *The New Republic*. He thought La Follette would have a big selling job to gain the support of these groups, but the emphasis on promoting private initiative and the production of wealth were admirable, and Philip La Follette was a man of "truly liberal spirit" who might give American democracy a new hope. Another major *Tribune* columnist, Dorothy Thompson, was not so approving as Lippmann. She criticized the lack of practical proposals and saw much in the governor's appeal that smacked of fascism, including the banners, the religious crusade, the emotional appeal, and the exaggerated nationalism. She warned that freedom came before, and was more important than, prosperity.[42]

The *Washington Post* called the governor's speech one of "glittering generalities," without any indication of the methods he would use to create more jobs, eliminate relief abuses, and give the people economic security. The paper indicated that it expected La Follette to issue a more substantive party platform. The *Washington Star* approved of La Follette's criticism of the New Deal but criticized the proposals for the granting of extra powers to the executive branch and the control of the banking system. *Star* columnist Owen L. Scott warned that the National Progressives could be the beginning of an American brand of fascism. He was concerned at the religious note in the speech and what he called the swastika-like banners on the platform from which La Follette spoke. *New York World Telegram* columnists Raymond Clapper and Heywood Broun were equally critical of the new party. The former thought the governor's appeal was along the same lines as that of Fascist and Communist dictators in speeches to the masses, even though that might not be the intention. The latter called La Follette's speech a "thoroughly reactionary utterance," one that Herbert Hoover could endorse. Distribution of goods was just as important as their production in the modern machine age, Broun asserted, but the Wisconsin governor seemed unaware of this. Columnist Jay Franklin of the *New York Post* was disturbed by La Follette's seeming endorsement of rugged individualism and his antilabor attitudes at a time when nearly three-fourths of the American people were living in an urban, industrial environment. Franklin declared: "Phil La Follette should be told that ours is an age of filling stations, not of covered wagons; of factories, not farms; of pay rolls, not frontiers."[43]

The leading liberal journals were no less critical of the new party. *The New Republic* feared the election of a reactionary in 1940 due to the potential liberal split between Roosevelt and the La Follette brothers. Although the New Deal could be attacked on many grounds, the journal doubted that the new party would offer a better program to the American people, and it was especially critical of the vagueness in the governor's speech. The journal published a column by Heywood Broun highly critical of the new party, and Bruce Bliven, *The New Republic*'s editor, wrote the governor asking for clarification of his attitude towards labor, small farmers, and the problem of relief. Bliven expressed concern over the Fascist orientation of the movement and asked for a more definite program of ideas. No formal reply was ever published in the pages of *The New Republic*.[44]

The Nation thought the new party was poorly timed and called upon progressives to be circumspect, since "The progressive cause and the American future are not to be identified with the political fortunes of any dynasty, whether it be the patrician Roosevelts or the fighting La Follettes. Whoever aspires to lead the progressives must earn that leadership by his concern for the interests of the vast American majority and by proof that he can unite the best resources of that majority." The journal did not like the governor's appeal to nationalism, the symbols and rhetoric of the Madison meeting, the call for a reinvigorated capitalism and a frontier-populist type of individualism, and the fact that conservatives were praising the new party while liberals were keeping their distance. Paul Anderson wrote in *The Nation* that the La Follette progressive party would prove to be a dud and would only contribute to a reactionary triumph in the 1940 presidential election. Anderson declared that the National Progressives were strictly a family enterprise and that Phil La Follette had sounded like a combination of Adolf Hitler, Huey Long, and Billy Sunday in his Madison speech.[45]

The Nation sent Max Lerner to Madison to learn more about the nature of the new party and its founder. Lerner came away convinced that La Follette was "a man of enormous ambition and personal mastery, grooming himself for a great destiny and believing utterly in that destiny." The governor seemed unconcerned that his party had received a bad reception. He was anxious to see the New Deal lose popularity and predicted that eventually his alternative would gain the support of most progressives. A concrete program was unnecessary for the present, he told Lerner, since only intellectuals and opponents of a new party were concerned about specific programs. Third parties had failed in the past, he said, because their programs were too specific. Lerner wrote that the governor's eyes glowed when he spoke of the creation of a mass movement around himself. La Follette defended the new party's symbol and said he was unconcerned that some commentators were labeling him a Fascist. His party, one based upon the middle class, would be the leading organization in the country within a few years, despite the attacks of the commentators. Lerner came away from his interview suspicious of the motives and views of Philip La Follette.[46]

Common Sense, a monthly magazine promoting advanced liberal thought, was equally suspicious of Phil La Follette. The editor, Alfred M. Bingham, was critical of the governor's failure to consult any leading national progressive figures in government or journalism and disliked his platform, manner of announcement, and organization of the new party. He wrote: "The general reminiscence of Fascism has struck all our intellectual friends. The adaptation of the swastika (unconscious no doubt) and the whole dependence on pronouncement by the one leader with no democratic formulation is obvious." In an editorial, Bingham declared that the new party was a trial balloon that would fail because it would alienate many potential supporters who were committed to an expansion of the New Deal.[47]

Faced with large-scale apathy among leading progressives and hostility from the nation's liberal press, the new party also came under a barrage of criticism from William Evjue, the editor of *The Progressive* and the *Madison Capital Times*. As indicated earlier, Evjue's opposition was evident before the April 28 speech. Now Evjue wrote of the "show" held in Madison, which "was suggestive of the thoroughness of the technique of Berlin or Munich." Evjue demanded a specific program from the governor rather than platitudes and asked him to refute the charge that the National Progressives would divide liberal forces in 1940. Evjue wrote: "Old Bob La Follette never asked the people to sign a blank check."[48]

Ignoring the criticism from many corners, Governor La Follette proceeded with plans to organize his personal vehicle for power. Visiting Iowa, delivering a nationwide radio address, and granting interviews to journalists within days of his address at Madison, he emphasized the organizational work needed on the state and local level before his party could be successful. He predicted that his party would run candidates in ten states in the fall elections. The present era could be compared to Revolutionary and Civil War times, when new parties were formed to deal with the prevailing crises. The final split with Roosevelt that had brought about this new movement dated from July 1937, the governor revealed, when President Roosevelt had rejected for the sixth time a plea from the La Follettes to adopt an aggressive program of relief and had asserted that the depression was over. Of course, the recession had hit a few months later.[49]

The governor's activities could not hide the reality that his party was not attracting support. When the official articles of association of the new party were published, the governor was listed as the founder, with no one listed as a co-founder. Still, he continued to believe that the party would succeed, writing his brother in May that much correspondence had been received and that most of the letters and telegrams were favorable. "Everything considered the reception was better than we could have expected. Of course the old guard papers have played it because of their dislike of Roosevelt. But we must not forget that they have been whacking at us for thirty or forty years and a few days news won't counter-act, but can't help improving, their onslaughts of three decades."[50]

The Roosevelt administration's public reaction to the new party was contradictory in nature. The president expressed a lack of concern that the New Deal might be threatened by the new organization. He welcomed any organization of liberals and progressives, and said the beginning of a new party was a healthy development for American politics. Interior Secretary Harold Ickes, on the other hand, asserted that the La Follette brothers were likely to retard or even wreck the cause of liberalism by forming a new party. The hope of the progressive movement lay in Franklin D. Roosevelt, not Philip La Follette, and Ickes hoped that liberals would remain united behind the president "as long as he shows the necessary qualities of leadership." Privately, Ickes considered Phil La Follette a "prima donna" with overpowering ambition and fascist tendencies.[51]

After ten days of exposure, the National Progressives of America seemed to need resuscitation, and Senator La Follette now delivered a nationwide radio address, appealing for support from liberals for his brother's organization. Reports lingered about the senator's lack of enthusiasm for the new venture. He tried to dispel these rumors in his speech, a sharp criticism of New Deal economic programs and the factionalism in the Democratic party that was, he said, preventing advanced liberal reform. The president was "one of the great liberal leaders of modern times," but he had lost his effectiveness due to party division over the Supreme Court and government reorganization proposals. While defending the need for his brother's new party, the Wisconsin senator was trying to avoid a complete break with the New Deal. In a letter to columnist John Chamberlain, he also tried to answer the charge that the National Progressive insignia was similar to a Fascist swastika. Then, in mid-May, he was invited aboard the president's yacht for a weekend cruise. This social occasion demonstrated the respect and admiration that the two men had for each other. The president, on the other hand, was very suspicious of Philip La Follette's motives, privately believing that the National Progressives of America was designed solely as the governor's vehicle for political power, and that Bob La Follette had reluctantly gone along with the move out of family loyalty.[52]

By the end of May, Governor La Follette had opened offices and produced literature for national distribution. He was encouraged by more than 25,000 letters received on the new party. But it continued to be a source of criticism in the nation's press, and a Gallup poll showed that while 60 percent of those questioned had heard of the National Progressives, less than 10 percent would be willing to join the organization. The governor then made a speaking tour of New England in June to recruit supporters, stating that he had found enthusiasm for change but had decided that he must first determine his own future in politics. Should he run for another term as chief executive of Wisconsin, or should he retire to plan his national effort for 1940? After a conference with the Wisconsin Progressive delegation in Congress, including his brother and editor William T. Evjue, he announced that he was seeking reelection.[53]

On Primary Day in September, the Progressive party lost 20,000 votes while the Republican party gained 50,000 votes, a sign that a tough reelection battle was evident and that Phil La Follette might indeed lose his bid for reelection. Evjue wrote in the *Capital Times*: "Bob and Phil must step on the gas between now and November if the Progressives are to emerge victorious at the general election." The Democratic candidate for governor, Robert Henry, withdrew in early October, throwing his support to conservative Republican Julius Heil in a blatant attempt to retire Philip La Follette from politics. Although the state Democrats later substituted another candidate, the alliance of conservative Democrats and Republicans held up until Election Day, and Heil easily defeated La Follette by a margin of about 183,000 votes. Virtually the whole Progressive ticket on the national and state level had gone down to defeat, with La Follette failing to achieve half of the vote of Heil in many formerly strong progressive areas of the state.[54]

After his crushing defeat, the governor said that the election results in Wisconsin and throughout the nation showed that reactionaries were assuming control of both major parties and that there was a need for a party such as his to unite liberals and progressives. But the new party failed to develop after its founder's loss of public office. Evjue published an editorial in the *Capital Times* blaming the governor's defeat on his formation of the National Progressives. Philip La Follette's dreams of the presidency remained just that, and he never held public office again. At the age of forty-one, his political career was over after six years as governor of Wisconsin. Who would have thought that such a bright career would come to an unfortunate early end?[55]

The failure of the National Progressives of America must have been a source of satisfaction to Franklin D. Roosevelt. He remained, as George Norris believed, the best hope of American liberalism. But the other progressive Republicans, with the partial exception of Bob La Follette, had already broken their ties with the New Deal. By the end of 1938, with the election of a majority conservative coalition in Congress, hopes of furthering the New Deal seemed a dream. The specter of fascism also presented new priorities for the United States. Should this country remain neutral while Fascist nations committed aggression in Europe and Asia? Foreign policy indeed proved to be a major battleground between the progressive Republican Senate bloc and Franklin D. Roosevelt as they came to different conclusions about what our aims should be.

[9]

The Neutrality Debate,
1933–1938

By the era of the New Deal, the members of the progressive Republican Senate bloc had acquired a well-deserved reputation as isolationists in foreign affairs. Although the isolationist spirit was widespread, claiming adherents across the political spectrum from left to right, the progressive Republicans were among the most outspoken in their disillusionment with the American experience in the First World War. Their belief that America must never again abandon the neutrality policy set forth by George Washington in his Farewell Address, that it must indeed follow a policy of noninvolvement in European affairs no matter what crisis arose, was an accepted creed which they would fight to maintain as America's foreign policy during the 1930s. A brief review of progressive views on foreign policy would clarify the situation as it stood in 1933.

Only three members of the progressive Republican bloc had had an opportunity to vote on American entrance into the First World War. George Norris was one of only six senators to vote against America's declaration of war, joining Robert La Follette, Jr.'s father in opposition, while William Borah and Hiram Johnson supported war against Germany in 1917. Norris and the elder La Follette were bitterly attacked for their opposition to the war, but in later years they were depicted as courageous figures who had stood against the overwhelming tide of war sentiment. After the elder La Follette's death in 1925, Norris became the sole remaining member of the Senate who had voted against war, and he was the subject of praise in editorials and speeches, becoming a kind of folk hero to isolationists. Norris had feared that America's democratic institutions would be endangered by war. He had been suspicious of the role that economic motives and British propaganda played in moving the United States toward entry into the war. In the early 1930s, the Nebraska senator still stood for a policy of nonintervention, a policy he believed had led to America's great achievements.

In contrast to Norris, Borah and Johnson had justified American entrance into war in 1917 on the rationale that German submarine warfare threatened America's national interest. America was fighting to preserve the national honor and the freedom of the seas, not to aid the British and French, of whose motives both senators were extremely suspicious. They would not have supported American involvement on any grounds other than national interest.

Borah and Johnson joined with Norris and La Follette in opposition to the Versailles Treaty and American entrance into the League of Nations. Along with others that made up a Senate bloc known as the Irreconcilables, they attacked the treaty as a victor's peace that possessed the seeds of war within it and the league as an organization that required the compromising of American sovereignty and independence and American support of Great Britain and France in future power struggles. America had undergone a loss of innocence by entrance into the war and had suffered the loss of many young men without bringing about the possibility of a just peace. Never again, these progressive senators vowed, should America go to war for other countries' national interests.

During the 1920s, the isolationist sentiment grew and spread in progressive Republican ranks. As new members were added to the progressive bloc, they expressed their support for the ideals set forth by the older progressive Senate spokesmen. Robert La Follette, Jr., entered the Senate holding the same views long pronounced by his father. He was determined to preserve democracy at home from international power conflicts and would be in the forefront of the struggle to keep America out of involvement in any future war in Europe. Arthur Capper, a Quaker and a pacifist, also worked for the same end. Opposed to American entry into the League of Nations without major changes in the League Covenant, he proposed a resolution in the late 1920s, calling for a trade embargo on nations that violated the Kellogg-Briand Pact renouncing war. Although he had a favorable attitude toward American involvement in the World Court, otherwise he followed the isolationist line.

Gerald P. Nye, a supporter of American entrance into World War I as a North Dakota journalist in 1917, had been converted to the isolationist cause by the time he entered the Senate in 1925. Nye's great moment as an isolationist spokesman would come during the New Deal, when he would become the most controversial member of the progressive bloc in foreign affairs. Henrik Shipstead was another vehement spokesman for isolationism, a true "irreconcilable" who insisted he was fighting for the maintenance of America's basic principles, as set forth in Washington's Farewell Address and the Monroe Doctrine. Lynn J. Frazier promoted peace resolutions and criticized internationalist sentiment during the late 1920s and early 1930s. Peter Norbeck expressed similar isolationist sentiments on those rare oc-

casions when he addressed the subject of foreign policy. The other progressives—Charles McNary, James Couzens, and Bronson Cutting—rarely dealt
with the subject, and their stand was therefore less certain and predictable.

Five of the progressive Republican senators—Borah, Capper, Johnson,
La Follette, and Shipstead—served as minority members of the Foreign
Relations Committee throughout the 1930s, a position that gave them great
publicity as isolationist spokesmen. After Borah's death in January 1940,
Nye replaced him on the committee. The North Dakota senator's activities
on the Munitions Committee and the Military Affairs Committee had already
given him public renown as a leading isolationist. George Norris never served
on the Foreign Relations Committee during the 1930s, but his status as an
elder statesman and the only surviving progressive who had voted against
entry into World War I gave him a platform for his views on foreign problems.
Although members of the minority party and few in number, the progressive Republican senators were able, because of their tremendous prestige
and reputation, to exert an influence on American foreign policy greater than
their numbers might indicate.

The first sign of future controversy over American foreign policy arose
soon after Roosevelt was inaugurated. In the spring of 1933, the administration considered consulting with major European powers about a collective
security policy, which would be promoted by presidential declaration of an
arms embargo against aggressor nations. Hiram Johnson blocked this idea in
the Foreign Relations Committee, offering an amendment stipulating that
any embargo had to apply impartially to all belligerents, thus changing what
was designed as an internationalist measure into an isolationist attempt to
avoid any entanglement in foreign wars. Key Pittman, Democratic chairman
of the committee, indicated to Roosevelt that the members would not accept
the arms embargo resolution without the Johnson amendment. The president
first approved the amendment, then dropped the whole embargo issue when
Secretary of State Cordell Hull, a confirmed believer in collective security,
attempted to change his mind. Roosevelt was apparently unwilling to go
all the way for the cause of collective security at a time when he was counting
on the support of progressives for his New Deal program. The Johnson
amendment had destroyed the administration's attempt to cooperate with
western European nations against potential aggression from the Fascist
powers.[1]

The first manifesto of progressive isolationist sentiment during the New
Deal years came in an address by Senator Borah, the former chairman of the
Foreign Relations Committee and now its ranking minority member, before
the Council on Foreign Relations in New York City on January 8, 1934. His
address, entitled "American Foreign Policy in a Nationalistic World," was

published in *Foreign Affairs* and also in the *Congressional Record* at the request of Senator Norris. Borah claimed that internationalists had been trying ever since the struggle over the League of Nations to draw the United States into the solution of Europe's problems, even though armaments build-up and the balance of power continued to dominate the continent's affairs as they had in 1914. Based upon the experience of the world war, there was no justification for the United States to engage again in a foreign conflict. Borah added that America must follow a nationalistic policy, concentrating on the solution of urgent domestic problems and pursuing a foreign policy of political isolation. Our foreign relations, he said, should be based on peace, trade, commerce, and friendship with all nations, but no political commitments to any countries. We must not name or chastise aggressor nations or accommodate our foreign policy to other nations' interests. Rather, we must retain our freedom of action and independence of judgment. Borah called for a return to Americanism, the foreign policy concept of George Washington and Thomas Jefferson.[2]

The growing strength of isolationist sentiment and the significant role of the progressive bloc in this crusade was further demonstrated by two developments during 1934. First, Hiram Johnson successfully sponsored the Johnson Act, which prohibited further loans to foreign nations that had defaulted on their debts to the United States. This effectively cut off financial activities with the major European powers, Great Britain and France. At the same time, the peace movement had grown in influence as a result of disillusionment over American involvement in the world war. The spreading revulsion against war as an instrument of national policy led to a call for a congressional investigation of the role of munitions makers and bankers in bringing about conflict between nations. Dorothy Detzer of the Women's International League for Peace and Freedom spoke with Senator Norris, and they settled upon Senator Nye as the man to promote the investigation. On February 8, 1934, the North Dakota senator introduced Resolution 179 to the Foreign Relations Committee.[3]

After Nye's resolution was combined with one proposed by Arthur Vandenberg of Michigan that advocated taking the profits out of war, Senate Resolution 206 was proposed on March 12, calling for a special committee to investigate the munitions industry. Senator Borah addressed the subject of the power of munitions makers before the world war and advocated the elimination of war profits in a speech during final debate over a naval construction bill. Attacking proponents of armaments as international criminals who made profits on people's deaths, he proposed government control of the munitions industry. Nye also opposed the naval bill as wasteful, its primary design being the financial relief of the munitions makers. An increased naval force would only encourage war and could not guarantee peace. Nye requested that the Senate abandon the naval construction program until a thorough investigation of the munitions makers could be undertaken. The Senate ignored his request and passed the bill 65 to 19, with seven progressive Republicans (Borah, Capper, Frazier, La Follette, Norris, Nye, and Shipstead) voting against the legislation.[4]

The Nye-Vandenberg resolution for a special Senate committee was adopted on April 12. Vice-President John Nance Garner was authorized to designate seven senators for the committee. Four Democrats and three Republicans were selected to serve, and Nye was named chairman, despite his minority party status, because he had promoted the original resolution for an investigation. The isolationist cause was thus given increased exposure and Nye now became probably the most controversial member of the Senate, his face and views known throughout the United States and supported by many Americans. Secretary of State Cordell Hull apparently was unhappy over the choice of a Republican isolationist to lead the investigation of the munitions industry but indicated that he would support and cooperate with the committee members.[5]

Nye created headlines with his early demands for confiscatory taxation of the wealthy in time of war, cash-and-carry laws to govern commerce in case of war abroad, the calling of a plebiscite of the American people before Congress could vote a declaration of war, and the creation of a Peace Division and appointment of an assistant secretary for peace in the State Department. The growing support for the Nye Committee investigation led President Roosevelt to praise the venture. In May, he indicated the executive branch would cooperate to the fullest possible extent with the committee.[6]

When the committee hearings began in September, the North Dakota senator gained plenty of publicity as he led harsh questioning of witnesses and delivered numerous public and radio addresses outlining the findings of the investigators and his proposals for removing the abuses practiced by munitions makers. The hearings showed that munitions makers indeed had had a close association with the War and Navy departments between 1914 and 1917. The profits of the industry were publicized for the first time, and it was shown that in times when America was at peace, the munitions makers were dependent upon foreign wars to remain prosperous. The sensational disclosures pushed the country deeper into an isolationist mood, and Nye would play a key role in the promotion of neutrality legislation during the next few years. The cause of collective security was seriously harmed by the Nye Committee hearings.[7]

Isolationists in Congress gained a major victory when, in January 1935, they blocked the Roosevelt administration's proposal for American entrance into the World Court. Created by the League of Nations, the Court was an independent judicial body open to all nations. To confirmed isolationists, it

represented political entanglement in the affairs of other nations and inter-
ference with the sovereignty of the United States. The president apparently
thought he would have no problem with the Democratic-dominated Senate
and was not expecting the isolationist forces to have such strength as they
now displayed. The progressive Republicans in particular played a key role
in the fight against the World Court. Hiram Johnson expressed bitterness over
the president's decision to push the issue, and along with all other progressive
Republicans on the Foreign Relations Committee except Arthur Capper, he
voted against reporting the World Court proposal favorably to the Senate
floor. However, the final vote of the committee was 14 to 7 in favor, and
now Johnson and Borah declared they would lead the isolationist struggle
against approval of American entrance. Charles McNary, who supported the
president's proposal, doubted that the progressives could gain enough supporters to prevent a two-thirds majority. Early indications were that no more
than twelve senators would vote against the administration, most of them
progressives.[8]

   Johnson began the struggle against the World Court by issuing a statement
to the newspapers before the beginning of Senate debate. He denounced
World Court membership as a violation of America's traditional foreign policy
of noninterference in international power politics. If America entered the
World Court, it would soon be in the League of Nations and would be
pledged to use its military force to back up the national interests of other
nations. In Senate debate, he delivered an impassioned speech against the
internationalist spirit that liked to "meddle and muddle" in the affairs of
other nations. At a time when "all Europe sits over a volcano" because of
concern over the intentions of Hitler and Mussolini, the United States, he
asserted, should vow to avoid all involvement in European affairs. The Treaty
of Versailles had caused the present problems that Europe faced, and the
World Court was derived from that ill-fated document. America must now
concentrate on solving its domestic economic problems, not on another
attempt to make the world safe for democracy.[9]

   George Norris submitted a resolution providing that no dispute or question affecting the interests of the United States should be submitted to the
World Court without prior approval by two-thirds of the Senate. However,
President Roosevelt soon declared his opposition to the Norris amendment,
terming it a limitation on the constitutional prerogatives of the executive
branch in foreign affairs. This statement seemed to rally the opposition.
Senators Borah and Shipstead had already issued scathing attacks on the administration proposal. Before crowded Senate galleries, Borah had been his
usually eloquent self. Shipstead called himself "an apostle of peace" who
was alarmed at the major arms build-up going on in the world. He remained
convinced that the League of Nations and the World Court were not instru-
ments of peace, and that the Versailles Treaty would eventually lead to war.

The victors of the world war were desperately attempting to gain American support for another crusade against tyranny, and this must not be allowed to occur.[10]

Before the Senate voted on the Norris reservation to the World Court proposal, Norris declared that he had complete faith in President Roosevelt but believed the Senate must consider the dangers of leaving to future presidents the power to determine which controversies would be submitted to the World Court. Norris feared that America would become entangled in international power politics through Court membership, and that its national interest would be ignored by judges who had lived under societies with different value systems. Despite his plea, the Senate defeated his amendment 47 to 37, with all twelve progressive Republicans in the minority. While this was a victory for the administration, it also signified that the progressives would refuse to support the president in foreign policy even if they often backed him on domestic programs. It still seemed likely that the Senate would ratify American membership in the World Court by a small margin.[11]

Johnson delivered another lengthy speech before the final vote, reciting the views toward internationalism of presidents from George Washington to Theodore Roosevelt. Then the Senate proceeded to reject a number of amendments designed to restrict the American connection with the Court, all of which received the unanimous support of the progressive Republican bloc. Norris announced that he was forced to vote against the administration because of the lack of restrictive amendments to the proposal. The final vote was a surprise 52 to 36, seven short of a two-thirds majority. Senate leaders declared that intense propaganda efforts by Father Charles Coughlin and the Hearst newspapers were responsible for defeat of the proposal. But probably just as significant was the opposition of eight progressive Republicans (Borah, Frazier, Johnson, La Follette, Norbeck, Norris, Nye, and Shipstead).[12]

Borah hailed the World Court vote as the most promising development in American foreign policy since the world war, a guarantee that the United States would never again enter into entangling alliances with European nations, while Johnson wrote his son: "I think, my lad, I won the toughest and the biggest and most far-reaching contest legislatively in which ever I have been engaged." The president had "used all his power, and I confess I did not like it." Norris again stated his regret over having to vote against the administration, while La Follette's journal, *The Progressive*, said the progressives had held the balance of power on the vote and criticized Roosevelt for raising the issue.[13]

Four progressives had broken away from the bloc on the issue. Bronson Cutting, James Couzens, and Charles McNary had never committed themselves to isolationist views as a general rule. They also never expressed specific reasons for supporting Roosevelt on the World Court. Arthur Capper, on the other hand, despite his general isolationist sentiments, had supported

American entrance into the World Court during the 1920s and still believed that membership "would have been a big step in the direction of World Peace and better understanding between nations."[14]

The World Court vote seemed to set the stage for neutrality legislation. The revelations of the Munitions Committee, Mussolini's threat to invade Ethiopia, and Hitler's announcement that Germany was rearming caused a progressive backlash against increased arms spending. They were a small minority, and not all of the progressive Republicans stayed together. Eight of them (Capper, Couzens, Cutting, Frazier, La Follette, Norris, Nye, and Shipstead) voted against the War Department appropriations bill in March 1935, but it easily passed by 68 to 15. In May, six voted against the Navy Department appropriations bill, but this group (Capper, Frazier, La Follette, Norris, Nye, and Shipstead) only had twelve others joining them in opposition on the 55 to 18 vote. A few days before the final vote on this bill, Nye made a motion to recommit it to committee, but only thirteen colleagues, including six progressive bloc members, backed him.[15]

It was obvious that fear of war plagued the minds of many of the progressives. Lynn Frazier introduced a resolution that proposed a constitutional amendment prohibiting war. Arthur Capper criticized the leading nations of the world for failing to honor the Kellogg-Briand Pact of 1928, which outlawed war. Nye was the most active spokesman for peace, delivering many addresses in the Senate and on the public platform during 1935, demanding a curb on army and navy spending, and urging Roosevelt to call an international disarmament conference. It was Nye who would propose and promote formal neutrality legislation through Congress to prevent America from going to war again.[16]

On March 19, 1935, President Roosevelt met with the Nye Committee members and suggested they study the neutrality issue. At the end of that month, the North Dakota senator proposed legislation in a public address. Asserting that the world situation was as dangerous as it was in 1914, he called for a strict neutrality policy for the United States. America must abandon all intentions of profiting through trade with belligerents, must forbid the use of the American flag on cargoes intended for nations engaged in war, must place an embargo on all munitions of war to belligerent nations, and must drastically curb passports to Americans wishing to travel in the war zone, in order to avoid the kind of incidents that brought about war between Germany and the United States in 1917.[17]

During April and May, Nye and Sen. Bennett Champ Clark, Democrat of Missouri, introduced three resolutions designed to implement the program of the Nye address. Secretary of State Hull wanted to postpone consideration of the resolutions because of his belief that a rigid neutrality policy impeded the executive branch in the conduct of foreign policy. A struggle ensued between administration forces urging a discriminatory arms embargo and the

Nye-Clark bloc, which demanded an impartial, mandatory policy in time of war. With the State Department and the Senate Foreign Relations Committee unable to reach a compromise, the Nye bloc threatened a filibuster until action was taken on a neutrality program. This filibuster lasted just three hours as the administration gave in, with the president unwilling to commit his prestige to a bitter struggle for the discriminatory legislation favored by Hull.[18]

Although the measure was limited to six months by a House amendment, the Neutrality Act was to a great extent the masterwork of Nye. All of the progressive Republicans present voted for the bill, although Hiram Johnson warned that no one should think that it guaranteed America would stay out of all future wars. He wondered whether an impartial arms embargo might not turn out to be partial to the side that could produce or buy its arms elsewhere. He also warned that never should one man be given the power to determine when and how neutrality should be practiced.[19]

The Neutrality Act of 1935—calling for a mandatory embargo on implements of war to belligerents, a ban on the shipment of munitions on American ships, and discretionary authority of the president to proclaim that American citizens traveling on belligerent ships did so at their own risk and to apply the arms embargo to other nations when they entered a war already in progress—was due to expire on February 29, 1936. The law had an immediate test when Italian troops invaded Ethiopia in October 1935. President Roosevelt, inconsistent and indecisive during the neutrality debate, now invoked the legislation without hesitation. Although war had not been officially declared, a proclamation was issued, imposing an arms embargo on both sides. Americans were warned to avoid travel on belligerent ships, and businessmen were told that trade with the belligerents, even in raw materials, would be conducted at their own risk.

Borah responded to the Ethiopian crisis by issuing a warning against propagandists who might try to draw America into the war. He demanded complete neutrality, expressed shock at Italy's use of planes to bomb women and children, and asserted that modern warfare was mass murder, savagery, and barbarism. Norris wrote that public opinion should stand behind the president's proclamation, that the country must sacrifice some profits if it wished to avoid sacrificing men in another European war. He feared that financial investment in the war would lead again, as in 1917, to military intervention to protect the interests of the investors. Nye, although expressing no sympathy for Italy's cause, proclaimed his emphatic opposition to any American cooperation in economic sanctions by the League of Nations against Italy. Johnson sent a friendly warning to the president:

> Will you pardon me for what I am sure is an utterly unnecessary suggestion; but I happen to *know* that certain gentlemen are on tinterhooks, hoping and praying that in the present world crisis something will be done which may be distorted into an endeavor on the part of

our country to be a part of the League of Nations or of England's policy. It will enable them to make an issue of internationalism next year, and while I feel sure that they are bound to be disappointed, nevertheless I felt that you would not take amiss this well-meant word of mine.

Borah warned publicly against any changes in the neutrality law during 1936 that might be interpreted as supportive of League sanctions against Italy. The progressive Republicans were primed to fight against any gestures toward internationalism as the 1936 congressional session opened.[20]

The State Department proposed new neutrality legislation in 1936. It called for a continuation of the impartial arms embargo and the ban on loans but allowed the president some discretion and flexibility in administering the law. The Nye-Clark neutrality bloc was strongly opposed to the concept of granting any discretionary powers to the president, wishing to force Roosevelt's adherence to a rigid policy, with all contingencies determined in advance by Congress. Two members of the progressive Republican bloc, Borah and Johnson, broke with the rest of the members of the group on the question of restrictions on traditional American trading rights in time of war. As during the world war, they were unwilling to surrender the nation's right to freedom of the seas. They were termed "belligerent" isolationists, while the Nye bloc members were known as the "timid" isolationists.[21] Johnson, while clearly disagreeing with the Nye bloc on the question of freedom of the seas, emphatically disagreed with the administration proposal because it could plunge the nation into war. Early in the session, he wrote his son:

> All the pacifist societies, all the internationalists, and the League of Nations' people, want a law which will give absolute discretion to the President to do anything he sees fit under any circumstances, and of course, this would transfer to him, in one fashion or another, the warmaking power. I will not give this power of the Congress to the Executive, no matter who the Executive is.[22]

Progressive sentiment was for permanent neutrality legislation, not just an extension of the 1935 law. Arthur Capper, calling war "a colossal crime and a stupendous folly, the curse of nations, and the misery of their people," cited a Midwest poll of 100,000 people who supported a strong neutrality law, as well as such ideas as the banning of compulsory military training in colleges and universities and a national referendum to gauge the popular view before Congress voted on a war declaration. Along with Nye, Frazier, La Follette, and nine other senators, Capper opposed a compromise resolution suggested by Utah's Sen. Elbert D. Thomas, calling for an extension of the 1935 neutrality law until May 1, 1937, with the addition of a ban on loans to belligerents. Instead, they proposed a three-month extension, but the Senate voted this down by 61 to 16. Other amendments to the Thomas resolution, calling for trade quotas to belligerents and warnings to Americans that they traded with warring nations at their own risk, were overwhelmingly defeated. On February 18, 1936, the Thomas resolution passed by voice vote, and President Roosevelt signed the extension legislation on February 29.[23]

The Neutrality Act of 1936 extended the arms embargo and travel restrictions of the 1935 law. Loans were also prohibited, and the president's freedom in the conduct of foreign policy in the event of war was further curbed. He could not restrict trade in raw materials, was limited in his discretion in invoking the arms embargo, and was compelled to extend the embargo to new belligerents in a war already in progress. While progressives had differed on the form of neutrality, all of them had held to the belief that presidential discretion in invoking the arms embargo should not be allowed. Fear of presidential power over foreign policy had united the progressives, even before the major domestic controversies on presidential power arose. Hiram Johnson expressed the progressive distrust toward Roosevelt's foreign policy views, when he wrote his son that he feared the president was gravitating toward an internationalist policy, and that he was "afflicted with delusions of grandeur."[24]

During the 1936 presidential campaign, Roosevelt delivered a major address on foreign policy in Chautauqua, New York, in which he indicated his basic disagreement with Congress over executive powers, while at the same time agreeing with Senator Nye and his followers that the neutrality problem was basically economic, one of bankers and financiers attempting to draw the nation into a defense of their interests. Despite this fact, Roosevelt said that only the executive branch could handle the day-to-day problems of war and peace, and that the concept of discretionary powers in the hands of the chief executive was essential for national security. Roosevelt was offering a bridge between the extreme viewpoints held by the isolationists and the collective security supporters. After the president won reelection, Nye reaffirmed his determination to fight for a strict neutrality program and to deny discretionary powers to the chief executive. He also called for a popular referendum before America again participated in a foreign war. The battle lines were clearly drawn as Roosevelt's second term began.[25]

In January 1937, Senate Foreign Relations Committee Chairman Key Pittman of Nevada introduced a comprehensive neutrality bill that continued the ban on arms, loans, and travel and added a mandatory cash-and-carry feature that was generally acceptable to the Nye-Clark bloc of senators. All members of the committee, with the exception of Borah and Johnson, supported the Pittman resolution that went to the floor of the Senate for debate. Johnson said the measure would not keep the nation out of war, as the cash-and-carry feature favored nations with large navies, specifically Great Britain and Japan. Americans should be permitted to trade as usual. Of course, our ships would be subjected to search and seizure by belligerents and to the perils of blockade, but we must be willing to take this risk in order to continue our right to freedom of the seas. This was better, Johnson insisted, than to "scuttle and run," and to become, ultimately, the allies of the strongest naval powers. He denounced the Nye neutrality bloc for being in favor of peace at any price.[26]

Borah denounced the Pittman bill for failing to control war profits, said it would cause a worsening of relations with nations opposed to the two leading naval powers, and instead called for defense of the traditional rights of trade, as he had in 1917. He rejected the Nye thesis that economics had caused American involvement in the world war. But Capper spoke up for the majority of progressive Republicans when he said that the Pittman resolution would preserve peace, that neutral rights could not be protected except by war, and that he was unwilling to cast his vote to send American boys abroad to fight for freedom of the seas. War was futile, brutal, degrading, and costly, and therefore the nation must adopt a definitive foreign policy to keep America isolated from war. On March 3, the Senate adopted the Pittman resolution by a vote of 63 to 6, Borah and Johnson being joined by four New England senators in vehement opposition.[27]

The House Foreign Affairs Committee adopted a different bill calling for discretionary, rather than mandatory, cash and carry. The House of Representatives proceeded to adopt this resolution later in March, therefore requiring a conference committee to come to some agreement acceptable to both houses. Finally, the House version was basically adopted, angering the Nye bloc in the Senate. Only five progressive Republicans were recorded on this vote. Nye, Frazier, Capper, and Johnson were on the losing side of a 41 to 15 tally, but Borah now switched to support of the legislation because discretionary cash and carry, which he had tried to add to the Senate bill before passage, had been accepted. Johnson denounced the final bill as he felt it gave the president the ability to steer the nation into a conflict. Nye expressed the same concern but disagreed with Johnson that the concept of freedom of the seas was lost—or mattered at all when compared to the chance to avoid war.[28]

The Neutrality Act of 1937 was obviously a compromise that satisfied no one entirely. The isolationists did not like the discretionary authority given to the president regarding cash and carry. Collective security advocates disapproved of the mandatory restrictions on arms, loans, and travel. Advocates of freedom of the seas, such as Borah and Johnson, were disturbed at the dangers to that principle embodied in the legislation.[29]

The split within progressive Republican ranks over freedom of the seas was further demonstrated by the vote on the naval appropriations bill in

March 1937. Nye, Frazier, and Capper attacked the expenditure of more than a billion dollars as unnecessary, ill conceived, and unjustified and as a sign that the government was preparing for another world war. Nye dismissed the argument that increased expenditures were essential because the nation was in danger of attack, especially from Japan. Robert La Follette, Jr., joined these three senators in opposition, but Borah, Johnson, and Charles McNary supported passage of the naval bill, which was adopted by a 64 to 11 vote.[30]

Within a few months after passage of the 1937 Neutrality Act, the international community was confronted with aggression in both the Far East, where Japan marched into North China, and in Spain, where the Fascist military forces of Gen. Francisco Franco were getting direct assistance from Hitler and Mussolini in their attack upon the Spanish Republic. These foreign crises only convinced the progressive Republicans of the righteousness of their isolationist cause. In a major Senate speech, Borah denounced fascism, nazism, and communism, saying there could be no compromise between democracy and these forms of government. Concentrating on fascism and nazism, he called these political philosophies a repudiation of civilization, a return to the barbarism of Attila the Hun. He described the massacre of Ethiopians by the Italian army as an example of "reversion to the savagery of the cave man" and denounced the bombing of Guernica, the ancient Basque capital in Spain, as the "most revolting instance of mass murder in all history." Borah told newsmen he deplored the fact that Fascist philosophy was popular and respectable in upper-class society. He supported the War Department appropriations bill as essential so that the United States would have an army and navy capable of defending the country from foreign and domestic threats. He was especially concerned that Fascist philosophy might infiltrate the minds of American youth. But this did not mean that he wished to see America abandon its isolationist policy and fight fascism abroad.[31]

After the Japanese-Chinese conflict began at the Marco Polo Bridge in July 1937, speculation arose as to whether President Roosevelt would invoke the discretionary aspects of the Neutrality Act in the absence of a declared war. Senator Nye advocated just such an action as the best means to keep America out of the conflict, but the administration believed Japan would benefit from that action, due to its large supply of arms and its control of the seas. Nye asserted: "Congress and the American people are being kept in the dark as to what policy this Government does intend to follow." Roosevelt refused to invoke the Neutrality Act, but during September he decided to curb the carrying of arms to either side by government-owned ships and warned that other vessels flying the American flag and attempting to transport arms were doing so at their own risk. Isolationists were angry at the government's limited action and were even more disturbed by the president's Quarantine Address delivered in Chicago on October 5, 1937, in which he compared the widespread terror and lawlessness in the world to physical disease and called for joint efforts to restrain those responsible, as well as positive efforts for peace.[32]

Johnson, Nye, Borah, and Shipstead responded to Roosevelt's speech with sharp comments. Johnson sent a telegram to former presidential adviser Raymond Moley in which he declared: "No responsible head of a government should ever threaten unless he is prepared to go the full length to carry his threat into execution." Johnson feared that the president had "taken the path to war and finally the whole situation will degenerate." Later, in a letter to Moley, he indicated he was ready for combat with the internationalists, who he believed were motivated by "a strange mixture of idealism and toady-ism, and, of course, in many instances these two traits are conmingled [SIC] with love for some foreign country and a lofty contempt for patriotism." Nye assailed Roosevelt for trying to bring America closer to another war, declaring: "The same forces which were at work destroying our spirit of neutrality and peace twenty years ago are once again engaged at that task."[33]

Borah wrote a Wall Street attorney explaining his isolationist views. America must attend to its own affairs, making sure it was well prepared in case of invasion, but only going to war if other nations attacked first. He was concerned about the welfare of mankind but more devoted to the best for America. He assessed the internationalist argument this way:

> But this running around over the world trying to placate every situation and adjust every controversy is not the business of a democracy. A democracy must live at home or have no life. Totalitarian states which have absolute control over their subjects and may send them into any way that personal discretion or ambition suggests may engage in combat against aggressors, and so forth, but democracies cannot do so.[34]

Shipstead, in a radio address, warned that war makers and politicians were propagandizing for American involvement in another crusade in order to take attention away from economic problems at home. The United States must not be "missionaries with bayonets," trying to force other nations to be virtuous. War was immoral, and the American people must ignore "high-powered salesmanship" promoting involvement in another major conflict against tyranny. The United States was in no danger of being attacked, Shipstead asserted, and should such an unlikely event occur, America could take care of itself, having no need for alliances.[35]

As the international situation worsened, progressive isolationists drew attention to a proposal set forth by a Democratic congressman from Indiana, Louis Ludlow, calling for a constitutional amendment requiring a nationwide referendum before Congress could declare war. The measure would not apply if the nation were attacked. The Progressive party platform of 1924 (on which Senator Robert L Follette, Sr., had run) contained this idea, and Senator Nye had been promoting it since 1934. Others, including Senators La Follette and Capper, had also endorsed the concept. Now the supposed change in the president's views on neutrality led to a renewed campaign for such an amendment. La Follette and Capper sponsored similar proposals, the former's being more precise. For example, it prohibited conscription until the referendum had been held. No more momentous decision loomed for American democracy, La Follette contended, than the question of when and how war should be waged abroad. A congressional declaration of war could transform America into an armed camp, curb civil liberties, send millions of men to their deaths, and burden the nation with billions of dollars in war loans and national debt. Therefore, the people should have the ultimate authority over the question of war.[36]

The Japanese attack on the American gunboat *Panay* in China in December 1937 strengthened the fear of war among isolationists. La Follette wrote his brother that the administration was promoting an increased armaments program for war preparation. *The Progressive* criticized the president's changing attitudes on foreign policy, contending that "Mr. Roosevelt astounds liberal supporters by his continual boosting of bigger navy and bigger army proposals, and it is pretty obvious that such military machines are not necessary for national defense." Capper blamed the *Panay* incident for causing the defeat of the Ludlow referendum resolution in the House of Representatives in January 1938 but said he was determined to continue the fight becasue, as he told the readers of *Capper's Weekly*: "I consider war the greatest evil of our time." Nye criticized the naval appropriations bill under consideration, claiming that American manufacturers were selling war supplies to Japan which were then being turned against Americans. The navy was already powerful enough to defend the nation, and additional funds would only give the administration the chance to pursue a program of adventurism in foreign policy. The promotion of a larger navy, Nye declared, was "part of a campaign of getting the United States ready for a slaughter of its men on foreign fields, to fulfill its hopes and ideas in foreign capitals. And it will get the food of the unemployed down to dry crusts in order that the money may be thrown into the ocean in useless ships."[37]

Even Hiram Johnson, long a supporter of a large navy, was surprised by the administration plan. He wrote his son:

> I don't know how long it will be before a minority in the Senate, in behalf of the Country, will have to filibuster on some outrageous plan of the President. He slowly but surely is taking us into a league of nations, and endeavoring to set at naught the long, gruelling fight we made seventeen years ago. While I favor a big Navy, I am somewhat alarmed by his activity in that direction now. We may need it to whip the Japs, but we don't need it as an auxiliary of Great Britain.

At the end of January 1938, in a Senate speech, Johnson declared that Congress was entitled to know what the foreign policy of the country was. Requesting passage of a resolution calling for information from the executive branch, he denounced the concept of foreign policy formulated in secret meetings of the president and his advisers. He also wanted to know whether the president was attempting to threaten Japan or Germany in his Quarantine speech. Borah joined the debate that ensued, warning that the nation was risking war by allowing the world to believe that it was in a tacit alliance with Great Britain in opposition to "aggressors." La Follette expressed fear that the naval expansion was related to a change in foreign policy, a move toward an alliance with the British. Nye indicated his intention to hold up the naval bill until the administration clarified its foreign policy. Frazier saw a war coming and cited the president's lobbying to defeat the Ludlow Amendment.[38]

Johnson pushed the issue of a resolution, stubbornly refusing to drop the idea until he had gotten a satisfactory answer from the government. He specifically wanted to know whether the State Department had any understandings involving naval cooperation with Great Britain or any other nations. Although Secretary of State Hull wrote Senator Pittman, the Foreign Relations Committee chairman, denying such an arrangement, Johnson indicated he would continue to observe events closely, because he did not believe that the true motivation behind the Quarantine speech had yet been explained. With news reports of secret alliances with the British, Johnson now demanded a better answer than Hull had provided. He told his fellow senators that he believed Hull had acted in good faith in denying the existence of secret agreements, but he thought that other government leaders might have entered into understandings without the secretary's knowledge. Johnson was convinced that Roosevelt, as he told his son, "does not know what his foreign policy is; and Hull, notwithstanding the newspaper praise heaped upon him, is simply a 'dumb Dora.' "[39]

Rumors of an Anglo-American alliance revived the movement in the Senate for a national referendum on war. On February 25, twelve senators introduced Joint Resolution 270, proposing a constitutional amendment for popular approval of entrance into an offensive foreign war. Capper, Frazier, La Follette, Nye, and Shipstead were among those sponsoring the resolution. The amendment, broader in scope than the Ludlow proposal, was not to apply when a nation in the Western Hemisphere was attacked. La Follette, the designated leader of the bloc, said the amendment would not affect national defense or harm representative government. It would, however, act as a "democratic check on a completely unlimited executive power." Disillusionment over the world war and its effects upon the world had led to a widespead feeling that America should not be "catapulted into future foreign wars by the oversight, decisions, or mistakes of any one man." La Follette saw the war referendum as "an attempt to reestablish the intent of the framers of the Constitution that the power of the President to make war singlehanded should be circumscribed by reasonable limitations."[40]

La Follette took his campaign for a war referendum to the public in March 1938. Speaking before an antiwar rally in New York City, he called for citizen resistance to a naval build-up, wartime taxation measures to take the profits out of war, and the preservation of democracy by government spending on conservation, housing, education, and social security. The missionary belief that the United States must police the world to bring peace would instead lead to war, which would cost the nation at least $100 billion and result in a greater depression than the present one.[41]

As war continued in Spain and China in the spring of 1938, a new crisis developed when Hitler annexed Austria. As the possibility of eventual conflict increased, the progressive Republicans persisted in demanding the continuation of an isolationist foreign policy. Borah criticized the naval expansion program as a major step toward war and economic bankruptcy. He now believed the president had more than national defense in mind. In a radio address, the Idaho senator deplored the German annexation of Austria but blamed it on the unjust Versailles Treaty. Democracy could not be saved in Europe by American intervention, but it could be retained at home if the government concentrated on solving economic and social problems. This would prove democracy to be the best form of government and would weaken the appeal of fascism and communism. Senator Nye engaged in a public debate with *New York Herald Tribune* columnist Dorothy Thompson, continuing his campaign against collective security. If America went to war, he said, fascism would come to America and we would be defending nations that had subjugated millions of people in Asia and Africa. Nye pointed out that Great Britain and France had attempted to bargain with Germany and Italy in the past. Ridiculing Roosevelt's concept of "quarantining" aggressors, he termed collective security as actually "collective suicide." America's historical and geographical position, he concluded, made it essential that we maintain the Western Hemisphere as one area of sanity in the world. Meanwhile, Arthur Capper told the readers of *Capper's Weekly* that "what is going on today in Europe is a strong warning to the United States to mind its own business and keep out of foreign wars."[42]

When the naval expansion bill reached the Senate floor in April, it was subjected to bitter attack by progressive Republicans. Nye called for an end to the discretionary aspects of the 1937 Neutrality Act, repeated his demands for legislation that would prevent America from defending its commerce and citizens anywhere in the world, and denounced what he viewed as the secrecy and deception in foreign policy that had developed in recent months. La Follette spoke at an antiwar meeting in Chicago and then attacked the advocates of a larger naval establishment in a Senate speech. Emphatically proclaiming that the nation was in no danger of attack in the near or distant future, he accused the administration of formulating a new foreign policy in violation of tradition and without the approval or knowledge of Congress or the

American people. Declaring that he was an isolationist only in the sense of wishing to keep the nation out of war, he rejected a role for America as "guardian angel of the world's morals." Attacking the advocates of collective security, he asserted that the United States should only cooperate with Great Britain when it had declared a love of peace and democracy and had agreed to yield its imperialistic, exploitive control of its colonies.[43]

Capper was concerned that passage of the legislation would convince Roosevelt that America should thrust itself into the maelstrom of world power politics. He feared financial bankruptcy and a presidential dictatorship if the bill passed. Frazier pleaded for world disarmament and peace, firmly believing that another war would lead to the annihilation of mankind. Borah said that passage of the naval bill would cause a new arms race. While the crisis in Europe might concern Americans as individuals, it should not have an effect upon government policy, as American security was not threatened. "The controversy in Europe," Borah affirmed, "is not between democracy and autocracies. The conflict is over the division of territories growing out of the World War."[44]

While the Senate was debating this question, twenty-seven members introduced a bill to take the profits out of war via heavy taxation. Senator Nye and others of similar persuasion had introduced this legislation in past years, and now the same five progressive Republicans who had backed the war referendum amendment—Capper, Frazier, Nye, La Follette, and Shipstead— endorsed this action. Despite the oratorical efforts of the progressives, the naval expansion bill was adopted by a vote of 56 to 28 on May 3. All eight bloc members who were present voted against the bill. Hiram Johnson, although a major critic of the administration's foreign policy and doubtful of the validity of a large navy, left word that he would have cast his vote for the legislation. This was probably due to his fear of Japan.[45]

As the Senate's progressive Republicans fought to maintain American neutrality and to curb the American arms buildup, their nominal leader, George Norris, showed signs of splitting with the bloc on foreign policy. In March 1938, in a letter to the editor of *The Nation*, he indicated that, while still opposed to naval expansion and to American intervention in foreign controversies, he believed that the policies pursued by Germany, Italy, and Japan would require an eventual modification in the Neutrality Act. In an interview in the magazine *U.S. News*, Norris expanded on this statement, asserting that America must be assured that it was always better armed than any of the Fascist powers, which he called wild, indecent, and dishonorable in their relations with other nations. There was already enough justification for a declaration of war against these international outlaws, more so than against the Kaiser in 1917, but Norris hoped that America could avoid war. He still upheld the progressive opposition to the naval bill and voted against it. In

July 1938, Norris wondered whether the United States should join with Great Britain, France, and the Soviet Union in a world war to destroy fascism, but he still insisted that he could not vote to put America into war again. Obviously, Norris was a troubled man, aware of the Fascist threat but reluctant to see Americans die in another mass slaughter. The slow evolution from isolationism to internationalism was evident, however, by the end of 1938, putting him on a collision course with his friends and colleagues in the progressive bloc.[46]

From 1933 to 1938, members of the progressive Republican Senate bloc had remained amazingly united on the major goals they sought in American foreign policy. There was some division on the question of freedom of the seas ("belligerent" isolationists such as Borah and Johnson versus "timid" isolationists such as Nye and La Follette). However, all of the progressives remained determined to promote neutrality legislation that would keep America out of foreign controversies, prevent presidential discretion in the invoking of neutrality restrictions, and avoid a tremendous arms buildup that might either provoke some other nation or tempt the American government to commit itself to the defense of other nations. Wanting to promote the success of democracy at home, the progressives saw the possibility of American involvement in a foreign war as a threat to the fulfillment of that goal. Triumphant in the accomplishment of their aims with the aid of others up through 1938, the progressive Republican Senate bloc would fight a lost cause beginning in 1939, once the Second World War began.

[10]

The Decline and Fall
of Western Republican Progressivism,
1939–1945

As 1939 began, the international situation remained unstable. During the previous fall, the British and French governments had come to an agreement with Adolf Hitler at the Munich Conference regarding the acquisition of part of Czechoslovakia and its immediate merger into the Third Reich. British Prime Minister Neville Chamberlain had called the Munich agreement "peace for our time." The whole series of events leading up to the conference seemed further proof to the progressive Republicans of the corrupt nature of European power politics, and they remained determined to fight against any modification of America's neutrality policy. A new world war threatened after Hitler marched into the rest of Czechoslovakia in March and began to threaten Poland, in violation of the spirit of the Munich agreements. The appeasement policy of the western democracies had failed, and President Roosevelt now attempted to focus attention on the need for a change in the nation's neutrality policy, so as to meet the threat of fascism. It was certain that the progressive Republicans in the Senate would vehemently oppose the president. The stage was set for a three-year struggle over whether America should go to war again, as it had in 1917.

When the new session of Congress opened in January 1939, President Roosevelt's annual message placed emphasis upon the march of aggressors in Europe and Asia and expressed concern for American security. While requesting a strengthening of the national defenses and a revision of the neutrality laws, FDR avoided promoting a specific program, seemingly unwilling to provoke a major battle in Congress at that time. Senator Key Pittman, the Foreign Relations Committee chairman, announced plans to conduct a series of hearings on neutrality revision that would last a few months.

A number of progressives expressed displeasure with the tone of the president's address. Said Capper: "I was not impressed by the alarm the President seemed to express as to the possibility of international disturbances. I don't think that we're in any great danger." Lynn Frazier, as on previous occasions, proposed an amendment prohibiting participation in foreign wars, and Nye again introduced two joint resolutions, one prohibiting the shipment of arms, ammunition, and implements of war to foreign nations, and the other calling for an amendment to the Constitution providing for the requisition of property in time of war. In a radio address, Nye criticized the administration request for a record defense budget. Demanding that Roosevelt issue a declaration of American foreign policy, subject to the approval of Congress and the American people, he speculated that the British Foreign Office was formulating the administration's program. An increased defense budget was unnecessary, Nye concluded, if the nation wished simply to protect itself from invasion.[1]

When an experimental American bomber crashed in California at the end of January, killing those aboard, including an official of the French Air Ministry, proof seemed available that the Roosevelt administration was promoting the sale of military aircraft to the western European democracies. News of the incident provoked the wrath of isolationists, including the progressive bloc. Hiram Johnson demanded to know if America was being pushed into a war without the approval of either Congress or the people. He wrote his son: "The President, in my opinion, cares no more for what may happen to us in a war, than the man in the moon. He has developed the dictator complex, . . . He will do anything for applause." Johnson believed that Jews were the primary group backing the president's changing foreign policy, terming them "the class which cheers him vociferously for aiding their people, who neither live here, nor have anything in common with our country." He said that he regretted the German persecution of the Jews but was unwilling to see America go to war over this issue. He admitted he was reluctant to express this view publicly for fear of invoking the wrath of American Jews. However, he issued a statement that advocates of collective security were encouraging hysteria and war propaganda.[2]

Senator Nye, as a member of the Military Affairs Committee, was invited to the White House for a conference on the airplane crash and its implications. He was irritated that the committee members were sworn to keep the briefing confidential. When the news leaked out that the president had stated that the frontier of American defense lay on the Rhine, the White House denied the accuracy of the story and denounced Nye for the leak. Actually, Sen. Ernest Lundeen of Minnesota had given out the information, but the ensuing war of words between Nye and the White House led to a break in personal relations. Nye accused the president of a complete retreat from his stated determination to keep America out of war, expressed in his 1936 reelection campaign. The president was making the same mistakes that Woodrow Wilson had committed between 1914 and 1917, Nye asserted, and he called upon him to be neutral in thought as well as action toward the international crisis. He said the United States could not and should not attempt to police the world. The North Dakota senator introduced a bill to put statutory restrictions upon the sale of American airplanes to foreign nations, and during debate on expansion of the Army Air Corps in late February, Nye declared his conviction that there would be no war in Europe within the next two years unless the United States encouraged it through arms trade.[3]

Capper and La Follette also commented on the controversy. In a letter to Alf Landon, Capper said he was opposed to secret conferences between congressional committees and the White House, as it denied members of Congress the right of public comment. Capper was convinced that "the President would not be very much disappointed if the international situation should result in dragging the United States into a foreign war." He hoped that the nation would stay out of any conflict, however, as "We owe it to our own people now to give attention to our own problems first." La Follette, commenting that "It is a burlesque of representative government if our foreign policies are formulated secretly by the Chief Executive," observed that if the United States continued to supply war materials to any group of nations, it was violating the neutrality laws and exposing the nation to certain involvement in any future foreign war, which could destroy American democracy. The same group of progressive Republicans—La Follette, Capper, Frazier, Nye, and Shipstead—that had sponsored a war referendum amendment in 1938 did so again in the midst of this controversy and was joined by seven other senators.[4]

While the progressive isolationists were attacking the administration's secretive foreign policy, George Norris was confirming the developing split with his colleagues. In February 1939, he confided to former Congressman Victor Murdock of Kansas his disillusionment with "some of our old Progressive 'war horses'" who had displayed "bitterness against President Roosevelt that I can not explain and do not understand." Norris declared:

> It seems to me all these party and all these petty jealousies ought to be forgotten in times like these. As I construe the past, all such differences were laid aside, at least temporarily, when the country was faced with danger such as that which confronts it now, and the thing that worries me and is almost heartbreaking to me is that such enmities and bad blood do not quiet down as I think they have quieted down in our past history. . . . I can not talk with some of the best friends I have in the Senate because they at once become angry, excited and illogical, if I dare to suggest that the President in any given action has not exceeded his constitutional right.

In March, Norris replied to a constituent's letter on the war referendum resolution, indicating his disagreement with the viewpoint of his progressive colleagues. During the interim period while such a resolution was being considered, Norris declared, the nation would be unable to prepare for military action to thwart a danger to our security. Once war had been declared, this would prove to be a serious handicap.[5]

In early March, the Senate debated the administration request for increased funds for defense, including an amendment for the manufacture of six thousand additional airplanes. Johnson, Capper, Frazier, and Shipstead spoke up in defense of their known views, while Johnson reviewed the developments within the previous year. Saying he was not a Nazi, Fascist, or Communist sympathizer and that he detested dictators of any stripe, Johnson contended there was no reason to increase production of airplanes, as there was no danger of the United States being attacked from the air. Recalling President Roosevelt's earlier commitments to remain out of European quarrels and entangling alliances, and demanding that America fight only defensive wars in the future, Johnson spoke of his passionate hate of war and his fear that dictatorship in America would be the result of involvement in another world war. He later wrote his son of his conviction that Roosevelt was allied secretly with Great Britain and France against Germany and Italy. Contending that Roosevelt wanted to take America into war to bring fame for himself as a great war leader, Johnson wrote that anyone courageous enough to fight against the tide "will be hooted down in the fashion with which we became so familiar twenty years or more ago . . . but some of the little fellows are so obstinate, they tempt their fate, and, of course, I am one of those."[6]

Capper, Frazier, and Shipstead all delivered statements with similar points: that America must not police the world, that it should not allow munitions makers to draw the nation into another European war, that America was safe from invasion, and that the country should concentrate on its domestic problems. The Senate proceeded to pass the aircraft amendment 54 to 28, with the six progressive Republicans present voting against and the other three leaving notice that they would have joined with their colleagues. On the final vote on the entire bill, the progressive Republicans split, with five (Borah, Capper, Frazier, Nye, and Shipstead) voting against and four (Johnson, La Follette, McNary, and Norris) supporting the legislation, which passed 77 to 8.[7]

Fearful of the repeal of the neutrality laws, a group of senators led by Nye announced plans to filibuster if necessary to prevent such a development. During March, with the backing of the administration, Key Pittman proposed what he termed the Peace Act of 1939. The measure called for revocation of the arms embargo and adoption of cash and carry for all trade with belligerent nations. The progressives immediately attacked this legislation. Borah, Johnson, Capper, Nye, and Shipstead denounced the concept of revision of the neutrality laws, and the latter three, along with La Follette and Frazier, were among the co-sponsors of a much-promoted bill to tax the profits out of war. Nye called for even stricter neutrality legislation, co-sponsoring a bill with Bennett Clark of Missouri and Homer Bone of Washington that would ban all arms trade with warring countries, prohibit American ships from transporting any commodities to belligerents, and forbid American citizens to travel on the ships of those nations. Nye thus revived once again the ideas he had been suggesting since 1934.[8]

The Pittman bill showed again the division of progressive Republicans over neutrality legislation. One group, consisting of Nye, Capper, La Follette, Frazier, and Shipstead, wanted rigid neutrality laws along the lines that Nye, Clark, and Bone had proposed. Borah and Johnson, as long-time defenders of freedom of the seas, demanded total repeal of all neutrality laws. Only Norris supported the Pittman bill, further evidence of his swing toward backing Roosevelt in foreign affairs. He expressed the belief that most Americans sympathized with Great Britain, France, and China in the prevailing international situation in Europe and Asia, and he added: "If we can pass a law that will rebound to their benefit, without violating the principles of neutrality, that is the kind of a law I want to pass." Borah warned against naming aggressors and granting economic support to their enemies. The European powers "all alike violate treaties, disregard the most fundamental principles of right, pursue methods which inevitably lead to war, and then call upon the United States . . . to save them from their own intolerable and vicious methods." The war threatening Europe was not over a question of democracy or totalitarianism, but rather a "sordid, imperialistic" conflict. In late April, Borah predicted that Hitler would avoid a major war and that Great Britain would continue its appeasement program.[9]

Widespread controversy over the Pittman neutrality bill led some legislators to call for early adjournment of the congressional session, with further study and investigation of the subject until early 1940. But Hiram Johnson denounced the suggestion, demanding that the legislative branch remain in session until the foreign situation clarified itself. In the spring of 1939, Hitler was making demands on Poland, and Great Britain and France were announcing a guarantee of that nation's borders. Johnson was apprehensive that if Congress was not in session, Roosevelt would take unauthorized action to involve the United States in war. In a dramatic statement that provoked widespread applause from a crowded Senate gallery, he proclaimed: "We must be on guard . . . every minute of the day and every minute of the night in the days to come, to see that we shall not participate in a war which is none of our concern, . . . Let us be ourselves and, for the people of the United States, let us keep out of war."[10]

At the end of May, the Roosevelt administration, determined to make a concerted effort for congressional passage of an arms embargo repeal and a cash-and-carry system, prodded the House of Representatives to take action. Senate isolationists now made plans for battle. Thirteen of them gathered in Nye's office on June 16 and announced the beginning of an "uncompromising fight." Seven progressive Republicans were present at this meeting. By early July, the opponents of the administration proposal had increased to an estimated thirty-four senators. The bloc met in Hiram Johnson's office and agreed to begin a filibuster to prevent passage of the administration proposal. Johnson wrote his son at this time: "There are of course not enough to whip the Administration in its foul designs, but we have enough to keep the subject indefinitely before the Senate." In concert with Nye, La Follette, and Arthur Vandenberg, he worked to promote a motion in the Foreign Relations Committee that called for postponing consideration of any neutrality legislation until the next session of Congress. On July 11, the committee voted 12 to 11 (including all five progressive Republicans) to defer the issue, thus spoiling months of Roosevelt administration effort.[11]

On July 14, Roosevelt took the offensive, sending a special message to Congress calling for an immediate amendment of the neutrality laws to eliminate the compulsory arms embargo. Borah and Johnson denounced the message. In a last-ditch effort to override the Senate Foreign Relations Committee's action, Roosevelt invited half a dozen Senate leaders up to the White House, including Republicans McNary and Borah. On the evening of July 18, the president and Secretary of State Hull spoke of the danger of war in Europe and attempted to enlist the support of the legislative leaders in bringing the issue to the Senate floor. But Borah disputed the view that war was imminent in Europe. Stating that he had his own sources of information that he kept confidential, Borah provoked an emotional scene in the White House, with Roosevelt and Hull obviously upset. Realizing finally that he would have no cooperation from the Republican leadership, the president reluctantly abandoned further attempts to promote neutrality revision for the time being. However, he indicated he might take the issue to the country.[12]

The progressive Republicans were extremely pleased at the turn of events. Johnson was ready for battle with the president if he went to the nation to appeal for his program. McNary wrote after the White House meeting: "It is not my intention, by vote, to transfer unusual powers to the President in the matter of neutrality." Nye declared that the administration obviously had been trying to assist Great Britain and France, and that the battle against unrestricted executive power in foreign affairs must continue. He suggested the formation of a joint congressional committee to consult secretly with the executive branch on all major decisions in foreign policy. Nye echoed Borah's view that a general war was unlikely, because of Congress's refusal to consider neutrality revision. This had served as a warning to the western nations that the United States would not be their arsenal in another military conflict. La Follette disagreed with the President's contention that a congressional coalition had tied his hands, preventing moves for world peace. America must remain out of European affairs, La Follette asserted, in order to promote democracy at home and peace abroad.[13]

On the morning of September 1, 1939, Nazi Germany invaded Poland. Within a few days, the Second World War began, as Great Britain and France declared war on Germany. President Roosevelt immediately called for a special session of Congress to change the neutrality laws in order to aid the western democracies, although his emphasis would be on the fact that the arms embargo harmed American security. A tough battle lay ahead, as the isolationist bloc was steadfastly dedicated to the prevention of American entanglement in the European crisis. The progressive Republicans, with the exception of George Norris, were in the forefront of the most significant foreign policy debate since the struggle over the Versailles Treaty and League of Nations in 1919 to 1920. Ultimately, their cause was a lost one.

At the outbreak of the European war, La Follette said he was convinced that if "we can but remain free from any foreign entanglements we can solve the problems of this country . . . We must avoid a blood transfusion that will bleed us white of man power and resources." Opposed to a repeal of the arms embargo and the sale of munitions and arms on a cash-and-carry basis, he felt that nonwar goods should be sold only for cash. Lynn Frazier termed the war "insane and futile," condemned the idea of war credits to any nation, and hoped that America would remain out of the conflict. However, he believed Roosevelt wanted to join on the side of Great Britain and France and agreed that the opponents of American involvement had the disadvantage in the forthcoming struggle. McNary reported that the president had phoned him, requesting the Republican leader's cooperation in expediting the neutrality issue in the special session. McNary agreed to this, but not to specific support of administration plans. Capper indicated he would fight repeal of the neutrality laws, vowing: "I am standing with Bill Borah, Bennett Clark and others in opposition to repeal. I feel very deeply on this question. It is not our war and we have no business breaking into it. We got the worst of it before and it would be very foolish to break into another war." Borah forecast another bitter donnybrook between the White House and the Senate isolationist bloc. He indicated that there would be no compromise, and that he and other members of the bloc would "fight to the last ditch" any effort to limit debate on amending neutrality. Nye also insisted on a full and open debate. Johnson called for a "prohibitory embargo against all nations at war." He stood with the Roosevelt of 1936 who favored an isolationist policy, he declared, rather than the Roosevelt of 1939, who was marching down the road to war.[14]

Borah delivered a radio address to set the mood for the "peace bloc" strategy. Repeal of the arms embargo would be the equivalent of entrance into the war, he contended, and America must base its national policies upon love of itself instead of hatred of other nations. After Roosevelt delivered his message requesting revision of the neutrality laws and repeal of the arms embargo, a group of twenty-four senators gathered in Hiram Johnson's office and resolved to prevent passage of the administration plan. All of the progressive Republicans except McNary and Norris were present. La Follette gave a pep talk, declaring that the group—if its campaign were well organized and aroused public opinion in a manner similar to the struggles against the League of Nations, World Court, Supreme Court bill, and government reorganization—could prevent modification of the neutrality laws. However, some senators disagreed on such a large-scale offensive, and the Wisconsin senator wondered if the battle were not already lost. He wrote his wife:

> The fight against the League of Nations, the World Court, the Supreme Court bill and the first reorganization bill were all won because there was a determined effort to make vocal the opposition in the country to these measures. I am convinced that an overwhelming majority of the people are against the repeal of the arms embargo but unless that opposition is brought to bear on the Congress the President has all the advantage in the struggle.

Abandoning his larger ideas, La Follette joined Borah, Johnson, and Nye in holding consultations with other isolationist senators during the next few days. At the conclusion of these conferences, Borah asserted that if the opponents of the president were granted a full debate, they would avoid the filibuster tactic. Johnson was confident, telling newsmen: "We are going to have a bully fight. We think it will last a long, long time, and we expect to win." On September 28, the Foreign Relations Committee favorably reported the administration bill to the Senate by a vote of 16 to 7, with all progressive Republican members opposed. However, they made no motions and offered no amendments in the committee room, deciding to record their vote quietly and to save their rhetoric for the struggle on the Senate floor.[15]

The campaign against Roosevelt's proposal lasted little more than a month. It was a futile battle from the beginning, as Roosevelt had a majority of Congress on his side. But whatever it lacked in strength the isolationists, and especially the progressive Republicans in the group, made up in dramatic and emotional rhetoric, as they denounced internationalism and increased executive power. They spoke over the radio, before peace organizations, and on the Senate floor. The Senate debate began on October 2, with the eyes of the nation focused on the acknowledged leaders of the two sides, Pittman and Borah. After Pittman had defended the administration program as essential, Borah rose to deliver what was to be his last great oration before his death in January 1940. A veteran of thirty-three years in the upper chamber of Congress, long regarded as one of the greatest public speakers in Senate history, he caused a great stir in the galleries as he denounced the "war hounds of Europe" who were crying for repeal of the American neutrality laws. The neutrality legislation enacted in previous years had the aim of keeping America impartial in European conflicts by preventing the sale of arms to any belligerent, he asserted, and therefore it was not America's business whether the laws operated neutrally in Europe. Repeal would demonstrate that the United States favored the western powers, and cash and carry would eventually draw the nation into the conflict. He saw the war as "nothing more than another chapter in the bloody volume of European power politics," cited the Munich conference as a perfect example of that power politics and of imperialism, and indicated that he did not see the war as a battle for democracy and civilization, as Great Britain and France were depicting it. When Borah completed his remarks, the galleries broke into widespread applause, colleagues rushed up to shake his hand, and it was obvious that he had made quite an impression on his listeners.[16]

The next day, Norris came to the defense of the Roosevelt administration proposal in a radio address. He believed the nation could stay out of the war but still assist the side that represented humanity, civilization, and liberty by repealing the arms embargo and providing for cash and carry. If the laws remained unchanged, Norris declared, then the United States would be aiding the Fascist forces in Europe. With this speech, Norris formally broke with the rest of the progressive Republican bloc on foreign policy. The great moral spokesman of opposition to American involvement in the First World War still hoped that America would stay out of the war, but believed that Nazism was too great a threat to be overlooked.[17]

The other progressive Republicans now took turns speaking for their cause on the Senate floor. La Follette, in a three-hour address, termed the supporters of arms embargo repeal "interventionists" who wanted the United States to become allies of Great Britain and France, nations he considered unworthy of our trust. The western powers professed to be democracies, but they did not practice it in their empires. Entrance into the war would lead to loss of civil liberties and greater economic crises, a repetition on a larger scale of the problems America had faced since World War I. La Follette created a stir in the galleries when he recalled his father's antiwar stand in 1917, and he received heavy applause at the conclusion of his address. Newsmen labeled it the most dramatic speech of the special session.[18]

Nye, the most active of the progressives during the session, delivered three lengthy speeches within twelve days. He challenged Roosevelt to think of America first. He suggested that the president act as a mediator for peace, a role that could be held only so long as the arms embargo continued. He blamed France and Great Britain for the rise of Hitler—the result, he believed, of the unjust Versailles Treaty imposed upon the Germans. As he had done many times within the previous five years, he spoke of the position of the munitions makers and financiers in drawing America into World War I, and asserted there was no such thing as steps short of war without ultimate involvement in it. He saw the conflict as a struggle for empire and thought it would be suicidal for the nation to get involved in it. When Nye claimed that everyone who favored the arms embargo repeal wanted to send American troops to fight in Europe, he aroused Norris's anger. The Nebraska senator's face was flushed as he abruptly interrupted Nye to say that he did not care whether Hitler would be displeased by such an action, and that he did not believe that repeal of the arms embargo would lead to American involvement in the war. Other proadministration senators also became engaged in heated debate with Nye.[19]

Frazier delivered a rare floor speech on October 14. Urging that the United States take no action that would appear to be in support of Great Britain and France, he warned against allowing profits or propaganda to sway America toward entrance into the war. War was a crime against humanity and the destroyer of democracy. Declaring that the nation had appropriated enough money in the previous six years to arm itself adequately against the unlikely possibility of foreign attack, Frazier pleaded that the United States divorce itself from European controversies, as it had throughout its history, except for World War I. Henrik Shipstead denounced propaganda that America must act as a missionary, or punish aggressor nations that violated treaties. He proceeded to a discussion of the Versailles Treaty and its aftermath during the 1920s and 1930s and a commentary on the worthlessness of peace treaties throughout history. All nations had at one time or another broken treaties and committed aggression, and he thus concluded: "I do not believe we can save democracy by a war of extermination, even though it is labeled a war to prevent a war of extermination."[20]

Arthur Capper followed Shipstead with a plea for defeat of the bill because it represented "a definite step toward war." Believing that America "cannot, logically or psychologically, be half in and half out of this war," he declared: "Let us save our boys for something better than fodder for Europe's battlefields during this latest of the long succession of wars that Europe has fought over boundaries and power." Although he professed personal sympathies for Great Britain and France, he believed in putting the nation's welfare first. Capper concluded with a pledge that he would never vote to send American soldiers to Europe.[21]

Hiram Johnson was given the honor of summing up the general case for the isolationist bloc. Speaking for more than an hour on October 20, he pleaded against taking "the first false step" to battle. In dramatic oratory, he said that America was in the "shadow, walking down the bloody path of war." He denounced Great Britain for playing power politics and the League of Nations supporters, who he believed were driving the nation toward participation in the conflict. Hitler would never conquer Europe, Johnson

insisted, and America was in no danger of attack from Germany. The isolationist bloc members, he promised, had only American interests in their
minds and hearts. Johnson joined Borah and Nye in final radio appeals for
support, while Norris told an interviewer that although America had more
justification to go to war now than in 1917, the psychology of the American
people would keep the nation out of the conflict.[22]

On October 25, the Senate defeated a La Follette amendment proposing
establishment of an export control board to place quota restrictions on all
exports to warring nations. Norris voted with the majority, and the Nebraska
senator also criticized another La Follette amendment providing for the
much-suggested war referendum before soldiers were sent overseas. Such
a requirement would impede the defense of the nation, giving the enemy
a strategic advantage, he claimed, and Congress already had the responsibility
as representatives of the people to declare war under the Constitution. Borah
and McNary supported Norris on this question, while the rest of the progressive Republicans joined the losing side of a 73 to 17 vote. Borah and Nye
now conceded that they could not prevent passage of the Pittman resolution,
as they had only thirty senators' support. By a 63 to 30 vote, the Senate
proceeded to pass the repeal of the arms embargo and the adoption of cash
and carry. Only Norris was on the winning side. On November 3, after House
passage, Congress gave final approval to the neutrality resolutions, with the
Senate vote of 55 to 24 showing the same lineup of progressive Republicans.
Borah and Johnson, as members of the conference committee on the legislation, refused to sign the report. A major blow had been dealt to the cause of
isolationism; however, the progressive Republicans had no intention of giving
up the fight, and they remained in the forefront of the struggle to keep
America out of war during 1940 and 1941.[23]

During the debate over changes in the American neutrality laws, Poland
had been occupied and divided between the Nazis and the Soviet Union, a
fulfillment of the German-Russian pact of late August that had allowed Hitler
to feel free to declare war on his eastern frontier. The next victim of attack
was Finland, which fought desperately for survival against Russian forces.
Since Finland had continued to pay its World War I debts to the United
States during the 1930s while other countries had defaulted, a great wave of
public sympathy developed for aid to that beleaguered nation. Seven of the
eight surviving progressive Republicans were present for a vote on financial
assistance to Finland in February 1940. They split 4 to 3 in favor of aid, with
Frazier, La Follette, McNary, and Shipstead going with the majority in the
49 to 27 vote, and Capper, Johnson, and Norris opposed. Nye, absent for the
vote, indicated that he opposed any assistance to Finland because it would be
regarded as another step toward war. Capper and Johnson echoed similar
sentiments in brief comments before the roll call was taken.[24]

To prevent any further trend toward war, La Follette introduced a resolution during March 1940, calling upon the Military Affairs Committee to conduct a full investigation of whether foreign purchase of arms was delaying the equipping of the American military forces. The committee rejected the resolution later in the month, however, because of the feeling that it would stir up another controversy over aid to Great Britain and France. Meanwhile, in the spring of 1940 Gerald Nye increased the pace and vehemence of his campaign to keep America out of war. Regarded as the most controversial member of the Senate during 1940 and 1941, he was subjected to much criticism and ridicule as he worked against American support for the western democracies, denied the danger to America of a Hitler victory, and insisted that the combined armies of all of the major powers of Europe, as well as Japan, could not come within striking distance of America's shores. In April 1940, Hiram Johnson wrote his son that he sensed the nation was coming closer to war, and certainly if Roosevelt campaigned for and won a third term in the White House, the country would be in the war by 1941.[25]

The struggle between isolationism and internationalism increased in fervor when German armies smashed through Denmark, Norway, Belgium, Holland, and France between April and June 1940. The miraculous retreat of British and Free French forces to safety from the German onslaught only showed the serious nature of the crisis that democratic forces faced in Europe. Benito Mussolini's declaration of war on the side of Germany only served to heighten the tension felt by internationalists in the United States. President Roosevelt now made a public statement ridiculing the policy of isolation, declaring his sympathy with Great Britain and France, and promising to send both nations all available equipment to aid them in their fight against fascism. He also announced the nomination of two internationalist Republicans to his cabinet, Henry Stimson as secretary of war and Frank Knox as secretary of the navy. This was seen as a bold move by the president to attract Republican support in Congress for aid to the western allies.[26]

The president's actions were strongly criticized by the progressive Republicans, especially Nye. He accused FDR of playing politics in his appointments of Stimson and Knox. Denouncing Roosevelt for pursuing a disastrous foreign policy of encouraging France to fight on when he knew the United States could not assist it under existing federal laws, he said that the president should resign and allow Vice-President Garner to restore confidence in the national government. Of course, no one, including Nye himself, really expected this to happen. The North Dakota senator was simply using rhetoric in an attempt to build up an atmosphere that would prevent any aid or comfort to the British. But many people began to question where Nye's loyalties lay, with democracy or with fascism. Despite his bitter attack upon the president, Stimson and Knox were confirmed for their posts, with all the progressive Republicans opposed, except for McNary and Norris. La Follette explained his vote by saying that Stimson and Knox were reactionaries and therefore he could not, in good conscience, support them for such responsible positions.[27]

During the summer of 1940, with the Battle of Britain commencing, Congress debated the administration's request for a Selective Service system and universal military training, a bill sponsored by Democratic Sen. Edward Burke of Nebraska. With the exception of Charles McNary, now the Republican vice-presidential nominee on Wendell Willkie's ticket, all the progressive Republicans bitterly opposed this legislation, which they believed would transform America into a military camp. Capper engaged in a radio debate with Burke, asserting that compulsory military training in peacetime was "repugnant" to American democracy, and "strikes at the heart of personal liberty and personal freedom." Lynn Frazier, in his last speech in the Senate (as he had been defeated for renomination by William Langer) indicated that the legislation was an abridgement of civil liberties and therefore unconstitutional. Hiram Johnson spoke twice in the Senate against the bill, terming it "the most sinister bill that ever was passed during my long service as a United States Senator."[28]

Nye was the most active opponent of the military conscription bill, delivering public and radio addresses as well as comments on the Senate floor on the issue. The call for military service in time of peace was the result of hysteria and propaganda encouraged by industrialists and munitions makers who wanted to drag America into the war, he declared, and he again demanded the taxation of war profits and the nationalization of war industries. Depicting the uncertainties that the nation's young men would face if military conscription was adopted, he said there was no need for such a large armed force unless someone had plans to take America into the war on the side of Great Britain.[29]

La Follette stated his opposition to the Selective Service bill in *The Progressive* in early August. Certain that the adoption of compulsory military training would produce drastic economic, social, and political consequences and would introduce regimentation into American life, he wrote his family: "It seems a crime to fasten such a system on the country when it is clear men can be gotten under the voluntary system." He admitted that the propaganda for the legislation was heavy, "but I am going to resist the drift to war all I can." In a radio address in early September, he spoke with great feeling of his conviction that America was proceeding down the path it had taken in 1917, when his father led the opposition to the war fever. Denouncing the propaganda that he said was bombarding the American people and fomenting fear and hysteria, he declared: "These fears we must resist, for they are designed to becloud our reason and if successful will end in disaster for our country. I appeal to the people who do not want our Nation plunged into the holocaust, not to be sucked along the road to war by easy stages and fake reasoning."[30]

George Norris, who had supported all administration proposals on defense in recent years, announced in mid-July that he was opposed to the Selective Service legislation, which surprised some Roosevelt supporters. America, said Norris, was not surrounded by hostile forces that could mount a surprise invasion, as was the case with Holland, Belgium, and Denmark. In a letter to a constituent that was released to the newspapers, Norris contended:

> To compel our young men to serve in the army in time of peace is to me abhorrent. I do not see the necessity or the reason for it. It is contrary to our history . . . the continuation of a policy of compulsory military training would gradually change our nation and the attitude of our people. To a very great extent, they would be drawn gradually but inevitably from their peace-loving ways into those of a nation whose chief object would be to destroy other nations.

Norris expressed his feelings twice on the Senate floor, once during general debate and again when the conference report was being discussed. Despite the protests of the progressives, the Senate adopted the bill 58 to 31 and the conference report 47 to 25. The isolationist views of the progressive Republicans had been dealt another blow. Time and events seemed to be turning against them in their struggle to keep America out of the Second World War.[31]

While the Battle of Britain was raging and the Selective Service bill was being debated, William Allen White had formed a Committee to Defend America by Aiding the Allies, which called for the sale of old destroyers to Great Britain in exchange for bases on various island possessions in the Western Hemisphere—this to be accomplished through an executive agreement rather than by treaty. Roosevelt, believing such an action was essential, arranged such a deal in September 1940. The announcement of this action seemed to mark the end of true American neutrality in the war in Europe. The United States, openly aiding Great Britain, was now a nonbelligerent instead of a neutral power. Isolationists, including the progressives, bitterly denounced the destroyers-for-bases deal. La Follette was upset because he believed it would take two years to replace the old equipment. He felt that America could have taken the British bases as payment for the World War I debt, and he added:

> Unless we stop in our tracks there will be no end to the policy of taking everything that Britain wants and labeling it surplus or overage and obsolete. . . . You and I have been told for months that this Nation must strengthen its defense, must build an impregnable military machine capable of protecting ourselves from any aggressor or combination of aggressors. . . . But all the while we are voting more money to prepare to

defend this hemisphere against all comers, we are dissipating strength
by sending huge quantities of guns, planes, and warships across the
ocean.

Nye said transferring the destroyers was equivalent to an outright declaration of war. Denying that Great Britain was or should be America's first line
of defense, he claimed that the war was simply a struggle to save the British
Empire.[32]

In the fall of 1940, after the announcement of the destroyers-for-bases
deal, isolationist spokesmen formed the America First Committee to campaign against further aid to Great Britain and to keep America out of the war
in Europe. Many of the nation's leading public figures spoke under the auspices of America First, contending that Germany represented no threat to
American security, that the European war was simply the typical power
struggle that had been going on for centuries, and that the American democratic system would be destroyed if it became involved in the conflict. The
progressive Republican Senate bloc had been promulgating these ideas since
the war began. Philip La Follette, Gerald Nye, Burton K. Wheeler, and
Charles Lindbergh were among the most prominent and active American
Firsters, but Senators Capper, Johnson, La Follette, and Shipstead also joined
the America First campaign through a general endorsement of its activities
and an occasional address or statement released through its headquarters.
They remained determined to fight for the cause despite the increasing odds
of ultimate failure. The America First Committee indeed acted as one of the
most powerful pressure groups in American political history.[33]

In the midst of the hot debate over American foreign policy, Roosevelt
decided to seek a third term, breaking the tradition that no president should
serve more than eight years. Rumors of such a decision had been prevalent
ever since the Second World War began. In November 1939, Arthur Capper
wrote Alf Landon: "There is a growing feeling that Roosevelt will run for a
third term. It is admitted that he can have the nomination with practically no
opposition if he wants it." The following February, the Kansas senator spoke
about the possibility of a third term in a Lincoln's Birthday address. Declaring that such action would represent a denial of the traditions of American
government, he characterized the president as a man who had "mesmerized"
himself with his own charm. Nye indicated his belief that Roosevelt should
not only refuse to run for a third term but should resign to restore faith in
American foreign policy. Shipstead, who was seeking reelection as a Republican after earlier campaigns as a Farmer-Laborite, also announced his opposition to a third term and came out for Wendell Willkie in the fall campaign,
despite his support of Roosevelt in 1932 and 1936.[34]

Hiram Johnson, who also was running for reelection in 1940, publicly split
with Roosevelt after the president said at a press conference that the Califor-

nia senator was no longer to be regarded as a progressive, as he had become reactionary in his views in the last three to four years. Johnson's response was to charge that the president again was attempting to purge his critics, as he had been so unsuccessful in doing within the Democratic party in the 1938 congressional elections. The president, Johnson remarked, would still consider him a liberal or progressive had he backed him on the Supreme Court reform and foreign policy, but the California senator proclaimed pride in his record and said the people of his home state did not wish him to be simply a blind supporter of any administration.[35]

Despite Roosevelt's comments, Johnson proceeded to win the nomination of the Democratic, Republican, and Progressive parties of his state by landslide proportions, guaranteeing his return to the Senate. After the primaries, Johnson told his son that while he lacked enthusiasm for Republican presidential nominee Wendell Willkie because of his general support of Roosevelt's foreign policy, "I could not be for a third termer, and I could not be for a man who asserted that I am unfit to be Progressive." Willkie, hopeful of gaining Johnson's endorsement, praised him in a Los Angeles campaign appearance, terming him a "great fearless liberal leader." Johnson then proceeded to announce his support of Willkie in mid-October in a nationwide radio address. His emphasis was not on Willkie but on the dangers of breaking the two-term tradition for American presidents. On Election Eve, he again endorsed the Republican nominee in a short statement warning that America could not trust Roosevelt to keep America out of war. He concluded: "I am convinced that a vote for Willkie means a vote for the real defense of our nation and a vote to keep the United States free from involvement in Europe's inferno." [36]

La Follette, the sponsor of an anti-third term resolution directed at President Coolidge in 1928, had become extremely critical of the Roosevelt administration's economic and foreign policies since 1936, when he had headed the Progressive National Committee campaign for the president. However, he had remained on friendly terms with Roosevelt even during the time when his brother Philip attempted to steer New Deal liberal support toward his ill-fated National Progressives of America in 1938. While he was far less enamored of Roosevelt by 1940, Senator La Follette declared his support for a third term in the fall of 1940. Despite his distaste for the foreign policy views of both major candidates, he believed that "On the record as made by the candidates for President, the American way of life has a better opportunity of working out its destiny in the next four years under the administration of Franklin D. Roosevelt." Running for reelection as a Progressive on a platform of continued resistance to sending American soldiers overseas, he had little difficulty winning reelection. In return for his endorsement of the president, vice-presidential nominee Henry A. Wallace went to Madison to endorse La Follette by inference after White House consultation with the La Follette campaign organization. This presidential decision represented both the repudiation of the state Democratic organization and the continuing close, though somewhat strained, relationship between the two men. However, La Follette did not campaign for Roosevelt, partially explainable perhaps by his own reelection campaign.[37]

George Norris was the sole progressive Republican who had remained loyal to Franklin D. Roosevelt through all the crises of confidence in his leadership and policies. Norris had undergone a fundamental transformation in his views on America's role in world affairs as a result of the threat of fascism. While opposed to the military conscription bill and expressing unwillingness to support sending American soldiers overseas, he avoided issuing denunciations of the British and French and defended Roosevelt's actions. As early as August 1939, Norris indicated he thought Roosevelt might be compelled to become a candidate for a third term because of the obstructionism of Republican and Democratic reactionaries. While opposed in principle to a third term, Norris believed that the conditions confronting the nation, as well as the lack of viable alternative progressive candidates, made the third-term idea less objectionable. He was convinced Roosevelt had no ulterior motives, that he had no desire to increase his power and become a dictator, as some progressive Republicans and many conservatives believed. In a letter to Interior Secretary Harold Ickes in September 1939, Norris said that he could not comprehend the maliciousness and hatred that so many men in public life expressed toward the president.[38]

In December 1939, Norris issued a public statement urging Roosevelt to avoid declaring his intentions for 1940 until the necessary time for decision, and also to ignore the attacks of his enemies. Norris implied that Roosevelt was indispensable to the continued triumph of progressivism on the national level. In May 1940, Norris said he did not see how the president could refuse another nomination, with such unsettled foreign conditions. Believing Roosevelt had no intention of running for a third term before the Nazi attack on France, Norris now felt that the nation needed his leadership during this crucial moment in history. In a letter to a constituent in June, the Nebraska senator affirmed his belief that Roosevelt had no intention of drawing America into the war. He was effusive in his praise of the president's leadership, asserting:

> He has done so many good things. He has made a fight for the common people of America under circumstances so exasperating and so difficult that it seems to me, even though it means his life, he ought to stay in the position where he is now. When we look over the field and see the candidates who are seeking the nomination in one party or the other for the office of President, it seems to me that every citizen with a drop of liberal blood in his veins ought to be convinced that our one hope in this dilemma is Roosevelt.

Following the President's renomination, Norris defended it, stating that most of the people opposed to a third term were long-standing enemies of the president.[39]

In September, an independent progressive movement for the reelection of the president was formed, with Norris and Mayor LaGuardia of New York as its leaders. They pledged support to the president at a White House meeting, and Roosevelt responded that the nation must remain progressive if democracy was to survive. The committee, of which Norris was honorary chairman, had representatives in twenty-two states and aimed at attracting progressive support to the president in a manner similar to that of the progressive organizations in 1932 and 1936. However, none of the remaining progressive Republicans in the Senate (Capper, Johnson, La Follette, Nye, and Shipstead) endorsed the Norris committee. Only La Follette backed Roosevelt for reelection, while Willkie's candidacy gained support from the other members of the bloc with the added attraction of Charles McNary as the vice-presidential nominee.[40]

During the fall, Norris set out on an ambitious series of public appearances, despite his seventy-nine years. In his addresses, as well as in a lengthy Senate speech, Norris denounced Willkie, accusing him of loyalty to the power trusts, corporations, and monopolies. He emphasized the inexperience in government and the corporate background of the Republican nominee, contrasting it with the successes of Roosevelt and his New Deal programs during the previous eight years. However, the president proceeded to win reelection to a third term with about 55 percent of the popular vote, nearly a five million margin over Willkie. His victory seemed to be a further blow to isolationist sentiment, even though he had promised during the campaign that he would not send American soldiers overseas to fight in another war. The progressive Republican isolationists, although gloomy about the future of their struggle, remained determined to continue it.[41]

As the Battle of Britain continued, Prime Minister Winston Churchill wrote President Roosevelt in December 1940, describing the grave condition of his nation in the face of the Nazi air attacks. He requested from the United States more war supplies, via loans of money and leasing of equipment. The president, convinced the the British were fighting on the front line for American security, now drew up the concept of Lend-Lease, in order to give Great Britain the munitions it needed to combat Hitler. On December 29, in a fireside chat to the nation, Roosevelt told the American people that it was our duty to be "the great arsenal of democracy." A Lend-Lease bill, numbered H.R. 1776, was introduced into Congress on January 10, 1941.[42]

Hiram Johnson predicted during December that America would soon be in World War II. He commented: "Those in command of us are perfectly mad to be a part of the game. When it is propitious, from their point of view, they'll take us in." The Lend-Lease bill seemed to him, as well as all other progressive Republicans except McNary and Norris, an obvious but dangerous step toward war. Calling the legislation "monstrous," Johnson denied he was an appeaser of totalitarian states, but said he was unwilling to change the American form of government just to please the desires of the British. He added: "The bill presents squarely to Congress whether it shall create a dictatorship. . . . It is up to Congress now to determine whether our government shall be as ordained or become a member of the totalitarian States." The day before Roosevelt's third inauguration, Johnson wrote his son about the coming "coronation": "Damn this ceremony tomorrow. . . . This probably may be the last ceremony of the inauguration of a President that we'll ever have. It is quite within the bounds of possibility." The Californian again took the leadership of the progressive isolationist opposition, including Capper, La Follette, Nye, and Shipstead. In mid-February, plans were readied to promote amendments prohibiting the transfer of any part of the American navy to Great Britain and barring the use of American warships to convoy goods abroad. In a radio address, Johnson appealed for public support of the small Senate bloc, including the progressives, who were fighting the Lend-Lease proposal. He declared: "Our band is small but determined, and will fight to the end. We need your help. This is your fight. Our backs are against the wall."[43]

Arthur Capper wrote William Allen White, head of the leading interventionist organization but also a close friend, of his view that the Lend-Lease proposal "goes too far in surrendering the powers of Congress. I believe it comes pretty close to setting up a dictatorship." In two radio addresses and two Senate speeches, Capper argued that the legislation gave the president absolute control of American foreign policy, that Great Britain should not be regarded as our Maginot Line, and that the nation would pay a heavy price in blood, sweat, tears, taxes, and postwar depression if it engaged in the war. Henrik Shipstead delivered two Senate speeches and one radio address, in which he denounced the Lend-Lease bill as "a blank check upon the entire resources of our country to guarantee the military victory of one of the belligerents." He warned that American sovereignty would be subordinated to other nations' interests in the foreign war, and "we will pay the cost with our money, our resources, and the precious blood of American boys."[44]

La Follette denounced the bill as one that called for abdication of congressional powers and for the creation of a presidential dictatorship in foreign affairs. He thought this bill the most crucial foreign policy issue since the armed ship bill of March 1917, which his father had bitterly attacked. He wrote Supreme Court Justice Felix Frankfurter of his "concern for the ultimate survival of the democratic spirit here at home." In a fiery Senate speech, the Wisconsin senator contended that he was not a pacifist, that he was for defending America in the Western Hemisphere, but that he continued to oppose any attempt to make the world "safe for democracy." Great Britain was fighting for herself and her empire. America must prove that democracy could function at home before it commenced to police the world. La Follette solemnly stated that he would never give his vote for another "bloodbath" or for a move toward totalitarianism.[45]

Nye delivered at least eight speeches against Lend-Lease over the radio or at public gatherings, as well as about twelve hours of oratory in the Senate— more than any other legislator. Administration supporters accused him of encouraging a war psychology by continued statements that war was imminent if the legislation passed. His continued attacks on Great Britain as the world's leading aggressor caused many people to continue to speculate whether he was a Fascist, which he heatedly denied. With Sen. Burton Wheeler, he demanded that President Roosevelt ask the belligerent nations for a statement of their war aims, their conditions for peace, and "any and all secret treaties for disposition of territorial spoils."[46]

McNary and Norris were the only progressive Republicans to support Lend-Lease aid to Great Britain. McNary, although originally against it "because it grants extraordinary and total power to one person," voiced the hope for modifications that would permit him to support the president. When some changes were made in the final form, the Oregon senator voted for the bill. Norris approved of the principle of Lend-Lease legislation, but thought a time limit should be placed on the powers given to the president. In a radio address, he endorsed the legislation as a way to help the British win the war and avoid American commitment of its own men to the battlefields of Europe. He denounced the Axis powers for their lack of humanity and civilization, and vowed that "The defeat of Hitler is necessary, not only to preserve a peace-loving world, but to preserve our own happiness, and ultimately, our own existence." Admitting to being troubled by the possibility of war, which he still dreaded as much as he did in 1917, Norris said the situation had changed since that time, and America must risk the possibility of involvement to preserve sanity in the world. To calm the fears of many that the Lend-Lease bill authorized Roosevelt to order the army to Europe, he proposed amending the legislation with a denial of that belief, but the Senate defeated his proposal 52 to 39. Norris still voted for the bill because of his faith in the president.[47]

Before the roll call vote on the bill, Hiram Johnson proposed an amendment that funds be provided to send American soldiers overseas only in time of actual hostilities. This amendment was designed to carry out Roosevelt's campaign pledge that he would never send American youths to fight another war in Europe. Speaking with emotion and indignation, the California senator pleaded with his colleagues to keep true to this promise, declaring: "All you need to do is to stand up, to have the guts that God gave you, to have the nerve which should be in you, to have the decency which should actuate you.

Every man of you should have all of these characteristics in order that you may save from bloody graves the boys of America." At the conclusion of his comments, the Senate galleries broke into widespread applause. But the Johnson amendment was voted down 56 to 35, all of the progressive Republicans supporting Johnson except Norris. The Senate proceeded to pass the bill by a 60 to 31 vote on March 8, 1941.[48]

After this defeat, La Follette wrote Gen. Robert E. Wood, head of the America First Committee, that the isolationist bloc had been beaten because "The ties of party loyalty combined with some Republican support and terrific Administration pressure proved to be more than the opposition could overcome." He believed the struggle against Lend-Lease had been essential, and that it was not appropriate to give up the fight of keeping America out of war. Capper wrote Alf Landon of his belief that American troops would be sent to Europe within a few months. Along with La Follette, Nye, Shipstead, and Democrats Bennett Clark and Burton K. Wheeler, Capper again sponsored a war referendum amendment, which had no chance of passage but remained a symbol of the die-hard isolationist spirit that still existed.[49]

Although cognizant of the fact that they were involved in a struggle that was unlikely to succeed, the progressive Republican isolationists refused to abandon their cause of keeping America out of World War II. Henrik Shipstead, for instance, delivered a bitter personal attack on Roosevelt, comparing him to Hitler, Mussolini, and Stalin in his desire for absolute power. He criticized the American occupation of Iceland, which had not received congressional approval. La Follette wondered whether Roosevelt's Four Freedoms speech meant anything once Russia had become an ally of the western powers after the Nazi invasion in June 1941. Capper denounced the president's orders that American ships be convoyed and shoot at Italian or German vessels that threatened attack. Johnson challenged those who favored intervention in Europe to present a resolution for a declaration of war to the Congress. In a radio address under the auspices of the America First Committee, he said that Roosevelt "speaks with the confidence of a Hitler or a Mussolini," and that he "puts to blush even these two braggarts." He denounced Roosevelt for speaking continually of his aim of bringing the Four Freedoms to everyone in the world, declaring: "How he is going to do it is a deep, dark mystery, but he speaks as if it were easy of accomplishment and never gives a thought to the agony and the anguish and bloodletting." He termed the Atlantic Charter, announced after conferences between Churchill and Roosevelt off Newfoundland in August, a violation of the Constitution.[50]

Although these senators kept their names and views in the public spotlight, refusing to remain silent, none was as active or involved in controversy as Gerald P. Nye. During the spring and summer of 1941, he pursued, amidst much criticism, his denunciation of Roosevelt's foreign policy. He introduced legislation to prohibit convoys and to investigate the public opinion polls and the motion picture and radio industries, which he believed were acting as propagandists for the interventionist cause. At an America First rally, he named the heads of the eight major film companies and was immediately accused of anti-Semitism since most were Jewish. In September, at the opening session of hearings on the motion picture resolution, Nye denied he was anti-Jewish and pro-Nazi. These charges were made, he claimed, by Jews who "were feeding their persecution complexes to their own detriment." To show that he was not biased, he requested that the inquiry undertake a thorough study of pro-Nazi, pro-Fascist, and pro-Communist, as well as antitotalitarian, films.[51]

Probably Nye's most controversial public appearance was at the Steuben Society Dinner in New York on September 20. Before this German organization and a nationwide radio audience, he appealed for "all loyal Amercans" to oppose President Roosevelt's policy of aiding those who were fighting Nazi Germany. He accused interventionists of labeling loyal Americans, such as Charles Lindbergh, Burton Wheeler, and himself as anti-Semitic and pro-Nazi. This charge had been revived when, the day before, Nye agreed with a Lindbergh speech which alleged that the Jews were the major factor in the movement toward intervention in World War II. While Nye was speaking, various groups were picketing outside, and a heavy police detail was on duty. This became a common sight wherever Nye spoke, as his speeches inspired such strong passions.[52]

Once Roosevelt had ordered the convoying of American ships and given "shoot on sight" orders to the navy, he was confronted with the problem that the 1939 Neutrality Act prohibited the arming of American merchant vessels and their entry into war zones. With Iceland under American control and Roosevelt's evident desire to help the British merchant marine by sending American ships with Lend-Lease supplies, the president decided to request revision of the remaining sections of the neutrality legislation. The attacks on the American ships *Greer*, *Kearny*, and *Reuben James* during September and October 1941 helped to increase pressure on Congress to do his bidding.

The progressive isolationists united in opposition to the president's request. La Follette attacked repeal or modification of the neutrality law as another step toward war and a violation of Roosevelt's pledge to keep America out of the conflict. It was the equivalent of war on the installment plan, he said. The Wisconsin senator, along with ten other isolationists who included Johnson, Capper, and Nye, caucused on strategy, fully aware that theirs was a losing battle. On October 25, the Senate Foreign Relations Committee approved 13 to 10 a measure to repeal the 1939 law. The five progressive Republicans on the committee—Capper, Johnson, La Follette, Nye, and Shipstead—voted against the measure. As the meeting ended, Shipstead declared: "This is the last of the many steps taken in the last three years leading us into war. And it may be the final step. The subtle program of the war party stands barefaced before the world."[53]

Despite defeat in committee, the progressives used yet their last ounce of strength to condemn the measure in floor debate. Nye declared that America would be in a shooting war as soon as the neutrality legislation was repealed. La Follette called the impending vote one on war or peace, and he warned again that democracy could not flourish if the nation went to war. Capper asserted he could not join in support of a "nightmare" brought about by subterfuge and lies. Shipstead said the isolationists had been "loyal to the sovereign," the American people. They would never regret their stand for peace, the Minnesota senator said of himself and his colleagues. Finally, Hiram Johnson declared his love of his country and his sadness at its future. Calling himself an "emotional, old man" and warning the Senate that every member who voted to repeal the Neutrality Act would live to regret it to the last day of his life, he affirmed: "There are not many more years of service that I can render or for which I shall survive, but so long as I live, and am a sentient being I shall stand up just as an American, let the abuse be what it may, and fight as well as God has given me the ability to fight, with every fiber of my being for my country."[54]

The Senate proceeded to approve the repeal of sections 2, 3, and 6 of the 1939 Neutrality Act by a 50 to 37 margin. Charles McNary joined the other progressive Republicans, with the exception of George Norris, on the losing side. Within a month, the academic question of whether and when America would enter the war had been resolved by the Japanese attack on Pearl Harbor. So much attention had been paid to Fascist aggression in Europe that little thought of a Japanese threat to American property had been expressed. Within a few days of Pearl Harbor, America was at war with Japan, Germany, and Italy. All the progressives supported the declaration of war despite earlier statements that they would not do so under any circumstances. The Japanese attack in Hawaii had destroyed the isolationist spirit and cause, which was never to recover. The public image and reputation of the progressive Republican Senate bloc had been dealt a mortal blow. During the war years, through death and electoral defeat, the progressives suffered a fall from grace, and the crushing repudiation of the remaining bloc members after the war only served to show that western Republican progressivism had gone into permanent eclipse. The decline and fall of the progressive Republicans of the Midwest and Far West was indeed an indication of a vast change in the nation and its two major political parties.[55]

The story of the fortunes of the progressive Republicans during and after World War II is a sad one. With the rise of an internationalist spirit among the American people, the spokesmen for isolationism suffered a quick oblivion,

accused of having misled the country as to its safety from attack and the true
threat of fascism. The progressive Republicans would remain true to their
principles although under attack, refusing to recant their beliefs despite the
rapid withering of public esteem.

The two progressives who had shown internationalist leanings, Charles
McNary and George Norris, both died during 1944. McNary, still minority
leader at his death in February, had endorsed, in a public statement five
months earlier, the concept of an international organization to maintain
peace. Norris, victim of a strong conservative tide in Nebraska in the 1942
elections, suffered the only political defeat in his career when Republican
Kenneth Wherry won his seat in the Senate. Disillusioned over his forced
retirement by the voters, Norris isolated himself for a period of months from
public view. However, he came into the public spotlight again when he endorsed the resolution of Sen. Tom Connally of Texas calling for American
involvement in a new international peace-keeping organization. He approved
of President Roosevelt's handling of the war effort and declared that unless
some outstanding individual presented himself within the next year, he was
willing and eager to back the president for a fourth term in the White House.
During the last year of his life, Norris worked on his memoirs and issued a
statement of support for Roosevelt, indicating that a change in leadership
during the war "would be a mistake, a tragic mistake." On September 3rd,
the "gentle knight of American Democracy" was dead. The *New York
Times* declared in an editorial: "Probably no Senator in his time left a deeper
impress on a changing America. . . . He was uncompromising and incorrup-
tible."[56]

Of the five progressive Republican isolationists who remained in the Senate, only Arthur Capper left public office by his own decision. Reelected to
a fifth Senate term in 1942, he joined in support of the Connally Resolution in the fall of 1943, and he supported the establishment of the United
Nations at the end of the war. In 1948, Capper, now eighty-three years
old, decided to retire, his public reputation intact. While he had been an isolationist before Pearl Harbor, he had never been as vehement in his advocacy
of that viewpoint as the other four surviving progressives. His closer ties to
the party establishment had also helped, as had his switch to internationalism,
to preserve his seat in the Senate. He died in retirement in 1951.[57]

When the Senate voted on the Connally Resolution, Gerald Nye had joined
Capper and McNary in supporting it, while Hiram Johnson, Robert La
Follette, Jr., and Henrik Shipstead had cast three of the six dissenting votes.
But Nye had challenged the need for such a resolution. As the most controversial member of the Senate because of his strong isolationist views, Nye
faced a tough reelection campaign, and despite his obvious shift to the right
politically, in apparent agreement with his North Dakota constituents, he
lost his seat in the 1944 election. In his farewell address to the Senate, Nye

told his colleagues that they stood between the United States and another world war. He predicted a return to the old balance-of-power system in Europe and imperialism in Asia. The only way to keep out of a third world war, he warned, was "by minding our own business, keeping out of entangling alliances, developing our markets in this hemisphere and devoting our strength honestly and solely to the defense of our own territories." It was obvious that the North Dakota senator's views had not basically changed at all since 1941. He retired to private life, becoming more and more conservative in his political attitudes during the years up to his death in 1971.[58]

Hiram Johnson, aging and sickly during most of the war, had little participation in Senate activities, spending much time in the hospital. However, he was present to speak out and vote against the Connally Resolution in the fall of 1943. His voice full of emotion, the old, bitter progressive of bygone days declared: "God save the United States of America. God give to her all she should have. God preserve her in the days to come. I know what they will bring. I have been through such days. But God be good to us and permit us to resist and permit us to be the country we have ever been." He indicated that if he still had his former strength, he would have fought the Connally Resolution in committee and on the floor. After the war was over, Johnson, again seriously ill in the hospital, declared in a public statement his opposition to American membership in the United Nations, which had recently been created in San Francisco. A few weeks later, the cantankerous old progressive died, marking the end of an era. On the day of his death, the atomic bomb had been dropped on Hiroshima. American foreign policy would never be restored to Hiram Johnson's dream of isolationism. The New York Times wrote in an editorial: "He went down with his colors flying. The veteran isolationist died as the dust arose over Hiroshima and the myth of isolation was shattered into bits."[59]

Robert La Follette, Jr.'s fortunes sagged during the war. In March 1943, he warned against American involvement in an international organization until it was clear what kind of peace would be established after the war. In May 1944, he expressed concern over the failure of the allies to make a clear statement of their war aims. He was critical of Roosevelt and refused to commit himself to an endorsement of the president for a fourth term. The Wisconsin Progressive Party platform of 1944 contained La Follette's critical comments on Roosevelt and his handling of the war. Turner Catledge of the New York Times commented that La Follette had not abandoned his isolationist beliefs, and that his criticism of the president demonstrated that the twelve-year alliance between the New Deal and the Wisconsin Progressives was over. When the senator addressed the Progressive state convention, he called for a foreign policy based strictly upon America's national interests. He declared the New Deal a casualty of the war effort. Roosevelt had reneged on his New Deal promises and had permitted the war effort to be directed by the forces of "monopoly and reaction." La Follette demanded that American foreign policy be divorced from the "imperial designs of Mr. Churchill" and the "Soviet drive for power of Mr. Stalin." He called for more of the Four Freedoms, instead of the Four Horsemen—imperialism, spheres of influence, special privilege, and exploitation. His refusal to endorse Roosevelt caused his opponents to allege that he was trying to keep the support of the German and Polish blocs in Milwaukee for his upcoming reelection campaign in 1946. Never had the Progressive party been so divided as it was in 1944.[60]

After the war ended, La Follette delivered a three-hour speech attacking the United Nations organizational setup, accusing the Soviet Union of violating the Yalta agreements, and claiming that Prime Minister Churchill had been dogmatic and arrogant in his position on the British Empire. Criticizing the United Nations plan that one of the five major powers in the Security Council could veto military action against a peace breaker, he warned that the world was traveling the same road as after World War I. But despite his bitter attacks on the U.N., he voted for American membership.[61]

By 1946, the Wisconsin Progressive party organization had become a shambles. The Progressives had lost their hold over the state during the war, and La Follette sensed that this third party could no longer win elections, that he must take the Wisconsin Progressives back into his former home, the Republican party. Henry Wallace and other Democrats tried to convince La Follette to bring his progressive following into the Democratic party, but to no avail. On March 17, the party convention voted to end its twelve-year independent existence and to rejoin the Republicans. La Follette said the Democratic party organization in Wisconsin was too weak to act as a vehicle for the passage of progressive ideas. He now announced his candidacy for reelection to the Senate as a "progressive Republican." He would run, he declared, on his record of service to the people of his state and his promotion of liberal causes.[62]

La Follette was challenged for the Republican nomination by an obscure circuit court judge, Joseph R. McCarthy, who would later become anathema to liberals. Few political observers thought the Wisconsin senator was in trouble, as the family had been in public office since 1900. However, the senator, involved in formulating congressional reorganization legislation, did not come home to campaign until a few days before the primary. Conservative elements in the Republican party emphasized La Follette's abandonment of their organization in 1934, and many progressives were critical of his decision to join the Republicans again. These progressives abandoned La Follette and agreed to back the liberal Democratic candidate. Thus, the La Follette reign in national politics came to a sudden, sad conclusion. On Primary Day, McCarthy eked out a victory by about 5,000 votes and went on to win in November. La Follette had lost much of his urban, liberal, and labor support to Howard McMurray, the Democratic nominee. Had he agreed to run on the Democratic ticket, he would have gained the united support of liberals and labor and would have continued his career in the Senate. The *New York Times* thought La Follette's isolationist record had harmed him among many liberals who had been Roosevelt supporters, "Yet not many hats will be thrown in the air to celebrate the Senator's defeat, despite his isolationism. . . . Among the isolationist group, La Follette was the best of the lot. No demagogue, an able and industrious Senator, he was unfortunate in inheriting his international position from his father." La Follette never returned to the Senate, and died a suicide victim in 1953.[63]

Henrik Shipstead continued his campaign for isolationism during and after World War II. During the 1944 presidential campaign, the Minnesota senator attacked Roosevelt's conduct of foreign policy over the previous twelve years. He blamed the president for the outbreak of the war, saying that Europe had been at peace, Germany had not been a military threat, and Japan had not been America's archenemy when Roosevelt took office. The diplomatic and economic policies of the administration, he asserted, had helped these countries to become threats to the peace of the world, and American backing of Great Britain and France had led to bloodshed. Shipstead was one of only two senators (along with William Langer of North Dakota) to vote against the ratification of the U.N. charter in July 1945. His rabid isolationist spirit remained his keynote.[64]

Shipstead was an excellent target for internationalists when he ran for reelection in 1946. The Minnesota Republican party was headed by Harold Stassen, a leading presidential possibility and prominent spokesman for internationalism. Stassen proceeded to promote Gov. Edward Thye for the Senate nomination. After nearly three Senate terms as a Farmer-Laborite, Shipstead had rejoined the Republican party in the late 1930s. But, as with La Follette in Wisconsin, Republicans saw no reason to feel loyalty to an individual who had abandoned them earlier in his career. Shipstead's isolationist stand made him seem outdated and illogical. During the primary campaign, he made a virtue of his isolationism, appealing to German and Scandinavian voters to support him because he had opposed the U.N. charter, a point that he boasted about. But the polls showed he would be defeated, and on Primary Day the voters of Minnesota repudiated him. He lost by a landslide vote in both urban and rural areas, winning only about 40 percent of the votes statewide. The *New York Times* seemed pleased that the "unreconstructed isolationist" had been removed from the Senate. Shipstead returned to private life and died in 1960. With the removal from the political scene of La Follette and Shipstead during 1946, western Republican progressivism had expired.[65]

[11]

Progressive Republicans
and the New Deal: An Assessment

The progressive Republican Senate bloc had come into the 1930s with a reputation as one of the leading reform elements of the American political system. Its agitation for change and its specific ideas had served as an important vehicle for the transition from Hoover Republicanism to Franklin D. Roosevelt's New Deal. Since the bloc members played a role as forerunners of the New Deal, it would have been expected that they would contribute much to the success of the Roosevelt programs and that they would be consulted often and remain strong supporters of the administration. But instead, the progressive Republicans would fail to be as influential as they might have hoped, would abandon the New Deal early in the second term (with the major exception of George Norris and occasionally Robert La Follette, Jr.), would become part of the conservative coalition in Congress that would thwart a furtherance of domestic reform, and would (again with the major exception of Norris) bitterly and vehemently oppose the administration in foreign affairs. The result was that by the end of World War II, the surviving progressive Republicans of the Midwest and West had experienced a rapid decline in public esteem and were regarded in liberal circles as foolish, irresponsible reactionaries out of tune with their time.

How had this come about? A general explanation can be developed from the available evidence. It is obvious that principles, personalities, and politics all played key roles in the reaction of the progressive Republicans to the New Deal.

The progressives had been nurtured on a belief in the basic goodness of the small town, agrarian West. They had grown to manhood in an atmosphere of mistrust of the eastern moneyed interests, large cities, and the "new" immigrant groups. They feared economic centralization of power in the form of trusts, holding companies, and other types of monopoly because it represented a departure from the provincial America that they wished to preserve,

203

a nation where economic competition and opportunities had flourished. As believers in a truly representative government, they were concerned lest reactionary machine elements and their immigrant supporters gain more political strength. As promoters of greater federal involvement in the economic and social affairs of the farmer, worker, and consumer, they welcomed strong presidential leadership, but they did not intend a vast centralization of power in the hands of the chief executive at the expense of the legislative branch. As firm supporters of political isolationism from international power politics, they were determined to keep America out of foreign war at all cost, convinced that otherwise the nation could not remain democratic and virtuous.

As firm individualists with a reputation as mavericks, the progressives would be unable to work closely together for common goals, since their own ambitions and egos had to be nurtured. As politicians who had never had much respect for the Democratic party and had made conscious decisions to become Republicans (even though three of them—La Follette, Norris, and Shipstead—later declared themselves to be independent of the party), they could not cooperate with a Democratic president in his aim to make the Democrats the majority party of the nation. Considering that they were destined to deal with Franklin D. Roosevelt, a man of strong will and enhanced ego who tended to take their support for granted, it should not be surprising that the progressive Republicans became his bitter enemies.

The progressives were disturbed that the national government's reaction to the onset of the Great Depression was to preach the virtues of individualism and laissez faire, while people were in dire need. The national government's lack of concern for the average American pushed the progressives toward a leadership role in promoting aid for the unemployed through relief and public works. The individualism of the progressives and their minority position in the Republican party prevented any success in a challenge to President Hoover's renomination. But Franklin D. Roosevelt represented a hope to many, if only his good intentions were pursued when he reached the White House. In advance of that aim, all but two progressive Republicans abandoned Hoover in the 1932 presidential campaign.

Roosevelt's campaign to attract progressive support and his overtures to several bloc members to join his cabinet were good signs for the future, but these fiercely independent men refused to join the cabinet so that they might be free to criticize the administration when deemed necessary and help promote legislative passage of his program when it was progressive. Wanting the New Deal to succeed, the progressives tried to steer Roosevelt toward reforms that they favored. The First New Deal program of cooperation with big business, economic planning, and deflation therefore disturbed the progressives. Roosevelt, however, cultivated good relations with a number of the bloc members and always seemed willing to listen. The president encouraged them to give advice and finally agreed in 1935 to their entreaties for a large-scale reform program that became known as the Second New Deal.

However, at the same time that the western progressives were experiencing their greatest triumphs, Roosevelt's handling of Bronson Cutting's reelection contest and his decision to push the World Court issue, as well as his denunciation of the Supreme Court's decision on the NRA, troubled many of the progressives. They began to evaluate Roosevelt as a personally charming man who nonetheless possessed a streak of egotism and ruthlessness and was determined to pursue his goals despite opposition from the progressive bloc. By the election of 1936, many of the progressives, formerly willing to grant powers to the president to deal with the depression, had begun to express public and private concern about the leanings of the New Deal. The executive power had increased tremendously, government bureaucracy had multiplied, and federal spending had skyrocketed, with Roosevelt creating larger deficit budgets every year. The powerful role of the corrupt city machines and Southern conservatives in the New Deal coalition had become apparent, and the actions of the Democratic National Chairman and Postmaster General James Farley promoting political patronage for loyal Democrats had irritated the progressive Republicans, who believed that the Democratic party organization was hopelessly reactionary, even if the president was a liberal with basically good intentions.

With the beginning of Roosevelt's second term, progressive faith in the president disintegrated when, without consulting them, he promoted the "packing" of the Supreme Court. Although the progressives agreed with Roosevelt that the Court was an impediment to the New Deal, all but La Follette and Norris feared his drive for increased presidential power. This concern over a too powerful presidency shaped their reaction to the government reorganization bill and to Roosevelt's desire for discretionary authority over American neutrality policy. Their deep suspicion and mistrust of Roosevelt's intentions was magnified by the president's growing internationalist stand and his denunciation of Fascist aggression in Europe and Asia. Convinced that Roosevelt was extending the executive branch's power to the detriment of Congress, and the political power of the Democrats to the disadvantage of the Republicans, the majority of the western progressives rejected any further extension of government authority over labor and agriculture, which the legislation of 1938 promised, and they attacked WPA involvement in politics. The left-leaning western progressives, the proponents of a "New Deal" before Roosevelt's election to the White House, now had moved to the right of Roosevelt, and had allied themselves with the conservative critics of New Deal reforms in the Democratic and Republican parties.

Unwilling to trust Roosevelt any longer, the members of the bloc, with the exception of La Follette and Norris, became more and more reactionary.

Roosevelt had destroyed their dream of a progressive democracy in which the president and Congress, working together, promoted economic equality and opportunity and destroyed the influence of political bossism. Instead, Roosevelt had catered to certain interest groups—labor unions, Southern conservatives, city machines, and urban dwellers, including the large immigrant masses. He had upset the balance of power between the executive and legislative branches, and his probable legacy was a powerful Democratic party, controlled by groups alien to western progressive ideals, and an America perverted by international involvement and committed to war, violence, and bloodshed in its role as an "international policeman."

The final blow to western progressivism in the Republican party was repudiation by the voters, who no longer felt that these men represented their views on national and international issues. Their progressive backgrounds hurt them in their conservative constituencies, and their isolationism harmed them in an era of growing internationalist spirit. American politics had indeed changed.

To this discussion of progressive principles as a factor in rejection of the New Deal by most members of the bloc must be added the all-important consideration of personality. As a group, the progressives were supreme moralists, extremely self-righteous, stubborn, strong headed, and strong willed. As usually proves true for all reformers, they saw their views as the forces of light against the forces of darkness. As mavericks and individualists, they were also the leading prima donnas of American politics. It would have been a major feat for any president to retain their support throughout his years in office. These senators, after all, were all leaders, not followers. They would not hitch their futures to the whims of any president, let alone one another. Many were regarded at one time or another as possible candidates for the White House. Borah, Norris, and Johnson had been potential candidates for many years, and younger progressives La Follette, Nye, and Cutting were the subject of speculation during the New Deal years. Such legislators would never give up their cherished independence to advance the fortunes of a leader who possessed as much egotism as they did.

A personality conflict was inevitable between the progressives, believers in their own righteousness, and Roosevelt, believer in his own leadership. As long as he consulted with them, humored and flattered them, they would cooperate with his administration. Once he began, after the sweeping mandate of 1936, to ignore them and to expand the executive branch's power in domestic and foreign affairs, their alienation from and animosity toward the New Deal was not surprising. They saw their own importance dwindling under Roosevelt's administration, and this convinced many of them to bolt the New Deal.

The role of politics cannot be ignored. Elected originally to public office under the banner of the Republican party, the majority party in the nation since the Civil War, the progressives had never had much regard or respect for Democratic leadership on the national or local level. Although constant critics of the Republican party's ties with big business and finance, they also had no faith or trust in the city machines-Solid South coalition that dominated the Democratic party organization. While both parties' leadership were reactionary and corrupt, the progressives believed that the Republican party had better potential as a reform party because of the historical record under Abraham Lincoln and Theodore Roosevelt and the large number of state Republican reformers during the Progressive Era.

Roosevelt represented such an improvement over Hoover that many of the progressives were willing to support him and ignore party lines in their desire to help the nation. But their suspicion of the Democratic party organization never waned. None of those who endorsed Roosevelt in 1932 or 1936 accepted Roosevelt's offer to join the Democratic party. They insisted on remaining Republican or ran as Independents or Progressives. The president was separated from his party in progressive minds. As the movement of the New Dealers toward institutionalizing a new and dominant reform coalition became obvious, the progressive Republicans either attacked Roosevelt personally or worried about the reactionary Democrats who might succeed him in national office. The New Deal alliance of the Solid South, city machines, labor, ethnic groups, and blacks represented the death of the western, small town, agrarian domination over political and social reform. The guarantor, welfare state had replaced the broker state. The old-style reform politics was dead.

The only progressives who remained Roosevelt supporters in the late 1930's—La Follette and Norris—were also those with the weakest Republican ties and the most advanced progressive philosophies. Both had left the Republican party to run as Independents. Both were willing to adjust to the changing nature of American society and the industrialization and urbanization of the country. They were often to the left of Roosevelt, wanting the New Deal to go further toward advanced economic and social reform than Roosevelt was willing to or able to accomplish. Bronson Cutting was the only other progressive who seemed to have the potential to accept the new America, due to his New York background. His premature death made it impossible to judge what his ultimate attitude toward the New Deal might have been.

The Second World War confirmed the transformation in American politics. The Democratic party emerged from the war with its coalition intact. The Republican party was determined to repeal the New Deal legislation under Roosevelt's successor, Harry Truman. Although controlled in presidential election years by eastern interests who backed New York Gov. Thomas Dewey, the Republican party had much of its strength in those western states which had formerly elected progressive Republicans to public office. Now those states and others in the heartland of the country elected Republicans of a conservative or reactionary nature to succeed such prominent progressives as Robert La Follette, Jr., George Norris, Hiram Johnson, and Gerald Nye. Joseph McCarthy, Kenneth Wherry, William Knowland, and Milton Young were the new representatives of western Republicanism. The western states, long known for their insurgency, had now turned to the political right, condemning what they called the "eastern liberals" who controlled both major party organizations for the benefit of urban America. Actually, the liberal coalition that controlled the Democratic party in national politics was more broadly based, taking in the surviving insurgency of the Midwest. However, in coalition with southern Democrats, the western conservative Republicans were to prove very effective in bottling up further reform legislation during the late 1940s and 1950s. Only with the nomination of Barry Goldwater in 1964 did the western Republicans again gain control over the national apparatus of the Republican party.

The Democratic party, expanding its commitment to liberal reform under the leadership of Harry Truman, Adlai Stevenson, John Kennedy, and Lyndon Johnson, gained strength in those western states where progressive Republicans had once been the prominent reform spokesmen. The states that had sent Republican insurgents to the nation's capital in the years before 1940 were later to be represented by liberal Democrats such as Frank Church, Philip Hart, John Tunney, Alan Cranston, William Proxmire, Gaylord Nelson, George McGovern, Hubert Humphrey, and Walter Mondale. In Oregon, Wayne Morse, elected as a progressive Republican in 1944 as McNary's successor, soon became disenchanted and joined the Democratic party during the early 1950s. An examination of the Senate's membership since the early 1950s would indicate that western Republicans have been overwhelmingly conservative, with only a rare exception such as Thomas Kuchel, Mark Hatfield, or Charles Percy. The main reform sentiment in the Republican party came instead from eastern liberals, such as Jacob Javits, Clifford Case, Edward Brooke, Charles Mathias, and Richard Schweiker.

The decline and fall of the western progressive Republican bloc in the Senate was a sign that American politics had been basically transformed. The Democratic party and the New Deal had supplanted the Republicans as the party of advanced liberal reform. But the progressive philosophy, while outmoded and insufficient to meet the problems of an industrialized, urbanized world power, did leave a legacy to the nation, which may not have been appreciated at the time of its decline in the 1940s but seems valid today. The progressives had expressed concern over the growing power of the president in domestic and foreign affairs and his ability to take power away from Congress and to involve the nation in foreign wars. America, having experienced the wounds of Vietnam and Watergate, certainly can now appreciate this concern. The power that big business and public utilities exert over the American people today was seen as a growing evil by the progressive Republicans. The progressive bloc's commitment to morality in government stands out in stark contrast to the record of many present-day figures in American politics. The issues and controversies that the progressive Republicans engaged in during their long, distinguished careers in the Senate are still far from solution. The progressive agenda still awaits fulfillment.

Notes

BDAC   *Biographical Directory of the American Congress, 1774-1961*
CB   *Current Biography*
CR   *Congressional Record*
CS   *Common Sense*
CW   *Capper's Weekly*
DAB   *Dictionary of American Biography*
MSS   Manuscript collection
N   *The Nation*
NR   *The New Republic*
NYHT   *New York Herald Tribune*
NYT   *New York Times*
P   *The Progressive*
WP   *Washington Post*

CHAPTER 1

1. *NYT*, Nov. 9, 10, 1929; *NYHT*, Nov. 9, 10, 1929. Journalistic accounts of the "Sons of the Wild Jackass" include the following: Ray Tucker and Frederick R. Barkley, *Sons of the Wild Jackass* (Boston: L. C. Page & Co., 1932); Drew Pearson and Robert S. Allen, *Washington Merry-Go-Round* (New York: Horace Liveright, 1931), chap. 8, pp. 184-216; anonymous, "The Progressives of the Senate," *American Mercury* 16 (Apr. 1929): 385-93.

Personal interviews with the following people gave me much information on the "Sons of the Wild Jackass": Sen. Burton K. Wheeler, Mar. 25, 1971, Washington, D.C.; Sen. Gerald P. Nye, Mar. 30, 1971, Washington, D.C.; Benjamin V. Cohen, Mar. 31, 1971, Washington, D.C.; Raymond Moley, May 14, 1971, New York City. I also had correspondence with the following people who gave me useful information: Bruce Bliven, May 4, 1971; Alfred Bingham, May 7, 1971; Sen. Burton K. Wheeler, May 10, 1971; Gov. Alf M. Landon, May 25, 1971.

Secondary sources that gave me important background details include Leroy Ashby, *The Spearless Leader: Senator Borah and the Progressive Movement in the 1920's* (Urbana: University of Illinois Press, 1972), which deals with the entire progressive group although concentrating on Borah; Otis L. Graham, Jr., *An Encore For Reform: The Old Progressives and the New Deal* (New York: Oxford University Press, 1967); Russel B. Nye, *Midwestern Progressive Politics: A Historical Study of Its Origins and Development, 1870-1958* (New York: Harper & Row, 1959); and the three-volume *Age of*

Roosevelt by Arthur M. Schlesinger, Jr.: *The Crisis of the Old Order, 1919-1933, The Coming of the New Deal*, and *The Politics of Upheaval, 1935-1936* (Boston: Houghton Mifflin Co., 1956-1960). A useful doctoral dissertation on the "Sons of the Wild Jackass" during the Hoover administration is Hugh James Savage, "Political Independents of the Hoover Era: The Progressive Insurgents of the Senate," University of Illinois, 1961.

2. James Holt, *Congressional Insurgents and the Party System, 1909-1916* (Cambridge, Mass.: Harvard University Press, 1967).

3. Biographical material on Borah is abundant and includes BDAC (Washington, D.C.: U.S. Government Printing Office, 1961), p. 573; William E. Leuchtenburg's article in *DAB* (New York: Charles Scribner's Sons, 1958), suppl. 2, vol. 2, pp. 49-53; *CB* (New York: H. W. Wilson Co.), 1940, pp. 99-102; obituaries in *NYT, NYHT*, and *WP* for Jan. 20, 1940; Tucker and Barkley, *Sons of the Wild Jackass*, chap. 4, pp. 70-95; Pearson and Allen, *Washington Merry-Go-Round*, chap. 8, pp. 210-14; anonymous, "Progressives of the Senate," p. 393; Claudius O. Johnson, *Borah of Idaho* (New York and Toronto: Longmans, Green & Co., 1936); John Chalmers Vinson, *William E. Borah and the Outlawry of War* (Athens: University of Georgia Press, 1957); Marian C. McKenna, *Borah* (Ann Arbor: University of Michigan Press, 1961); Robert James Maddox, *William E. Borah and American Foreign Policy* (Baton Rouge: Louisiana State University Press, 1969); Ashby, *The Spearless Leader;* Orde S. Pinckney, "William E. Borah and the Republican Party, 1932-1940," Ph.D. diss., University of California, Berkeley, 1958. Numerous other dissertations and journal and magazine articles have been written on Borah over the years.

4. Biographical material on Norris is extensive and includes *BDAC*, p. 1393; Richard Lowitt's article in *DAB* (New York: Charles Scribner's Sons, 1973), suppl. 3, vol. 23, pp. 557-61; obituaries in *NYT, NYHT,* and *WP* for Sept. 3, 1944; Tucker and Barkley, *Sons of the Wild Jackass*, chap. 3, pp. 43-69; Pearson and Allen, *Washington Merry-Go-Round*, chap. 8, pp. 214-16; anonymous, "Progressives of the Senate," pp. 390-91; Richard L. Neuberger and Stephen B. Kahn, *Integrity: The Life of George W. Norris* (New York: Vanguard Press, 1937); Richard L. Neuberger, "A Politician Unafraid: George W. Norris, Senator from Nebraska," *Harper's Magazine*, Oct. 1936, pp. 540-50; Alfred Lief, *Democracy's Norris: The Biography of a Lonely Crusade* (New York: Stackpole Sons, 1939); Richard Lowitt, *George W. Norris: The Making of a Progressive, 1861-1912* (Syracuse, N.Y.: Syracuse University Press, 1963); idem, *George W. Norris: The Persistence of a Progressive, 1913-1933* (Urbana: University of Illinois Press, 1971); idem, *George W. Norris: The Triumph of a Progressive, 1933-1944* (Urbana: University of Illinois Press, 1978); Norman L. Zucker, *George W. Norris: Gentle Knight of American Democracy* (Urbana: University of Illinois Press, 1966). The Nebraska senator also wrote his memoirs shortly before his death: *Fighting Liberal: The Autobiography of George W. Norris* (New York: Macmillan Co., 1945).

5. Biographical material on Johnson is not extensive, considering the significant role he played in American politics. It includes *BDAC*, p. 1126; George E. Mowry's article in *DAB*, 1973, pp. 393-98; *CB*, 1941, pp. 439-41; obituaries in *NYT, NYHT*, and *WP* for Aug. 7, 1945; Tucker and Barkley, *Sons of the Wild Jackass*, chap. 5, pp. 96-122; George E. Mowry, *The California Progressives* (Berkeley and Los Angeles: University of California Press, 1951); Spencer C. Olin, Jr., *California's Prodigal Sons: Hiram Johnson and the Progressives, 1911-1917* (Berkeley and Los Angeles: University of California Press, 1968); Irving McKee, "The Background and Early Career of Hiram Warren Johnson, 1866-1910," *Pacific Historical Review* 19 (Feb. 1950): 17-30; Clifford B. Liljekvist, "Senator Hiram Johnson: His Career in California and National Politics," Ph.D. diss., University of Southern California, 1953; Richard Coke Lower, "Hiram Johnson and the Progressive Denouement, 1910-20," Ph.D. diss., University of California, Berke-

ley, 1969; Peter Gerard Boyle, "The Study of an Isolationist: Hiram Johnson," Ph.D. diss., University of California, Los Angeles, 1970; Howard A. DeWitt, "Hiram W. Johnson and American Foreign Policy, 1917-1941," Ph.D. diss., University of Arizona, 1972.

6. Biographical material on McNary is limited and includes *BDAC*, p. 1314; Earl Pomeroy's article in *DAB*, 1973, pp. 496-97; *CB*, 1940, pp. 542-44; obituaries in *NYT*, *NYHT*, and *WP* for Feb. 26, 1944; Walter K. Roberts, "The Political Career of Charles Linza McNary, 1924-1944," Ph.D. diss., University of North Carolina, 1954; Roger Taylor Johnson, "Charles L. McNary and the Republican Party During Prosperity and Depression," Ph.D. diss., University of Wisconsin, 1967.

7. Biographical material on Capper is limited and includes *BDAC*, p. 660; Homer E. Socolofsky's article in *DAB* (New York: Charles Scribner's Sons, 1977), suppl. 5, vol. 25, pp. 100-101; *CB*, 1946, pp. 91-93; obituaries in *NYT*, *NYHT*, and *WP* for Dec. 20, 1951; Homer E. Socolofsky, *Arthur Capper: Publisher, Politician, and Philanthropist* (Lawrence: University of Kansas Press, 1962); article on Capper by William Allen White in *Kansas City Star*, Apr. 22, 1942, published in *CR*, Appendix, Apr. 27, 1942, pp. 1559-60.

8. Biographical material on Norbeck is limited and includes *BDAC*, pp. 1392-93; Gilbert C. Fite's article in *DAB*, 1958, pp. 491-92; obituaries in *NYT*, *NYHT*, and *WP* for Dec. 21, 1936; Gilbert C. Fite, *Peter Norbeck: Prairie Statesman* (Columbia: University of Missouri Press, 1948).

9. Biographical material on Couzens is adequate and includes *BDAC*, p. 742; Harry Barnard's article in *DAB*, 1958, pp. 125-27; obituaries in *NYT*, *NYHT*, and *WP* for Oct. 23, 1936; Tucker and Barkley, *Sons of the Wild Jackass*, chap. 10, pp. 221-44; Harry Barnard, *Independent Man: The Life of Senator James Couzens* (New York: Charles Scribner's Sons, 1958).

10. Biographical material on Frazier is extremely limited and includes *BDAC*, p. 913; Theordore Saloutos's article in *DAB* (New York: Charles Scribner's Sons, 1974), suppl. 4, vol. 24, pp. 308-9; obituaries in *NYT, NYHT, WP*, and the *Bismarck (N.D.) Tribune* for Jan. 13, 1947; Robert L. Morlan, *Political Prairie Fire: The Non Partisan League, 1915-1922* (Minneapolis: University of Minnesota Press, 1955); George Creel, "The Old Homesteader," *Collier's*, Oct. 3, 1936, p. 22; Pearson and Allen, *Washington Merry-Go-Round*, chap. 8, p. 203; anonymous, "Progressives of the Senate," pp. 389-90; two-page memorandum on Frazier's career in Philip La Follette MSS, State Historical Society of Wisconsin.

11. Biographical material on Shipstead is limited and includes *BDAC*, p. 1596; obituaries in *NYT*, *NYHT*, and *WP* for June 27, 1960; Martin Ross, *Shipstead of Minnesota* (Chicago: Packard & Co., 1940); Tucker and Barkley, *Sons of the Wild Jackass*, chap. 8, pp. 171-95; Pearson and Allen, *Washington Merry-Go-Round*, chap. 8, pp. 206-9; anonymous, "Progressives of the Senate," pp. 391-93; Sister Mary Rene Lorentz, "Henrik Shipstead, Minnesota Independent, 1923-1946," Ph.D. diss., Catholic University of America, 1963; two long memoranda on Shipstead's background and career in the Shipstead MSS, Minnesota Historical Society.

12. Biographical material on La Follette is quite extensive and includes *BDAC*, p. 1184; Roger T. Johnson's article in *DAB*, 1977, pp. 403-4; *CB*, 1944, pp. 368-72; obituaries in *NYT*, *NYHT*, and *WP* for Feb. 25, 1953; Tucker and Barkley, *Sons of the Wild Jackass*, chap. 7, pp. 148-70; Pearson and Allen, *Washington Merry-Go-Round*, chap. 8, pp. 190-95; anonymous, "Progressives of the Senate," pp. 386-88; Edward N. Doan, *The La Follettes and the Wisconsin Idea* (New York and Toronto: Rinehart and Co., 1947); Roger T. Johnson, *Robert M. La Follette, Jr. and the Decline of the Progressive Party in Wisconsin* (Madison: State Historical Society of Wisconsin, 1964); Jerold S. Auerbach, *Labor and Liberty: The La Follette Committee and the New Deal* (Indianapolis: Bobbs-Merrill, 1966); Patrick J. Maney, *"Young Bob" La Follette: A Biography of*

Robert M. La Follette, Jr., 1895-1953 (Columbia: University of Missouri Press, 1978); Mauritz A. Hallgren, "Young Bob La Follette," *N*, Mar. 4, 1931, pp. 235-37; Oswald Garrison Villard, "Issues and Men: Robert M. La Follette, Jr.," ibid., Aug. 8, 1934, p. 147; Francis Brown, "La Follette: Ten Years a Senator," *Current History* 42 (Aug. 1935): 475-80; Donald Young, ed., *Adventure in Politics: The Memoirs of Philip La Follette* (New York: Holt, Rinehart & Winston, 1970); Theodore Rosenof, "The Ideology of Senator Robert M. La Follette, Jr.," M.A. thesis, University of Wisconsin, 1966; Alan E. Kent, "Portrait in Isolationism: The La Follettes and Foreign Policy," Ph.D. diss., University of Wisconsin, 1957; personal interviews with Morris H. Rubin and Mrs. Isen (Philip F.) La Follette, Aug. 6, 1970, both in Madison, Wisconsin. There are a number of journal and magazine articles on the Progressive party of Wisconsin and the National Progressives of America, as well as two dissertations on the Progressive party, cited elsewhere in the text.

13. Biographical material on Nye is quite extensive and includes *BDAC*, p. 1397; *CB*, 1941, pp. 618-21; obituaries in *NYT* and *WP* for July 19, 1971; Tucker and Barkley, *Sons of the Wild Jackass*, chap. 13, pp. 292-315; Pearson and Allen, *Washington Merry-Go-Round*, chap. 8, pp. 197-200; anonymous, "Progressives of the Senate," p. 389; Wayne S. Cole, *Senator Gerald P. Nye and American Foreign Relations* (Minneapolis: University of Minnesota Press, 1962); John E. Wiltz, *In Search of Peace: The Senate Munitions Inquiry, 1934-1936* (Baton Rouge: Louisiana State University Press, 1963); Francis Brown, "The Crusading Mr. Nye," *Current History* 41 (Feb. 1935): 521-27; Daniel Rylance, "A Controversial Career: Gerald P. Nye, 1925-46," *North Dakota Quarterly* 36 (Winter 1968): 5-19; personal interview with Sen. Nye, Mar. 30, 1971, Washington, D.C.

14. Biographical material on Cutting is quite good, considering his short career in the Senate. It includes *BDAC*, p. 770; the article by Charles O. Paullin in *DAB*, 1958, pp. 215-16; obituaries in *NYT, NYHT, WP*, and the *St. Louis Post-Dispatch* for May 7, 1935; Tucker and Barkley, *Sons of the Wild Jackass*, chap. 9, pp. 196-220; Pearson and Allen, *Washington Merry-Go-Round*, chap. 8, pp. 204-6; Patricia Cadigan Armstrong, *A Portrait of Bronson Cutting through His Papers, 1910-27* (Albuquerque: Division of Research, Department of Government, University of New Mexico, June 1959); Gustav Leonard Seligmann, Jr., "The Political Career of Senator Bronson M. Cutting," Ph.D. diss., University of Arizona, 1967; Robert W. Larson, "The Profile of a New Mexico Progressive, Bronson M. Cutting," *New Mexico Historical Review* 45 (July 1970): 233-34.

15. T.R.B., "Washington Notes," *NR*, Feb. 20, 1929, pp. 15-16.

16. Anonymous, "Progressives of the Senate," pp. 385-86.

17. Tucker and Barkley, *Sons of the Wild Jackass*, chap. 1, p. 8; Pearson and Allen, *Washington Merry-Go-Round*, chap. 8, pp. 184-87.

CHAPTER 2

1. Hiram Johnson to Hiram Johnson, Jr., Feb. 9, 1929, Johnson to his Boys, Feb. 23, Mar. 5, 1929, Hiram Johnson MSS, Bancroft Library, University of California, Berkeley.

2. Hiram Johnson to his Boys, Oct. 26, 1929, Johnson to Hiram Johnson, Jr., Nov. 16, 23, 30, 1929, Johnson MSS.

3. *NYT*, Nov. 23, 1930; *P*, Dec. 6, 13, 20, 27, 1930; "A Progressive Program," *N*, Dec. 3, 1930, p. 598.

4. *CR*, Dec. 3, 1930, p. 80; Dec. 16, 1930, pp. 802-3, 807; Feb. 3, 1931, p. 3856. The major works dealing with President Hoover's relations with Congress and the progressive bloc specifically are: Jordan A. Schwarz, *The Interregnum of Despair: Hoover, Congress, and the Depression* (Urbana: University of Illinois Press, 1970), and Hugh James Savage, "Political Independents of the Hoover Era: The Progressive Insurgents of the Senate," Ph.D. diss., University of Illinois, 1961.

5. Robert La Follette, Jr., to Fola La Follette, Nov. 4, 1930, La Follette Family MSS, Manuscript Division, Library of Congress; *CR*, Dec. 9, 1930, p. 426.

6. *CR*, Dec. 15, 1930, pp. 703, 707; *NYT*, Dec. 15, 16, 1930.

7. *CR*, Dec. 16, 1930, p. 859; Dec. 20, 1930, pp. 1173-1207; *NYT*, Dec. 21, 1930.

8. *NYT*, Jan. 5, 1931; *CR*, Jan. 9, 1931, pp. 1662-1711; *NYT*, Jan. 17, 1931.

9. *CR*, Jan. 14, 1931, pp. 2140-43; Feb. 2, 1931, pp. 3759-60; *NYT*, Feb. 3, 1931.

10. *CR*, Feb. 7, 1931, pp. 4229-30; *NYT*, Feb. 8, 11, 1931.

11. *NYT*, Feb. 15, 1931.

12. Hiram Johnson to Hiram Johnson, Jr., Feb. 15, 1931, Johnson MSS.

13. *CR*, Feb. 20, 1931, pp. 5462-63; Feb. 26, 1931, p. 6100; *NYT*, Mar. 1, 1931.

14. For background on the League For Independent Political Action, see the following: Donald R. McCoy, *Angry Voices: Left-Of-Center Politics in the New Deal Era* (Lawrence: University of Kansas Press, 1958); Karel Denis Bicha, "Liberalism Frustrated: The League For Independent Political Action," *Mid-America* 48 (Jan. 1966): 19-28; R. Alan Lawson, *The Failure of Independent Liberalism, 1930-1941* (New York: G. P. Putnam's Sons, 1971).

15. John Dewey to George Norris, Dec. 23, 1930, George Norris MSS, Manuscript Division, Library of Congress; *NYT*, Dec. 26, 1930.

16. George Norris to John Dewey, Dec. 27, 1930, Norris MSS; *NYT*, Dec. 27, 1930; *NYHT*, Dec. 27, 1930; *P*, Jan. 3, 1931.

17. *NYT*, Dec. 29, 1930; *NYHT*, Dec. 29, 1930.

18. *NYT*, Jan. 1, 1931; "The Need For a New Party," *NR*, Jan. 7, 1931, pp. 203-4; "Toward A New Party," *N*, Jan. 14, 1931, p. 32.

19. Form letter invitation to Progressive Conference, Feb. 25, 1931, Edward Costigan MSS, Western Historical Collections, University of Colorado, Boulder; *NYT*, Mar. 3, 1931; *NYHT*, Mar. 3, 1931; *P*, Mar. 7, 1931.

20. *NYT*, Mar. 8, 1931.

21. Progressive Conference lists, Costigan and Norris MSS; *NYT*, Mar. 9, 12, 1931; *NYHT*, Mar. 9, 12, 1931; Hiram Johnson to Harold Ickes, Mar. 8, 1931, Johnson MSS (also in Harold Ickes MSS, Manuscript Division, Library of Congress); *NYHT*, Mar. 11, 1931.

22. *Proceedings of a Conference of Progressives* (Washington, 1931), and other materials in Costigan and Norris MSS.

23. *NYT*, Mar. 10, 11, 12, 1931; *NYHT*, Mar. 10, 11, 12, 1931; *Proceedings of a Conference of Progressives*.

24. *NYT*, Mar. 13, 1931; *NYHT*, Mar. 13, 1931; *Proceedings of a Conference of Progressives*, and other materials in Costigan and Norris MSS.

25. *NYT*, Mar. 12, 1931; *St. Louis Post-Dispatch*, Mar. 11, 1931; *New York World Telegram*, Mar. 13, 1931.

26. "The Progressive Conference," *NR*, Mar. 25, 1931, pp. 137-39; "Progressivism Awakes," *N*, Mar. 25, 1931, p. 316; Mauritz A. Hallgren, "Progressives Turn to the Left," ibid., pp. 320-21; *The New Leader*, Mar. 21, 1931.

27. *NYT*, Mar. 14, 1931; *NYHT*, Mar. 14, 1931; *NYT*, Mar. 15, 1931.

28. *Washington Evening Star*, Mar. 15, 1931; *NYT*, Mar. 16, 1931.

29. *NYT*, Mar. 17, 1931; T.R.B., "Washington Notes," *NR*, Apr. 1, 1931, pp. 181-82.

30. *NYT*, Mar. 8, 22, 1931; Robert La Follette, Jr., to his mother and sister, Apr. 14, 1931, La Follette Family MSS; *NYT*, Apr. 15, 24, 27, 1931.

31. *NYT*, May 22, 24, 1931; Robert La Follette, Jr., to Fola and George Middleton, May 15, 1931, La Follette Family MSS.

32. *NYT*, May 26, 1931; George Norris to Fred S. Hunter of the *Omaha Bee-News*, June 11, 1931, Norris MSS.

33. *P*, June 20, 1931; *NYT*, Aug. 5, 1931; Charles McNary to James Couzens, Aug. 5, 1931, Couzens to McNary, Aug. 12, 1931, James Couzens MSS, Manuscript Division, Library of Congress; *NYT*, Aug. 23, 1931; Couzens to Robert Klinkhardt, Sept. 2, 1931, Couzens MSS.

34. *NYT*, Sept. 6, 8, 1931; William Borah to Herbert Bayard Swope, Sept. 10, 1931, William Borah MSS, Manuscript Division, Library of Congress.

35. Robert La Follette, Jr., "President Hoover's Record: IV: The President and Unemployment," *N*, July 15, 1931, pp. 61-63; *P*, Aug. 8, 1931; *NYT*, Oct. 7, 1931.

36. Arthur Capper to Herbert Hoover, Nov. 6, 1930 and June 1, 1931, Herbert Hoover MSS, Herbert Hoover Presidential Library, West Branch, Iowa.

37. Arthur Capper to William Allen White, Sept. 15, 1931, William Allen White MSS, Manuscript Division, Library of Congress; Capper to Hoover, Dec. 31, 1931, Hoover MSS.

38. T.R.B., "Washington Notes," *NR*, Oct. 21, 1931, p. 262, and Nov. 11, 1931, pp. 351-52.

39. *NYT*, Nov. 24, Dec. 20, 1931.

40. Ibid., Dec. 23, 1931; *CR*, Dec. 22, 1931, pp. 1070, 1126-29; *P*, Dec. 26, 1931; "The Week," *NR*, Jan. 6, 1932, p. 198.

41. *CR*, Jan. 5, 1932, pp. 1292-93; Jan. 12, 1932, pp. 1760-63; *NYT*, Jan. 12, 1932; *CR*, Jan. 15, 1932, p. 1997; *NYT*, Jan. 22, 1932; Robert La Follette, Jr., to Fola and George Middleton, Dec. 30, 1931, La Follette Family MSS.

42. *NYT*, Feb. 1, 2, 1932; *CR*, Feb. 2, 1932, pp. 3068-95; Robert La Follette, Jr., to Fola and George Middleton, Feb. 5, 1932, La Follette Family MSS.

43. *CR*, Feb. 10, 1932, pp. 3666-73; Feb. 12, 1932, pp. 3810-13; *NYT*, Feb. 11, 13, 1932.

44. *CR*, Feb. 11, 1932, pp. 3756-57; Feb. 16, 1932, pp. 4018-21.

45. *CR*, Feb. 16, 1932, p. 4052; *NYT*, Feb. 17, 1932; *P*, Feb. 20, 1932; Robert La Follette, Jr., to Fola and George Middleton, Feb. 19, 1932, La Follette Family MSS.

46. *NYT*, May 19, 23, 24, 31, 1932; *CR*, May 23, 1932, pp. 10919-23; May 30, 1932, p. 11538.

47. *NYT*, June 11, 1932; *CR*, June 10, 1932, pp. 12534-35.

48. *NYT*, June 19, 1932; *CR*, June 22, 1932, pp. 13674-90; *NYT*, July 10, 1932.

49. *CR*, Dec. 17, 1931, p. 670; Feb. 23, 1932, p. 4489; May 26, 1932, p. 11262; June 4, 1932, p. 11948; "The Week," *N*, March 16, 1932, p. 297.

CHAPTER 3

1. *NYT*, Nov. 23, 1930, Mar. 17, May 3, 1931.

2. Ibid., May 31, June 2, 3, 1931; *NYHT*, June 2, 1931. On Pinchot in 1932, see Martin N. McGeary, *Gifford Pinchot: Forester-Politician* (Princeton, N.J.: Princeton University Press, 1960).

3. *NYT*, Oct. 21, Dec. 30, 1931.

4. Harold Ickes form letter, Mar. 14, 1932, Gifford Pinchot MSS, Manuscript Division, Library of Congress; *NYT*, Mar. 23, 1932; Ickes to William Allen White, Mar. 18, 1932, William Allen White MSS, Manuscript Division, Library of Congress.

5. Harold Ickes to Gifford Pinchot, Mar. 23, 1932, Pinchot to Ickes, May 3, 1932, Ickes to Pinchot, May 7, 1932, Pinchot MSS.

6. *NYT*, May 24, Sept. 14, 1931; *NYHT*, Sept. 14, 1931.

7. *NYT*, Oct. 5, Nov. 1, 1931, Jan. 14, Feb. 26, 1932.

8. Ibid., Nov. 10, 1931; George Norris to Arthur G. Wray, Feb. 4, 1932, Norris to Kenneth Harlan, Mar. 29, 1932, George Norris MSS, Manuscript Division, Library of Congress.

9. Harold Ickes to Hiram Johnson, June 19, 1931, Hiram Johnson MSS, Bancroft Library, University of California, Berkeley, and Harold Ickes MSS, Manuscript Division, Library of Congress. On Johnson in 1932, see Marty Hamilton, "Bull Moose Plays an Encore: Hiram Johnson and the Presidential Campaign of 1932," *California Historical Society Quarterly* 41 (Sept. 1962): 211-21. On Ickes's attempt to persuade Johnson to run, see Harold Ickes, *The Autobiography of a Curmudgeon* (New York: Reynal & Hitchcock, 1943).

10. Harold Ickes to Hiram Johnson, Nov. 5, 1931, Johnson MSS; Ickes to Johnson, Nov. 20, 1931, Johnson and Ickes MSS; Johnson to Ickes, Nov. 23, 30, 1931, Ickes MSS.

11. *NYT*, Nov. 20, 1931.

12. Harold Ickes to Hiram Johnson, Dec. 7, 1931, Ickes and Johnson MSS; Ickes to Johnson, Dec. 11, 14, 23, 1931, Johnson to his Boys, Dec. 27, 1931, Johnson MSS; Johnson to Ickes, Dec. 28, 1931, Johnson and Ickes MSS.

13. Hiram Johnson to his Boys, Jan. 9, 18, 1932, Johnson MSS; Bronson Cutting to Harold Ickes, Jan. 21, 1932, Ickes MSS.

14. Harold Ickes to Mrs. Hiram Johnson, Jan. 24, 1932, Ickes MSS; Ickes to Hiram Johnson, Jan. 28, 1932, Johnson MSS; Ickes to Johnson, Jan. 29, 1932, Johnson and Ickes MSS; Ickes to Johnson, Feb. 8, 1932, Johnson MSS; Bronson Cutting to Ickes, Jan. 29, 1932, Ickes MSS.

15. Hiram Johnson to Charles K. McClatchy, Feb. 2, 1932, Johnson MSS; *NYT*, Jan. 14, Feb. 13, 1932; Johnson to Harold Ickes, Feb. 13, 1932, Johnson MSS.

16. *NYT*, Feb. 26, 1932.

17. Ibid., May 6, 1932.

18. Ibid., Sept. 9, 1931; Hiram Johnson to Charles K. McClatchy, Feb. 14, 1932, Johnson to his Boys, April 17, May 1, 1932, Johnson MSS.

19. *NYT*, March 22, 28, 1932.

20. Ibid., May 24, 31, June 16, 21, 1932; *P*, May 28, June 25, 1932.

21. Hiram Johnson to Hiram Johnson, Jr., July 3, 1932, Johnson to Charles K. McClatchy, July 3, 1932, Johnson MSS; *NYT*, July 5, 3, 1932; *NYHT*, July 3, 1932; *NYT*, June 15, 1932.

22. Speech of Arthur Capper, June 14, 1932, Arthur Capper Papers, Kansas State Historical Society.

23. *P*, July 9, 1932.

24. *NYT*, Sept. 23, 24, 1932; *NYHT*, Sept. 23, 24, 1932.

25. *NYT*, Sept. 28, 25, 1932; *NYHT*, Sept. 28, 1932; *Santa Fe New Mexican*, Sept. 27, 24, 1932.

26. *NYT*, Sept. 29, 1932; *NYHT*, Sept. 29, 1932.

27. Harold Ickes to Hiram Johnson, Apr. 30, 1932, Johnson MSS.

28. Eleven-page memorandum on Formation of the National Progressive League, Frank P. Walsh MSS, Manuscript Division, New York Public Library; George Norris to Basil Manly, Sept. 1, 1932, Walsh and Norris MSS.

29. Memo on formation of National Progressive League and typed press release for morning papers of Sept. 26, 1932, Walsh MSS.

30. *NYT*, Sept. 26, 1932; *NYHT*, Sept. 26, 1932; typed carbon list of national committee members of National Progressive League, Walsh MSS.

31. *NYT*, Sept. 27, 1932; *P*, Oct. 1, 1932; T.R.B., "Washington Notes," *NR*, Oct. 12, 1932, pp. 232-33.

32. Memo on formation of National Progressive League, Walsh MSS.

33. Ibid.

34. Ibid.

35. *NYT*, Oct. 13, 15, 1932; *NYHT*, Oct. 15, 1932; Hiram Johnson to representatives of seventy southern California newspapers, Oct. 13, 1932, Franklin D. Roosevelt MSS, Roosevelt Presidential Library.

36. *NYT*, Oct. 29, Nov. 3, 5, 1932; *NYHT*, Oct. 29, Nov. 5, 1932.

37. Hiram Johnson to Peter Norbeck, Oct. 3, 1932, Peter Norbeck MSS, Western Historical Manuscripts Collection, University of Missouri; Johnson to Charles McNary, Oct. 7, 1932, Charles McNary MSS, Manuscript Division, Library of Congress; Johnson to Bronson Cutting, Oct. 18, 1932, Bronson Cutting MSS, Manuscript Division, Library of Congress.

38. Bronson Cutting to his mother, Oct. 5, 10, 21, 1932, Cutting MSS; *Santa Fe New Mexican*, Oct. 21, 1932; typed press release on Cutting support of Roosevelt, Walsh MSS.

39. *NYT*, Oct. 27, Nov. 7, 1932; *NYHT*, Oct. 27, 1932; *Santa Fe New Mexican*, Oct. 26, Nov. 7, 1932.

40. Robert La Follette, Jr., to Bronson Cutting, Oct. 1, 1932, La Follette Family MSS, Manuscript Division, Library of Congress.

41. *NYT*, Oct. 20, 25, 1932; *NYHT*, Oct. 20, 25, 1932; *P*, Oct. 22, 1932.

42. Memo on Formation of National Progressive League, Walsh MSS; copies of Norris campaign speeches in Norris MSS.

43. *Bismarck (N.D.) Tribune*, Sept. 29, 1932; *NYT*, Nov. 7, 1932; typed carbon list of national committee members of National Progressive League, Walsh MSS.

44. *NYT*, Aug. 3, 1932.

45. Arthur Vandenberg to William Borah, Aug. 23, 1932, Arthur Vandenberg MSS, Bentley Library, University of Michigan.

46. Vandenberg to Borah, Oct. 21, 1932, Borah to Alfred J. Dunn, Oct. 2, 1932, William Borah MSS, Manuscript Division, Library of Congress.

47. *NYT*, Oct. 27, Nov. 7, 1932; William Borah to Walter Lippmann, Nov. 9, 1932, Borah MSS.

48. Gerald Nye to George Norris, Oct. 5, 1932, Norris MSS; *Bismarck (N.D.) Tribune*, Oct. 19, 25, 1932; personal interview with Senator Nye, Washington, D.C., Mar. 30, 1971.

49. Arthur Vandenberg to James Couzens, Sept. 22, 1932, Donald Richberg to Couzens, Oct. 11, 1932, John Carson to Couzens, Oct. 13, 1932, Couzens to Vandenberg, Sept. 26, 1932, Couzens to John Carson, Oct. 1, 17, 1932, Couzens to Richberg, Oct. 12, 1932, James Couzens MSS, Manuscript Division, Library of Congress.

50. *NYT*, Oct. 23, 1932.

51. Peter Norbeck to W. R. Ronald, July 11, 1932, Peter Norbeck MSS, University of South Dakota; *Sioux Falls (S.D.) Daily Argus-Leader*, Oct. 8, 24, 1932.

52. Speeches of Charles McNary, Oct. 31, Nov. 1, 1932, Charles McNary MSS; *NYT*, Nov. 2, 1932.

53. *NYT*, Sept. 27, 1932; *Topeka (Kan.) Daily Capital*, Sept. 27, 28, Oct. 8, 19, Nov. 2, 8, 1932; *NYT*, Nov. 8, 1932; *CW*, Sept. 24, Oct. 1, 15, 22, Nov. 5, 1932; Arthur Capper to William Borah, Sept. 30, 1932, Borah MSS.

CHAPTER 4

1. *NYT*, Nov. 10, 30, Dec. 9, 1932; *P*, Dec. 10, 1932; Hiram Johnson to Charles K. McClatchy, Dec. 4, 1932, Hiram Johnson MSS, Bancroft Library, University of California, Berkeley.
2. George Norris to Bertrand V. Tibbels, Dec. 27, 1932, George Norris MSS, Manuscript Division, Library of Congress; Franklin D. Roosevelt to Philip La Follette, Nov. 19, 1932, P. La Follette MSS, State Historical Society of Wisconsin; Roosevelt to Robert La Follette, Jr., Nov. 19, 1932, La Follette Family MSS, Manuscript Division, Library of Congress; *P*, Nov. 12, 19, 1932.
3. Bronson Cutting to Philip La Follette, Nov. 10, 1932, P. La Follette MSS; Cutting to his mother, Nov. 11, 1932, Cutting to Clara D. True, Nov. 19, 1932, Bronson Cutting MSS, Manuscript Division, Library of Congress.
4. *CW*, Dec. 3, 1932; *Capper's Farmer*, Feb. 1933. See also *CW* editorials for Nov. 12, 26, 1932, and *Capper's Farmer* editorial for Jan. 1933; Franklin D. Roosevelt to Arthur Capper, Dec. 22, 1932, Arthur Capper MSS, Kansas State Historical Society; Charles McNary to John H. McNary, Jan. 25, 1933, Charles McNary MSS, Manuscript Division, Library of Congress; James Couzens to Thomas W. Payne, Jan. 3, 1933, James Couzens MSS, Manuscript Division, Library of Congress; Peter Norbeck to Lauritz Swenson, Dec. 29, 1932, Peter Norbeck MSS, University of Missouri.
5. *NYT*, Dec. 1, 1932; George Norris to Bertrand V. Tibbels, Dec. 27, 1932, Norris MSS.
6. Franklin D. Roosevelt to Bronson Cutting, Nov. 19, 1932, Cutting MSS; *NYT*, Dec. 5, 1932; typed memorandum on "1932-33 Offer of Cabinet Post. Relations with F.D.R.," undated, Cutting MSS; ten-page statement by Clifford McCarthy, undated but entitled "1932-1935," Cutting MSS; Robert La Follette, Jr., to Philip La Follette, Jan. 20, 1933, La Follette Family MSS and P. La Follete MSS.
7. *NYT*, Jan. 23, 1933; *NYHT*, Jan. 23, 1933; *P*, Jan. 28, 1933; Robert La Follette, Jr., to Philip La Follette, Jan. 24, 1933, La Follette Family MSS and P. La Follette MSS; *NYT*, Feb. 18, 19, 1933; memo on "1932-33 Offer of Cabinet Post," Cutting MSS; undated statement by Clifford McCarthy, Cutting MSS. On Roosevelt's consideration of Cutting to be interior secretary, see also Raymond Moley, *After Seven Years* (New York and London: Harper & Brothers, 1939) and *The First New Deal* (New York: Harcourt, Brace & World, 1966). My interview with Moley on May 14, 1971, in New York City indicated much the same information as in his two books.
8. Hiram Johnson to his Boys, Dec. 18, 1932, Johnson MSS.
9. Hiram Johnson to Hiram Johnson, Jr., Jan. 15, 22, 1933, Johnson MSS; Moley, *The First New Deal*, p. 73.
10. Hiram Johnson to Hiram Johnson, Jr., Jan. 22, 1933, Johnson to Charles K. McClatchy, Jan. 29, 1933, Johnson MSS.
11. Harold Ickes to Hiram Johnson, Jan. 30, 1933, Johnson to Ickes, Feb. 12, 1933, Johnson to his Boys, Feb. 12, 1933, Ickes to Johnson, Feb. 14, 1933, Johnson MSS; Moley, *The First New Deal*, pp. 94, 126-27; Harold Ickes, *The Autobiography of a Curmudgeon* (New York: Reynal & Hitchcock, 1943), pp. 266-68, 270; interview with Raymond Moley, May 14, 1971, New York City.
12. *NYT*, Feb. 23, 1933; Hiram Johnson to his Boys, Feb. 26, 1933, Johnson MSS; T.R.B., "Washington Notes," *NR*, March 8, 1933, pp. 100-101.
13. Philip La Follette to Robert La Follette, Jr., Dec. 9, 1932, John F. Sinclair to R. La Follette, Jr., Dec. 15, 1932, R. La Follette, Jr., to P. La Follette, Dec. 22, 1932, La Follette Family MSS.
14. Philip La Follette to Robert La Follette, Jr., Jan. 4, 1933, P. La Follette to Fola and George Middleton, Jan. 4, 1933, Henry Morgenthau to R. La Follette, Jr., Jan. 9,

1933, R. La Follette, Jr., to Morgenthau, Jan. 9, 1933, La Follette Family MSS.

15. John F. Sinclair to Robert La Follette, Jr., Jan. 10, 1933, P. La Follette MSS; R. La Follette, Jr., to Sinclair, Jan. 17, 1933, P. La Follette MSS, La Follette Family MSS and Franklin D. Roosevelt MSS, Roosevelt Presidential Library; Sinclair to Roosevelt, Jan. 18, 1933, Roosevelt MSS.

16. Robert La Follette, Jr., to Philip La Follette, Jan. 20, 1933, P. La Follette MSS and La Follette Family MSS; Moley, *The First New Deal*, p. 73; *P*, Jan. 21, 1933.

17. Robert La Follette, Jr., to Philip La Follette, Jan. 24, 1933, P. La Follette MSS and La Follette Family MSS; R. La Follette, Jr., to Fola and George Middleton, Jan. 26, 1933, La Follette Family MSS.

18. Ibid.

19. Ibid.

20. Philip La Follette to Robert La Follette, Jr., Feb. 5, 1933, La Follette Family MSS; R. La Follette, Jr., to P. and Isen La Follette, Feb. 7, 1933, La Follette Family MSS and P. La Follette MSS.

21. Robert La Follette, Jr., to Philip La Follette, Feb. 22, 1933, P. La Follette MSS and La Follette Family MSS; P. La Follette to R. La Follette, Jr., Feb. 23, 1933, R. La Follette, Jr., to Fola and George Middleton, Feb. 24, 1933, La Follette Family MSS; R. La Follette, Jr., to Franklin D. Roosevelt, Mar. 6, 1933, La Follette Family MSS and Roosevelt MSS.

22. Philip La Follette's notes on interview with FDR on return from Europe, Mar. 20, 1933, La Follette Family MSS and P. La Follette MSS; *NYT*, Mar. 21, 1933; *P*, Mar. 25, 1933.

23. Rexford Guy Tugwell, *The Brains Trust* (New York: Viking Press, 1968), pp. 489-92, 496.

24. *NYT*, Jan. 22, 1933; Hiram Johnson to Hiram Johnson, Jr., Feb. 4, 1933, Johnson MSS.

25. T.R.B., "Washington Notes," *NR*, Feb. 15, 1933, pp. 16-17; *P*, Mar. 4, 1933; *NYT*, Feb. 19, 1933.

26. Phil D. Swing to Gifford Pinchot, Dec. 14, 1932; Pinchot to Swing, Dec. 16, 1932, Gifford Pinchot MSS, Manuscript Division, Library of Congress.

27. Harold Ickes to Hiram Johnson, Jan. 13, 1933, Johnson MSS; Ickes to Robert La Follette, Jr., Jan. 24, 1933, R. La Follette, Jr., to Ickes, Jan. 27, 1933, La Follette Family MSS; Ickes to Johnson, Jan. 30, 1933, Johnson MSS.

28. *NYT*, Jan. 29, 1933; *P*, Feb. 4, 1933; Robert La Follette, Jr., to Harold Ickes, Jan. 30, 1933, Ickes to R. La Follette, Jr., Feb. 1, 1933, La Follette Family MSS.

29. Robert La Follette, Jr., to Harold Ickes, Feb. 6, 1933, La Follette Family MSS; *NYT*, Feb. 26, 1933; *NYHT*, Feb. 26, 1933; *P*, Mar. 4, 1933; *CS*, Mar. 2, 1933.

30. Robert La Follette, Jr., to Phil and Isen La Follette, Feb. 7, 1933, P. La Follette MSS and La Follette Family MSS.

31. Hiram Johnson to his Boys, Feb. 12, 19, 1933, Johnson MSS; *NYT*, Feb. 23, 1933.

32. *P*, Mar. 11, 1933; Hiram Johnson to his Boys, Mar. 5, 1933, Johnson MSS.

33. *CR*, Mar. 9, 1933, pp. 67, 46, 63-65; *P*, Mar. 18, 1933; *NYT*, Mar. 11, 1933; William Borah to Joseph J. Turner, Apr. 3, 1933, William Borah MSS, Manuscript Division, Library of Congress.

34. Hiram Johnson to his Boys, Mar. 12, 1933, Johnson MSS; *CR*, Apr. 27, 1933, pp. 2434-35.

35. *CR*, Mar. 14, 1933, pp. 322-23, 346-48, 336-37; William Borah to L. C. Macomber, Apr. 3, 1933, Borah MSS.

36. *CR*, Mar. 15, 1933, pp. 442-43, 449, 466, 468; Robert La Follette, Jr., to Thomas Duncan, Mar. 17, 1933, La Follette Family MSS; Bronson Cutting to Dr. E. S.

Bullock, Apr. 28, 1933, Cutting MSS.
37. *CR*, May 31, 1933, pp. 4651-55, 4658; *NYT*, June 1, 1933.
38. *CR*, May 31, 1933, p. 4662; June 2, 1933, pp. 4815, 4832.
39. Ibid., June 5, 1933, p. 4970; June 14, 1933, pp. 6002-3; Bronson Cutting to Col. J. D. Attwood, June 16, 1933, Cutting MSS.
40. Bronson Cutting to his mother, Mar. 25, Apr. 8, 1933, Cutting MSS.
41. Hiram Johnson to his Boys, Mar. 19, 1933, Johnson to Hiram Johnson, Jr., Mar. 25, 1933, Johnson MSS.
42. George Norris to A. Barnett, Apr. 8, 1933, Norris MSS; *CR*, Apr. 12, 1933, pp. 1548-50; Apr. 13, 1933, pp. 1636, 1630; Apr. 17, 1933, p. 1831; Apr. 13, 1933, pp. 1632-33.
43. *CR*, Apr. 14, 1933, pp. 1730-32; Apr. 22, 1933, p. 2160; Apr. 28, 1933, p. 2558; Apr. 22, 1933, p. 2157; May 10, 1933, p. 3121.
44. *CR*, May 3, 1933, p. 2808; *P*, Apr. 15, 1933; *CR*, Apr. 6, 1933, p. 1350; William Borah to L. F. Ingersoll, Apr. 7, 1933, Borah MSS.
45. *P*, Mar. 18, 1933; *CR*, Mar. 27, 1933, p. 860; Mar. 30, 1933, p. 1042; *P*, Apr. 8, 22, 1933; Robert La Follette, Jr., to Fola and George Middleton, Apr. 3, 1933, La Follette Family MSS.
46. Robert La Follette, Jr., to Fola La Follette, Apr. 10, 1933, La Follette Family MSS; R. La Follette, Jr., to Philip La Follette, Apr. 13, 1933, La Follette Family MSS and P. La Follette MSS; *NYT*, Apr. 15, 1933; R. La Follette, Jr., to Alfred T. Rogers, Apr. 20, 1933, P. La Follette to R. La Follette, Jr., May 3, 1933, La Follette Family MSS.
47. *CR*, May 8, 1933, p. 2966; Robert La Follette, Jr., to Dear Ones, May 8, 1933, La Follette Family MSS; *NYT*, May 14, 1933; *P*, May 27, 1933.
48. Robert La Follette, Jr., to Fola and George Middleton, June 6, 1933, La Follette Family MSS; *CR*, June 7, 1933, pp. 5162-65; June 8, 1933, p. 5246; *NYT*, June 8, 1933; *CR*, June 13, 1933, p. 5842.
49. *CR*, June 9, 1933, p. 5424; June 13, 1933, pp. 5861, 5834-37; *NYT*, June 14, 1933.
50. William Borah to George Record, June 19, 1933, Borah MSS and Amos Pinchot MSS, Manuscript Division, Library of Congress; *CR*, June 9, 1933, pp. 5419-20; June 13, 1933, p. 5851.
51. Harold Ickes, *The Secret Diary of Harold L. Ickes* (New York: Simon & Schuster, 1954), Vol. 1, pp. 33, 42, 43; Moley, *After Seven Years*, p. 218; idem, *The First New Deal*, p. 407; *NYT*, May 22, 25, 1933; Hiram Johnson to his Boys, May 26, 1933, Johnson MSS.
52. Philip La Follette to Robert La Follette, Jr., May 28, 1933, R. La Follette, Jr., to P. La Follette, May 29, 1933, La Follette Family MSS; *NYT*, May 30, 1933; *P*, June 3, 1933; *NYT*, May 30, 31, 1933.
53. Hiram Johnson to Hiram Johnson, Jr., Apr. 1, 1933, Johnson to his Boys, Apr. 16, 1933, Johnson MSS; *CR*, Apr. 28, 1933, p. 2541; Johnson to Hiram Johnson, Jr., May 2, 1933, Johnson to Charles K. McClatchy, June 4, 1933, Johnson MSS.
54. *P*, June 17, 24, 1933.
55. *NYT*, June 20, 1933; *CW*, June 17, 24, 1933.
56. Charles McNary to John H. McNary, Apr. 10, 1933, McNary MSS; Peter Norbeck to James E. Stewart, May 25, 1933, Peter Norbeck MSS, University of South Dakota.
57. James Couzens to A. L. Couzens, May 26, 1933, Couzens MSS; William Borah to Hunter Woodson, May 1, 1933, Borah MSS.
58. *NYT*, June 27, 1933.

CHAPTER 5

1. *P*, July 15, Aug. 5, 19, 1933.

2. James Couzens to John Carson, Aug. 24, 1933, James Couzens MSS, Manuscript Division, Library of Congress.

3. Arthur Capper Radio Address, Sept. 17, 1933, Arthur Capper MSS, Kansas State Historical Society; *NYT*, Sept. 27, 1933.

4. *NYT*, Nov. 6, 18, 26, 1933.

5. Robert La Follette, Jr., to Dearest, Nov. 8, 1933, La Follette Family MSS, Manuscript Division, Library of Congress; *P*, Dec. 16, 1933.

6. *NYT*, Dec. 27, 1933.

7. "The Week," *N*, Jan. 3, 1934, p. 1.

8. *NYT*, Jan. 17, 1934; *CR*, Jan. 18, 1934, pp. 866-71, 871-74; *NYT*, Jan. 19, 1934.

9. *CR*, Jan. 22, 1934, pp. 1075-77; *NYT*, Jan. 23, 25, 1934; *CR*, Jan. 27, 1934, pp. 1442-44; T.R.B., "Washington Notes," *NR*, Jan. 31, 1934, p. 333.

10. *CR*, Feb. 2, 1934, p. 1824; *NYT*, Feb. 3, 1934; *CR*, Feb. 6, 1934, pp. 2059-60.

11. *NYT*, Feb. 7, 8, 1934; *CR*, Feb. 8, 1934, pp. 2156-58, 2182-85.

12. *CR*, Feb. 20, 1934, p. 2831; Feb. 21, 1934, p. 2945; *NYT*, Feb. 21, 22, 1934; T.R.B., "Washington Notes," *NR*, Feb. 7, 1934, pp. 361-62.

13. *CR*, Mar. 21, 1934, pp. 4999-5000; *NYT*, Mar. 22, 23, 1934.

14. *NYT*, Apr. 15, 1934; Arthur Capper Radio Address, May 1, 1934, Capper MSS; Gerald P. Nye to Franklin D. Roosevelt, May 16, 1934, Roosevelt to Nye, May 18, 1934, Franklin D. Roosevelt MSS, Roosevelt Presidential Library.

15. *NYT*, May 23, 1934; *CR*, May 22, 1934, pp. 9234-40; May 23, 1934, pp. 9320-23, 9327, 9328; *NYT*, May 25, 1934; *CR*, June 16, 1934, pp. 12051-52.

16. *NYT*, July 5, 6, 25, Aug. 7, 4, 1934.

17. Ibid., Jan. 11, 1935; *CR*, Feb. 14, 1935, pp. 1905-6; *NYT*, Feb. 15, 16, Mar. 1, 9, 1935; *CR*, Mar. 8, 1935, pp. 3201-3.

18. *NYT*, Mar. 10, 22, 1935; *CR*, Mar. 21, 1935, p. 4166; George Norris to Richard W. Grant, Apr. 4, 1935, George Norris MSS, Manuscript Division, Library of Congress.

19. *NYT*, Apr. 1, May 1, 21, 1935.

20. Hiram Johnson to Hiram Johnson, Jr., June 2, 1935, Hiram Johnson MSS, Bancroft Library, University of California, Berkeley.

21. *Capper's Farmer*, July 1933; *P*, Oct. 21, 1933; *NYT*, Mar. 20, 1934.

22. *CR*, Mar. 23, 1934, pp. 5218-20; William Borah to J. R. Durk, Apr. 21, 1934, William Borah MSS, Manuscript Division, Library of Congress.

23. George Norris to Charles E. Franklin, Apr. 12, 1935, Norris MSS.

24. *CR*, Feb. 26, 1934, p. 3212; Feb. 27, 1934, pp. 3296-97, 3292-93.

25. Ibid., Mar. 27, 1934, p. 5554; Mar. 28, 1934, pp. 5606, 5573-74.

26. *P*, July 22, 1933; Robert La Follette, Jr., to Franklin D. Roosevelt, July 8, 1933, R. La Follette, Jr., to Fola and George Middleton, Dec. 11, 1933, La Follette Family MSS; *CR*, Feb. 8, 1934, pp. 2162-68, 2169-74; *NYT*, Feb. 8, Apr. 12, 1934.

27. *CR*, Apr. 13, 1934, p. 6547; Apr. 12, 1934, pp. 6464, 6468; Apr. 5, 1934, p. 6084; Apr. 12, 1934, pp. 6460, 6486; Apr. 13, 1934, pp. 6543-46; Apr. 4, 1934, pp. 5973-75; Apr. 24, 1934, pp. 7198-7200; Apr. 5, 1934, p. 6091.

28. Ibid., Jan. 27, 1934, p. 1484; May 12, 1934, p. 8714; June 4, 1934, p. 10395; Hiram Johnson to Charles K. McClatchy, Mar. 11, 1934, Johnson MSS.

29. *NYT*, Mar. 18, 1934; *CR*, May 17, 1934, pp. 9006-12, 8996-9005; *NYT*, May 18, 1934.

30. *CR*, May 30, 1934, p. 9960; *NYT*, May 31, 1934; *CR*, May 31, 1934, pp. 10084-90; June 4, 1934, pp. 10375-76.

31. *CR*, June 4, 1934, pp. 10378-80.

32. Charles McNary to John H. McNary, Dec. 19, 1933, Senator McNary Radio Speech, June 8, 1934, Charles McNary MSS, Manuscript Division, Library of Congress; *NYT*, June 9, 1934; *CR*, June 16, 1934, pp. 11968-69; *NYT*, July 17, 1934; McNary to James Couzens, Aug. 14, 1934, McNary MSS and Couzens MSS.

33. *CW*, July 8, 1933; Arthur Capper Radio Address, Jan. 16, 1934, Capper MSS; *NYT*, Feb. 24, Mar. 4, 1934; *Capper's Farmer*, Mar. 1934; *NYT*, May 4, 1934.

34. Arthur Capper to William Allen White, June 1, 1934, William Allen White MSS, Manuscript Division, Library of Congress; *Capper's Farmer*, Aug. 1934; Capper Radio Address, Aug. 6, 1934, Capper MSS.

35. George Norris to Franklin D. Roosevelt, Sept. 22, 1933, Norris to James Farley, Sept. 22, 1933, Roosevelt MSS; *CR*, Apr. 30, 1934, pp. 7666-67, 7672-73.

36. George Norris to A. F. Buechler, June 8, 1934, Norris MSS.

37. James Couzens to Marguarite Meagher, Feb. 1, 1934, Couzens MSS; Couzens to Charles McNary, Aug. 23, 1934, Couzens MSS and McNary MSS; *NYT*, Aug. 26, 1934; Couzens to Violet M. Wood, Sept. 4, 1934, Couzens MSS; Couzens to McNary, Oct. 5, 1934, Couzens MSS and McNary MSS.

38. "The Week," *NR*, July 18, 1934, p. 247; Oswald Garrison Villard, "Issues and Men: Borah Goes on the War Path," *N*, July 25, 1934, p. 91; William Borah to James F. McCarthy, Sept. 29, 1934, Borah MSS.

39. T.R.B., "Washington Notes," *NR*, Jan. 10, 1934, pp. 250-51; Oswald Garrison Villard, "The Senate Progressives' Dilemma," *N*, Jan. 17, 1934, p. 63; "The Progressives' Dilemma," *NR*, Jan. 17, 1934, pp. 267-68; *NYT*, Jan. 15, 1934.

40. Microfilm copy of *Press Conferences of the President*, vol. 3, June 27, 1934, p. 435.

41. Harold Ickes to Hiram Johnson, July 10, 1933, Johnson MSS; T.R.B., "Washington Notes," *NR*, July 12, 1933, pp. 233-34; Johnson to Franklin D. Roosevelt, Aug. 26, 1933, Johnson MSS.

42. Franklin D. Roosevelt to Hiram Johnson, Nov. 5, 1933, Johnson to Charles K. McClatchy, Nov. 9, 1933, Johnson MSS; Johnson to Roosevelt, Nov. 16, 1933, Johnson and Roosevelt MSS; Harold Ickes to Johnson, Nov. 30, 1933, Johnson MSS; Johnson to Roosevelt, Dec. 22, 1933, Johnson and Roosevelt MSS.

43. *NYT*, Jan. 27, June 24, Mar. 4, 1934.

44. Ibid., Sept. 4, 1934.

45. Robert La Follette, Jr., to Philip La Follette, Oct. 18, 1933, P. La Follette MSS, State Historical Society of Wisconsin; R. La Follette, Jr., to Dearest, Nov. 7, 1933, La Follette Family MSS.

46. Sample letter and list of people it was sent to, Nov. 1933, P. La Follette MSS; Thomas R. Amlie to John Kent, Dec. 15, 1933, Thomas Amlie MSS, State Historical Society of Wisconsin; "The Progressives' Dilemma," *NR*, Jan. 17, 1934, p. 268.

47. Philip La Follette to Robert La Follette, Jr., Feb. 12, 1934, R. La Follette, Jr., to P. La Follette, Feb. 16, 1934, P. La Follette to R. La Follette, Jr., Feb. 24, 1934, La Follette Family MSS.

48. R. La Follette, Jr., to P. La Follette, Feb. 27, 1934, La Follette Family MSS and P. La Follette MSS; R. La Follette, Jr., to Dearest, Mar. 2, 1934, La Follette Family MSS.

49. Thomas Amlie to Howard Y. Williams, Mar. 5, 1934, Amlie MSS; *P*, Mar. 10, 1934; Francis Scott, "Making History in Wisconsin: The Third Party Movement Gathers Headway," *CS* 3 (Apr. 1934): 16-17; *Madison Capital Times*, May 1, 2, 5, 1934; *P*, May 5, 12, 1934.

50. Philip La Follette to Robert La Follette, Jr., Mar. 31, 1934, La Follette Family MSS; *Madison Capital Times*, May 12, 20, 1934; *NYT*, May 20, 1934; *NYHT*, May

20, 1934; *Madison Capital Times*, May 21, 1934; *P*, May 26, 1934; Mark Rhea Byers, "A New La Follette Party," *North American Review* 237 (May 1934): 401-9; *Madison Capital Times*, May 21, 1934.

51. Robert La Follette, Jr., to Philip La Follette, June 4, 1934, La Follette Family MSS and P. La Follette MSS; *Press Conferences of the President*, p. 434; *Madison Capital Times*, July 1, 1934.

52. *Madison Capital Times*, July 12, Aug. 9, 1934; *NYT*, Aug. 10, 13, 1934; *Madison Capital Times*, Aug. 13, 1934; *P*, Aug. 25, 1934.

53. *Madison Capital Times*, Aug. 14, 16, 1934; *NYT*, Aug. 17, 1934; Philip La Follette, "Capital on Strike," *CS* 3 (July 1934): 6-9; *Madison Capital Times*, Oct. 4, 5, 9, 14, 19, 22, 23, 30, 31, 1934; *P*, Sept. 29, Oct. 13, 20, Nov. 3, 1934.

54. Robert La Follette, Jr., to Franklin D. Roosevelt, Oct. 21, 1934, La Follette Family MSS and Roosevelt MSS; *Madison Capital Times*, Nov. 2, 9, 1934; *NYT*, Nov. 9, 1934; *P*, Nov. 10, 1934.

For other details on the Progressive party of Wisconsin, see Donald McCoy, "The Formation of the Wisconsin Progressive Party in 1934," *The Historian* 14 (Autumn 1951): 70-90; Charles H. Backstrom, "The Progressive Party of Wisconsin, 1934-1946," Ph.D. diss., University of Wisconsin, 1957; John E. Miller, "Governor Philip F. La Follette, The Wisconsin Progressives, and the New Deal, 1930-1939," Ph.D. diss. University of Wisconsin, 1973; Donald .Young ed., *Adventure in Politics: The Memoirs of Philip La Follette* (New York: Holt, Rinehart & Winston, 1970), pp. 204-16; Wallace S. Sayre, "Left Turn in Wisconsin," *NR*, Oct. 24, 1934, pp. 300-302; Harold M. Groves, "Wisconsin's New Party," *N*, Aug. 1, 1934, pp. 122-24; E. Francis Brown, "The Progressives Make a New Bid," *Current History* 41 (Nov. 1934): 149-54. The biographical materials on Robert La Follette, Jr., listed in the notes for chapter 1 and in the bibliography also offer material on the Progressive party.

55. Ten-page statement by Clifford McCarthy, undated but entitled "1932-1935," Bronson Cutting MSS, Manuscript Division, Library of Congress.

56. Bronson Cutting to Philip La Follette, Nov. 1, 1933, P. La Follette MSS; Cutting to his mother, Nov. 12, 29, 1933, Cutting MSS; *CR*, Jan. 27, 1934, pp. 1476-77.

57. George Norris to Franklin D. Roosevelt, Jan. 19, 1934, Roosevelt to Norris, Jan. 24, 1934, Roosevelt MSS; Bronson Cutting to his mother, Mar. 21, 1934, Cutting MSS.

58. Bronson Cutting to H. Phelps Putnam, Apr. 22, 1934, Cutting MSS.

59. *Santa Fe New Mexican*, July 17, 1934; Bronson Cutting to Dottori, July 19, 1934, Cutting to his mother, July 24, 1934, Cutting MSS; *Santa Fe New Mexican*, July 21, 1934.

60. *Santa Fe New Mexican*, Sept. 24, 25, 1934; text of Bronson Cutting's acceptance speech, Sept. 24, 1934, Cutting MSS; *Santa Fe New Mexican*, Sept. 26, 1934.

61. *Santa Fe New Mexican*, Oct. 1, 1934; letters and telegrams in Cutting MSS.

62. Hiram Johnson to George Norris, Oct. 23, 1934, Norris MSS; Johnson to Edgar F. Puryear (Cutting's secretary), Oct. 27, 1934, Cutting MSS; *Santa Fe New Mexican*, Oct. 27, 1934; Norris to Bronson Cutting, Oct. 29, 1934, Norris MSS; "Sinclair, La Follette, and Cutting," *N*, Nov. 7, 1934, p. 522; Fleter Campbell Springer, "Through the Looking Glass," *NR*, Nov. 7, 1934, pp. 357-58.

63. *Santa Fe New Mexican*, Nov. 13, 15, 16, 17, 1934; William Borah to Bronson Cutting, Nov. 16, 1934, Hiram Johnson to Cutting, Nov. 16, 1934, Cutting MSS; *NYT*, Nov. 22, 1934.

64. *NYT*, Nov. 23, 1934; *NYHT*, Nov. 24, 1934; *Santa Fe New Mexican*, Nov. 23, 1934; *NYT*, Nov. 25, 1934.

65. *NYT*, Nov. 27, 1934; George Norris to David K. Niles, Nov. 30, 1934, Norris MSS; T.R.B., "Washington Notes," *NR*, Dec. 12, 1934, p. 128.

66. *Santa Fe New Mexican*, Dec. 11, 31, 1934, Jan. 1, 1935; *NYHT*, Dec. 10, 1934; *NYT*, Jan. 1, 1935.

67. Hiram Johnson to Hiram Johnson, Jr., Dec. 22, 1934, Johnson MSS; undated statement by Clifford McCarthy, Cutting MSS; typed memorandum by Clifford McCarthy to H.S.C., sheet on 1934-35–"The Contest. Role of F.D.R. Efforts at Reconciliation," undated, Cutting MSS.

68. Harold Ickes, *The Secret Diary of Harold L. Ickes* (New York: Simon & Schuster, 1954), vol. 1, p. 217; statement by Clifford McCarthy, Cutting MSS.

69. *NYT*, Jan. 1, 1935; *Santa Fe New Mexican*, Jan. 11, Feb. 25, 26, 1935; *NYT*, Feb. 26, 1935; *Santa Fe New Mexican*, Apr. 11, 17, 1935; *NYT*, Apr. 12, 1935; U.S. Senate, Privileges and Elections Committee, 74th Congress, 1st session, *Hearings on New Mexico Senator Election*, U.S. Government Printing Office, 1935.

70. Hiram Johnson to Hiram Johnson, Jr., Apr. 16, 1935, Johnson MSS.

71. Undated statement by Clifford McCarthy, Cutting MSS; memo by Clifford McCarthy to H.S.C., Cutting MSS.

72. Ibid.

73. *CR*, May 6, 1935, p. 6999; *NYT*, May 7, 1935; *NYHT*, May 7, 1935; *NYT*, May 10, 1935.

74. Ickes, *Secret Diary*, vol. 1, pp. 358-59: *NYT*, May 7, 1935; statement by the president for immediate release to the press, May 6, 1935, Roosevelt MSS.

75. See the following newspaper editorials for May 7, 1935: *NYT*, *NYHT*, *New York World-Telegram*, *New York Post*, *St. Louis Post-Dispatch*, *WP*. Also see the following liberal periodicals: *N*, May 15, 1935, p. 557; Oswald Garrison Villard, "Issues and Men: Senator Cutting," *N*, May 22, 1935, p. 591; "The Week," *NR*, May 15, 1935, p. 1; *P*, May 11, 18, 1935; *CS* 4 (June 1935): 2-3, 6; *NYT*, May 21, 1935; *NYHT*, May 21, 1935; *P*, May 25, 1935.

For further treatment of the Cutting reelection contest, see Gustav Leonard Seligmann, Jr., "The Political Career of Senator Bronson M. Cutting," Ph.D. diss., University of Arizona, 1967; William H. Pickens, "Bronson Cutting vs. Dennis Chavez: Battle of the Patrones in New Mexico, 1934," *New Mexico Historical Review* 46 (Jan. 1971): 5-36; and G. L. Seligmann, Jr., "The Purge That Failed: The 1934 Senatorial Election in New Mexico–Yet Another View," ibid. 47 (Oct. 1972): 361-81.

CHAPTER 6

1. *CR*, Mar. 21, 1935, pp. 4148-52, 4160; *P*, Feb. 23, 1935; *CR*, Mar. 23, 1935, p. 4366; Apr. 5, 1935, p. 5135; Hiram Johnson to Hiram Johnson, Jr., Jan. 26, Apr. 7, 1935, Hiram Johnson MSS, Bancroft Library, University of California, Berkeley.

2. Hiram Johnson to Hiram Johnson, Jr., Mar. 3, 10, Apr. 28, 1935, Johnson MSS; Charles McNary to John H. McNary, Feb. 26, 1935, Charles McNary MSS, Manuscript Division, Library of Congress; T.R.B., "Washington Notes," *NR*, Mar. 6, 1935, p. 101.

3. Harold Ickes, *The Secret Diary of Harold L. Ickes* (New York: Simon & Schuster, 1954), vol. 1, p. 363; George Norris to Franklin D. Roosevelt, May 15, 1935, Felix Frankfurter to Roosevelt, May 16, 1935, Felix Frankfurter MSS, Manuscript Division, Library of Congress.

4. *CR*, June 18, 1935, pp. 9541-43; June 19, 1935, pp. 9634, 9650; May 16, 1935, p. 7681.

5. *NYT*, Mar. 13, 14, 1935; *CR*, Mar. 27, 1935, pp. 4509-12, 4526; *NYT*, Mar. 28, Apr. 29, 1935.

6. *NYT*, June 22, 1935.

7. Ibid., June 24, 1935; *P*, June 29, 1935; *NYT*, July 1, 16, 17, 28, 1935; *P*, Aug. 10, 1935; *CR*, Aug. 15, 1935, pp. 13201-2, 13254.

8 *NYT*, Aug. 16, 1935.

9. *CR*, June 3, 1935, pp. 8491-8519; *NYT*, June 4, 1935; *CR*, June 11, 1935, pp. 9049, 9053, 9065; *NYT*, June 12, 1935; *CR*, Aug. 24, 1935, pp. 14470-71; *NYT*, Aug. 25, 1935.

10. *CR*, May 4, 1934, pp. 8051-53 (reprint of article entitled "Is Private Banking Doomed?" in Mar. 31, 1934, issue of *Liberty Magazine*); *P*, Apr. 14, 1934; Gerald P. Nye, "Under the Banker's Thumb: A Progressive Points a Way Out," *CS* 3 (Mar. 1934): 12-13; *CR*, May 22, 1934, pp. 9225-27; June 6, 1934, p. 10557; Mar. 8, 1935, p. 3180; July 26, 1935, p. 11935; Aug. 19, 1935, p. 13655.

11. *CR*, Aug. 22, 1935, p. 14084.

12. Ibid., July 23, 1935, p. 11658; July 16, 1935, p. 11219; *NYT*, Sept. 29, 1935; *Capper's Farmer*, Nov. 1935.

13. *CR*, Feb. 15, 1936, p. 2165; Feb. 12, 1936, pp. 1882-84; Feb. 14, 1936, pp. 2029, 2037-38; Feb. 15, 1936, pp. 2139, 2141-43, 2161; *NYT*, Feb. 13, 8, 1936; *CR*, Feb. 6, 1936, p. 1576.

14. *CR*, June 5, 1936, p. 9110; June 20, 1936, p. 10476.

15. *NYT*, Nov. 9, 10, Dec. 2, 1934.

16. Ibid., Dec. 2, 3, 5, 1934; *NYHT*, Dec. 2, 5, 1934; *P*, Dec. 8, 1934.

17. *NYT*, Dec. 14, 1934; *NYHT*, Dec. 14, 1934; *P*, Dec. 22, 1934; Arthur Capper to Charles F. Scott, Jan. 11, 1935, Arthur Capper MSS, Kansas State Historical Society.

18. *NYT*, July 21, 1935; William Allen White to William Borah, July 22, 1935, White to Borah, Sept. 23, 1935, Borah to White, Sept. 26, 1935, William Borah MSS, Manuscript Division, Library of Congress.

19. "Will Borah Run?", *N*, Sept. 11, 1935, p. 285; *P*, Oct. 26, 1935.

20. *WP*, Oct. 15, 1935; *NYT*, Nov. 4, 1935.

21. *NYT*, Nov. 16, Dec. 8, 1935; *NYHT*, Dec. 8, 1935; *NYT*, Dec. 20, 23, 1935, Jan. 4, 1936, Nov. 29, Dec. 27, 1935, Jan. 5, Feb. 21, 5, 1936.

22. *NYT*, Mar. 20, 22, 1936.

23. Johnathon Mitchell, "Borah Knows Best," *NR*, Jan. 29, 1936, pp. 333-34; "Borah as a Candidate," ibid., Mar. 4, 1936, pp. 97-98; Oswald Garrison Villard, "Issues and Men: Senators Wagner, Nye, and Others," *N*, Sept. 4, 1935, p. 259; Herbert C. Pell, "Judas Goat: Is Borah Leading the Progressives to the Slaughter?" *CS* 5 (May 1936): 24-25. Other articles on Borah in 1936 include Richard L. Neuberger, "Behind the Borah Boom," *Current History* 43 (Feb. 1936): 463-66, and William Hard, "Borah and '36 and Beyond," *Harper's Magazine* 172 (Apr. 1936): 575-83. See also Hiram Johnson to Hiram Johnson, Jr., Dec. 27, 1935, and Mar. 29, Apr. 19, 1936, Johnson MSS.

24. *NYT*, Apr. 21, 22, May 10, 29, 1936.

25. Ibid., June 9, 12, 1936.

26. Ibid., Apr. 22, July 15, 1935; Arthur Capper to Amos Pinchot, July 23, 1935, Amos Pinchot MSS, Manuscript Division, Library of Congress; Capper to C. A. Brewer, July 26, 1935, Capper to Will Morton, Aug. 19, 1935, Capper MSS; Capper to Victor Murdock, Sept. 10, 1935, Victor Murdock MSS, Manuscript Division, Library of Congress; *Capper's Farmer*, Nov. 1935; *NYT*, Dec. 29, 1935.

27. Arthur Capper to Alf Landon, Jan. 4, 1936, Capper to Landon, June 13, 1936, Alf Landon MSS, Kansas State Historical Society; *CW*, Oct. 17, 24, 31, 1936; *NYT*, Oct. 18, 1936; *Topeka (Kan.) Daily Capital*, Oct. 18, Nov. 3, 1936; *CW*, Nov. 14, 1936; Arthur Capper Radio Speech, Nov. 8, 1936, Capper MSS; Capper to William Allen White, Dec. 1, 1936, William Allen White MSS, Manuscript Division, Library of Congress.

28. Charles McNary statement to the press, July 15, 1935, McNary MSS; *NYT*, Aug. 18, 1935, Oct. 18, 1936; *Portland Morning Oregonian*, Oct. 29, 1936.

29. *Bismarck (N.D.) Tribune*, Oct. 3, 1936; *NYT*, Oct. 4, 1936.

30. *NYT*, July 2, 7, 26, Sept. 6, 1936.

31. Dispatch from *Philadelphia Record* printed in *NYT*, Oct. 4, 1936; *NYT*, Oct. 5, 1936.

32. *NYT*, Oct. 10, 17, 1936.

33. Ibid., July 7, 1935; *P*, Aug. 17, 1935; *NYT*, June 13, 1936; Harold Ickes, *Secret Diary*, vol. 1, pp. 655-56.

34. Personal interview with Senator Gerald P. Nye, Mar. 30, 1971, Washington, D.C.; Franklin D. Roosevelt to Nye, Aug. 17, 1936, Franklin D. Roosevelt MSS, Roosevelt Presidential Library; Nye to Robert La Follette, Jr., Sept. 10, 1936, La Follette Family MSS, Manuscript Division, Library of Congress; *NYT*, Oct. 2, 1936; Harold Ickes, *Secret Diary*, vol. 1, p. 698; *Bismarck (N.D.) Tribune*, Nov. 5, 1936; *P*, Dec. 5, 1936.

35. Hiram Johnson to Hiram Johnson, Jr., May 5, June 29, 1935, Johnson MSS.

36. *NYT*, July 7, 1935; Johnson to Hiram Johnson, Jr., July 8, 1935, Johnson MSS; Johnson to Franklin D. Roosevelt, July 8, 1935, Johnson MSS and Roosevelt MSS; Johnson to Hiram Johnson, Jr., July 13, 1935, Johnson MSS; *NYT*, Sept. 1, 1935; Roosevelt to Johnson, Nov. 14, 1935, Roosevelt MSS.

37. *NYT*, Dec. 22, 1935; Hiram Johnson to Hiram Johnson, Jr., Jan. 5, Mar. 1, May 9, 31, 1936, Johnson MSS.

38. Hiram Johnson to Hiram Johnson, Jr., Aug. 2, 1936, Johnson MSS; Johnson to Robert La Follette, Jr., Aug. 13, 1936, La Follette Family MSS; Johnson to Hiram Johnson, Jr., Aug. 24, 1936, Johnson MSS.

39. Hiram Johnson to Hiram Johnson, Jr., Aug. 26, 1936, Johnson MSS; *NYHT*, Aug. 27, 1936; *NYT*, Oct. 22, 1936.

40. Ickes, *Secret Diary*, vol. 1, pp. 693, 697-98; Elliott Roosevelt, ed., *F.D.R.: His Personal Letters, 1928-1945* (New York: Duell, Sloan, and Pearce, 1950), vol. 1, pp. 622-23; Johnson to Hiram Johnson, Jr., Oct. 24, 1936, Johnson MSS.

41. William Gibbs McAdoo to James Farley, Nov. 5, 1936, William Gibbs McAdoo MSS, Manuscript Division, Library of Congress; Hiram Johnson to Hiram Johnson, Jr., Nov. 10, 1936, Johnson MSS.

42. Peter Norbeck to Herman D. Eilers, July 15, 1935, Peter Norbeck MSS, University of South Dakota; *NYT*, Aug. 11, 1935; Norbeck to S. X. Way, Nov. 13, 1935, Norbeck MSS; *Sioux Falls (S.D.) Daily Argus-Leader*, Oct. 14, 1936; *NYT*, Oct. 19, 1936.

43. *NYT*, Nov. 8, 1934; Franklin D. Roosevelt to James Couzens, July 13, Aug. 5, 24, 1935, Couzens to Roosevelt, Oct. 9, 1935, Roosevelt MSS; Couzens to George R. Averill, Feb. 20, 1936, James Couzens MSS, Manuscript Division, Library of Congress.

44. Couzens to George R. Averill, Feb. 20, 1936, Couzens MSS.

45. *NYT*, May 11, 1936; James Couzens to Thomas W. Payne, June 15, 1936, Couzens MSS; *NYT*, July 30, Aug. 23, 1936.

46. Roosevelt, ed., *F.D.R.: His Personal Letters*, vol. 1, pp. 611-12 (letter dated Sept. 8, 1936) and pp. 616-18 (letter dated Sept. 17, 1936); *NYT*, Sept. 17, Oct. 16, 17, 1936; Franklin D. Roosevelt to James Couzens, Oct. 20, 1936, Roosevelt MSS; *NYT*, Oct. 23, 1936.

47. Henrik Shipstead to Franklin D. Roosevelt, Sept. 5, 1935, Roosevelt MSS; Shipstead to Robert La Follette, Jr., Sept. 11, 1936, La Follette Family MSS; *NYT*, Sept. 15, 1936; *Minneapolis Tribune*, Oct. 9, 10, 1936; *NYT*, Oct. 19, 1936.

48. Speech of Sen. Henrik Shipstead, Oct. 20, 1936, Roosevelt MSS; *Minneapolis Tribune*, Oct. 21, 1936; Franklin D. Roosevelt to Shipstead, Nov. 4, 1936, Roosevelt MSS.

49. Philip La Follette to Isen La Follette, Dec. 7, 1934, Philip La Follette MSS,

State Historical Society of Wisconsin.

50. *NYT*, Mar. 23, 1935; Francis Brown, "Old Wars For 'Young Bob,' " *NYT Magazine*, Aug. 18, 1935; *P*, Sept. 7, 1935; Felix Frankfurter to Robert La Follette, Jr., May 22, 1936, Frankfurter MSS.

51. *NYT*, July 14, 1935.

52. Ibid., Oct. 20, 1935; *P*, Oct. 26, 1935; *NYT*, Nov. 9, 16, 1935; Franklin D. Roosevelt to George Norris, Nov. 22, 1935, Roosevelt MSS, and George Norris MSS, Manuscript Division, Library of Congress; *NYT*, Dec. 7, 1935.

53. George Norris to Sen. Robert F. Wagner, June 12, 1936, Norris MSS; *NYT*, June 15, 1936; *P*, June 20, 1936.

54. *NYT*, July 12, Aug. 26, Sept. 12, Oct. 2, 11, 1936; copy of FDR speech in Omaha, Oct. 10, 1936, Roosevelt MSS.

55. Donald R. McCoy, "The Progressive National Committee of 1936," *Western Political Quarterly* 9 (June 1956): 454-69; *NYT*, Jan. 29, 1936; Donald Richberg to George Norris, Jan. 27, 1936, Norris MSS; *NYT*, May 21, 1936; Franklin D. Roosevelt to James Farley, May 8, 1936, Frank P. Walsh MSS, Manuscript Division, New York Public Library; confidential memorandum by Frank P. Walsh, June 4, 1936, Walsh MSS; Walsh to Farley, June 5, 1936, Walsh to Judson King, July 9, 1936, Robert La Follette, Jr., to Walsh, July 25, 30, Aug. 18, 1936, Walsh MSS; Richberg to R. La Follette, Jr., Aug. 24, 1936, Donald Richberg MSS, Manuscript Division, Library of Congress.

56. George Norris to Frank Walsh, Aug. 31, 1936, Walsh MSS; Progressive National Committee telegram to Philip La Follette, Aug. 31, 1936, P. La Follette MSS; *NYT*, Sept. 2, 1936; *P*, Sept. 5, 1936; *NYT*, Sept. 11, 1936; *NYHT*, Sept. 11, 1936.

57. *NYT*, Sept. 12, 1936; *NYHT*, Sept. 12, 1936; *P*, Sept. 19, 1936; Norris to the Conference of Progressives, Sept. 11, 1936, Norris MSS; Resolution of Progressives' meeting, Sept. 11, 1936, P. La Follette MSS; Declaration of Principles Adopted at Chicago Conference, Sept. 11, 1936, Progressive National Committee MSS, Manuscript Division, Library of Congress; Robert La Follette, Jr., to Franklin D. Roosevelt, Sept. 11, 1936, Roosevelt MSS.

58. *NYT*, Sept. 19, 28, 29, 1936; text of La Follette speech, Progressive National Committee pamphlet, P. La Follette MSS; *P*, Oct. 3, 1936; *NYT*, Oct. 29, 1936.

59. *NYT*, Nov. 3, 1936; Robert La Follette, Jr., speech of Nov. 2, 1936, Progressive National Committee MSS; R. and P. La Follette to Franklin D. Roosevelt, Nov. 2, 1936, P. La Follette MSS.

CHAPTER 7

1. *NYT*, Jan. 31, 1935, Feb. 6, 1937.

2. Ibid., May 28, 30, 31, June 3, 1935.

3. Ibid., June 3, 1935; *P*, June 8, 1935; *NYT*, June 18, 1935; *CR*, June 17, 1935, p. 9415.

4. *NYT*, May 28, 30, 31, June 1, 2, 1935; *P*, June 29, 8, 1935.

5. *NYT*, Jan. 7, 1936; *CR*, Jan. 17, 1936, p. 553; *NYT*, Jan. 18, 1936; Hiram Johnson to Hiram Johnson, Jr., Jan. 11, 1936, Hiram Johnson MSS, Bancroft Library, University of California, Berkeley; *P*, Feb. 1, Jan. 11, 1936.

6. *NYT*, Jan. 7, 1936.

7. Ibid., Jan. 3, 1936; *NYHT*, Jan. 3, 1936; *CR*, Jan. 6, 1936, pp. 57-59; *NYT*, Jan. 8, 1936.

8. George Norris to William Ritchie, Jan. 7, 1936, Norris to Jessie Cales, Jan. 11, 1936, George Norris MSS, Manuscript Division, Library of Congress; *NYT*, Jan. 12, Feb.

13, 1936; *NYHT*, Feb. 13, 1936; *NYT*, Feb. 15, 1936; Norris to editors and editorial associates of *The Nation*, May 21, 1936, Norris MSS.

9. Hiram Johnson to Hiram Johnson, Jr., Nov. 15, 1936, Johnson MSS; *NYT*, Jan. 8, 16, 17, 1937; *P*, Feb. 6, 1937.

10. William Borah to J. Reuben Clark, Feb. 1, 1937, William Borah MSS, Manuscript Division, Library of Congress; *NYT*, Feb. 2, 1937; *NYHT*, Feb. 2, 1937; *WP*, Feb. 2, 1937; *CR*, Appendix, Feb. 3, 1937, pp. 131-33.

11. *NYT*, Feb. 6, 1937.

12. Ibid., Feb. 6, 1937; *NYHT*, Feb. 6, 1937; Hiram Johnson to Hiram Johnson, Jr., Feb. 6, 1937, Johnson MSS; *CR*, Appendix, Feb. 8, 1937, p. 180.

13. *NYT*, Feb. 6, 1937.

14. *NYHT*, Feb. 7, 1937; *NYT*, Feb. 8, 1937; Joseph Alsop and Turner Catledge, *The 168 Days* (Garden City, N.Y.: Doubleday, Doran & Co. 1938), p. 97.

15. *NYT*, Feb. 9, 1937; *NYHT*, Feb. 9, 1937; *Washington Evening Star*, Feb. 9, 1937.

16. *NYT*, Feb. 10, 1937; *NYHT*, Feb. 9, 1937; *Washington Evening Star*, Feb. 10, 1937; Arthur Capper to Alf Landon, Feb. 10, 1937, Alfred Landon MSS, Kansas State Historical Society; *NYHT*, Feb. 11, 1937.

17. *NYT*, Feb. 12, 1937; *NYHT*, Feb. 12, 1937; Alsop and Catledge, *The 168 Days*, pp. 94-96.

18. *NYT*, Feb. 13, 1937; *NYHT*, Feb. 13, 1937; Lynn Frazier to Amos Pinchot, Feb. 13, 1937, Amos Pinchot MSS, Manuscript Division, Library of Congress; *NYT*, Feb. 14, 1937.

19. *NYT*, Feb. 14, 1937; *NYHT*, Feb. 14, 1937; *CR*, Appendix, Feb. 15, 1937, pp. 211-13; *P*, Feb. 20, 1937.

20. *NYT*, Feb. 15, 1937.

21. *NYHT*, Feb. 21, 1937; *NYT*, Feb. 21, 1937; *Washington Evening Star*, Feb. 21, 1937; personal interview with Sen. Gerald P. Nye, Mar. 30, 1971, Washington, D.C.

22. *NYT*, Feb. 22, 1937; *NYHT*, Feb. 22, 1937; *Bismarck (N.D.) Tribune*, Feb. 22, 1937; *CR*, Appendix, Feb. 24, 1937, pp. 311-14.

23. *NYT*, May 12, 1937; Henrik Shipstead to George Norris, May 17, 1937, Norris MSS.

24. Hiram Johnson to Hiram Johnson, Jr., Feb. 14, 1937, Johnson MSS; Arthur Capper to Amos Pinchot, Feb. 16, 1937, A. Pinchot MSS; *NYT*, Feb. 17, 19, 1937; *NYHT*, Feb. 17, 19, 1937.

25. William Borah to Henry L. Stoddard, Feb. 20, 1937, Borah MSS; reminiscences of Louis J. Taber, Columbia University Oral History Collections, 1956, vol. 2, pp. 321-24.

26. George Norris to Gerald F. Harrington, Feb. 19, 1937, Norris MSS; *CW*, Feb. 20, 1937; Arthur Capper radio address, Feb. 25, 1937, Arthur Capper MSS, Kansas State Historical Society; *NYT*, Feb. 26, 1937.

27. *NYT*, Feb. 23, 1937; *CR*, Feb. 26, 1937, pp. 1649, 1644; *NYT*, Feb. 27, 1937; *NYHT*, Feb. 27, 1937; Hiram Johnson to Hiram Johnson, Jr., Feb. 27, 22, 1937, Johnson MSS.

28. *NYT*, Feb. 26, 1937; *NYHT*, Feb. 26, 1937.

29. William Allen White to George Norris, Feb. 22, 1937, White to Gerald Nye, Feb. 22, 1937, White to Norris, Feb. 23, 1937, William Allen White MSS, Manuscript Division, Library of Congress.

30. William Allen White to George Norris, Feb. 22, 1937, White MSS.

31. *NYT*, Feb. 25, 1937; George Norris to William Allen White, Feb. 27, 1937, Arthur Capper to White, Feb. 26, 1937, White MSS.

32. *NYT*, Feb. 28, 1937; *NYHT*, Feb. 28, 1937; *P*, Mar. 6, 1937; *CR*, Appendix, Mar. 1, 1937, pp. 355-57.

33. William McAdoo to Clifford C. Anglim, Feb. 10, 1937, William Gibbs McAdoo MSS, Manuscript Division, Library of Congress; Harold Ickes, *The Secret Diary of Harold L. Ickes* (New York: Simon & Schuster, 1954), Vol. 1, pp. 69-70; Ickes to William Allen White, Feb. 25, 1937, White MSS; Josephus Daniels to Franklin D. Roosevelt, Mar. 8, 1937, Franklin D. Roosevelt MSS, Roosevelt Presidential Library; "Progressives and the Court," *NR*, Mar. 3, 1937, pp. 96-97.

34. *NYT*, Mar. 1, 4, 1937; *CW*, Mar. 6, 1937.

35. Robert La Follette, Jr., to Franklin D. Roosevelt, Mar. 5, 1937, Roosevelt MSS; *NYT*, Mar. 6, 1937; *NYHT*, Mar. 6, 1937; Hiram Johnson to Hiram Johnson, Jr., Mar. 7, 1937, Johnson MSS.

36. Text of speech of Robert La Follette, Jr., Mar. 8, 1937, La Follette Family MSS, Manuscript Division, Library of Congress; *CR*, Appendix, Mar. 11, 1937, pp. 499-502; *NYT*, Mar. 9, 1937; *NYHT*, Mar. 9, 1937; R. La Follette, Jr., to Franklin D. Roosevelt, Mar. 16, 1937, La Follette Family MSS and Roosevelt MSS; *NYT*, Mar. 25, 1937; *NYHT*, Mar. 25, 1937.

37. George Norris to J.B.S. Hardman, Mar. 5, 1937, Norris MSS; *CR*, Mar. 12, 1937, pp. 2139-45; *NYT*, Mar. 13, 1937; *NYHT*, Mar. 13, 1937; *CR*, Mar. 15, 1937, p. 2196; *NYT*, Mar. 16, 1937; Hiram Johnson to Raymond Moley, Mar. 13, 1937, Johnson to Hiram Johnson, Jr., Mar. 15, 20, 1937, Johnson MSS.

38. *NYT*, Mar. 23, 1937.

39. Ibid., Apr. 13, 16, 1937; *NYHT*, Apr. 13, 16, 1937; *NYT*, Apr. 20, 1937; Philip La Follette to J. B. Boscoe, Apr. 17, 1937, P. La Follette MSS, State Historical Society of Wisconsin; Hiram Johnson to Hiram Johnson, Jr., Apr. 16, 1937, Johnson MSS.

40. Hiram Johnson to Hiram Johnson, Jr., Apr. 16, 18, 23, 1937, Johnson MSS.; Arthur Capper to Victor Murdock, Apr. 20, 1937, Victor Murdock MSS, Manuscript Division, Library of Congress; Capper to Alf Landon, May 1, 1937, Landon MSS; George Norris to Lewis Westwood, May 14, 1937, Norris MSS.

41. Alsop and Catledge, *The 168 Days*, p. 206; *NYT*, May 19, 1937; Hiram Johnson to Hiram Johnson, Jr., May 21, 1937, Johnson MSS; *NYT*, May 23, 1937; *NYHT*, May 23, 1937.

42. *NYT*, June 5, 6, 1937; *NYHT*, June 5, 6, 1937; Alsop and Catledge, *The 168 Days*, pp. 86, 103; Ickes, *Secret Diary*, vol. 2, pp. 125, 135; Hiram Johnson to Hiram Johnson, Jr., June 5, 12, 1937, Johnson MSS; Arthur Capper Radio Address, July 11, 1937, Capper MSS; Johnson to Hiram Johnson, Jr., June 23, 1937, Johnson MSS; *NYT*, July 7, 1937; Henrik Shipstead press release, July 14, 1937, Henrik Shipstead MSS, Minnesota Historical Society; *CW*, July 17, 1937; William Borah to Victor J. Smith, July 19, 1937, Borah MSS.

43. *NYHT*, July 22, 23, 1937; *NYT*, July 23, 1937; *CR*, July 22, 1937, p. 7381; Alsop and Catledge, *The 168 Days*, pp. 293-94; *NYT*, Sept. 2, 1937.

44. William Allen White to Felix Frankfurter, Oct. 11, 1937, Felix Frankfurter MSS, Manuscript Division, Library of Congress.

CHAPTER 8

1. *CR*, Mar. 17, 1937, p. 2337; *NYT*, Mar. 18, 1937; Hiram Johnson to Hiram Johnson, Jr., Mar. 26, 1937, Hiram Johnson MSS, Bancroft Library, University of California, Berkeley.

2. *CR*, Mar. 19, 1937, pp. 2476-78; *NYT*, Mar. 20, 1937; *CR*, Apr. 1, 1937, pp.

3021-22; Apr. 2, 1937, pp. 3062-65, 3076-77, 3087; *NYT*, Apr. 2, 1937; *CR*, Apr. 5, 1937, p. 3127; *P*, Apr. 3, 1937.

3.   *CR*, Apr. 5, 1937, p. 3136; Apr. 7, 1937, p. 3248; Hiram Johnson to Hiram Johnson, Jr., Apr. 9, 1937, Johnson MSS.

4.   Hiram Johnson to Hiram Johnson, Jr., May 29, 1937, Johnson MSS; *CR*, July 29, 1937, pp. 7793-95; *NYT*, July 30, 1937.

5.   *CR*, July 31, 1937, pp. 7954, 7957; *P*, Aug. 7, 1937.

6.   Arthur Capper speech, Aug. 29, 1937, Arthur Capper MSS, Kansas State Historical Society; Hiram Johnson to Hiram Johnson, Jr., Aug. 1, 1937, Johnson MSS; *NYT*, July 23, 1937; *CR*, July 28, 1937, pp. 7734-38; *P*, Aug. 14, 1937.

7.   *NYT*, Oct. 22, Nov. 16, 1937; Arthur Capper to Victor Murdock, Nov. 2, 1937, Victor Murdock MSS, Manuscript Division, Library of Congress.

8.   *CR*, Dec. 3, 1937, p. 803; Dec. 16, 1937, p. 1639; *NYT*, Dec. 4, 8, 1937; *CR*, Dec. 15, 1937, pp. 1533-34; Dec. 7, 1937, p. 987; Hiram Johnson to Hiram Johnson, Jr., Dec. 18, 1937, Johnson MSS; *CR*, Dec. 6, 1937, pp. 906-8; Dec. 10, 1937, pp. 1236-39; Dec. 17, 1937, p. 1768.

9.   *CR*, Feb. 11, 1938, pp. 1839-41; Feb. 14, 1938, pp. 1868, 1870-71, 1871-73, 1881.

10.   Ibid, Feb. 14, 1938, p. 1881.

11.   *CW*, Jan, 8, 1938.

12.   *NYT*, Feb. 21, 1938; *CR*, Mar. 8, 1938, p. 3028; Hiram Johnson to Hiram Johnson, Jr., Feb. 26, 1938, Johnson MSS; *CR*, Mar. 11, 1938, pp. 3247-48; Mar. 15, 1938, pp. 3398-3400; Mar. 17, 1938, pp. 3575-76.

13.   *NYT*, Mar. 18, 1938; *CR*, Mar. 18, 1938, p. 3645; Hiram Johnson to Hiram Johnson, Jr., Mar. 19, 1938, Johnson MSS.

14.   *CR*, Mar. 21, 1938, p. 3733; William Borah to Prof. E. D. Schock, Mar. 25, 1938, William Borah MSS, Manuscript Division, Library of Congress; Hiram Johnson to Hiram Johnson, Jr., Mar. 26, 1938, Johnson MSS.

15.   Henrik Shipstead statement, Mar. 28, 1938, Henrik Shipstead MSS, Minnesota Historical Society; *CR*, Mar. 28, 1938, pp. 4196-97, 4193, 4194-95, 4195-96.

16.   *CR*, Mar. 28, 1938, p. 4204; Hiram Johnson to Hiram Johnson, Jr., Apr. 2, 1938, Johnson MSS.

17.   Hiram Johnson to Hiram Johnson, Jr., Apr. 2, 1938, Johnson MSS.

18.   *NYT*, Apr. 10, 1938; Hiram Johnson to Hiram Johnson, Jr., Apr. 10, 1938, Johnson MSS; George Norris to John M. Leyda, Apr. 30, 1938, George Norris MSS, Manuscript Division, Library of Congress.

19.   *NYT*, Apr. 26, 1937; *CW*, May 1, 1937; Hiram Johnson to Hiram Johnson, Jr., May 7, 1937, Johnson MSS.

20.   *NYT*, Dec. 31, 1937; Charles McNary to George Putnam, Jan. 28, 1938, Charles McNary MSS, Manuscript Division, Library of Congress.

21.   *NYT*, Apr. 15, 1938; Hiram Johnson to Hiram Johnson, Jr., Apr. 16, 1938, Johnson MSS; *NYT*, May 23, 1938; Arthur Capper speech, May 22, 1938, Capper MSS; *CR*, May 26, 1938, p. 7547.

22.   *CR*, June 3, 1938, p. 8152; June 2, 1938, p. 8000.

23.   Personal interview with Sen. Gerald P. Nye, Mar. 30, 1971, Washington, D.C.; *NYT*, Oct. 23, 1938; Arthur Capper speech, Oct. 22, 1938, Capper MSS; *NYT*, Sept. 18, 1938; Hiram Johnson to Harry Byrd, Aug. 13, 1938, Johnson to Hiram Johnson, Jr., June 18, 1938, Johnson MSS; *NYT*, Dec. 23, 1938.

24.   *P*, Jan. 1, 1938; *NYT*, Nov. 29, 1938.

25.   *Madison Capital Times*, Nov. 8, 1934; Louis Adamic, "A Talk with Phil La Follette," *N*, Feb. 27, 1935, pp. 242-45.

26. *NYT*, July 28, Oct. 13, 27, Nov. 2, 1935.

27. *Washington Evening Star*, Oct. 3, 1936; Francis Brown, "The La Follettes Survey New Horizons," *NYT Magazine*, Jan. 3, 1937, p. 9; *CR*, Appendix, Mar. 24, 1937, pp. 628-29.

28. *NYT*, May 20, 1937; *Madison Capital Times*, May 20, 1937; *P*, May 29, 1937; Message from Governor Philip La Follette on the Occasion of the Third Anniversary of the Founding of the Progressive Party, May 1937, P. La Follette to Franklin D. Roosevelt, June 3, 1937, P. La Follette MSS, State Historical Society of Wisconsin; P. La Follette to Robert La Follette, Jr., June 4, 1937, La Follette Family MSS, Manuscript Division, Library of Congress; *CR*, June 16, 1937, pp. 5825-28; R. La Follette, Jr., to Dearest, June 19, 1937, P. La Follette to R. La Follette, Jr., June 25, 1937, La Follette Family MSS; Donald Young, ed., *Adventure in Politics: The Memoirs of Philip La Follette* (New York: Holt, Rinehart & Winston, 1970), pp. 246-47.

29. George F. Rowe to Gordon Sinykin (Governor La Follette's assistant), June 25, 1937, Rowe to P. La Follette, June 25, 1937, P. La Follette MSS; Donald R. McCoy, "The National Progressives of America, 1938," *Mississippi Valley Historical Review* 44 (June 1957): 80; Young, ed., *Adventure in Politics*, p. 252; *NYT*, Oct. 17, 1937; P. La Follette to R. La Follette, Jr., Nov. 27, Dec. 5, 1937, La Follette Family MSS.

30. David Niles to P. La Follette, Dec. 6, 1937, P. La Follette MSS and La Follette Family MSS; R. La Follette, Jr., to P. La Follette, Dec. 7, 1937, La Follette Family MSS.

31. *P*, Dec. 11, 1937.

32. *NYT*, Jan. 3, 14, 1938; *CR*, Appendix, Jan. 13, 1938, pp. 188-190; copy of R. La Follette, Jr., address, Jan. 13, 1938, La Follette Family MSS; *P*, Jan. 22, 1938; *NYT*, Feb. 20, 21, 1938; *CR*, Appendix, Feb. 21, 1938, pp. 732-33.

33. *NYT*, Mar. 1, 1938; *P*, Mar. 5, 1938.

34. Philip La Follette to Robert La Follette, Jr., Mar. 17, 22, 1938, La Follette Family MSS; *Madison Capital Times*, Mar. 27, 1938; *NYT*, Apr. 9, 1938; personal interview with Morris H. Rubin, editor of *The Progressive*, Aug. 6, 1970, Madison, Wisc.; P. La Follette to R. La Follette, Jr., Apr. 8, 18, 1938, La Follette Family MSS.

35. *NYT*, Apr. 21, 22, 23, 1938; *NYHT*, April 21, 22, 23, 1938; *Madison Capital Times*, Apr. 21, 22, 23, 1938; *NYT*, Apr. 24, 1938.

36. *Madison Capital Times*, Apr. 25, 1938; *NYT*, Apr. 26, 1938; *Madison Capital Times*, Apr. 26, 1938; *NYT*, Apr. 27, 1938.

37. *Madison Capital Times*, Apr. 28, 1938; *NYT*, Apr. 28, 1938; *NYHT*, Apr. 28, 1938.

38. *NYT*, Apr. 29, 1938; *Madison Capital Times*, Apr. 29, 1938; *NYHT*, Apr. 29, 1938; Robert La Follette, Jr., to Alvin C. Reis, chairman of Progressives' meeting, Apr. 28, 1938, La Follette Family MSS and P. La Follette MSS; *P*, Apr. 30, 1938.

39. *NYT*, Apr. 29, 1938; *NYHT*, Apr. 29, 1938; *Madison Capital Times*, Apr. 29, 1938; *CR*, Appendix, Apr. 28, 1938, pp. 2002-6.

40. *NYT*, Apr. 29, 1938; *NYHT*, Apr. 29, 1938; *Madison Capital Times*, Apr. 29, 1938.

41. *Madison Capital Times*, Apr. 29, 1938; *NYT*, Apr. 30, 1938; *NYHT*, Apr. 30, 1938; *NYT*, May 1, 5, 1938.

42. *NYT*, Apr. 30, 1938; *NYHT*, Apr. 30, May 2, 1938.

43. *WP*, Apr. 30, 1938; *Washington Evening Star*, Apr. 30, May 8, 1938; *New York World Telegram*, Apr. 30, 1938; *New York Post*, May 12, 1938.

44. "A Third Party in 1940?" *NR*, May 4, 1938, pp. 382-83; "The Progressives and the Future," ibid, May 11, 1938, pp. 3-4; Robert Morss Lovett, "April Hopes in Madison: The National Progressives Are Launched," ibid., pp. 13-14; Heywood Broun,

"Phil La Follette Sounds Off," ibid., p. 16; Bruce Bliven to Philip La Follette, May 10, 1938, P. La Follette MSS.

45. "La Follette Thunder," *N*, Apr. 30, 1938, pp. 492-93; "The New Progressives," ibid., May 7, 1938, pp. 519-20; Paul Y. Anderson, "La Follettes' Bid For Power," ibid., pp. 524-25.

46. Max Lerner, "Phil La Follette: An Interview," ibid., May 14, 1938, pp. 552-55.

47. Alfred M. Bingham to Mrs. Kate Richards O'Hare, May 4, 1938, Thomas R. Amlie MSS, State Historical Society of Wisconsin; "Progressives, What Now?" *CS* 7 (June 1938): 3-5; Ruben Levin, "A New Party is Launched," ibid., pp. 17-19.

48. *Madison Capital Times*, May 1, 1938; William T. Evjue, *A Fighting Editor* (Madison, Wisc.: Wells Printing Co., 1968), pp. 562-68.

49. *NYT*, Apr. 30, 1938; *Madison Capital Times*, Apr. 30, May 1, 1938; *NYT*, May 1, 2, 1938; *NYHT*, May 1, 2, 1938.

50. *NYT*, May 3, 1938; *Madison Capital Times*, May 3, 1938; *P*, May 7, 1938; Philip La Follette to Robert La Follette, Jr., May 5, 1938, La Follette Family MSS.

51. *P*, May 7, 1938; *NYT*, May 6, 1938; Harold Ickes, *The Secret Diary of Harold L. Ickes* (New York: Simon & Schuster, 1954), vol. 2, pp. 379-89, 385.

52. Speech of Sen. Robert La Follette, Jr., May 9, 1938, P. La Follette MSS and La Follette Family MSS; *CR*, Appendix, May 9, 1938, pp. 2675-2677; *Madison Capital Times*, May 10, 1938; *P*, May 14, 1938; R. La Follette, Jr., to John Chamberlain, May 13, 1938, La Follette Family MSS; *NYT*, May 14, 15, 16, 1938; *Madison Capital Times*, May 14, 16, 1938; *P*, May 21, 1938; Ickes, *Secret Diary*, vol. 1, pp. 393-95; personal interview with Morris H. Rubin, editor of *The Progressive*, Aug. 6, 1970, Madison, Wisc.

53. *NYT*, May 27, 29, 1938; *Madison Capital Times*, May 29, 1938; *NYT*, June 4, 5, 6, 23, 1938; *Madison Capital Times*, June 22, 23, July 22, 1938; *NYT*, July 24, 1938.

54. *Madison Capital Times*, Sept. 21, 1938; *NYT*, Sept. 25, Oct. 2, 29, Nov. 9, 1938; *Madison Capital Times*, Nov. 9, 1938.

55. *NYT*, Nov. 10, 1938; *Madison Capital Times*, Nov. 10, 1938; *NYT*, Nov. 13, 1938; *P*, Nov. 12, 1938.

CHAPTER 9

1. *NYT*, May 25, 26, 1933; Robert A. Divine, *The Illusion of Neutrality* (Chicago: University of Chicago Press, 1962), pp. 53-55.

2. *NYT*, Jan. 9, 1934; William E. Borah, "American Foreign Policy in a Nationalistic World," *Foreign Affairs* 12 (Jan. 1934): 3-12; *CR*, Jan. 10, 1934, pp. 315-17.

3. *CR*, Feb. 8, 1934, p. 2153; *NYT*, Feb. 9, 1934.

4. *CR*, Mar. 12, 1934, p. 4229; Wayne S. Cole, *Senator Gerald P. Nye and American Foreign Relations* (Minneapolis: University of Minnesota Press, 1962), pp. 69-72; *CR*, Mar. 5, 1934, pp. 3688-91; *NYT*, Mar. 6, 1934; *CR*, Mar. 6, 1934, pp. 3780-84, 3813.

5. Cole, *Nye and American Foreign Relations*, pp. 71-72; *NYT*, Apr. 24, 1934.

6. *CR*, Apr. 12, 1934, pp. 6472-75, 6454; Apr. 19, 1934, p. 6898; *NYT*, May 19, 1934.

7. Divine, *Illusion of Neutrality*, pp. 74-76, 80; John E. Wiltz, *In Search of Peace: The Senate Munitions Inquiry, 1934-1936* (Baton Rouge: Louisiana State University Press, 1963).

8. Hiram Johnson to Hiram Johnson, Jr., Jan. 6, 1935, Hiram Johnson MSS, Bancroft Library, University of California, Berkeley; *NYT*, Jan. 10, 12, 1935; *NYHT*, Jan. 13, 1935.

9. *NYT*, Jan. 13, 17, 1935; *NYHT*, Jan. 13, 17, 1935; *CR*, Jan. 16, 1935, pp. 479-83.

10. *CR*, Jan. 17, 1935, p. 562; *NYT*, Jan. 18, 24, 22, 1935; *NYHT*, Jan. 22, 1935; *CR*, Jan. 21, 1935, pp. 695-96, 702; Jan. 24, 1935, pp. 873-76.

11. *CR*, Jan. 25, 1935, pp. 964-66, 977; *NYT*, Jan. 26, 28, 1935; *NYHT*, Jan. 26, 1935.

12. *CR*, Jan. 28, 1935, pp. 1039-44; *NYT*, Jan. 29, 1935; *CR*, Jan. 29, 1935, pp. 1142-43, 1147; *NYT*, Jan. 30, 1935; *NYHT*, Jan. 30, 1935.

13. *NYT*, Jan. 30, 1935; Hiram Johnson to Hiram Johnson, Jr., Jan. 31, Feb. 10, 1935, Johnson MSS; George Norris to Rev. Ray J. Harmelink, Feb. 5, 1935, George Norris MSS, Manuscript Division, Library of Congress; *P*, Feb. 2, 1935.

14. Arthur Capper to R. M. Parks, Feb. 7, 1935, Arthur Capper MSS, Kansas State Historical Society.

15. *CR*, Mar. 8, 1935, p. 3214; *NYT*, Mar. 9, 1935; *CR*, May 24, 1935, p. 8161; May 20, 1935, p. 7833.

16. *CR*, Jan. 4, 1935, p. 104; Jan. 15, 1935, pp. 444, 444-61; *NYT*, Feb. 10, 1935; *CR*, Mar. 8, 1935, pp. 3189-93.

17. Divine, *Illusion of Neutrality*, p. 86; *NYT*, Mar. 31, 1935.

18. *CR*, Apr. 9, 1935, pp. 5286-87; May 7, 1935, p. 7042; *NYT*, May 8, 1935; Divine, *Illusion of Neutrality*, pp. 98-108; *NYT*, Aug. 19, 1935; Divine, *Illusion of Neutrality*, pp. 109-15; *NYT*, Aug. 22, 1935.

19. *CR*, Aug. 24, 1935, p. 14434, 14430-32.

20. *NYT*, Oct. 8, 1935; George Norris to Richard Manthey. Oct. 14, 1935, Norris MSS; *NYT*, Oct. 27, 1935; Hiram Johnson to Franklin D. Roosevelt, Nov. 18, 1935, Franklin D. Roosevelt MSS, Roosevelt Presidential Library; *NYT*, Nov. 29, 1935.

21. Divine, *Illusion of Neutrality*, pp. 136-39; *NYT*, Jan. 5, 12, 14, 26, 1936.

22. Hiram Johnson to Hiram Johnson, Jr., Jan. 26, 1936, Johnson MSS.

23. *CR*, Jan. 16, 1936, pp. 500-501; *NYT*, Jan. 17, Feb. 14, 1936; Divine, *Illusion of Neutrality*, pp. 152-58.

24. Hiram Johnson to Hiram Johnson, Jr., Oct. 5, 1936, Johnson MSS.

25. Divine, *Illusion of Neutrality*, pp. 163-65; *NYT*, Nov. 12, 1936.

26. Divine, *Illusion of Neutrality*, pp. 173, 175, 179; *NYT*, Feb. 21, 1937.

27. *CR*, Mar. 1, 1937, pp. 1677-83; *NYT*, Mar. 2, 1937; *CR*, Mar. 3, 1937, pp. 1778-79, 1784-85, 1807; *NYT*, Mar. 4, 1937.

28. Divine, *Illusion of Neutrality*, pp. 190-92; *CR*, Apr. 29, 1937, pp. 3942-43, 3954, 3957, 3959-61, 3962; *NYT*, Apr. 30, 1937.

29. Divine, *Illusion of Neutrality*, pp. 193-98.

30. *NYT*, Mar. 23, 1937; *CR*, Mar. 22, 1937, pp. 2540-42, 2548, 2554.

31. *CR*, May 6, 1937, pp. 4236-37; *NYT*, May 7, 1937; *P*, May 15, 1937; *CR*, June 23, 1937, pp. 6214-15; *NYT*, June 24, 1937.

32. *CR*, Appendix, Aug. 20, 1937, pp. 2257-58.

33. Hiram Johnson to Raymond Moley, Oct. 11, Nov. 1, 1937, Johnson MSS; *NYT*, Nov. 3, 1937.

34. William Borah to Robert Reed, Nov. 9, 1937, William Borah MSS, Manuscript Division, Library of Congress.

35. *CR*, Appendix, Dec. 1, 1937, pp. 257-58.

36. *CR*, Nov. 16, 1937, p. 24; Nov. 17, 1937, p. 61; *NYT*, Nov. 17, 1937; *P*, Dec. 4, 1937.

37. Robert La Follette, Jr., to Philip La Follette, Jan. 6, 1938, P. La Follette MSS, State Historical Society of Wisconsin; *P*, Jan. 15, 1938; Arthur Capper to William Allen White, Jan. 8, 1938, William Allen White MSS, Manuscript Division, Library of Congress; *CW*, Jan. 22, 1938; *NYT*, Jan. 17, 1938; *CR*, Appendix, Jan. 16, 1938, pp. 238-39.

38. Hiram Johnson to Hiram Johnson, Jr., Jan. 29, 1938, Johnson MSS; *CR*, Jan. 31, 1938, p. 1263; Feb. 1, 1938, pp. 1326-27; *NYT*, Feb. 1, 2, 4, 1938.

39. *CR*, Feb. 7, 1938, p. 1532; Feb. 8, 1938, p. 1622; Feb. 10, 1938, pp. 1764-65; *NYT*, Feb. 8, 9, 11, 1938; Hiram Johnson to Hiram Johnson, Jr., Feb. 12, 1938, Johnson MSS; *NYT*, Feb. 14, 1938; Johnson to Hiram Johnson, Jr., Feb. 19, 1938, Johnson MSS.

40. *CR*, Feb. 25, 1938, pp. 2410-11; *NYT*, Feb. 26, 1938; *P*, Mar. 5, 1938.

41. *CR*, Appendix, Mar. 6, 1938, pp. 898-99; *NYT*, Mar. 7, 1938; *NYHT*, Mar. 7, 1938; *P*, Mar. 12, 1938.

42. *NYT*, Mar. 7, 1938; *NYHT*, Mar. 7, 1938; *CR*, Appendix, Mar. 28, 1938, pp. 1217-19; Mar. 24, 1938, pp. 1177-78; *NYT*, Mar. 25, 1938; *NYHT*, Mar. 25, 1938; *CW*, Mar. 26, 1938.

43. *CR*, Apr. 20, 1938, pp. 5571-74; Apr. 21, 1938, p. 5623; Apr. 27, 1938, pp. 5826-27; *NYT*, Apr. 21, 25, 1938; *NYHT*, Apr. 25, 1938; *CR*, Apr. 28, 1938, pp. 5890-5901; *NYT*, Apr. 29, 1938; *P*, Apr. 30, 1938.

44. *CR*, Apr. 28, 1938, pp. 5906-9; *NYT*, Apr. 29, 1938; *CR*, Apr. 26, 1938, pp. 5778, 5780-82; *NYT*, Apr. 27, 1938; *CR*, May 2, 1938, pp. 6044-45; *NYT*, May 3, 1938.

45. *CR*, Apr. 27, 1938, p. 5824; May 3, 1938, p. 6135.

46. George Norris to Freda Kirchwey, Mar. 19, 1938, Norris MSS; *NYT*, Mar. 28, 1938; *NYHT*, Mar. 28, 1938; *CR*, Appendix, Mar. 28, 1938, pp. 1193-94; "How to Keep Out of War," *N*, April 2, 1938, pp. 376-77; *CR*, Apr. 27, 1938, p. 5854; *NYT*, July 12, 1938.

CHAPTER 10

1. *NYT*, Jan. 5, 1939; *CR*, Jan. 4, 1939, p. 70; *CR*, Appendix, Jan. 24, 1939, pp. 282-83.

2. *CR*, Feb. 1, 1939, pp. 1015-16; Hiram Johnson to Hiram Johnson, Jr., Feb. 11, 1939, Hiram Johnson MSS, Bancroft Library, University of California, Berkeley; *NYT*, Feb. 24, 1939.

3. Personal interview with Sen. Gerald P. Nye, Mar. 30, 1971, Washington, D.C.; *CR*, Feb. 1, 1939, p. 1010; *NYT*, Feb. 2, 1939; *NYHT*, Feb. 2, 1939; *NYT*, Feb. 13, 1939; *CR*, Appendix, Feb. 12, 1939, pp. 558-59; *NYT*, Feb. 19, 1939; *NYHT*, Feb. 19, 1939; *CR*, Appendix, Feb. 18, 1939, pp. 648-50; *NYT*, Feb. 21, 1939; *CR*, Feb. 28, 1939, pp. 2001-3; *NYT*, Mar. 1, 1939; *NYHT*, Mar. 1, 1939.

4. Arthur Capper to Alf Landon, Feb. 9, 1939, Alfred Landon MSS, Kansas State Historical Society; *NYT*, Feb. 6, 12, Mar. 1, 1939; *NYHT*, Mar. 1, 1939; *CR*, Feb. 28, 1939, p. 1976; *P*, Mar. 4, 1939.

5. George Norris to Victor Murdock, Feb. 11, 1939, George Norris MSS, Manuscript Division, Library of Congress, and Victor Murdock MSS, Manuscript Division, Library of Congress; Norris to Dr. Leland H. Evans, Mar. 17, 1939, Norris MSS.

6. *CR*, Mar. 2, 1939, pp. 2131-33, 2137-39; *NYT*, Mar. 3, 1939; *NYHT*, Mar. 3, 1939; Hiram Johnson to Hiram Johnson, Jr., Mar. 19, 1939, Johnson MSS.

7. *CR*, Mar. 3, 1939, pp. 2204-5; Mar. 6, 1939, pp. 2271-72, 2277, 2285; Mar. 7, 1939, p. 2377.

8. *NYT*, Mar. 10, 20, 1939; *NYHT*, Mar. 20, 1939; *CR*, Mar. 20, 1939, p. 2926; *NYT*, Mar. 22, 1939; *CR*, Mar. 21, 1939, p. 3020; Mar. 28, 1939, p. 3395; *NYT*, Mar. 29, 1939; *CR*, Appendix, Apr. 4, 1939, pp. 1317-19; Apr. 2, 1939, pp. 1316-17.

9. Form letter reply on neutrality by Robert La Follette, Jr., May 1939, La Follette Family MSS, Manuscript Division, Library of Congress; *NYT*, May 11, 1939; *NYHT*,

May 11, 1939; *P*, May 13, 1939; *CR*, Appendix, May 18, 1939, pp. 3544-45; Apr. 20, 1939, pp. 1727-29; *CR*, May 9, 1939, pp. 5276-77; *CR*, Appendix, May 16, 1939, pp. 2025-26; speech of Sen. Henrik Shipstead on neutrality, May 16, 1939, Henrik Shipstead MSS, Minnesota Historical Society; *NYT*, Apr. 30, 1939; *NYHT*, Apr. 30, 1939; *CR*, Apr. 8, 1939, p. 3970; *NYT*, Apr. 9, 14, 1939; *CR*, Appendix, Apr. 13, 1939, p. 1468; *NYT*, Apr. 24, 1939.

10. *NYT*, May 3, 1939; *NYHT*, May 3, 1939; *CR*, May 2, 1939, pp. 4999-5000.

11. *NYT*, June 17, July 8, 1939; *NYHT*, July 8, 1939; Hiram Johnson to Hiram Johnson, Jr., July 8, 1939, Johnson MSS; *NYT*, July 9, 12, 1939; *NYHT*, July 9, 12, 1939.

12. *NYT*, July 15, 1939; Cordell Hull, *The Memoirs of Cordell Hull* (New York: Macmillan Co., 1948), vol. 1, pp. 649-650; *NYT*, July 19, 20, 1939; *NYHT*, July 19, 20, 1939.

13. *NYT*, July 20, 1939; *NYHT*, July 20, 1939; Charles McNary to Mrs. Harriet Gilbert, July 21, 1939, Charles McNary MSS, Manuscript Division, Library of Congress; *CR*, July 29, 1939, pp. 10399-406; *NYT*, July 30, 1939; *NYHT*, July 30, 1939; *NYT*, Aug. 17, 10, 1939; *P*, Aug. 19, 1939.

14. *NYT*, Sept. 4, 1939; *P*, Sept. 9, 1939; *NYT*, Sept. 6, 8, 1939; *NYHT*, Sept. 6, 1939; Arthur Capper to Victor Murdock, Sept. 12, 1939, Murdock MSS; *NYT*, Sept. 12, 13, 18, 1939; *NYHT*, Sept. 12, 13, 18, 1939.

15. *NYT*, Sept. 15, 22, 1939; Robert La Follette, Jr., to Dearest, Sept. 23, 1939, La Follette Family MSS; *NYT*, Sept. 23, 24, 1939; R. La Follette, Jr., to Dearest, Sept. 24, 1939, La Follette Family MSS; *NYT*, Sept. 27, 29, 1939; *NYHT*, Sept. 27, 1939.

16. *NYT*, Oct. 3, 1939; *CR*, Oct. 2, 1939, pp. 66-75; *NYHT*, Oct. 3, 1939.

17. *NYT*, Oct. 4, 1939; *NYHT*, Oct. 4, 1939; *CR*, Appendix, Oct. 3, 1939, pp. 128-29.

18. *NYT*, Oct. 13, 1939; *NYHT*, Oct. 13, 1939; *P*, Oct. 21, 1939; *CR*, Oct. 12, 1939, pp. 321-35.

19. *NYT*, Oct. 6, 1939; *NYHT*, Oct. 6, 1939; *CR*, Oct. 5, 1939, pp. 113-14; Oct. 13, 1939, pp. 360-83; Oct. 23, 1939, pp. 728-55; Oct. 25, 1939, pp. 846-50; *NYT*, Oct. 14, 24, 26, 1939; *NYHT*, Oct. 14, 24, 26, 1939.

20. *NYT*, Oct. 15, 1939; *NYHT*, Oct. 15, 1939; *CR*, Oct. 14, 1939, pp. 397-403; *NYT*, Oct. 17, 1939; *NYHT*, Oct. 17, 1939.

21. *CR*, Oct. 16, 1939, pp. 449-56, 461-66; *NYT*, Oct. 22, 1939.

22. *NYT*, Oct. 21, 1939; *NYHT*, Oct. 21, 1939; *CR*, Oct. 20, 1939, pp. 628-32; *CR*, Appendix, Oct. 24, 1939, pp. 561-63; Oct. 22, 1939, pp. 461-63; *NYT*, Oct. 23, 1939; *NYHT*, Oct. 23, 1939.

23. *NYT*, Oct. 26, 1939; *CR*, Oct. 25, 1939, p. 856; Oct. 27, 1939, pp. 986-89, 994-96, 998, 999; *P*, Nov. 4, 1939; *NYT*, Oct. 26, 28, 1939; *NYHT*, Oct. 26, 28, 1939; *CR*, Oct. 27, 1939, pp. 1024, 986; Nov. 3, 1939, p. 1356; *NYT*, Nov. 4, 1939.

24. *NYT*, Jan. 11, 1940; *CR*, Feb. 13, 1940, pp. 1389, 1401-2, 1405.

25. *CR*, Mar. 13, 1940, p. 2765; *NYT*, Mar. 14, 29, 24, 1940; Hiram Johnson to Hiram Johnson, Jr., Apr. 28, 1940, Johnson MSS.

26. *NYT*, June 21, 1940.

27. *CR*, June 21, 1940, pp. 8791-98; *NYT*, June 22, 1940; *CR*, July 9, 1940, pp. 9313-16, 9324-25, 9337-39, 9341; July 10, 1940, pp. 9411-12; *P*, July 13, 1940.

28. *NYT*, July 1, 1940; *CR*, Appendix, July 29, 1940, pp. 4601-2; *CR*, Aug. 19, 1940, pp. 10474-78, 10485-87; Aug. 9, 1940, pp. 10090-91; Sept. 9, 1940, p. 11777.

29. *CR*, Appendix, Aug. 9, 1940, pp. 4996-98; *CR*, Aug. 23, 1940, pp. 10804-12, 10819-22.

30. *P*, Aug. 10, 1940; Robert La Follette, Jr., to Dearest Ones, Aug. 13, 1940, R.

La Follette, Jr., to Dear Ones, Aug. 24, 1940, La Follette Family MSS; *CR*, Appendix, Sept. 11, 1940, pp. 5649-50.

31. *NYT*, July 14, 26, 1940; *NYHT*, July 26, 1940; George Norris to Rev. G. A. Moon, July 23, 1940, Norris MSS; *NYT*, Aug. 13, 1940; *CR*, Aug. 12, 1940, pp. 10113-19; Sept. 13, 1940, pp. 12106-7; Aug. 28, 1940, p. 11142; Sept. 14, 1940, p. 12160.

32. *NYT*, Aug. 6, 1940; *P*, Aug. 24, 1940; *CR*, Appendix, Sept. 11, 1940, pp. 5649-50; Aug. 25, 1940, p. 5660; *NYT*, Aug. 26, Sept. 2, 1940.

33. See Wayne Cole, *America First: The Battle against Intervention* (Madison: University of Wisconsin Press, 1953).

34. Arthur Capper to Alf Landon, Nov. 7, 1939, Landon MSS; *NYT*, Feb. 13, 22, June 22, 1940; *CR*, June 21, 1940, pp. 8791-98; *NYT*, Aug. 2, 28, 1940.

35. *NYT*, Aug. 3, 4, 1940; *NYHT*, Aug. 3, 4, 1940.

36. *NYT*, Aug. 29, 1940; Hiram Johnson to Hiram Johnson, Jr., Sept. 1, 1940, Johnson MSS; *NYT*, Sept. 20, Oct. 19, 1940; *NYHT*, Oct. 19, 1940; *CR*, Appendix, Oct. 18, 1940, pp. 6472-74; Johnson to Tom Lewis, Nov. 4, 1940, Johnson MSS.

37. *NYT*, Oct. 1, 1940; *NYHT*, Oct. 1, 1940; *P*, Oct. 5, 1940; *NYT*, Oct. 23, 1940; *NYHT*, Oct. 23, 1940.

38. George Norris to Claude Pepper, Aug. 11, 1939, Norris to Pepper, Aug. 28, 1939, Norris to Harold Ickes, Sept. 8, 1939, Norris MSS.

39. *NYT*, Dec. 4, 1939, May 26, 1940; George Norris to Jackson H. Ralston, June 8, 1940, Norris MSS; *NYT*, July 19, 1940.

40. *NYT*, Sept. 25, 28, 1940; *NYHT*, Sept. 25, 1940.

41. *CR*, Sept. 27, 1940, pp. 12723-43; text of speeches of Senator Norris in 1940 campaign, Norris MSS; *CR*, Appendix, Oct. 15, 1940, pp. 6401-3; *NYT*, Oct. 27, Nov. 3, 1940.

42. *NYT*, Dec. 30, 1940, Jan. 11, 1941.

43. *NYT*, Dec. 5, 1940; *NYHT*, Dec. 5, 1940; *NYT*, Jan. 11, 12, 1941; Hiram Johnson to Hiram Johnson, Jr., Jan. 19, 1941, Johnson MSS; *NYT*, Feb. 15, 25, 1941; *CR*, Appendix, Feb. 24, 1941, pp. 826-28.

44. Arthur Capper to William Allen White, Jan. 11, 1941, William Allen White MSS, Manuscript Division, Library of Congress; *NYT*, Jan. 15, 1941; *NYHT*, Jan. 15, 1941; *CR*, Appendix, Jan. 21, 1941, pp. 168-70; Feb. 7, 1941, pp. 612-13; *CR*, Feb. 22, 1941, pp. 1271-75; *NYT*, Jan. 13, 1941; *CR*, Jan. 16, 1941, p. 150; Feb. 25, 1941, pp. 1346-50; *CR*, Appendix, Mar. 8, 1941, p. 1078; *NYT*, Feb. 26, 1941; *NYHT*, Feb. 26, 1941.

45. *NYT*, Jan. 11, 12, 1941; *P*, Jan. 18, 1941; Robert La Follette, Jr., to Felix Frankfurter, Jan. 30, 1941, Felix Frankfurter MSS, Manuscript Division, Library of Congress; *CR*, Feb. 24, 1941, pp. 1299-1308; *NHYT*, Feb. 25, 1941; *NYT*, Feb. 25, 1941; *P*, Mar. 1, 1941.

46. *NYT*, Jan. 11, 12, 20, 27, Feb. 2, 19, 21, 23, 26, 27, Mar. 2, 3, 9, 1941; *CR*, Jan. 27, 1941, pp. 310-11; Feb. 18, 1941, pp. 1108-12; Feb. 25, 1941, pp. 1363-68; Feb. 26, 1941, pp. 1406-13, 1420-22, 1423-25, 1432-35; Mar. 4, 1941, pp. 1722-33; Mar. 8, 1941, pp. 2082-96; *CR*, Appendix, Mar. 24, 1941, pp. 1333-39.

47. *NYT*, Jan. 23, 1941; *NYHT*, Jan. 23, 1941; Charles McNary statement to the press, Jan. 22, 1941, McNary to Alfred A. Huber, Apr. 2, 1941, McNary MSS; *NYT*, Jan. 23, 1941; *NYHT*, Jan. 23, 1941; *NYT*, Feb. 27, 1941; *CR*, Appendix, Feb. 26, 1941, pp. 873-75; Thomas N. Guinsburg, "The George W. Norris 'Conversion' to Internationalism, 1939-1941," *Nebraska History* 53 (Winter 1972): 477-90; *CR*, Mar. 7, 1941, pp. 1975-78; *NYT*, Mar. 8, 1941.

48. *CR*, Mar. 7, 1941, pp. 1961-62; *NYT*, Mar. 8, 1941; *CR*, Mar. 8, 1941, p. 2097; *NYT*, Mar. 9, 1941.

49. Robert La Follette, Jr., to Gen. Robert E. Wood, Mar. 11, 1941, La Follette

Family MSS; *P*, Mar. 15, 1941; Arthur Capper to Alf Landon, Mar. 12, 1941, Landon MSS; *NYT*, Mar. 28, 1941; *CR*, Mar. 27, 1941, p. 2610; *NYHT*, Mar. 28, 1941.

50. *NYT*, May 11, 1941; *NYHT*, May 11, 1941; *NYT*, July 5, 1941; *CR*, Appendix, July 4, 1941, pp. 3506-8; July 19, 1941, pp. 3539-40; statement of Robert La Follette, Jr., to Richard Neuberger of the *Portland Oregonian*, Aug. 15, 1941, La Follette Family MSS; *CR*, Sept. 15, 1941, p. 7404; *CR*, Appendix, May 31, 1941, pp. 2594-96; *NYT*, June 1, 1941; *NYHT*, June 1, 1941; *CR*, Aug. 19, 1941, pp. 7206-8; *NYT*, Aug. 20, 1941.

51. *CR*, Apr. 29, 1941, p. 3374; May 6, 1941, p. 3606; June 9, 1941, p. 4851; Aug. 1, 1941, p. 6565; *CR*, Appendix, Aug. 1, 1941, pp. 3736-38; *NYT*, Aug. 2, Sept. 10, 1941; *NYHT*, Sept. 10, 1941; *CR*, Oct. 6, 1941, pp. 7627-30.

52. *NYT*, Sept. 21, 1941; *NYHT*, Sept. 21, 1941; *CR*, Oct. 6, 1941, pp. 7626-27; *CR*, Appendix, Sept. 23, 1941, pp. 4567-68; *NYT*, Sept. 23, 1941; *NYHT*, Sept. 23, 1941.

53. *NYT*, Sept. 28, Oct. 13, 1941; *P*, Oct. 18, 1941; *NYT*, Oct. 15, 26, 1941; *NYHT*, Oct. 15, 26, 1941.

54. *NYT*, Oct. 30, 1941; *NYHT*, Oct. 30, 1941; *CR*, Oct. 29, 1941, pp. 8305-8, 8316-18, 8321-25; Oct. 31, 1941, pp. 8385-89; Nov. 3, 1941, pp. 8421-23, 8425-26; Nov. 7, 1941, pp. 8602-7, 8671; *CR*, Appendix, Nov. 7, 1941, pp. 5040-42; *NYT*, Nov. 8, 1941; *NYHT*, Nov. 8, 1941.

55. *CR*, Nov. 7, 1941, p. 8680; *NYT*, Nov. 8, 1941; *NYHT*, Nov. 8, 1941.

56. *NYT*, Sept. 11, Nov. 8, 1943, July 9, Sept. 4, 1944.

57. Ibid., Oct. 29, 1943, July 27, 1945.

58. Ibid., Nov. 5, 6, 1943, Dec. 20, 1944.

59. Ibid., Nov. 6, 1943, July 15, Aug. 7, 1945.

60. Ibid., Mar. 24, 1943, May 8, 9, 10, Oct. 16, 20, 1944.

61. Ibid., June 1, July 29, 1945.

62. Ibid., Mar. 17, 18, Apr. 1, 1946.

63. Ibid., June 19, Aug. 13, 15, 1946.

64. Ibid., Sept. 20, 1944, July 29, 1945.

65. Ibid., June 17, July 8, 9, 10, 1946.

Bibliography

PRIMARY SOURCES

Manuscript Collections

Thomas R. Amlie MSS, State Historical Society of Wisconsin
William Borah MSS, Manuscript Division, Library of Congress
Arthur Capper MSS, Kansas State Historical Society
Edward Costigan MSS, Western Historical Collections, University of Colorado
James Couzens MSS, Manuscript Division, Library of Congress
Bronson Cutting MSS, Manuscript Division, Library of Congress
Felix Frankfurter MSS, Manuscript Division, Library of Congress
Herbert Hoover MSS, Herbert Hoover Presidential Library
Harold Ickes MSS, Manuscript Division, Library of Congress
Hiram Johnson MSS, Bancroft Library, University of California, Berkeley
Philip La Follette MSS, State Historical Society of Wisconsin
La Follette Family MSS, Manuscript Division, Library of Congress:
    La Follette Family Letters; Robert La Follette, Jr., MSS
Alfred Landon MSS, Kansas State Historical Society
William Gibbs McAdoo MSS, Manuscript Division, Library of Congress
Charles McNary MSS, Manuscript Division, Library of Congress
Victor Murdock MSS, Manuscript Division, Library of Congress
Peter Norbeck MSS, Western Historical Manuscripts and State Historical Society of Missouri Manuscripts, University of Missouri
Peter Norbeck MSS, Richardson Archives, I. D. Weeks Library, University of South Dakota
George Norris MSS, Manuscript Division, Library of Congress
Amos Pinchot MSS, Manuscript Division, Library of Congress
Gifford Pinchot MSS, Manuscript Division, Library of Congress
Progressive National Committee MSS, Manuscript Division, Library of Congress
Donald Richberg MSS, Manuscript Division, Library of Congress
Franklin D. Roosevelt MSS, Franklin D. Roosevelt Presidential Library
Henrik Shipstead MSS, Minnesota Historical Society
Louis J. Taber Memoirs, Oral History Collections, Columbia University
Arthur Vandenberg MSS, Michigan Historical Collections, Bentley Historical Library, University of Michigan

Frank P. Walsh MSS, Manuscript Division, New York Public Library
William Allen White MSS, Manuscript Division, Library of Congress

Public Documents

U.S. Congress, *Congressional Record*, 71st Congress, 3rd session, through 77th Congress, 1st session (Dec. 1930-Dec. 1941)
U.S. Senate, Privileges and Elections Committee, 74th Congress, 1st session, *Hearings on New Mexico Senator Election*, U.S. Government Printing Office, 1935.
While not cited in the notes, the various hearings on neutrality legislation and other foreign policy controversies conducted by the Senate Foreign Relations Committee are useful in understanding progressive Republican attitudes on foreign policy issues.

Newspapers

Bismarck (N.D.) Tribune
Madison Capital Times
Minneapolis Tribune
New York Herald Tribune
New York Post
New York Times
New York World Telegram
Portland Morning Oregonian
St. Louis Post-Dispatch
Santa Fe New Mexican
Sioux Falls (S.D.) Daily Argus-Leader
Topeka (Kan.) Daily Capital
Washington Evening Star
Washington Post

Periodicals

American Mercury
Capper's Farmer
Capper's Weekly
Collier's
Common Sense
Congressional Record
Current Biography
Current History
Foreign Affairs
Harper's Magazine
The Nation
New Leader
The New Republic
North American Review
The Progressive

Personal Interviews

Benjamin V. Cohen, Mar. 31, 1971, Washington, D.C.
James A. Farley, May 14, 1971, New York City
Mrs. Isen (Philip) La Follette, Aug. 6, 1970, Madison, Wisc.
Raymond Moley, May 14, 1971, New York City
Gerald P. Nye, Mar. 30, 1971, Washington, D.C.
Morris H. Rubin, Aug. 6, 1970, Madison, Wisc.
Burton K. Wheeler, Mar. 25, 1971, Washington, D.C.

Correspondence

Alfred Bingham to the author, May 7, 1971
Bruce Bliven to the author, May 4, 1971
Alf Landon to the author, May 25, 1971
Morris H. Rubin to the author, Aug. 28, 1970
Burton K. Wheeler to the author, May 10, 1971

Autobiographies, Memoirs, Collected Letters, Diaries, Contemporary Journalistic Studies, and Conference Proceedings

Alsop, Joseph, and Catledge, Turner. *The 168 Days*. Garden City, N.Y.: Doubleday, Doran & Co., 1938.

Evjue, William T. *A Fighting Editor*. Madison, Wis.: Wells Printing Co., 1968.

Freedman, Max, annotator. *Roosevelt and Frankfurter: Their Correspondence, 1928-1945*. Boston: Little, Brown & Co., 1967.

Hull, Cordell. *The Memoirs of Cordell Hull*. 2 vols. New York: Macmillan Co., 1948.

Ickes, Harold. *The Autobiography of a Curmudgeon*. New York: Reynal & Hitchcock, 1943.

_____. *The Secret Diary of Harold L. Ickes*. 3 vols. New York: Simon & Schuster, 1954.

Moley, Raymond. *After Seven Years*. New York and London: Harper & Brothers, 1939.

_____. *The First New Deal*. New York: Harcourt, Brace & World, 1966.

Nixon, Edgar, ed. *Franklin D. Roosevelt and Foreign Affairs*. 3 vols. Cambridge, Mass.: Belknap Press of Harvard University Press, 1969.

Norris, George W. *Fighting Liberal: The Autobiography of George W. Norris*. New York: Macmillan Co., 1945.

Pearson, Drew, and Allen, Robert S. *Washington-Merry-Go-Round*. New York: Horace Liveright, 1931.

Proceedings of a Conference of Progressives. Washington, D.C., 1931.

Roosevelt, Elliott, ed. *F.D.R.: His Personal Letters, 1928-1945*. 2 vols. New York: Duell, Sloan & Pearce, 1950.

Rosenman, Samuel, ed. *The Public Papers and Addresses of Franklin D. Roosevelt*. 13 vols. New York: Random House (vols. 1 to 5), Macmillan Co. (vols. 6 to 9), Harper & Brothers (vols. 10 to 13), 1938-1950.

Tucker, Ray, and Barkley, Frederick R. *Sons of the Wild Jackass*. Boston: L. C. Page & Co., 1932.

Tugwell, Rexford Guy. *The Brains Trust*. New York: Viking Press, 1968.

_____. *The Democratic Roosevelt*. Garden City, N.Y.: Doubleday & Co., 1957.

Wheeler, Burton K., and Healy, Paul F. *Yankee from the West*. Garden City, N.Y.: Doubleday & Co., 1962.

Young, Donald, ed. *Adventure in Politics: The Memoirs of Philip La Follette*. New York: Holt, Rinehart & Winston, 1970.

SECONDARY SOURCES

Biographies and Studies of Individual Progressive Republican Senators

Armstrong, Patricia Cadigan. *A Portrait of Bronson Cutting through His Papers, 1910-1927*. Albuquerque: Division of Research, Department of Government, University of New Mexico, June 1959.

Ashby, Leroy. *The Spearless Leader: Senator Borah and the Progressive Movement in the 1920's*. Urbana: University of Illinois Press, 1972.

Auerbach, Jerold S. *Labor and Liberty: The La Follette Committee and the New Deal*. Indianapolis: Bobbs-Merrill, 1966.

Barnard, Harry. *Independent Man: The Life of Senator James Couzens*. New York: Charles Scribner's Sons, 1958.

Cole, Wayne S. *Senator Gerald P. Nye and American Foreign Relations*. Minneapolis: University of Minnesota Press, 1962.

Doan, Edward N. *The La Follettes and the Wisconsin Idea*. New York and Toronto: Rinehart & Co., 1947.

Fite, Gilbert C. *Peter Norbeck: Prairie Statesman*. Columbia: University of Missouri Press, 1948.

Johnson, Claudius O. *Borah of Idaho*. New York and Toronto: Longmans, Green & Co., 1936.

Johnson, Roger T. *Robert M. La Follette, Jr. and the Decline of the Progressive Party in Wisconsin*. Madison: State Historical Society of Wisconsin, 1964.

Lief, Alfred. *Democracy's Norris: The Biography of a Lonely Crusade*. New York: Stackpole Sons, 1939.

Lowitt, Richard. *George W. Norris: The Making of a Progressive, 1861-1912*. Syracuse, N.Y.: Syracuse University Press, 1963.

_____. *George W. Norris: The Persistence of a Progressive, 1913-1933*. Urbana: University of Illinois Press, 1971.

_____. *George W. Norris: The Triumph of a Progressive, 1933-1944*. Urbana: University of Illinois Press, 1978.

McKenna, Marian C. *Borah*. Ann Arbor: University of Michigan Press, 1961.

Maddox, Robert James. *William E. Borah and American Foreign Policy*. Baton Rouge: Louisiana State University Press, 1969.

Maney, Patrick J. *"Young Bob" La Follette: A Biography of Robert M. La Follette, Jr., 1895-1953*. Columbia: University of Missouri Press, 1978.

Morlan, Robert L. *Political Prairie Fire: The Non Partisan League, 1915-1922*. Minneapolis: University of Minnesota Press, 1955.

Mowry, George E. *The California Progressives*. Berkeley and Los Angeles: University of California Press, 1951.

Neuberger, Richard L., and Kahn, Stephen B. *Integrity: The Life of George W. Norris*. New York: Vanguard Press, 1937.

Olin, Spencer C., Jr. *California's Prodigal Sons: Hiram Johnson and the Progressives, 1911-1917*. Berkeley and Los Angeles: University of California Press, 1968.

Ross, Martin. *Shipstead of Minnesota*. Chicago: Packard & Co., 1940.

Socolofsky, Homer E. *Arthur Capper: Publisher, Politician, and Philanthropist*. Lawrence: University of Kansas Press, 1962.

Vinson, John Chalmers. *William E. Borah and the Outlawry of War*. Athens: University of Georgia Press, 1957.

Wiltz, John E. *In Search of Peace: The Senate Munitions Inquiry, 1934-1936*. Baton Rouge: Louisiana State University Press, 1963.

Zucker, Norman L. *George W. Norris: Gentle Knight of American Democracy*. Urbana: University of Illinois Press, 1966.

Studies of Political History
of the 1930s and Early 1940s

Baker, Leonard. *Back to Back: The Duel between FDR and the Supreme Court*. New York: Macmillan Co., 1967.

Burns, James MacGregor. *Roosevelt: The Lion and the Fox*. New York: Harcourt, Brace & World, 1956.

————. *Roosevelt: The Soldier of Freedom*. New York: Harcourt, Brace, Jovanovich, 1970.

Freidel, Frank. *Franklin D. Roosevelt: Launching the New Deal*. Boston: Little, Brown, 1973.

Goldman, Eric F. *Rendezvous With Destiny: A History of Modern American Reform*. New York: Vintage Books, 1956.

Graham, Otis L., Jr. *An Encore For Reform: The Old Progressives and the New Deal*. New York: Oxford University Press, 1967.

Greenbaum, Fred. *Fighting Progressive: A Biography of Edward P. Costigan*. Washington, D.C.: Public Affairs Press, 1971.

Hofstadter, Richard. *The Age of Reform: From Bryan to F.D.R.* New York: Vintage Books, 1955.

Huthmacher, J. Joseph. *Senator Robert F. Wagner and the Rise of Urban Liberalism*. New York: Atheneum, 1968.

Jackson, Robert H. *The Struggle for Judicial Supremacy*. New York: Alfred A. Knopf, 1941.

Lawson, R. Alan. *The Failure of Independent Liberalism, 1930-1941*. New York: G. P. Putnam's Sons, 1971.

Leuchtenburg, William E. *Franklin D. Roosevelt and the New Deal, 1932-1940*. New York: Harper & Row, 1963.

McCoy, Donald R. *Angry Voices: Left-of-Center Politics in the New Deal Era.* Lawrence: University of Kansas Press, 1958.

———. *Landon of Kansas.* Lincoln: University of Nebraska Press, 1966.

McGeary, Martin N. *Gifford Pinchot: Forester-Politician.* Princeton, N.J.: Princeton University Press, 1960.

Nye, Russel B. *Midwestern Progressive Politics: A Historical Study of Its Origins and Development, 1870-1958.* New York: Harper & Row, 1959.

Patterson, James T. *Congressional Conservatism and the New Deal: The Growth of the Conservative Coalition in Congress, 1933-1939.* Lexington: University of Kentucky Press, 1967.

Polenberg, Richard. *Reorganizing Roosevelt's Government: The Controversy over Executive Reorganization, 1936-1939.* Cambridge, Mass.: Harvard University Press, 1966.

Rauch, Basil. *The History of the New Deal, 1933-1938.* New York: Capricorn Books, 1963 (originally published in 1944).

Schlesinger, Arthur M., Jr. *The Coming of the New Deal.* Boston: Houghton Mifflin Co., 1958.

———. *The Crisis of the Old Order, 1919-1933.* Boston: Houghton Mifflin Co., 1956.

———. *The Politics of Upheaval, 1935-1936.* Boston: Houghton Mifflin Co., 1960.

Schwarz, Jordan A. *The Interregnum of Despair: Hoover, Congress, and the Depression.* Urbana: University of Illinois Press, 1970.

Studies on American Foreign Policy in the 1930s and Early 1940s

Adler, Selig. *The Isolationist Impulse: Its Twentieth Century Reaction.* New York: Macmillan Co., 1957.

———. *The Uncertain Giant, 1921-1941: American Foreign Policy between the Wars.* New York: Macmillan Co., 1965.

Beard, Charles A. *American Foreign Policy in the Making, 1932-1940: A Study in Responsibilities.* New Haven, Conn.: Yale University Press, 1946.

Cole, Wayne. *American First: The Battle against Intervention.* Madison: University of Wisconsin Press, 1953.

Dallek, Robert. *Franklin D. Roosevelt and American Foreign Policy, 1932-1945.* New York: Oxford University Press, 1979.

Divine, Robert A. *The Illusion of Neutrality.* Chicago: University of Chicago Press, 1962.

———. *The Reluctant Belligerent: American Entry into World War II.* New York: Wiley, 1965.

———. *Second Chance: The Triumph of Internationalism in America during World War II.* New York: Atheneum, 1967.

Drummond, Donald F. *The Passing of American Neutrality, 1937-1941.* New York: Greenwood Press, 1955, 1968.

Fehrenbach, T. R. *FDR's Undeclared War, 1939-1941*. New York: David McKay, 1967.
Johnson, Walter. *The Battle against Isolation*. Chicago: University of Chicago Press, 1944.
Jonas, Manfred. *Isolationism in America, 1935-1941*. Ithaca, N.Y.: Cornell University Press, 1966.
Kimball, Warren F. *The Most Unsordid Act: Lend-Lease, 1939-1941*. Baltimore: Johns Hopkins Press, 1969.
Rauch, Basil. *Roosevelt from Munich to Pearl Harbor*. New York: Creative Age Press, 1950.
Wiltz, John E. *From Isolation to War, 1931-1941*. New York: Thomas Y. Crowell Co., 1968.

General Reference Works

Biographical Directory of the American Congress, 1774-1961. Washington, D.C.: U.S. Government Printing Office, 1961.
Dictionary of American Biography. 25 vols. New York: Charles Scribner's Sons, 1928-1977.

Articles in Historical Journals

Bicha, Karel Denis. "Liberalism Frustrated: The League For Independent Political Action." *Mid-America* 48 (Jan. 1966): 19-28.
Feinman, Ronald L. "The Progressive Republican Senate Bloc and the Presidential Election of 1932." *Mid-America* 59 (Apr.-July 1977): 73-91.
Guinsburg, Thomas N. "The George W. Norris 'Conversion' to Internationalism, 1939-1941." *Nebraska History* 53 (Winter 1972): 477-90.
Hamilton, Marty. "Bull Moose Plays an Encore: Hiram Johnson and the Presidential Campaign of 1932." *California Historical Society Quarterly* 41 (Sept. 1962): 211-21.
Larson, Robert N. "The Profile of a New Mexico Progressive, Bronson Cutting." *New Mexico Historical Review* 45 (July 1970): 233-44.
McCoy, Donald. "The Formation of the Wisconsin Progressive Party in 1934." *The Historian* 14 (Autumn 1951): 70-90.
_____ . "The National Progressives of America, 1938." *Mississippi Valley Historical Review* 44 (June 1957): 75-93.
_____ . "The Progressive National Committee of 1936." *Western Political Quarterly* 9 (June 1956): 454-69.
McKee, Irving. "The Background and Early Career of Hiram Warren Johnson, 1866-1910." *Pacific Historical Review* 19 (Feb. 1950): 17-30.
Pickens, William H. "Bronson Cutting vs. Dennis Chavez: Battle of the Patrones in New Mexico, 1934." *New Mexico Historical Review* 46 (Jan. 1971): 5-36.
Rylance, Daniel. "A Controversial Career: Gerald P. Nye, 1925-46." *North Dakota Quarterly* 36 (Winter 1968): 5-19.

Seligmann, G. L., Jr. "The Purge That Failed: The 1934 Senatorial Election in New Mexico—Yet Another View." *New Mexico Historical Review* 47 (Oct. 1972): 361-81.

Doctoral Dissertations

Backstrom, Charles H. "The Progressive Party of Wisconsin, 1934-1946." Ph.D. diss., University of Wisconsin, 1957.

Boyle, Peter Gerard. "The Study of an Isolationist: Hiram Johnson." Ph.D. diss., University of California, Los Angeles, 1970.

DeWitt, Howard A. "Hiram W. Johnson and American Foreign Policy, 1917-1941." Ph.D. diss., University of Arizona, 1972.

Johnson, Roger Taylor. "Charles L. McNary and the Republican Party during Prosperity and Depression." Ph.D. diss., University of Wisconsin, 1967.

Kent, Alan E. "Portrait in Isolationism: The La Follettes and Foreign Policy." Ph.D. diss., University of Wisconsin, 1957.

Liljekvist, Clifford B. "Senator Hiram Johnson: His Career in California and National Politics." Ph.D. diss., University of Southern California, 1953.

Lorentz, Sister Mary Rene. "Henrik Shipstead, Minnesota Independent, 1923-1946." Ph.D. diss., Catholic University of America, 1963.

Miller, John E. "Governor Philip F. La Follette, The Wisconsin Progressives, and the New Deal, 1930-1939." Ph.D. diss., University of Wisconsin, 1973.

Pinckney, Orde S. "William E. Borah and the Republican Party, 1932-1940." Ph.D. diss., University of California, Berkeley, 1958.

Roberts, Walter K. "The Political Career of Charles Linza McNary, 1924-1944." Ph.D. diss., University of North Carolina, 1954.

Savage, Hugh James. "Political Independents of the Hoover Era: The Progressive Insurgents of the Senate." Ph.D. diss., University of Illinois, 1961.

Seligmann, Gustav Leonard, Jr. "The Political Career of Senator Bronson M. Cutting." Ph.D. diss., University of Arizona, 1967.

Index

Agricultural Adjustment Act of 1933, 60-61, 65, 66, 68, 73, 74, 77, 96, 97, 98, 101, 118, 119, 120, 121
Agricultural Adjustment Act of 1938, 138-39
Agricultural Bloc, 8
Allen, Robert S., 17, 56
America First Committee, 190, 196, 197
American Federation of Labor, 20, 61
American Labor Party, 132
American Mercury, 17
Amlie, Thomas R., 150
Anderson, Paul, 152
Associated Press, 45
Atlantic Charter, 196
Austria, 173

Baker, Ray Stannard, 41
Banking Act of 1935, 95
Barkley, Frederick R., 17
Battle of Britain, 188, 189, 193
Belgium, 187, 189
Berle, Adolf, 149, 151
Bingham, Alfred M., 153
Black, Hugo, 61, 112; and thirty-hour work week, 61, 65
Blaine, John J., 56
Bliven, Bruce, 152
Bone, Homer, 83, 86, 112, 127, 180
Borah, William E., 106, 110, 144, 175, 206; and Agricultural Adjustment Act of 1933, 61, 73-74; and Agricultural Adjustment Act of 1938, 138-39; and Black's thirty-hour-work-week bill, 61; compared with Johnson, 6; compared with Norris, Johnson, and La Follette, Jr., 13; compared with other progressives, 16; and Congress of Industrial Organizations sit-down strikes, 137; considers running against Hoover, 33, 35; on Cordell Hull, 55; and Cutting reelection controversy, 87, 89, 90;

death of, 183; and defense appropriations, 161, 169, 173-74, 179; and drought relief, 21; early career, beliefs, and mentality of, 2-4; and Economy Act, 59, 74; and Emergency Banking Act, 58; endorses Cutting for reelection, 86; and Ethiopian crisis, 165; and Fair Labor Standards Act, 137-38; and Fascism, 169; on First Hundred Days, 66-67; on first two years of New Deal, 78; and First World War, 157-58; and Gold Reserve Act, 75; and government reorganization bill, 140-42; and Guffey-Snyder Coal Act, 96; on Hoover's tax policy, 27; on isolationism, 159-60; on Johnson's 1932 presidential candidacy, 37; Johnson envious of, 7; and La Follette-Costigan relief bill, 30, 31; and La Follette's Progressive Party of Wisconsin, 82; on League For Independent Political Action's proposal for progressive party, 22; on liberalization of Republican Party, 97-98; and movement to form permanent organization of progressives, 57; and National Labor Relations Act, 93; and National Progressives of America, 150; and National Recovery Act, 63-64, 69-73; on neutrality, 100; and neutrality legislation, 166-68, 179-86; *New York Times* on his view of Supreme Court in 1923, 121; and Pinchot's bid for presidential nomination, 34; on power of munitions makers, 160; and presidential campaign in 1936, 98-101; and presidential election of 1932, 28, 33-35, 37-39, 45, 47; and presidential election of 1936, 100-103; and Progressive Conference of 1931, 24, 26; and Public Utilities Holding Company Act, 95; and recession of 1937-1938, 143; and Reciprocal Trade Agreements

Ronald L. Feinman is assistant professor of history at the New York Institute of Technology, Old Westbury, New York.

The Johns Hopkins University Press

This book was set by Culpeper Publishers in IBM Selectric Press Roman and printed on 50-lb. #66 Eggshell Offset paper and bound by Universal Lithographers, Inc.